The Financial Time Machine

Predicting Our Economic Future

ROBERT D. OBERST

First Addition

For information contact
Global Future Press
34750 Cannon Rd.
Solon, Ohio 44139
RobOberst@sbcglobal.net

Library of Congress Number: 2013912026
ISBN-13: 978-1490594989
ISBN-10: 1490594981

Edited by Tom Hoeler

Table of Contents

About the author

--

As a management consultant, Rob Oberst served as the regional practice manager for Watson Wyatt (currently Towers Watson.) He wrote the white paper, business plan, and directed the marketing efforts used to found the successful $100+ million consulting practice. Earlier, he managed the design and implementation of nearly every financial application.

As a leader in three national associations, Rob published works on strategic reengineering, and emerging technologies including a book entitled *2020 Web Vision: How the Internet will Revolutionalize Future Homes, Business, and Society.* He has presented to dozens of management groups and universities. Rob has a BS in Operations Research from Miami University along with a MBA in Policy and Organizational Behavior from Case Western Reserve University.

Clients include JP Morgan Chase, Bank America, Citi Bank, PNC, Key Corp, GE, Kraft, Sherwin Williams, Goodyear, Bridgestone Firestone, Toyota, BP, Callaway Golf, Qualcomm, Eaton, Parker Hannifin, Ryder Truck, TRW, Scripps Clinic, and the Cleveland Clinic.

Introduction:

The Genesis of the Financial Time Machine

The existence of a financial time machine is a bold premise, and one I would not normally believe myself, but let's just say for the purposes of conjecture that there is such a device. Not a Jules Verne, bumper-car sized contraption, but a simple physical representation of a complex model you could easily operate that told you what financial challenges you were likely to face over the next 20 years. And, let's say that operating the machine does not rely on complex mathematical formulas, but rather could be maneuvered by anyone with moderate intelligence and motivation along with a minimal amount of training.

What is proposed is not a day-trading tool to predict stock vicissitudes on an hourly, daily, or even monthly basis. You may have seen an infomercial promoting a program to manage your stocks on late-night TV. If a stock's color is green, you buy. When it is red, you sell, implying that all you need to become rich is to purchase this software tool and start trading. It's certainly not that.

The assembly of the Financial Time Machine (FTM) relies on generational economics. Essentially, it looks at whole generations such as the War Boom Baby Generation, Generation X, or the Millennials based on their progress through the Financial Life Cycle in order to predict where the economy is heading. The book discusses how the time machine predicts past events, what it predicts for the future and the corresponding implications.

What could you do with such a device? The reason I developed it was to manage our portfolio. It predicts broad economic cycles. Therefore, if you had a variety of investments (Stocks, Bonds, Real Estate, 401(k)s, IRAs, Pensions, Commodities) you could use it to manage and rebalance your portfolio avoiding pitfalls, recessions, and taking advantage of expansions.

This macro-foresight would give you the kind of perspective that most financial advisors allude to when they counsel clients to look at "the big picture", like don't wait until the year you retire to transfer funds from equities to bonds. Imagine if you had waited until 2009 to perform the conversion after the market lost 60% of its value and missed the recovery until 2013 where it regained those losses.

It may be too much to hope for, but the other potential application of the FTM is for our national leadership to hopefully plan for our financial future. If you are reading these paragraphs, you are likely a reasonably intelligent person who by yourself or with the help of a financial advisor has a financial plan for your house, retirement, and children's education taking into account downward cycles. Having a plan that can adapt over time is a valuable concept. You would think our elected leaders would have a plan, but due to our gridlocked political system, they never seem to develop one fully.

My hope is that they will finally do something about the major long-term financial crisis we see unfolding. All you have to do is look at the financial challenges Europe and most of the states faced as their debt soared, to see where we are heading. The Financial Time Machine can help plan for inevitable future financial cycles and stave off disaster without bankrupting the future, by making the obvious more vivid and soluble.

Origins of the Financial Time Machine

At the turn of the 21st century, the stock market surged with optimism after we survived the ludicrous Y2K crisis where the computer dependent world would supposedly fall apart at its digital seams. This presented an ideal time to perform the recommended periodic investment rebalancing, which I never quite found the time to do. I wondered where the long-term economy tracked, so in 2001, I developed a model to understand its future direction.

What I call generational economics forms the basis of the model, which predicts people's financial behavior throughout their lifetime. According to my generational economic concept, people will borrow, save, or draw off their investments according to their stage in life. The most obvious effect was as the Baby Boomers neared retirement they would stop spending wildly, be forced to save more, and start downsizing, which would take air out of the consumer based economic bubble, but the time machine reveals much more.

The model predicted a massive recession or even a depression starting in **2008**, so in 2001, I wrote a note to myself on the Excel spreadsheet to divest most of the equities prior to that time. In 2007, when clouds started to form resembling my model's predictions, I withdrew most of our funds from the market. When it lost 50%, I put these back in and by the time the Dow hit 10,000 I had fully recovered. Unfortunately, many of the large pension and corporate funds (the smart money) did not fare as well.

There were 11 recessions between the Great Depression and Great Recession, but these were relatively minor, averaging less than a year and 7 ½% unemployment. What is astounding is that five years after the start of the Great Recession, unemployment still hovered near 8% with anemic GDP growth. Unlike the previous brief recessions, the model predicted the effects of this recession would last for several years. Curiously, at the heart of the tangled morass was housing -- which interestingly was a key factor in the model.

The effect was much larger than we could imagine, because we did not know the full extent of the dangerous games Wall Street was playing and how blindly greedy they were. Without going into all of the causes, they and their investors essentially bet trillions of dollars that the housing market would continue to rise, which the model said would collapse in 2008. Because the investment banks were "too big to fail," the American taxpayer in effect paid off those losses. So at the core of all that happened was housing.

Since the crash, I tried to figure out when we will truly prosper again which most people would define as full employment -- something under 5% and sustained growth over 3.0%. I also wanted to know what the risks of additional recessions were.

Additional questions included when the bond bubble would pop, how the equity market would perform over the long term and if possible how the developed versus developing economies would perform. I started thinking about the model again to see if it could possibly predict these scenarios.

The new model turned out to be much more complex, based on detailed economic analysis largely supported by governmental economic and demographic data. There are thousands of figures and calculations, which most people would find boring, so I needed something to make it simple to relate to. The time machine metaphor made it much easier to understand the implications of the model. As a result, the depiction and manipulation of the model is surprisingly easy to understand and relate to. Similarly, an automobile, although a complex piece of machinery, is relatively easy to operate.

To test the model, I went back 60 years when the first Boomers were toddlers. I examined each of the 20th century's five generations throughout their Financial Life Cycle. It accurately predicted two economic cycles from 1950 to 2013. I wondered if the Financial Time Machine applied to earlier decades and generations. For instance, could it have predicted the Great Depression in advance too? The Financial Time Machine remarkably predicted the five economic cycles back to the 1840s including the Great Depression, and the remarkable boom of 1870 - 1890 when the U.S. economy became the dominant economy of the world.

The main purpose of driving the time machine back in time was to ascertain its accuracy, which exceeded expectations. Initially I expected it to predict inflection points (when the economy shifts), within a five-year period, but it often predicted these within a year. The ultimate goal consisted of driving the time machine into the future to find the full recovery and beyond. Encouraged by the results, I set off into the future. The book portrays the results of this journey along with its long-term implications.

Since the Financial Time Machine did so well at predicting America's economic course, I wondered if it applied to other nations. I tried the principles of the Financial Time Machine on twelve other major world economies, including China, Japan, Germany, the UK, France, Italy, and Spain. To my surprise, it predicts where these economies are heading over time too.

Generational Economics

There is not much literature regarding generational economics, but the few economists who discuss it attach a specific meaning to the term. The primary context is as a way to look at funding or the lack of funding for the global War Boom Baby's retirements by the younger generations. This book applies a much more expansive definition of generational economics, looking at how generations of varying size affect the economy as a whole as they pass through their financial lives. The previous context focuses one key event, whereas the Financial Time Machine applies generational economics throughout time (200 years) encompassing numerous economic events and the broader economy as a whole.

The Book's organization

The Financial Time Machine consists of five sections each composed of a few chapters. Here is a summary of each of these sections.

Section One

In the first section, we delve into the two primary concepts used to construct the time machine - the Financial Life Cycle and the generations who pass through the life cycle. The Financial Life Cycle follows our economic state from childhood through our career and eventually into retirement. There are five generations born in the 20th century of varying size and behaviors. Where a particular generation is in its Financial Life Cycle has a profound impact on the economy. After exploring these two primary concepts, we assemble the Financial Time Machine and show how it operates.

Section Two

In the second section, we drive our time machine back for each of the first four 20th-century generations. Here we establish how well the time machine predicts major economic shifts thereby establishing its credibility while gaining an appreciation for the true engine powering our economy.

Section Three

In the third section, we peer into the future with the Millennial generation and then build a multi-generational version of the Financial Time Machine before driving into the future. Throughout the second and third sections, we follow two families, one blue collar, and one white, to see how economic events of the past, present, and future affect them. Hopefully, this approach eases the complexity of the model and makes the resulting economic cycles more relatable in human terms. The calculations represented in the model are necessarily cold, but the economy is not only influenced by the cycles, but how people, businesses, and national leaders react to the cycles.

Sections Four and Five

The fourth section presents future implications unearthed by the machine, including policy and leadership implications along with recommendations. The final section applies the discovered principles to uncover global implications for Europe, Japan, and the BRIC nations of Brazil, Russia, India, and China.

Notes

An asterisk (*) indicates a reference to Notes at the end of the book. These are listed by chapter and numbered in the order of their appearance in the chapter.

Section One

1

The Financial Lifecycle

As we journey through our lives, we pass through successive developmental stages from our early childhood until our late retirement. Simultaneously, we proceed through successive financial stages as our capacity to earn a living steadily inclines and then rather suddenly declines. Where a particular generation progresses in their financial life, proves to be a vital component of the Financial Time Machine.

When we are children, our parents provide for our needs, and they, along with society fund our education so that we will be productive adults and in turn cultivate the next generation. Most of us acquire our first jobs in high school or college when we earn a little money, start to spread our financial wings, and learn to be independent.

As we enter our twenties and thirties, many of us settle down and raise our own families. We earn more, but it is not enough to buy and furnish a house, so we take out mortgages and use our credit cards to remodel, buy appliances, and purchase our electronic gadgets. In our forties and fifties, we reach our peak earning years, start to pay off that debt, and, if all goes as planned, save diligently for our children's education and our own retirement. Hopefully by our sixties we have saved enough to retire and live an enjoyable life into our eighties or even nineties.

Next is a depiction of the Financial Life Cycle, followed by an explanation of each of the eight stages. For each, we will highlight the earning, spending, debt, and savings characteristics of the stage. These four factors, along with the Financial Life Cycle, will become vital components in assembling the Financial Time Machine.

Financial Life Cycle

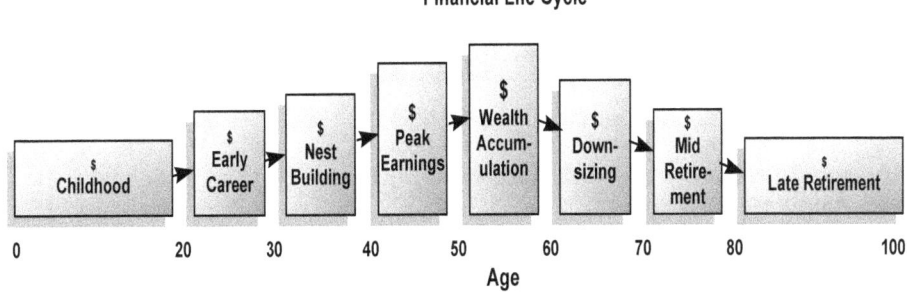

Age

Years 1-20, Childhood

During our childhood and teen years, we depend upon our parents for our food, clothing, shelter, education, entertainment, transportation, and moral development. Children have little direct economic impact other than through their parents' heightened spending to care for them.

According to the U.S. Department of Agriculture, it will cost between $163,000 and $377,000 to raise a child born in 2010. Depending upon the family's income level, having more than one child reduces the cost per child by up to 20%. This costs the average income parents $13,300 per year until age 18. It does not include public or private educations costs, which vary from $6,000 to $25,000 per year depending upon the location. The average K – 12 expense is about $10,000 per student per year or $130,000 in total.*

As we enter our teens, we start earning a little money, contributing to our community through part-time jobs such as babysitting, delivering papers, working at McDonald's, or working at the supermarket.

During these formative years, most individuals earn little compared to what they will later in life. Few will save or incur large debt other than college loans. With relatively minor earnings, these individuals tend to spend for immediate consumption rather than long-term investments like housing. When we think of teen spending, we think of electronic gadgets, games, food, entertainment, movies, clothes, gas, smart phone charges, and pizza. Many teens work to afford these items and save for their college educations, too. One relatively large purchase is that first automobile, which their parents may provide.

High school graduation is the culmination of childhood, celebrated with the rites of passage of prom, in which teens shed their jeans in favor of grownup tuxedos and ball gowns. We say goodbye to our childhood friends as each chooses their next path in life to a job, military, or a college. Depending upon the times, some may go off to war to fight for their country. Parents throw a graduation party for family and friends announcing to the world that their child is heading out into the world, while they also plan for the empty nest and the vacant bedroom.

In the past, teens earned enough through part-time and summer jobs to work their way through a state college. Now it is nearly impossible to do so and complete college in four years.

An asterisk (*) indicates a reference to Notes at the end of the book. These are listed by chapter and numbered in the order of their appearance in the chapter.

Years 20 – 30, Early Career

After living under their parents' wings, young adults construct their own lives semi-independent of their families. This comprises the period when we find our way in the world: choose a major, make career decisions, travel, and decide where and how we will live. It's the time to acquire that first job, learn the profession, and gain vital experience. It's the time to determine if the job fits and, if it does not, to try a new path. Some in their 20s fortunately know what they want to do and pursue their destiny, whereas others struggle to find themselves.

For those that do not attain a degree, they may choose a trade, medical, or office job. Many of these jobs require six months to two years of education for a certificate or an associate's degree with a direct path into the profession, and an apprenticeship may still be required. After a few years of education and toil at the lower levels, if successful, they obtain the full status, pay and respect the profession affords. Others may enter jobs requiring only on-the-job training such as assembly, retail, food, or customer service.

For those who complete college, they have chosen a major, which usually implies a profession. The challenge then becomes finding that first job, which often entails choosing where they will live. One of the problems recent graduates face is a lack of experience, so obtaining that first two years of experience is vital. With a degree and experience, they launch their career. If they become unemployed, finding that next position will be incrementally easier, although they may have to move to a more receptive market to do so.

During this period, they often form lifelong friendships and relationships, reaching career decisions that influence their general direction from then on. Those who graduate from college increase their salaries dramatically but still gain minor relative purchasing power compared to future earnings

For the generations prior to the World War II baby boomers (Boomers) and for the early Boomers who behaved like their predecessors, their twenties was the time when people married, started nesting and having children. However, for the subsequent generations, nesting became less prevalent as many continued to live at home. In the 1950s and 1960s, the median age at marriage was 23 for a male and 20 for a female. By 2010, this advanced to 28 for men and 26 for women.

Marriage rates have decreased over time as well. In the 1960s, 94% of upper middle class whites in their 30s and 40s were married, while today it is 83%. The marriage decline is even more dramatic: for working class Caucasians. Eighty-four percent were married in the 1960s, but less than half were married as of 2012. *

From society's viewpoint, when you live until nearly 80, it is not as important to marry young to propagate the species. The extended lifespan, a benefit of improved healthcare and nutrition, allows an extended maturation process and more advanced education. It, in effect, leads to an extended childhood not viable in developing countries or prior to the 1950s, when there were not enough societal resources to sustain delayed contributions. Society benefits from those with advanced educations who improve healthcare, science, technology, education, the arts, and business. This process offers a reinforcing loop - those who obtain more education produce scientific and healthcare innovations which lead to longer lives, which, in turn, enable more individuals to seek additional education and work longer in their field.

Those who do not follow the college path will likely have low earnings through this period. Their unemployment and turnover rates tend to be higher. Educational achievement varies within a generation. With many well-paying manufacturing and service jobs outsourced to other countries, individual earning potential depends greatly upon the level of educational attainment. As Warren Buffet says, "Someone in America who has a 90-point IQ is qualified for many fewer jobs today than he was 100 years ago." *

Adjusted for inflation, the average male earned $40,081 in 2011 versus about $47,000 in 1999. Wages are down for all, but the uneducated are particularly disadvantaged.*

Approximately 25% of teens will drop out of high school, while another 25% will not attend college. Another 20% will obtain an associate's degree or drop out of college. The remaining 30% will enter the workforce with a bachelor's degree. Unemployment among the less educated is typically higher and wages are typically lower, as the following chart portrays.

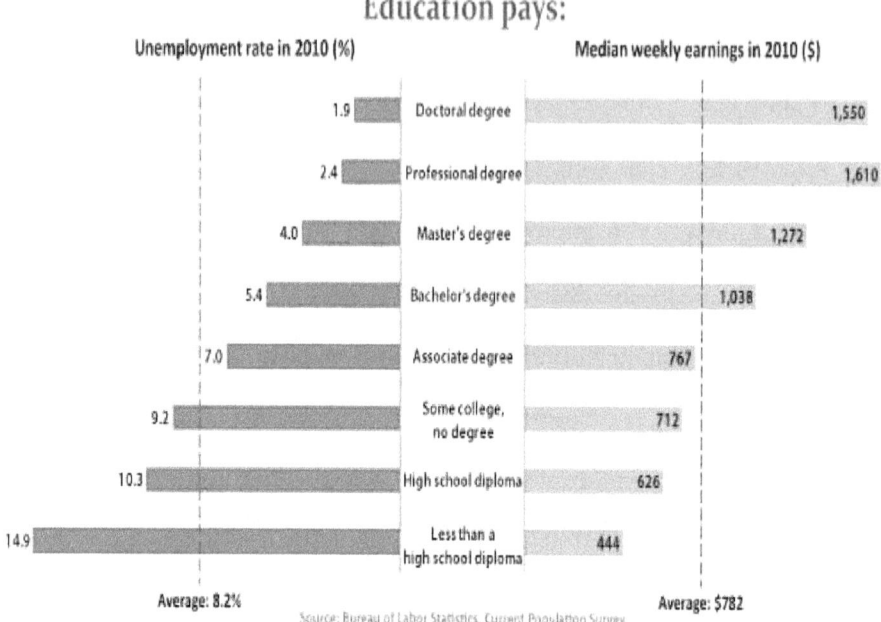

Education pays:

Unemployment rate in 2010 (%)   Median weekly earnings in 2010 ($)

Unemployment rate	Education	Median weekly earnings
1.9	Doctoral degree	1,550
2.4	Professional degree	1,610
4.0	Master's degree	1,272
5.4	Bachelor's degree	1,038
7.0	Associate degree	767
9.2	Some college, no degree	712
10.3	High school diploma	626
14.9	Less than a high school diploma	444

Average: 8.2%   Average: $782

Source: Bureau of Labor Statistics, Current Population Survey

Someone with a high school diploma can expect to earn 29% more annually than someone without one, and those with a bachelor's degree can expect to earn a whopping 66% more than that person with only a high school diploma.

The 2010 census figures taken at the end of the Great Recession are dramatic, emphasizing not only the difference in earnings but also the disparity in unemployment. Unemployment for someone with a degree was nearly half of that of those with a diploma, which in turn was half of someone without a diploma.

Layoffs and time out of the workforce dramatically reduce lifetime savings as those out of work live off the savings it took years to accumulate. If someone was laid off for a year and had saved 10% of their salary, even if with unemployment benefits, it would take 4 ½ years to make up for the lost savings. Over time, the education a person achieves dramatically affects their lifetime earnings potential and, consequently, the lifestyle they can afford.

Those who go to college tend to take longer to graduate these days, and a record number of upper middle-class kids must take out loans. The propensity to save for the entire group is low, debt is high, and savings are low or nonexistent.

Years 30-40, Nest Building

Up until the 1970s, people settled down, marrying in their 20s. Now many delay this rite of passage until their 30s. Often those who do marry delay having children and buying homes. This phenomenon was popularized in the 1990s by the term DINKs – **D**uel **I**ncome **N**o **K**ids. They may live in stimulating urban environments, meeting many people and enjoying the multitude of activities the cities offer. When they have their first child, they might continue to live in an apartment or condominium, but as their possessions and children grow, their limited space shrinks, so they seek a home in the suburbs with more room and a more child-friendly community.

By now, workers gain expertise. If they have a blue-collar job, they completed their training, apprenticeships, and likely garnered respect in their profession. For professionals, they obtained their degree and established a foundation of experience to build upon.

In the past, most workers settled into the company with which they spent the entirety of their career, finding a stable manufacturing, office, government, or union job. Today, you cannot depend upon a single company for lifetime employment but rather depend upon the skills you build over your career to guarantee employment. By their 30s, most people establish a career direction, so if the employer changes, they can port their skills to another role depending on the market.

For the 50% who did not attend college, wages stabilize. Since many of the manufacturing and higher paid office jobs flow overseas, wages tend to be lower than previous generations. According to the IRS, incomes for the average American taxpayer have been stagnant for over 30 years. The average was $33,400 in 1988, whereas in 2008 it was $34,000 (adjusted for inflation). Since the recession, it has become worse. According to the Wall Street Journal, from 2000 to 2010, median income adjusted for inflation declined 7%.*

For college and postgraduates entering the workforce, wages continue to rise. Many thirty-somethings who delayed nesting are finally marrying and having children. When they nest, they buy houses, taking on mortgages and spending on remodeling, durable goods, appliances, decorations, and furnishings. They also spend on their children's food, clothes, toys, tuitions, family outings, and vacations. These are extreme consumers, acquiring massive amounts of housing, auto, student, and credit card debt.

The more prudent thirty-somethings start to save, but for many their needs peak as their earnings build and retirement remains a distant prospect. Hopefully, they at least contribute enough to their savings plans to obtain the company match.

Years 40-50, Peak Earnings

The 40s typify stabilization. Many will acquire larger homes as their earnings increase, and their families grow in size, but the moves and relocations become less frequent. Up until the 1980s, it was common for same sex middle class siblings to occupy the same bedroom, but now parents expect to provide a separate bedroom for each child. Most will settle into a house, a neighborhood, and a school system, effectively growing roots.

Wages usually peak in the 40s even for those in the professional ranks. Earlier in their careers, it was relatively easy to acquire the next promotion. If the promotion did not come, they would find a higher-level job at another employer. But as you rise in your career, there are fewer jobs at the next level because most companies still operate like a pyramid. You may have risen to a position as a director or Vice President, but there is only one President.

Spending remains high but supported by higher incomes. Since they likely have their house, furniture, appliances, and a lot of stuff, they no longer need to buy all of these but merely repair or replace them. Now, they pay down debts such as their student and housing loans.

They also begin saving for the children's education and retirement, now more likely defined contribution (401(K)) versus defined benefit pension plans with lower company contributions. The number of private sector workers covered by pension plans declined to 17%, down from 40% in the 80s. Public pension plans cover 90% of public employees. With each younger generation, the typical mother, father, and two child family constitutes a smaller percentage of households. More singles, partnerships, and divorced households comprise the population, which sometimes implies dual households with duplicate rooms for each child. According to the Census Bureau, while 45% of all adults over 18 are married, only about half of the population in their 40s is married.*

Years 50-60, Wealth Accumulation

The settling process continues, and even though 50 may be the new 30, people start to slow down. Aches and pains linger longer and it takes a little longer to complete physical tasks than before. Some of those who married in their 20s are having their first grandchildren, shocking for those who think they are still virtually in their 30s.

Thirty years ago, managers and executives after a long career in their corporation, would begin to float. They occupied a high-level position in their company, put in their hours, completed the tasks they had done for years, and then spent most of their time enjoying their families, friends, vacations, clubs, and high salaries. Lower levels in the organization competed fervently to attain these golden positions.

For these managers, dramatic shifts erupted in the 80s. Once placid, generous corporations now faced global competition and suddenly survival required increasing productivity and cutting costs. At first, they cut the lower levels, holding higher positions sacrosanct, relying on their computer systems to provide added productivity. Soon this was not enough, so they hired management-consulting firms like Booz Allen and McKinsey to streamline their operations.

From the management consulting company's perspective, these corporations grew obese, could not compete effectively, or move quickly, and needed to go on a strict diet, restricting the intake of human resources and losing the "fat."

Typical recommendations included staff cuts of 25 to 35%. Numerous corporations who previously offered employment for life with no management layoffs faced wrenching decisions. They realized that they could cut one floating executive or two or three lower level, highly productive employees. For the first time, they cut the execs en masse. The result was a massive culture shock through the 80s and 90s as one after another great American corporation endured the downsizing trauma.

Nowhere was the culture shock more difficult to absorb than for the American auto industry, who until the mid-1970s dominated the world. General Motors, the largest of the world's corporations, held over 50% of the U.S. market. Due to a lack of competition, consistently over-generous union contracts, and floating management, they were ripe for a sea shift. The quality declined, exemplified by planned obsolescence, in which the automakers designed cars to rust out in just 5 years so that they could sell another. It took 30 years for this drama to play out until 2008, when the government saved GM and Chrysler from bankruptcy.

Some workers retire in their 50s. They may start working in their early 20s as a fireman, policeman, teacher, factory, or government worker. These are typically union jobs, which guarantee up to 80% of their salary after working 30 to 35 years.

Many of these folks retire from their initial career to commence another. A local fireman retired after 35 years at 55 and started a well-known restaurant in the area with a fire station theme. Jim, a teacher, and his wife retired at 59 and opened a gift shop in a Carolina beach town where they had vacationed over the previous ten years. Hank, a pneumatic plumber for GM's robots, retired after 30 years and opened a shop repairing the type of valves he worked on at the Chevy plant.

Others, symbolized as a midlife crisis, leave their initial career for a new more interesting one. Due to relentless restructuring, many do not have a choice. There were 19 million high paying manufacturing jobs in 1980, accounting for 25% of all employment; now, there are fewer than 12 million, representing only 10%. As the jobs vanish, the remaining ones pay relatively less. This downward trend accelerated over the last decade with a loss of 20% of the manufacturing jobs. Laid-off workers had no choice other than to find a new profession. Some went back to school and initiated a new career in health care or technology, while others settled for positions in retail at a lower wage.

For the majority of those in their 50s, earnings do not increase much. Children are leaving to go to college or left the nest and support themselves. Houses are largely paid-off. Consumption slows to a replacement versus an acquisition mode. The emphasis finally shifts to saving for retirement.

As the more fortunate people pass through their 50s, much of their income derives from investments. Their salaries may peak, but the money they saved and invested earns interest and dividends. This also applies to their defined contribution plans such as IRAs, 401(k)s and 403(b)s. Under normal circumstances, their company pension plan will accrue earnings on their behalf, although they do not have to worry, since if they are fortunate enough to have a pension plan, the company guarantees their payout.

Years 60-70, Downsizing

The average retirement age has been 62. Some retire in their 50s, whereas others labor into their 80s. Joe just turned 94. Until 85, he worked full-time at his business selling paper products to customers he formed a close bond with over 60 years. His 30-year-old grandson, also named Joe, took over the business, and grandpa Joe still works part-time.

Fred Crawford formed TRW, a *Fortune 50* aerospace/industrial/automotive company bought by Northup Grumman. He started at the fledgling company after graduating from Harvard and serving in the Army in World War I. As he approached 100, the sprightly Crawford received a perpetual clock in honor of his 75th anniversary with the organization. He still spent 15 -20 hours a week in his old office giving welcome advice to a myriad of younger executives and walking the halls and plant floors, where he recalled the names of the workers and made passes at flattered secretaries. This is not something anyone but Mr. Crawford could do without fear of a harassment suit.

Most people look forward to retiring in their 60s, although some will work part-time at their previous job or start a new endeavor. Many northern retirees dream of a retirement home in Florida, the Carolinas, or Arizona, away from cold winters and snow.

Those who work into their sixties continue to save at a high rate as they start to downsize. The children have left the nest and have families of their own, so they no longer need the extra space or want to provide burdensome maintenance on their aging homes. Many will trade the center hall four-bedroom-colonial and yard for a stair-less condominium. Spending will decline as they shed goods accumulated over decades, although they may travel more while they still can. Plus, when they retire, they no longer have all of the associated work expenses. By their sixties, debts should be paid off.

Since the Great Recession, the face of retirement changed. Many of those who are currently retired have generous pension benefits, but with only 17% of current private employers offering pensions, the burden of saving for retirement shifted from the investment experts at the company to the individual. Even those who possess private pension plans find it difficult to accrue 30 years of continuous service with the same organization.   In addition, numerous companies froze pension plans, meaning workers will accrue no additional benefits for future years of service. Therefore, the monthly pension benefit for a private employee retiring in the future will be a fraction of what it is today.

The Great Recession and lack of state tax revenue hit public pension funds hard as employment and property taxes plummeted. Some like those in Indiana and Illinois were only 50% funded. Many states faced with large deficits cut back on pension funding requirements by increasing age requirements, reducing benefits, or increasing employee contributions. This came to a head in Ohio and Wisconsin. Ohio public employees were successful in mounting a referendum campaign to reduce the Republican governor's, John Kasich, and the legislator's drastic cutbacks. In Wisconsin, they mounted a campaign to recall the Republican governor Scott Walker and some of the representatives. They succeeded in Ohio and recalled some Wisconsin legislators, but not the governor.

Therefore, retirees must rely to a large extent upon their defined contributions savings such as 401(k)s tied to the stock market. However, the S&P was down over the first decade of the twenty-first century. A dollar invested in the S&P at the start of the decade was worth only 90 cents at the end of the decade.* Since then the market climbed, but not enough to compensate for inflation over the lost decade.

As we come closer to retirement, common financial wisdom tells us to invest less in market securities and more into fixed investments. Unfortunately, the return for 12-month CDs in 2012 is less than one percent at a time when inflation runs up to 3%. Retirees depending upon interest income drastically reduce their spending and live off their dwindling principal.

Bonds have done well, outpacing the stock market over the last 30 years.   But these too are at historical lows, and with rates tied to Treasury yields, will decline when interest rates climb.   Due to the European Sovereign debt crisis, there have been few safe havens to flock to other than U.S. treasuries, which the S&P downgraded for the first time in several decades. The U.S. debt-to-GDP ratio has been over the 100% level, comparable to many of the struggling European economies. Therefore, it is only a matter of time until inflation rears its ugly head and bond rates climb. Rising rates will help retirees on fixed incomes as long as they are not tied to long-term bonds.

Declining portfolios, anemic fixed asset returns, an increased Social Security retirement age, plus high unemployment forced many potential retirees to work longer than they anticipated prior to the Great Recession.   Gary, a three-generation distribution company owner, partially retired in his 50s, but after the Great Recession, market and business losses, plans to work fulltime until age 70. This unfortunate situation is keeping more workers in the workforce longer, clogging up the job market for younger workers trying to enter the market. At the end of 2011, the unemployment rate was 8.5%, but for those 16 to 20 years old it was 23.1%, and for those 21to 25 it was 14.4%.*

Years 70-80, Mid Retirement

From the date of retirement until the mid-70s are the golden years – the reward for a life spent working, contributing to society, and rearing children; a time to enjoy and perhaps spoil our grandchildren. In the past, most of the family lived in the same city and grandparents might even live in a three-generation home. These days, families spread apart and time together during the holidays and vacations is precious.

Retirement income typically flows from a combination of savings, defined contribution plans, social security, stocks, and pensions. Not all stocks are sold, but at 70 ½ some IRA, 401(k), 403(B) plans dictate that a portion of assets must be sold every year. There is little need or desire to buy many new goods. The average debt is relatively low.

Many early and mid-retirees enjoy traveling, as they were unable to do in the past due to limited time and children. Some now take to the road in fully outfitted RVs, spending time in their home city during the summer and traveling towards the sun in the winter, seeing friends and the sights along the way.   Others will enjoy cruises to Caribbean or Mediterranean ports.

Some retirees travel overseas perhaps for the first time to visit Europe, South America, Africa, or Asia. They see fascinating destinations through group tours that provide transportation, lodging, meals, and guides. These tours may be multidimensional, in which the experience includes visits with locals, seminars, and cultural encounters. Garry's parents formed the BETS group (Boozing, Eating, and Talking Society), many of whose members served in the Foreign Service. They would arrange trips to cities a member was familiar with, meet with mayors, and even the presidents of these countries.

My sister-in-law, a world traveler, takes her grandchildren on a trip of their choosing when they come of age at 16. So far, they explored Germany, the Baltic, England, and France. The youngest wants to travel to Japan and perhaps China.

Many retirees will move to or winter in the warmth of the south, often in a retirement community providing a wealth of organized activities like golf, bingo, tennis, horseshoes, shuffleboard, and cards. Communities offer periodic events celebrating each holiday in turn. The community's members form tight bonds and help each other. As time goes by, retirees frequently sell one home and choose to live in the other, which could be the original, but is usually the smaller retirement home.

We may be witnessing the golden age of retirement. Prior to the 1950s, few could afford to retire, rather they continued to work as long as they could. When they were unable to work any longer, they lived with their families. When enacted in 1932, less than half of the elderly could expect to draw Social Security benefits, since the life expectancy was only 60.

The current life expectancy is 78. Over half of those currently retired have a pension benefit in addition to Social Security. These provide relatively rich benefits, since many retirees stayed with a single company for decades. In addition, many of the companies included retiree health care, which is vanishing for future retirees as medical costs skyrocket.

Up until now, over three workers support each recipient on Social Security. In 1965, there were four. In 2010, for the first time, the ratio dropped under three to one. By 2030, there will be only two workers paying into the system for each recipient. It is arguable whether Social Security is solvent, since the government spends the receipts, promising to reimburse these in the future. The interest they pay to the fund is a low rate comparable to the Treasury bond rate, currently around 3%, versus the historically higher pension plan assumption corporations and the state funds used of 8%. Social Security was solvent until 2034, but due to the tax reductions over the last two years, there is less in the fund.

The past retirees received full social security at 65. Those who retired in 2012 must be 66, which will become 67. To fund the system in the future requires either reducing benefits or extending the age to 68 or 69. Europe, too, faces the retirement challenge. Greece, the focus of the sovereign debt crisis, proposes to raise its full retirement age from 65 to 67. Currently, some Greeks can retire as early as 50. Other Euro countries look to change their retirement ages, too. As a result of the Great Recession, many states increased public employee retirement ages from as low as 50.

There is a sense of justice to the retirement picture. Those who lived through the deprivations of the Great Depression and World War II are having a well-deserved, lucrative retirement. They made the United States a magnificent place for those who followed. Their children, who did not live though such nationally tough times and lived in unparalleled times of abundance will likely have to work longer to receive a similar reward, but will on average live longer.

How people age varies widely. Some people remain extremely agile and healthy in their 80s, able to play golf and make demanding repairs on their houses, whereas others face disease, Alzheimer's, and the ravages of age prior to their 70s. By their late 80s, most retirees become less mobile, travel is unlikely, and even a trip to the grocery store becomes challenging.

With past life expectancies at birth in the 60s, many current retirees will pass away in their 70s. When they die, their inheritance passes to their children, which if they do not spend it will increase the children's wealth. For some it may be their major source of retirement savings.

Years 80 and beyond, Late Retirement

The number of people living to old age increased by 30% over the last decade, with more than 11 million over 80. For most, mobility slowed considerably and many substantially downsize, live with children, or in nursing homes. If they had two homes, they usually choose to live in one and sell the other. Some are still able to travel and enjoy activities like golf, whereas others deal with disabilities, illnesses, and the death of their spouse. Thankfully, their religion offers comfort for many.*

When they first retire, their savings may increase due to investment income, but by their 80s they continue to draw down their savings balance as constant inflation deflates fixed incomes. Unforeseen medical expenses and rising rates for Medicare supplemental plans also take a toll. Large corporations and public retirement plans usually paid for retiree medical supplemental insurance, but as these became increasingly more expensive they either eliminated coverage or increased the portion the retiree pays, further reducing retiree income.

Between 75 and 85, 4% of the elderly occupy nursing homes. After 85, 21% of women and 11.6% of men live in nursing homes. Those who run out of funds may end up on Medicaid; indeed, 20% of Medicaid costs are for those over 65.*

As their numbers decrease, the elderly constitute less economic impact other than on healthcare costs. Increasingly, inheritances flow to the younger generations.

The Financial Life Cycle Ruler

Earning, spending, debt, and saving habits change as we pass through the stages of life. These characteristics alter over time, such that the Greatest Generation's behavior vastly differs from the Millennials, with a progressive shift towards lower or flat real earnings, higher spending, more debt, and less savings.

The ruler below depicts phases with each increment representing a decade and a new stage of the Financial Life Cycle as defined above. The Financial Life Cycle constitutes half of the Financial Time Machine. This will come in handy after we discuss the generations in the next chapter, conceptually the other half of the Financial Time Machine. When we assemble these two together, we will possess a surprisingly powerful tool for predicting future financial cycles.

The Financial Life Cycle

```
Age
0.... l....10....l....20....l....30....l....40....l....50....l... 60....l....70....l....80....l....90....l..10(
CHILDHOOD        | EARLY  |  NEST  |  PEAK  |WEALTH | DOWN-  |  MID   |   LATE
                  CAREER  BUILDING EARNING  ACCUM.  SIZING  RETIREMENT  RETIREMENT
```

2

Generations

Two primary elements comprise the Financial Time Machine. The first is the Financial Life Cycle – the subject of the last chapter, exploring the stages we pass through from birth to death. The second major component is composed of the five 20th Century generations, the subject of this chapter. When we assemble the two together, we will possess a powerful long-term economic indicator: The Financial Time Machine.

We think of generations spanning 20 to 25 years, the time it takes one generation to replicate itself in the next. We occupy a generation along with our siblings, cousins, and our friends. Our parents occupy the previous generation and our grandparents occupy the one preceding theirs. Our children constitute the next generation as their children, our grandchildren, compose the following one.

The boundaries of a generation are porous. For instance, my father was the youngest in his family of 11 children with a brother nearly 25 years older than he was. My father even had a nephew older than he was. So his nephew and he were in the same chronological generation even though they were not in the same genetic generation – of the same parents.

My father's situation was not unusual at the dawn of the twentieth century when people had many children over a broad span of years. Today, with divorce and blended families, parents might have children with large separations in ages too. I was at a clambake recently talking to a fun-loving middle-aged fellow who said he and his wife had to leave because his grandson was babysitting his son. Of course, I was shocked: the reaction he greatly enjoyed. He explained that he married young and soon had a daughter, who also married young and had a son. He divorced his first wife and in his forties married someone younger with whom he had another son. This son was six years younger than his grandson, who by then was old enough to baby sit.

Some women have children in their teens, whereas others choose to concentrate on their careers and hold off bearing children until their late 30s. So designating clear-cut generations is somewhat arbitrary.

The most pronounced generation is the Boomers, who were born from 1946 until 1964 in the period following World War II. During the depression and subsequent war when the men were abroad fighting the war, birth rates were naturally low. When the servicemen returned, they started having children.

Those who fought in the war were the "Greatest Generation," a term coined by Tom Brokaw in his similarly named book. They were the Boomers' parents. The fewer children born during the tough time of the depression and war were the Silent Generation. Silent may be a misnomer, describing those sandwiched between the more noticeable Greatest and Boomer generations, who only by virtue of their larger numbers had more economic, sociological, and political impact.

Generally, the Silents' kids are Generation X and the Boomers' kids are the Millennials. So if you are a Millennial your parents are likely Boomers and your grandparents are likely Greatests, although they could be Silents too.

Opinions differ as to how long a given generation is. The Xers and the Millennials are the most controversial. The time span for the Xers is anywhere from 13 to 20 years, which makes pinning the start of the Millennials difficult. A 13-year generation is too short.

Looking at the census records offers a better clue of where the generations should fall, as displayed below. The most dramatic difference occurred between 1945 and 1947 when the number of births escalated by a whopping **39%** at the end of the war leading into the War Boom Baby Generation. In the middle of the Silent generation in 1935, there were only 2.1 million births versus 4.3 million in 1957 during the middle of the Boomer generation. That is over twice as many. Being a Boomer, I always thought there was too much attention paid to our self-absorbed generation, but alas, this was a major demographic event that had broad and long lasting effects. The War Boom Generation is from 1946 through 1964.*

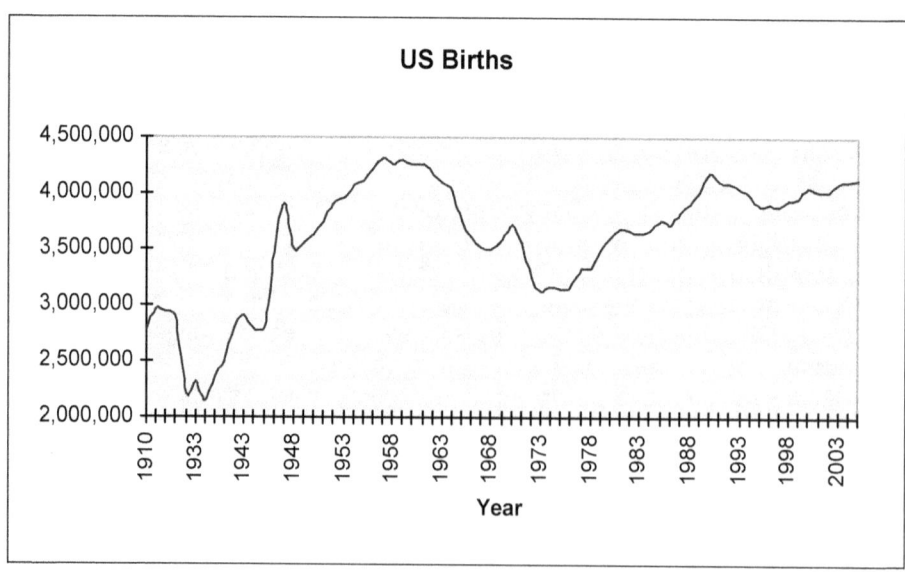

Around the middle of the 1960s, during the social turmoil of that time, you notice the number of births declines and does not pick back up until the 80s. This is because the much fewer Silents were now having their children. Choosing an end date for the Xers is somewhat arbitrary, but I chose 1979, which results in a 15-year generation (1/1/1965-12/31/1979.)

20th Century Generations Timeline

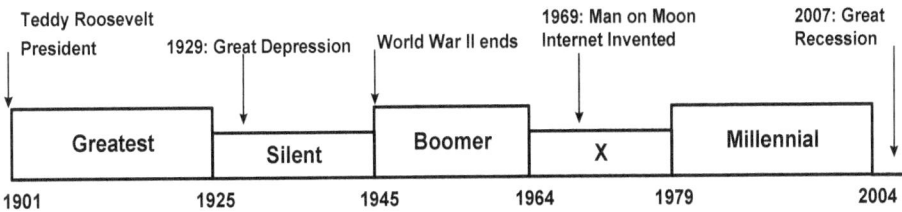

The Millennials are generally considered the children of the Boomers, but unlike their predecessors, not all Boomers started having children in their 20s. Many of the early Boomers did, but many late Boomers delayed their first childbirths until their 30s and even 40s. Others had children in their 20s, divorced, and started new families in their 30s or even 40s. Therefore, the Boomers children spread over a broad period of time – 40 years and mix with the children of the late Silents and early Xers. By now, the generational effect is not well demarcated. Even though the number of births is consistently over four million, the birthrate declined, such that the birthrate for the Millennials is less than the Xers by about 10%.

It is difficult to characterize an entire generation made up of many vastly different individuals from various social strata, locations, races, religions, politics, and nationalities, but there are some common characteristics that generally apply to the majority of those in a particular generation. They all share the same timeframe and are affected by the same events that occur in that period. How old they are when the events occur shape their view and reaction to those events, just as the events shape them. The events that occur during adolescence and early adulthood are particularly influential, for this is when personal identities and value systems develop, which impact how the cohort views and reacts to future events throughout their lives. They also share the common technology, attitudes, and culture of the time.

The Greatest Generation

It is not really when the generations are born, but rather the events they face that shape them. Born from 1901 to 1925, the Greatest Generation grew up in the early 1900s. Even in the early days of the twentieth century, there was a spirit in the air that this was to be an amazing century for the United States and that it would become a great or perhaps even the dominant world power. The British Empire comprised the premier power of the 19th century. The monarch of the Empire, Queen Victoria, who reigned since 1838, died at the turn of the century, signaling the end of the Victorian era, decline of the British Empire, and indeed the end of the Age of Empires for the major European powers.

If Queen Victoria was the predominant power of the 19th century, Teddy Roosevelt symbolizes the dominant power of the 20th. He was the hero of the Spanish American War, brashly charging up San Juan Hill when the upstart Americans surprised the developed world by beating a European power - Spain. Teddy was later known for his "Speak softly and carry a big stick" policy. This was a time when anything the Greatest generation could imagine was possible, a time of invention and promise. They grew up reading Jules Verne's tales of magnificent undersea voyages and trips to the moon, thinking that these remarkable stories could come true. Unbelievably, these did come to pass and they made it happen.

Teddy, also known as the Trust Buster, thwarted the Robber Barons of the 19th century, making it a fairer game for the average Joe - calling it a "Square Deal." Up until that time, the industrialists who built the country's oil, steel, railroad, electric, and financial industries, like Carnegie, Rockefeller, Aston, Morgan, Vanderbilt, and Mellon, had immense economic and political power. Just three of these men, Carnegie, Rockefeller, and Morgan, had fortunes worth over $1 trillion today. One Cleveland iron, oil, and coal magnet, Mark Hanna, allegedly elected and controlled Ohioan, President McKinley in 1896. Carnegie, Rockefeller, and Morgan, fearing the anti-monopoly candidate, William Jennings Bryan, each donated $20 million (in today's dollars) to the McKinley campaign. They were also concerned about the up and coming New York Governor, Theodore Roosevelt, so they persuaded McKinley to replace his first Vice President, Garret A. Hobart, with Roosevelt in his second term, a do-nothing position at the time.

McKinley was shot by a laid off steel worker turned anarchist six months into his second term, after which Teddy assumed the office of the Presidency. Roosevelt came from an upper-class family but felt that these industrialists wielded too much power over the American political system. He thereby moved to reduce their influence, most notably by breaking up the Standard Oil monopoly originated in Cleveland, the largest company in the world at the time. Just one of its many pieces, Exxon, is still one of the world's largest companies. If whole, the estimated value of Standard Oil's pieces and parts is over one trillion dollars. Even though Rockefeller lost his monopoly, his stake in the 30 split companies became worth $600 billion today, far more than riches Gates and, Buffet, accumulated together.*

Although not old enough to fight as children, the Greatests went through the 'war to end all wars', World War I. Following the war that redefined Europe and the Middle East, the post-war twenties were an optimistic boom time, which ended when Wall Street, banking gamesmanship, and greed plunged this generation into the Great Depression. The Depression ended when America started manufacturing war supplies for Europe during the first battles of World War II, followed by our entry into that war, where the Greatest Generation became heroes in the worst conflagration the world ever endured.

The servicemen who fought World War II came from every strata of society -- young men from different cultures, religions, races, ethnicities, and classes depending upon each other for their lives while fighting a common, ferocious enemy. This was a horrendous war, in which 62 to 78 million people died.* Battles like D-Day and Iwo Jima were brutal blood baths. The gruesome war ended with two atomic bombs falling on Nagasaki and Hiroshima, killing 150,000 – 250,000 people.

The young men and teenagers who fought in World War II lost many of their best friends, carrying unsavory memories with them throughout their lives. They rarely talked about those they lost or killed or the brutality of this war to their children or even their wives, locking the horrors deep within their psyche. They lost the innocence of youth reflected in their sometimes-harsh and unapproachable manner.

Many of the returning GIs took advantage of the GI bill to attend college, and when they graduated, for most the first in their family, they entered the booming upper-middle class professions of engineering, business, law, and advertising with the corresponding entrée to the more affluent suburbs and neighborhoods. To pay for the war and maintain a large industrial military complex against the Soviet threat, the top tax bracket was around 90% throughout the 50s, which seems excessive, but had an equalizing effect. More people were middle class than ever before.

During the Depression and subsequent war, few babies were born, due to a lack of prosperity and men away at war. It is interesting that during times of hardship, there is a natural tendency towards reduced birthrates, which tends to apply to any species. With less available resources, there is less to nurture the next generation. When resources are abundant, birthrates explode.

The end of the war came to define a generation born into unparalleled prosperity. Since it was a world war, the same population boom occurred throughout Europe, Japan, China, Russia, India, and the South Pacific, except there was a major difference. The rest of the developed world lay in ruins, creating a tremendous opportunity for the United States, whose infrastructure was intact and running at full speed to supply the war effort throughout the world.

As returning GIs married their childhood sweethearts, those 'Rosie the Riveters" left the factories and had children in record numbers. The world no longer needed boatloads of weapons, but they needed everything else the U.S. could supply, who, as a result, dominated the world economy with its converted factories and established shipping routes. One of the best examples were the tank and munitions plants throughout the Midwest that were converted from producing jeeps, trucks, tanks, and bombs, to making cars, domestic trucks, and farm equipment for the world to buy. Converted aircraft assembly plants spawned the burgeoning domestic airlines. Factories adopted the planning techniques, such as the PERT charts, an efficient war effort required. The top down military structure became the structure of the huge manufacturing conglomerates.

One by-product of the boom helped labor. Since American manufacturers could sell anything they produced to much larger domestic and foreign populations, there was a shortage of U.S. labor and since they could charge any reasonable price due to a lack of worldwide competition, there was room to pay labor more. The downtrodden laborers of the 30s banded together and demanded a seat at the bountiful table, thereby increasing union membership.

Another powerful force lay in the background – Communism, which conquered country after country in Eastern Europe and Eastern Asia. By the mid-1950s, led by China and Russia, nearly half of the world's population lay in Communist-controlled countries, not including India, who leaned towards Communism and was under the sphere of influence of Russia. Living in the U.S., it is difficult to understand the appeal of Communism, which was consistently portrayed as evil. Communism was a response to the greed of the capitalists at the end of the nineteenth century and in the 30s. It along with socialism became a credo of many abused American workers who toiled 6 days a week, 12 hours a day in deplorable and dangerous conditions for a pittance barely enough to support their families in their pollution laden, teeming tenements.

During the cold war, the union movement seemed like the lesser of two evils to executives and politicians. At the height of the communist threat in the late 1940s and early 1950s, Europe adopted socialistic measures. The U.S. under Johnson adopted the Great Society, which included welfare, Medicare, Medicaid, school lunches, and public housing in the sixties. It is likely that much of this social legislation passed because of the abundant wealth and charitable nature of the U.S., but it also mollified people at a time during the 60s when civil protests and riots were rampant.

The unions initially bargained for fair wages, reasonable working conditions, reasonable hours, and moderate benefits, but in contract after contract, union leaders, justifying their existence, negotiated for constantly more. With little competition, they had an effective monopoly and corporations, dependent upon their scarce labor, who had little global competition, gave into their escalating demands and merely raised their prices. Whatever the union negotiated also applied to the salaried employees, so in effect, giving into the unions enriched management, too.

In a tight labor market, to keep scarce-trained employees longer, companies developed benefits like pension plans, health care insurance, sick time, vacation time, and seniority. Wages and benefits went higher creating a huge middle class, whose kids benefited from the boom. These kids, unlike their previously poor parents and encouraged by their parent's ambitions, dreamed of going to college, the cornerstone of the American dream.

The Greatests experienced an unprecedented amount of progress in their lifetime, to which they contributed immensely. Many were born on farms and in small towns across America when there were no electric lights, telephones, radios, indoor plumbing, automobiles, or airplanes. They helped establish all of these innovations along with televisions, computers, jets, and the landing of a man on the moon.

According to "Generations" by Strauss and Howe and their characterization of this generation as Heroes, they tend to be pragmatic, self-reliant, laissez-faire, team-oriented, optimistic during a crisis, energetic, overly confident, and politically powerful.* **Seven** American Presidents from Kennedy through George H. W. Bush were Greatests.

The Silent Generation

The term "Silent Generation" first appeared in a November 1951 Time cover article, when this generation was just coming of age and applied to those born between 1926 and 1945. Unlike the Greatest Generation, they were born during the Great Depression and WWII, growing up in a time of deprivation when their parents, facing high unemployment, eked out a generally meager living. The article characterized this generation as fatalistic and conventional, possessing confused morals, expecting disappointment but desiring faith.

They were too young to remember the boom times of the 20s and grew up during the 30s, when one out of four men was unemployed and few women worked. Even those who had jobs worked for reduced wages and struggled daily. Many of the wealthy lost everything to the stock market crash and joined the ranks of the poor. Millions of people lost all of their savings as thousands of banks evaporated. It seemed everyone was poor. For many families who prospered during the 20s, the purchase of a new pair of shoes, a dress, or meat for the table became luxuries. Many children did not know they were poor, because it seemed everyone they grew up with was in the same condition.

In the cities, people huddled in their ethnically and racially demarcated neighborhoods, many looking to their faith for sustenance. Many lost their farms to the dust bowl or because they were unable to make payments to the banks. At the dawn of the Great Depression, there was no social net to catch families – no Social Security, unemployment compensation, Workers Compensation, welfare, Medicaid, or Medicare. The Democrats, led by another Roosevelt, Franklin D, passed most of these during the Depression.

World War II started in 1939, ending the Great Depression as U.S. factories hired workers to produce war goods purchased by Europeans. During the war, life improved dramatically. Many of the Silents' dads were too old to fight and found high paying jobs in the war industries. Even if their dads went off to the war, their mothers could find good factory jobs.

Families now had plenty of money, but there was little to spend on due to the war effort. Everyone on the home front including the kids united, growing victory gardens, collecting recyclables, and buying war bonds. Many goods were either not available or rationed like rubber, sugar, cheese, milk meat, fish, fuel, nylon, autos, and shoes.

The silent theme extends to politics as no American President was from the Silent Generation. Unlike their predecessors and followers, when the bulk of social legislation passed in response to generational political pressure, they did not rock the boat.

This was also the "beat" generation, frequently called the artistic generation. Prominent members of the generation included the Beatles, Jimmy Hendrix, James Dean, Elvis Presley, Marilyn Monroe, Marlon Brando, Clint Eastwood, Bob Dylan, the Rolling Stones, Colin Powell, Gloria Steinem, and Woody Allen.*

The Silents fought in the Korean War when the draft and GI Bill sere still intact. As a result, they went to college in record numbers. Following the example of their Rosie the Riveter predecessors, many Silent generation women became the first generation to enter the workforce en masse. Even though still not paid well, they experienced a degree of economic freedom uncommon until then. Partially due to their independence and the burgeoning women's movement, the divorce rate zoomed from 9 to 23 (divorces per 1000 married women.)*

Even though the Silent generation did not have to fight in World War II, they benefited from the prosperity. Despite their moniker and tough start, the Silents grew up during a time when conditions became progressively better. The Silents went to smaller schools that were more personable and grew up in close-knit proud communities. In the wake of the Greatests, due to the economic stimulus of the Boomers and rebuilding of the world, the Silents had numerous job and advancement opportunities. They received benefits unheard of by their grandparents including generous retirement packages along with Social Security and Medicare.

The Silents were the first true teenagers. They grew up in the big band era, listened to folk music in college, and invented rock and roll. Silents like the Stones, Beach Boys, and Paul McCartney still perform today. Many graduated from high school for the first time in their families, but they expected to go to work, get married, and start a family right after high school or college at the latest. They married at a younger age than any generation. The lack of security through the depression and war and a yearning for the stability of a family may explain this phenomenon, along with an unconscious natural urge to reproduce following times of deprivation during times of abundance.

Boomers

When GIs returned, they married and started families, begetting the War Boom Baby generation or Boomers, born from 1946 until 1964 in unprecedented numbers. With housing stocks depleted by the depression and war, the new parents moved from their balkanized neighborhoods and farms into mass housing developments in newly minted suburbs, enabled by affordable autos and newly paved roads. There were fewer ethnic, religious, and social boundaries in newly minted suburbs, which were not as important for the more worldly, fraternal, and bloodied GIs. There were still, however, racial and class boundaries defined by adjacent upscale suburbs and now relatively poorer cities. These young families needed everything: appliances, furniture, autos, gasoline, clothing, toys, books, schools, food etc. As a result, the economy exploded.

The boomers grew up in a more socially equal society. Many of their grandparents were immigrants growing up in nationality-based neighborhoods, where many still spoke their native language. Others grew up in the still segregated South. This is the world their parents were born into and where they visited on the weekends and holidays with all of the old world traditions and flavors. Their parents grew up in American melting pot schools learning English, American history, and culture. The ethnically integrated war and factories also helped to form the Greatests' character and opinions. The friends Boomers grew up with came from different nationalities and religions. When they went to high school and college, they might even be on a team or cheer squad with those from another race.

Growing up in the 50s was the golden age of childhood. The suburbs were brand spanking new with all of the modern, timesaving conveniences, close enough to the cities to experience all of its wonders yet close enough for a ride in the country in the new family car. When they were young, most moms were home and kids roamed neighborhoods free, with dozens of kids to play ball and games with. There was little childhood obesity, since kids wanted to play as much as they could, disappointed at having to go home when the streetlights came on. Vacations, formerly a luxury, became commonplace as American families explored all of the wonders of the nation or at least their region. As Dinah Shore sang on the first TVs, "See the USA in your Chevrolet!".

These were optimistic and bountiful times. In the 30s, it seemed everybody was poor, and meals were meager or frugal. In the 40s, goods were rationed, and even if you could afford it, hard to acquire. Now, most people could afford meat every day, few worried about buying children's clothes, and loved lavishing their children with the toys they themselves rarely received at Christmas. A new invention, television, opened a window to the world. Disney stimulated young imaginations with shows like the Mouseketeers and Davy Crockett.

There were still worries for this fortunate generation. Anticommunist fervor and witch-hunts peaked with periodic practice air raids, for which Boomers huddled under their school desks fearing atomic bombs bursting over their heads.

In 1957, the Russians launched Sputnik and the United States panicked, fearing that the Russians would occupy space, potentially raining A-Bombs down upon us. People went to parks and school fields at dusk to see Sputnik, a tiny star flying though the autumn sky. The nation feared we did not have enough scientists to compete and a call went out to educators and the Boomers emphasizing the importance of scientific education as a patriotic duty, vital for national defense. Less than twelve years after Sputnik, the Boomers saw the miraculous event on TV of Neil Armstrong walking on the moon, a crescendo to the American optimism of the age.

When the Boomers entered their teen years en masse, many expected the extended period of delayed financial responsibility to last for another 10 years until they graduated from college and started their careers. Is it any wonder that rock and roll, drug, sexual and life exploration exploded for the first time, stimulated by an unequalled mass of hormonal teenagers throughout the world? Silent girls screamed for Elvis, but the hysteria became deafening when the Beatles visited the UK, U.S., Canada, Germany, and France.

Most of the Boomers grew up during a time of overwhelming opportunity and optimism as contrasted with prior periods, partially because their parents had just gone through hell and wanted a well-deserved peaceful life for themselves and their children. Some sensed they were growing up in a Pollyannic world and had the luxury of seeing injustices that few could focus on before. The ethnic and class boundaries that kept their predecessors in silos were dissolving, so they formed tighter bonds among themselves and less of a bond to their multigenerational nationalities and classes. Plus, they also had the added luxury of an education that most of their forefathers, who went to work full-time at 13, 16, or 18, could not afford.

Prior to the GI Bill, few lower and middle class families considered college an option, certainly not in the Great Depression. During the optimistic 50s and early 60s, with expanded affluence, burgeoning middle class families expected their Boomer kids to go to college - it was part of the American Dream towards continuous upward mobility. With many states building new campuses and subsidizing tuition, college became affordable. Up until 1971-72, tuition at California state universities was free, then it was $600 a year, so the young adults could readily work their way through college. Professor salaries were on a par with factory wages and professors frequently had to obtain second jobs to support a family. Currently, full professor's salaries are three to four times a standard factory wage.

Radically increasing Boomer angst was the Vietnam War, in which they, due to the draft, expected to fight. Vietnam constituted the longest U.S. war thus far with men dying for an unclear, amorphous goal. The U.S. involvement lasted from 1961 until 1974. **8,744,000** men served during the war. **58,193** lost their lives, and over **300,000** were wounded. At first, Boomer men obtained draft deferrals to attend college, leading to bulging college enrollments. Late In 1969, when the War required more young men, those in power did away with the deferrals and replaced it with a lottery. If your number came up, you were heading for Vietnam and might be killed or maimed. The following spring, protests spread throughout the nation like wild fire, until four students died at Kent State, sapping the nation's will for war.

Unlike their fathers, the Vietnam veterans were not welcomed back as heroes, and millions still dealt with the psychological terror and questionable purpose of the war. The Boomers made sure that their children who served in Afghanistan and Iraq received warm welcomes home.

John Kennedy, who began U.S. involvement in Vietnam, died after his shooting in Dallas. His successor, Lyndon Johnson massively escalated the war. Drained and gaunt by Vietnam, Johnson decided not to run for a second term. Robert McNamara, then Secretary of Defense, later apologized for Vietnam stating, "We were wrong, terribly wrong about the Vietnam War." Nixon, who promised to end the war in his first term then secretly expanded the war to Cambodia and Laos leading to the protests, finally ended it in his second and soon afterwards drew impeachment and resigned.*

The Vietnam War became the first the U.S. ever lost and as a result, we finally lost our taste for war for at least a couple of decades. Similar to the Greatests' WWII, the Viet Nam war came to define the Boomer generation, but in a negative fashion, even though it was not the Boomer's war. They fought it, but they did not plan nor direct it.

Antiestablishmentism peaked in the late sixties and early 70s, including not only the war, but also civil rights protests and riots after the Martin Luther King shooting, women's liberation, and gay rights. The term "generation gap" described what seemed to be a chasm between the Boomers and their overwrought Greatests parents.

Many Boomers, persuaded to obtain a technical education to support the aerospace industry, which developed the jet liners and space program, entered engineering and math programs. By the early seventies after reaching the moon, spending on aerospace rapidly declined. Thousands lost their positions. Young scientists and technicians who graduated from college in the late sixties and seventies, sought new employment in the burgeoning computer industry. They flocked from the aerospace companies in Seattle, LA, and San Diego, and colleges throughout the country to the greener pastures of Silicon Valley and Boston's beltway. In 1975, Bill Gates and Paul Allen started Microsoft in Seattle just as the city's aerospace industry declined. Millions of Boomers became computer engineers, analysts, salesmen, entrepreneurs, and managers. Thousands became the first computer millionaires and billionaires like Bill Gates, Paul Allen, Steve Jobs, Steve Wozniak, and Steve Case. The Boomers were the first digital generation.

Many of same Boomers who protested against the establishment in college became the workaholics of the 80s and 90s. The women became the first to seek and succeed at careers en masse. These women also became soccer moms, ferrying their kids from one scheduled event to another, working unbelievable hours both at home and work and never really resting. Boomer dads, perhaps feeling the lack of attention from their war-bruised dads and guilt about their exhausted wives, paid uncustomary attention to their kids, becoming their sometimes too boisterous coaches and cheerleaders. Following the example of their parents, they lavished their Millennial kids with goods and opportunities along with the praise they craved but rarely received. Together they became hover parents as their kids metamorphosed off to college.

The Boomers, accustomed to the abundance of their childhood, became mass consumers like no others. It is not difficult to understand this phenomenon since Madison Avenue bombarded them with ads on TV selling cereal and toys before they could read, then cars, beer, cigarettes, cosmetics, and fast food by the time they were teenagers.

Their predecessors saved heavily and paid in cash. Boomers bought now and paid later with newly minted bank credit cards. When these maxed out, the financial industry invented a new and more deadly instrument, the home equity loan, to further stretch their credit. Consumption grew to 70% of GDP and the leadership of the early 2000s encouraged continuous, conspicuous, corrosive consumption. Their parents settled into suburban bungalows and ranches with a family room. They moved up to McMansions with private bedrooms for each kid, an equal number of bathrooms, guest rooms, home offices, game rooms, work out rooms, and home theaters.

Many Boomers did not save for retirement, perhaps due to their optimistic upbringing, never enduring major generational hardships, and youth-obsessed narcissistic self-image (50 was, after all, the new 30). They never really thought about growing old. Many unwisely thought housing prices would continue to soar indefinitely and escalating equity in their McMansion would provide their retirement when they finally downsized.

Generation X

Following the Boomers, the Xers were born from 1965 through 1979. The first reference to Generation X was by Coupland in his book, "Generation X: Tales for an Accelerated Culture."* In France, they were generation Bof or "whatever", a typical global response from the generation symbolizing their view of the world in general.

These were children of the seventies and eighties when the U.S. was in a funk following the end of the Viet Nam War, the first ever lost by United States, revealing its vulnerability to the rest of the world. The Arab Oil Embargo added to the sense of the malaise as OPEC cut the supply of oil to the United States in response to the U.S.'s arming of Israel during the Yom Kippur War. With multi-block lines leading into gas stations, the price of a barrel of oil quadrupled to $12.

Until then, everyone wanted a large powerful automobile that may travel as little as seven miles on a gallon of gas. The more power the better. Gas was plentiful and cheap at as little as 25 cents per gallon. Teenagers drooled over muscle cars like the Mustang, Vet, and GTO. Then, after the embargo, attitudes dramatically changed and everyone wanted a compact car with the high mileage, few of which American profit-driven automakers produced.

Gas-guzzlers were suddenly no longer popular as Americans started to see that higher mileage, less expensive, longer lasting, and more reliable, Japanese models could replace the "planned obsolescent" products of Detroit. The Japanese, facing complaints of cheaply made products in the 1950s, rigorously adopted the quality principles of Deming, an American and protégé of Bell Lab's Shewhart, the father of quality control. It was not until 30 years later during the early 80s that U.S. manufacturers (initially Ford) adopted Deming's quality and leadership transformative principles, recapturing a vital advantage previously surrendered to the Japanese.*

In reality, since WWII, the U.S. enjoyed an unprecedented term of economic prosperity with little global competition. By the mid-70s, the developed world finally caught up. Management and labor became complacent and a lack of national leadership made it easy for other countries to compete, an inevitable prospect. For the first time, the United States had formidable economic competition and high paying manufacturing jobs in steel, automotive, and manufacturing started to flow overseas.

During the late 70s, the U.S. faced rampant double-digit inflation and then stagflation settled in, which added slow growth to the discouraging mix. Adding insult to injury, the decade ended with another shock to the country's psyche when Iran captured 52 American hostages in the embassy during November of 1979. Some link Iran's actions to the defeat of President Carter. Iran held the hostages for 444 days until President Reagan's inauguration day in 1981, when Carter left office.

As children, the Xers felt the full brunt of their parents high divorce rates. They typically lived with their mothers, staying with their fathers on weekends. Since most mothers were now working, they became the latchkey kids. Even those whose parents stayed together did not have full-time mothers and sensed what was happening to their classmates.

They saw their dads lose long-time jobs due to cutbacks and became skeptical of the system. Xers became self-reliant and entrepreneurial. Realizing that there were no guarantees for marriage or employment, they became pragmatic. Seeing pension plans discontinue and doubting Social Security would remain fully intact, they became savers, unlike the elder Boomers. As teenagers, they wore jeans and flannel shirts while they listened to grunge music on MTV. They were the first kids to have home PCs and computer games.

Certainly, the problems of the 70s did not compare to those of the Xer's parents, the Silents, during the depression, but these were neither the optimistic 50s of the Boomers nor the buoyant turn of the century of the Greatests. Following the Boomer-induced expansion, there were fewer initial opportunities for the Xers as they entered the workforce in the mid-80s. The 80s started with two relatively severe depressions separated by only one year in 1980 and 81, when unemployment grew to 10.8%, the worst since the Great Depression.

As the first Xers finally graduated from college, they found it difficult to obtain jobs partially because of the larger preceding generation. Many worked as waiters or waitresses for a couple of years until they found a position in their chosen field. Then the economy started to boom again in the mid-80s and 90s.

This generation did not have the job security, wage increases, and benefits of their Silent parents. When they entered the job market, American business was downsizing, right sizing, reengineering, reorganizing, etc. They could no longer depend upon one corporation to offer them lifetime employment, but had to depend upon the knowledge and skills they possessed to build a career and provide job security.

A nephew graduated from college with dual degrees in chemistry and art in the late 80s but was unable to find a position in either field. At the time, his mother had 3rd stage colon cancer and his father had five heart attacks, so he took out loans to finish school, which his younger brother, who attended the same university, could not afford. He worked as a waiter and built decks, working up to 60 hours a week, while living at home and helping to support his ailing parents. At the same time, he studied for a 3rd degree in graphic arts. In the 90s, he found employment in New York as a 3-D graphic artist creating many of the ads seen on TV, like the introduction to NFL football. He eventually rose to director-level positions in the industry. His story is typical of many determined Xers who found it difficult at first, then obtained success later.

By the early 90s, the economy improved, unemployment was generally low, and Ronald Reagan occupied the presidency. In 1989, the Berlin Wall and European communism fell, ending the 45-year long cold war with a victory for the United States. Two years later, the U.S. under George H.W. Bush led a worldwide, world-paid, coalition in a blitzkrieg war against Saddam Hussein, conquering Iraq in months. Winning the Cold War and the Gulf War restored self-confidence to the U.S. The way George Bush won the war with funding and cooperation of the world restored the world's confidence in the U.S.

The '90s became the longest period of expansion in U.S. history. Now ensconced in their jobs and professions, the Xers were doing well. Xers were better educated than their predecessors. Seeing how older generations felt betrayed by their employers, they were less likely to become workaholics, more likely to seek balance and were more family-oriented. They also tended to save more and live within their means.

The Millennial Generation

By the time the Millennials arrived in the 1980s, the effects of the Great Depression and World War II, the two major shaping events of the twentieth century, faded into history. As the children of the massive Boomers wave, there were 25 -30% more Millennials born per year than there were Xers at their low point. There is no clear population demarcation that distinguishes the Millennials from the next generation. The number of newborns hovers a little over four million, as the birth rate gradually declines. The Millennials begin in 1980 and end in 2004, both of which are somewhat arbitrary, but there is no consensus as to exactly when they start or end. This results in a 25-year generation like the Greatests, which seems like the maximum for a generation.

Millennials were born during the longest period of economic expansion in U.S. history. These were prosperous years and by the end of the 90s, the nation even had a balanced budget.

Many Boomers delayed marriage until their late 20s and 30s. When they did marry, the now two income couples (DINKs – dual income no kids) delayed having children. Then when they had children, they were further along economically with more resources for their children. Workaholic Boomer parents, somewhat guilty about their careers lavished their children with toys, video games, private bedrooms, computers, TVs, and a myriad of post-school activities. Many Millennials grew up in merged families with one natural parent, stepparents, and stepsiblings. Such families, a rough adjustment for Xers, became the norm.

Parents, now, had fewer children. There was little random play but rather scheduled events to fill a child's free time. These mothers were the soccer moms and dads who carted kids from one event to another in oversized SUVs. It was no longer important whether you won or lost, everyone got a trophy and praise. School grades were raised a full letter, so what used to be a C became a B and a B became an A.

This was truly the digital generation who grew up attached to the internet and texting on smart phones. Social media such as Facebook and Twitter became an integral part of their lives. With an extensive amount of screen-time spent on the internet, video games, and TV, and with less time spent in outdoor play, this was the first generation to have a high percentage of obesity. When they went off to college, hover parents called them daily and continued to intercede in their lives. College professors and some bosses heard complaints regarding their children's grades and reviews.

Millennials are more tolerant of other races and gays. They are multitaskers participative decision makers, confident, realistic, and seek balance in their lives.

Pew Research performed extensive research on the Millennial Generation. Here are some of their findings*:

- They are the most ethnically and racially diverse cohort of youth in the nation's history. Among those ages 13 to 29: 18.5% are Hispanic; 14.2% are black; 4.3% are Asian; 3.2% are mixed race or other; and 59.8%, a record low, are white.
- They are starting out as the most politically progressive age group in modern history. In the 2008 election, Millennials voted for Barack Obama over John McCain by 66%-32%, while adults ages 30 and over split their vote's 50%-49%. In the four decades since the development of Election Day exit polling, this is the largest gap ever seen in a presidential election between the votes of those under and over age 30.
- They are the least religiously observant youths since survey research began charting religious behavior.
- They are more inclined toward trust in institutions than were either of their two predecessor generations. They are significantly less cynical about government and political leaders than are other Americans or the previous generation of young people.
- Their heroes are close and familiar. When asked to name someone they admire, they are twice as likely as older Americans to name a family member, teacher, or mentor.
- They are more comfortable with globalization and new ways of doing work. They are the most likely of any age group to say that automation, the outsourcing of jobs, and the growing number of immigrants have helped and not hurt American workers.

The first decade of their new millennium started with a tragedy on September 11, 2001, when three jets exploded into the Pentagon and the World Trade Towers murdering 2,977 innocent people. The 9/11 assault preceded the dot com crash and the discrediting of companies like Enron,

WorldCom, and Arthur Anderson. It started out with the dotcom bust and a recession, followed by two of the longest wars in U.S. history, Afghanistan, and Iraq, which led to record deficits.

The first decade of the twenty-first century ended with the Great Recession, continuingly high unemployment, hugely expensive Wall Street bailouts, even higher deficits, and a sky-high National Debt approaching 100% of GDP. Continuing a trend started in the 90s, millions of manufacturing jobs disappeared, and then professional jobs like programming, accounting, customer service, radiology, architecture, editing, and engineering started to flow overseas.

Parents and grandparents hoped that this generation would continue to be more prosperous than their own but have doubts. Like the Xers when they graduated, many of the highly educated Millennials found it difficult to acquire a job in their chosen field and their unemployment continues to be much higher than their elders. They cannot expect to be at the same job for their lifetime and will likely face periodic layoffs. Few will receive pensions, and even public pension benefits are reducing since state and local governments budgets contracted due to less tax revenues. They will likely need to work until after 68 or 70 to collect full Social Security benefits, and they may face a huge national debt to pay off, which will likely reduce their security net leaving them more exposed with less unemployment, Medicare, Medicaid, healthcare and Workers Compensation.

For those that do not have degrees, middle class wages have stagnated or declined for decades, and for many, jobs like manufacturing substantially decreased. Still, this cohort's professionals and executives should do well, although the gap between the wealthy and middle classes may continue to grow, with the likelihood of continued civil unrest, exemplified by the Occupy Wall Street movement, increasing.

It is still too early to underestimate this talented, highly educated, technically gifted, collaborative, socially networked, optimistic generation for they will likely find solutions their elders have not been able to fathom, leading to something better we cannot envision. I believe that vision lay with digital technology, productivity, and sustainability, covered in the last chapter. As we will see in the coming chapters, this generation will eventually lead us out of the current stagnation.

Summary

One of the themes you may have noticed is that the living generations pass through the same events, but due to their age, these events affect them differently. The Greatests grew up in marvelous times, weathered the Great Depression and War, then relished the post war boom. The Silents grew up during the bad times, so even though life for them got consistently better, they were understandably less optimistic.

Except for the 70s malaise, the Boomers' lives were full of boom times until the Great Recession. The manner parents treat their children also changes depending upon the times. Boomer parents spoiled many of their Millennial children, but now these children must face at least a decade of lean years, a difficult adjustment.

By necessity, the Financial Time Machine focuses upon numbers to build its model, but subtle generational characteristics influence these figures.   Much of the time machine relates to the size of each generation, but the generation's financial texture also matters.   Each generation processes a set of economic circumstances and events, whether favorable or unfavorable, that influence their financial behaviors.   The financial landscape and history one generation faces determines the world the next will inherit.   For instance, the lack of global competition, record prosperity, and technological advancements the Greatest Generation enjoyed during the 50s and 60s allowed them to provide material, security, and educational advantages to their children, to a degree not experienced by any previous generation.

The four recessions, stagflation, divorce, rampant layoffs, and lack of security Generation X's children endured in the 70s affected their financial perception of the world.   Certainly, members of a generation exist as individuals, but each possesses a common experience they share repeatedly amongst themselves, thereby reinforcing and bonding the generation together.

The rebellion the War Boom Generation exhibited during their coming-of-age changed their attitude towards the financial world, although they later became workaholics, the Wizards of Wall Street, and digital technological pioneers, perhaps in some ironic way because they experienced the rebellion. Steve Job's genius stemmed partially from his experiences with LSD, marijuana, counterculture, and Eastern religions, including a monastic journey to India. He credited his "artistic" side as the reason he designed such imaginative, attractive, and supremely practical products. His company, Apple, is now the largest in the world.

The general attitudes the Boomers developed regarding sexuality, religion, childcare, materialism, religion, gender roles, and discrimination greatly affected their Millennial offspring.   This, too, affected the economy. Female Boomers entered the workplace in record numbers, many acquiring advanced education and credentials. In many cases, they were the first women to occupy professional and managerial positions in numerous traditional companies. This opened up the world of work to their Millennial daughters who expected to work whether they had children or not.   Women working dramatically increased the workforce and therefore the GDP.

3

Generational Megatrends

Several pervasive trends transcend the events shaping individual generations to span all of the generations. These megatrends affect each generation's financial behavior, significantly impacting the Financial Life Cycle.

World War II

The first megatrend consists of the war that defined the War Boom Baby Generation, although it seems odd to apply the term baby to, now, 60-year old grandparents. Following the largest global war in history, the baby boom phenomenon occurred not only in the U.S., but also in Europe, Russia, China, Japan, parts of the Middle East, Africa, and the South Pacific. Countries like the Soviet Union, Japan, and Germany lost millions and even tens of millions of their citizens, so the baby boom was an even larger event for them as they repopulated their devastated nations.

World War II represents the seminal event of the twentieth century. The effects of the war and its aftermath, like ripples from a rock thrown into a pond, permeate to the twenty-first century. Atomic power, space exploration, rapid technological advancement, jet planes, American affluence, Israel, Communist Eastern Europe, the Cold War, the Korean War, and the Viet Nam War all have roots in World War II. The huge population wave the war induced dominated economic cycles for 60 years, creating prosperity and the Great Recession. It will continue to affect the economy for another 20 years.

There have been many wars and conflicts throughout the latter half of the 20th and early 21st century, but there has not been a war on a developed nation's soil for nearly 70 years. The fact that Europe has not had a major international conflict within its borders is in itself an amazing accomplishment, considering European nations fought each other for centuries. War is devastating and destructive, after which it takes decades to recover, thereby stunting human productive progress.

This period of relative worldwide peace enabled unprecedented technological advancement and globalization in which trade routes remain largely open and free flowing. The entire world benefits immensely from this sustained period of relative peace and trade, allowing many underdeveloped nations to prosper like never before. Indeed, most of the developed countries like those in Europe now have miniscule military budgets, less than a tenth of previous levels. In 2011, the U.S.'s defense budget was three times that of all of the Eurozone's defense spending combined, more than that of the entire world and nine times our nearest competitor, China.*

One result of World War II are the world's War Boom Babies who are just starting to retire, stressing European and U.S. economies as they try to fund promised Boomer retirements. Prior to the war, during the Great Depression, Franklin Roosevelt and a Democratic Congress passed numerous social legislative bills such as Social Security and Unemployment Compensation. Following the war, Lyndon Johnson under his Great Society policy passed additional social legislation including Medicare and Medicaid. The European countries became even more socialistic adding programs like universal healthcare and restrictive labor practices. By the time these programs peaked in the 70s, the huge Boomer population wave had entered the workforce. Since most of the benefits accrue for the elderly, as earnings increased, these countries were able to afford the generous social benefits of the smaller preceding generations. The progress of this huge wave into the latter stages of its financial life cycle creates stress upon social benefit programs throughout the developed world.

Globalization

The world became more globally connected, as the world wide Baby Boomers progressed through the successive stages of their Financial Life Cycle. This began during the war when the U.S. sent tens of thousands of ships to supply its allies. Global connectivity continued to strengthen after the war as the U.S. helped Europe rebuild their infrastructure with the Marshall Plan.   The trend accelerated as nations like Japan, Germany, Korea, and then China and India joined the global economy.

Boomers like Microsoft's Allan and Gates, Apple's Jobs and Wozniak, Oracle's Ellison, Amazon's Bezos, and thousands of entrepreneurs like them became catalysts for the digital age. Millions of Boomers labored in software companies, hardware companies, and corporations to design and build the millions of devices and billions of lines of code powering the digital revolution. Their technology shrunk the country and then the world, making it possible for people throughout the globe to work together.   Their technology made it possible for capital to flow effortlessly around the world seeking opportunity.   Globalization represents the second mega-trend.

With the rest of the developed infrastructure and industrial capacity in ruins, U.S. corporations and labor had a huge competitive advantage. U.S. companies found willing markets for their goods and started expanding overseas, eventually building plants throughout Europe and parts of Asia. By the 70s, the rest of the world, particularly Germany,

Korea, and Japan, started to catch up. As their industrial capacity, innovation, and quality climbed, they acquired U.S. companies and built plants in the U.S. Multinational corporations started to dominate business, for there are few large or even medium sized companies in the U.S. or overseas, who do not derive a significant portion of their revenue from foreign operations.

Enabled by technology such as the Internet, globalization rapidly increased in the 90s when notably China, India, Mexico, Russia, and Brazil entered the global economy. Many business operations could now be performed anywhere and flowed overseas to the lowest-priced labor provider. To be competitive, even small manufacturers produced goods overseas. Wal-Mart became a leader, acquiring hundreds of billions of dollars' worth of Chinese goods streaming in a continuous flow of ships across the Pacific. As a consequence, whole industries like furniture manufacture, apparel, shoe making, and electronics, nearly vanished from American shores.

By the 2000s, intellectual tasks also flowed overseas. India offered a huge population of educated English-speaking people who worked for a fraction of American wages. Millions of Indians became programmers, accountants, clerks, research analysts, radiologists, medical transcriptionists, data entry clerks, and customer service representatives for U.S. operations. Even engineering and innovation, previously a U.S. competitive advantage started to migrate overseas. The U.S. produces about 14% of the world's engineers, whereas Asia provides over 50%, so now some U.S. companies build research facilities in China and India to increase their innovative capacity.*

By 2010, wages in China and India rose, as did consumerism. Energy prices also climbed so that it no longer made financial sense to manufacture bulky items overseas and ship these to the U.S. Notably Japanese, Korean, and German companies shifted some operations to the U.S. Fortunately, many jobs like those in retail, restaurants, healthcare, sales, education, government, and local services cannot be outsourced overseas.

Globalization initially increased wages in the United States, particularly for blue-collar jobs. Later it tended to decrease these earnings, which is a dominant component in the Financial Time Machine.

Life Expectancy

Our third generational mega-trend relates to life expectancy. Two hundred years ago in George Washington's era, the average life expectancy was just over **35**. At the turn of the Twentieth Century, it was **48**. By 1950 during the baby boom, it was **68**, and now it is nearly **79** years.* In 200 years, life expectancy more than doubled. The Millennials can expect to live over thirty years longer than their Greatest Generation great grandparents did – what an amazing gift.

Expanding Life Expectancies

Year	Life Expectancy	Increase
1800	35	
1900	48	37%
1950	68	42%
2010	79	16%

Like previous generations, some of our forefathers such as Franklin, Jefferson, and Adams lived to ripe old ages, but many died while children or in their 20s and 30s. That's why few in society could afford extended educations or teenagers that did not work and start reproducing. In the Twentieth Century, thanks to ever-improving healthcare, sanitation, and nutrition, an individual's prospects began to change. Society could finally afford to have a large percentage of its children graduate from high school, college, and even receive advanced degrees, delaying jobs, marriage, and children. Higher educational achievement leads to further innovations, which in turn leads to longer life expectancies. Scientists think they may have discovered the cure of Alzheimer's and aging itself. The trend to longer life expectancies seem to have slowed, but some think there may be a dramatic genome induced increase within the next ten years.

There is probably no other megatrend that has a larger impact upon society than the blessings of a longer life. This really changes the ballgame of life. Parents can expect to work long enough to afford college educations for their children. Children can afford to graduate from high school and college and establish themselves in a career before they marry and have children themselves. They can expect to work into their 60s and save enough for retirement then expect to enjoy their golden years. Unlike previous generations, we can expect to travel through life with most of our siblings and friends before we eventually die. We even expect to have an extended relationship with and the support of our parents well into our middle-age. At the start of the Twenty-first Century, we think it is tragic if parents die before their children reach 30. At the start of the Twentieth Century, it was not uncommon for children to become orphans before they reached ten.

Life insurance costs are proportional to the expanded life expectancy. For those who unfortunately die before their time, they can more readily afford life insurance to cover their families until the children are old enough to be independent.

Before the Twentieth Century, generational economics did not make as much sense, because there were no large, long-living generations. There were certainly many devastating wars with population spikes following the wars when nations tried to recover and build up the next generation of warriors. But when half of the population dies by 40 or 50, the preceding generations do not have much long-term impact, because their numbers are so small. This is less true for the wealthy class, who could afford sanitation, good food, and health care. For the poorer majority struggling to survive, few thought of retirement other than living with their children if they made it that long.

Now with people expecting to live into their 80s or even 100, a Financial Life Cycle and focusing on more than a couple of generations makes sense. None of my grandparents were alive when I was born, but it is not unusual for today's children to know their great-grandparents.

Declining Birthrates

Birthrates declined substantially over the last 60 years. The following chart displays the lowest and highest birthrates for each of the generations when they were born.

Generational Birthrates (live births per 1,000 women)*

Generation	Birthrate		
	High	Median	Low
Greatest	28	25	30
Silent	20	19	21
Boomer	24	22	25
X	17	15	18
Millennial	15	14	17

Generational Birth Rates

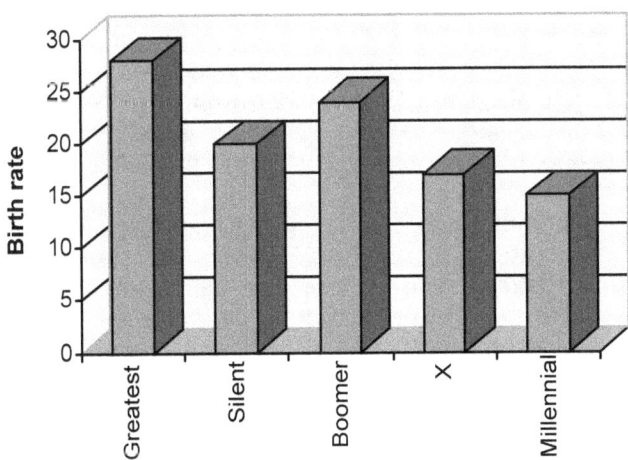

With the exception of the Boomers, birthrates decline dramatically over the 20th century. The number of Millennials born per year was over 4

million, nearly that of the Boomers, but there are about twice as many people in the U.S. in 2000 as there were in 1950. The current birthrate approaches half of what it was for the Greatests and two-thirds of the Boomers. A declining birthrate is an indicator of a declining civilization like those of Rome, Greece, or France in the 19th Century, and perhaps Europe today.

The declining birthrate is no doubt partially contributable to birth control, but also because of a preference for fewer children and later marriages. At an average cost of $200,000, children are unfortunately expensive and although it is less expensive to raise an additional child, stretched modern American families dependent upon two incomes have less time and psychological resources. Preschool childcare is particularly expensive. The typical American family has two children, which, since not everyone has children, is not enough to maintain current population levels.   Immigration helps compensate for the lower birthrates, plus immigrants traditionally have higher birthrates.

One consequence of declining birthrates is that as Boomers retire, which millions have already done, there will be fewer workers to support them.   Up until recently, there were three workers contributing into Social Security for each recipient. This slides to two in the future.

Delayed Marriage

The fifth Mega Generational trend closely relates to the fourth. As mentioned in the previous chapter, the average age people marry today is about 28 for males and 26 for females. In 1960, it was 23 for males and 20 for females. There are 104 million unmarried Americans over age 18, representing over 45% of the adult population, according to the U.S. Census Bureau's 2008 American Community Survey.

The first inference is that when females delay marriage for six of their prime childbearing years, they are likely to have fewer children, although 58% of first births are to unmarried women. Still the average age of the first births increased by four years since 1970.*   Many Greatests and Silents had two or three children in their early twenties and then went on to have more.

There are numerous reasons for delaying marriage. Certainly the nearly 50% divorce rate over the last 50 years constitutes a factor. Children of broken homes tend to associate pain with their parent's divorce, which may make them reluctant to enter marriage. Since the 60s when the use of birth control skyrocketed, more couples live together prior to marriage, which in many cases discourages future marriage. The first year of marriage or living together is a rough adjustment.

Society is more tolerant of living together and marrying later. Today's young adults do not face the same degree of parental pressure to marry young or the social stigma of a 30-year old spinster.

Many women and men delay marriage until they have had a chance to spread their wings and concentrate on their careers. It used to be when you graduated from high school or college at the latest, the next item on your life's agenda was to marry. Many people thought this way during the 1950s and 60s. Into the 70s, young adults married early in rural America. Even in the 70s, many people thought that college was the last best opportunity they had to find a suitable mate.

My non-fraternity college roommates mocked our fraternity and sorority friends who thought they had to acquire a fiancée before graduation. It seemed like a form of Greek rites of passage that began with pinning. The thinking even extended to which sorority or fraternity you married into – Betas married Pi Phis, whereas a Fegie might marry a DZ (Delta Zeta). During the spring, many seniors scrambled to find their mates, frequently becoming engaged to someone they only started dating spring quarter.

Two of my three roommates who mocked the system married within a year after we graduated --one to a Pi Phi and the other to a DZ. Don, a Navy fighter pilot, flew his jet to Belgium to pick up his Pi Phi fiancée who studied at the university's extension there. Together like a knight in shining armor with his damsel in bliss, they flew back across the Atlantic on his trusty white fighter jet for the wedding.

One good friend, the president of her sorority, also thought this way. As we talked on the walk back to our apartments from campus, she explained that she was majoring in elementary education and there would be few if any eligible bachelors in grade school where she would teach, whereas there were thousands of eligible bachelors on campus. She was very worried. I explained to her that she was a beautiful, bright young woman who would meet plenty of young men no matter where she worked. She took my advice and then spent two years as a stewardess before teaching. It did not take her long after that to find her ideal man. They now have three beautiful daughters. The manner people thought about marriage changed in the 70s and 80s.

Delaying marriage has two financial effects upon one's Financial Life Cycle. First, those who delay marriage into their late 20s and early 30s are able to pay down those school loans and build some savings for when they do marry and buy a house. Children do not perceive their economic surroundings for some time, but older parents are able to provide more opportunities and perhaps a better school system for them.

The second point relates to the biological clock. By delaying child bearing for 6 years, women significantly reduce their childbearing years. It is certainly possible for women to have their first children in their early 40s, but it becomes more difficult, and if artificial means are utilized, much more expensive. This delay also dampens the effect of the Millennial generation's population boost. Since the Millennial generation is spread over a longer and later period of time, the size of the cohort to rescue the economy is smaller.

Single majority?

In 1960, married couples comprised 74% of all households.* According to the Census Bureau, by 2005, unmarried households constituted the majority of all households and by 2007, there were 51 million single households.* Of course, divorced parents who were previously married head many of these families. The fact that people continue to marry later contributes to the single majority.

More single households have a negative economic impact, for it is easier for two people to live on less when they live together than when they live separately. Fewer people are getting married these days, as the following chart displays.

Marriage rate by Class for 30-49 year olds

Class	1960	2010
Upper middle	94%	83%
Working	84%	48%

The effect has been much more dramatic for the working class, with astoundingly less than half those in this age bracket married.*

After the Great Recession, there had been a reverse housing trend, with more people seeking roommates and young adults moving back in with their parents due to a high, sustained underemployment of 15% or above. There had also been a trend towards older adults, who, having lost their jobs moved in with their children. The doubling up effect reduces the amount of housing needed, thereby continuing to depress the housing market and its recovery. From a societal viewpoint, it is inefficient to have all of these adults in different domiciles with twice as many household items. It increases spending and loans on housing and related items but reduces funds available savings and investments.

Changing spending and savings habits

As we will see in the next chapter, in addition to earnings, two of the most important components in constructing the Financial Time Machine are spending and savings behaviors. Spending and saving habits shifted dramatically over the last 100 years. The Greatests were in their formative adolescent and early adult years during the roaring 20s when it seemed everyone made money in the stock market. Bootleg gin flowed at the speakeasies where young flappers' skirts shimmied above the knee while they twisted shamelessly to the suggestive jazz beats of the Charleston.

For the first time, the common man entered the stock market and initially made unfathomable profits as the market increased five-fold in a mere six years. Some even left their jobs to become day traders. They traded on margin, which multiplied their bets and subsequent profits until the market crashed in 1929, when it lost half of its value. Because they bought on margin, putting up only a fraction of the stock's price, they lost all of their investment when the price declined by the margin amount and owed even more when it went below that price. By 1932, the market stood at a mere tenth of its 1929 peak.

By 1934, one third of all banks failed, with many families losing all of their life savings. Similar to the Great Recession, housing prices also fell, losing nearly 50% of their value. In 1939, you could buy a new house for $3,800. A complete,"modern" 10-piece bedroom set cost only $79.85.*

These events greatly shaped the Greatests spending and savings habits. My father, laid off from his job as college coach, lost half of his savings to margin calls as a day trader in 1929. He never again invested in the stock market, instead rooting against it. Learning from these drastic lessons, Greatests tended to save and then pay in cash, being very careful about what they spent. They understandably avoided risk.

The Silents, having been born during times of distress, saved heavily and did not spend frivolously either. Except for their childhood, things had always improved, so they were inclined to use credit cards as these became popular in the 70s.

Boomers were a disappointing story though. As a group, they never went through any truly terrible times, so many never became savers. They bought big houses and had high credit card balances. As manufacturing declined, many left the cold climate of the North and Midwest for the sunnier climes of California, Arizona, Nevada, Florida, and Texas.

By 2000, the California economy had been booming for 50 years. Recessions did not seem to affect them much. Housing prices continued to rise with only periodic setbacks. Then, a typical three-bedroom, 1,600 square foot California ranch on a postage stamp lot cost over $750,000 - far beyond what most people could afford even on two incomes. So Californian's stretched their budgets, putting 35% or even an ill-advised 40% of their income toward the mortgage payments, expecting their wages would continue to increase and that their budget would become more affordable over time. Many even gambled on Adjustable Rate Mortgages (ARMs) that would increase in 2 or 4 years. Housing values continued to ascend by 10% a year, so they took out home equity loans to buy that pool or vacation in Hawaii.

Boomers hoped ever-increasing wages and housing values would provide for their retirement. Consumption comprised 70% of GDP and they felt it was their patriotic duty to keep the economy moving ever upwards by spending ever more.

As of 2008 when the Great Recession commenced, the Boomers had saved an average of $38,000. Those who had a qualified retirement plan had an additional average savings of $88,000.* Taken together, this would generate a little over $6,000 a year - along with Social Security, not enough to live well in retirement. Of course, most Boomers still have some time to build retirement savings, but not much.

According to the Federal Reserve, Americans lost $16.4 trillion of net worth during the great recession. The stock market recovered its losses since then, but $6 trillion of the loss was in real estate values.* For most of the years between 2005 and 2008, the average savings rate was less than 3%. In 2005, it dipped below zero. By 2009, it increased to 4%.

As children at a time when they formed their financial character, the Xers encountered the relatively bad times of the 70s. They experienced four recessions, gas prices doubling, stagflation, the loss of manufacturing jobs and their dad's loosing long-time jobs. As a result, they are more likely to save more and spend less.

It is too early to judge the Millennials. They were children during the longest period of economic expansion in history and often spoiled by their Boomer parents. They also went through the Great Recession during their formative adolescence and early adulthood, similar to their Greatest great-grandparents in the Great Depression. They know how expensive college is and how difficult it is for many families to afford. Their unemployment is much higher than the national rate. In 2010, over a year after the Great Recession, employment for Millennials aged 16 -25 approached 20% for those not is school, and this did not include those who either gave up or went back to school.*

Unemployment is less for those Millennials who graduated from college, but unless they had an in-demand major, it might have taken a year to find an appropriate position. Since this is the most socially connected generation, it is unlikely that these lessons escaped the generation. Financially, they will probably be more like their Silent grandparents than their Boomer parents - more likely to spend less and save more.

Up until the Great Recession, the trend was to spend more than we had and save less, which at one point was zero. If they ever expect to retire, the free-spending Boomers have no choice. The Xers have been and will continue to be great savers and it is likely the Millennials will adopt the Xer's habits or a balanced approach, carrying the lessons of the Great Recession throughout their lifetime.

Expanding Productivity

Prior to 1880, nearly half of Americans lived on farms and over half of the labor force consisted of farmers. From 1890 to 1930, the United States population nearly doubled, but the number of farmers feeding that population remained constant. By 1990, the population more than doubled again, but the number of farmers feeding those folks dropped to **2.6%** of the labor force, only 1/20th of what it took one hundred years earlier to grow all of the nation's food.

What happened over a hundred years is an amazing testament to the productivity of American farmers and American ingenuity. In 1890, it required 40 -50 hours to produce 100 bushels of wheat; now it takes only 3 hours. This is a 15-fold improvement or a whopping 1500%. American farms not only feed us, but also are one of the nation's largest exporters, helping to reduce our imbalance of trade, particularly with China and Japan.* In addition to the unbelievable productivity, the quality and variety of our food supply is better than ever.

Employment by Industry

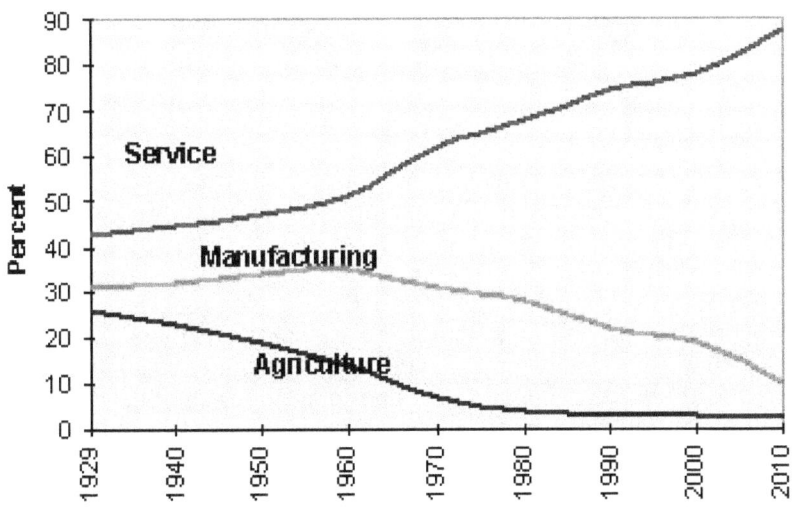

Robert D. Oberst, *2020 Web Vision: How the Internet Will Revolutionize Future Homes, Business & Society*

The productivity story is similar in manufacturing. In 1929, about a third of the jobs were manufacturing, which peaked at 35% in 1960. By 2000, manufacturing represented only about 20% of the workforce.*. Over the last decade, the number of manufacturing jobs fell from 17.3 to 11.7 million.* According to the Bureau of Labor Standards, manufacturing employment fell to just 9.25% in March of 2009 at the bottom of the Great Recession.* Since then, manufacturing employment has increased.

Part of the story is the outsourcing of American manufacturing overseas, which started in the 70s with Japan and accelerated in the 21st century with China, but another factor in this tale is productivity improvement. Between 1950 and 1997, worker productivity quadrupled. From 1997 to 2010, it doubled again, but this time it only took 13 years.*

Manufacturing Output

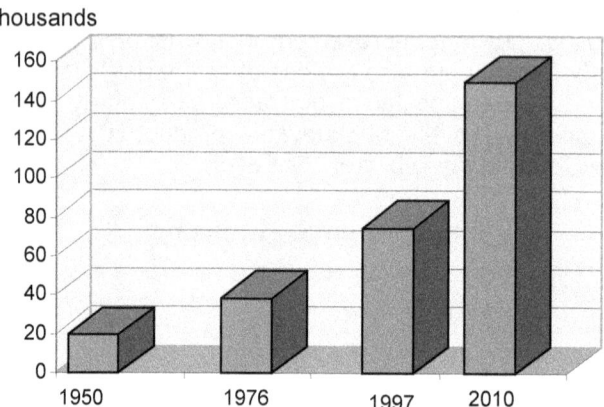

Many of the improvements are due to robotics and Enterprise Resource Planning systems (ERP) that provide an integrated stream of data to the organization as it routes materials through the production lines to the customers. The major reason corporations fared so well during the Great Recession is that their ERPs provided real time data that allowed them to respond immediately to changes in demand. Over the last 50 years, the variety and complexity of manufactured goods has increased as the price declined. Just consider all a smart phone that fits in your pocket can do – it possesses more power than a multi-million dollar 1970s mainframe.

In 2009, the U.S. was still the manufacturing leader with $2.3 trillion if manufactured goods, whereas China had $1.64 trillion.* After being the world's largest manufacturer for 110 years, in 2010 China became the largest, producing a little over $2 trillion of goods.* The United States produced a little less – $1.95 trillion. The loss of the title is no doubt due to the recession, but it was bound to happen since the U.S. companies transferred so much of their manufacturing to China.

In 2010, the U.S. and China produced approximately the same amount of manufactured goods, but China employed 100 million people versus 11.5 million in the U.S. The U.S. is therefore much more productive.

With manufacturing employment down to around 10% from a high of 35% and agricultural employment down from 38% to less than 3% since the turn of the last century, where are the jobs? The remaining jobs are in the services. Therefore, over 87% of us now work in various services.*

Thanks to technology, services have become more productive too. Jobs that once employed millions of people like file clerks, data entry operators, phone operators, secretaries, typists, and bookkeepers barely exist. Other jobs like bank tellers, grocery checkout clerks, administrative assistants, assembly workers, customer service reps, and medical transcriptionists improved radically through technology.

Mankind advanced agricultural techniques over thousands of years, most dramatically over the last 200 years. Manufacturing improved exponentially over the last 100 years. With 85% of us now in service industries, the current reengineering focus is upon services, which will experience similar exponential enhancements. This has been happening over the last 20 years and the pace is only increasing.

Corporations eliminated millions of managerial and administrative positions during the 80s and 90s. The typical process consisted of a study conducted by major management consulting firms like Booz Allen or McKinsey, who, based on benchmarks, recommended cutting 25 – 40% of the positions. Unspecified technological improvements would take up the slack. I helped several mega-sized companies work through the aftermath of downsizing by finding technical solutions to reengineer their processes. One worldwide oil client cut staff in one department from 250 to 101. The technologies and systems helped dramatically. Over 30 years, the typical IT system was radically reengineered from six to two steps, a 66% savings.* Often the remaining people just picked up the tasks of their departed associates, prioritizing all they had to do.

Take the first jobs for many teens: working in a fast-food restaurant like McDonald's or a grocery store. In a grocery store, the checkout counter has a scanner that uses the latest prices, immediately updates inventory, and then prints out a summary of everything just bought. When you order fast food, the order is immediately visible to those who fill the order then checked by the person who took your order before handing it to you. A few fast food restaurants and grocery stores skip a step by providing a touch screen to their customers to enter their order. For others, you can use a store-specific app on your smart phone or tablet to order and pay for your purchase.

Most fine dining establishments also have digital systems to enter orders. Some waitresses use iPads at the table connected through WiFi to take the order, again skipping a step. ATMs have been around for decades and some are now touch screens, but many people bank online or through their smart phone. Customer service reps have been in touch with the system for years, and we all hate the annoying voice response systems, a result of poor design, but these finally have some intelligence with Siri-like voice recognition and responses.

Not long ago there were record/disk stores and photo stores like Fotomat, but these are long gone and Kodak tragically declared bankruptcy. Now, there are fewer bookstores, newspapers, and movie theatres because music, digital photos, news articles, and movies are all available on your Kindle, iPhone, iPad, or similar device.

Online sales grow dramatically every year. Amazon, the largest online retailer, sold approximately $50 billion of items in 2011, and it still grows at a 40% clip. They just spent billions of dollars on distribution facilities. Retail stores are not going away soon, but their numbers are declining. For many busy Americans, it is much easier to shop online and have items appear at their doorstep. When gas prices are high, it is much less expensive than driving around shopping. FedEx and UPS, who deliver most of these goods, have sophisticated systems tracking packages at each delivery point into which the buyer can tap.

The various levels of government are even reengineering their processes with web-based technologies. You no longer need to stand in line at a license station for renewal, see a clerk for a form, register in person for unemployment, or buy stamps at the post office. All of these processes are online. Police have digital devices in their cars. The military use robots to sniff out bombs and drones to conduct air missions, thereby saving friendly lives. Email has eliminated much of the mail, leaving the post office less solvent, which will likely lead to cutbacks of service, offices, and staff. Email itself has morphed into texting, tweets, and Facebook updates on a smart phone.

Teaching too is changing. In some communities, it costs over $20,000 per year to educate a child -- $250,000 through high school. It will cost the community $1,000,000 to educate a family of four's children. You see more commercials for online education at the college level, but also at the K-12 level. For years, home schoolers have taken advantage of online educational resources helping to advance the techniques. Many home scholars achieve the highest marks on standardized tests like the SATs. With local budgets stretched thin, more communities will rely upon online education.

Nearly every service is experiencing productive improvement. We recently had our water meter replaced with a new meter that requires no meter reader but will send a signal with the reading on a periodic basis to the utility company.

Summary

To summarize the generational megatrends:
- World War II had a significant effect upon subsequent generations which still ripples through the economy.
- We now live in a global economy with interconnected labor and commodity markets governed by international corporations.
- Life expectancies increased by over 30 years in just a century, enabling prolonged life stages and the Financial Life Cycle.
- Couples marry later, allowing them to build careers and acquire more resources before nesting.
- Birth rates are down, providing more resources per child.
- A single person now heads most households.
- Spending and savings habits, atrocious leading into the Great Recession, are improving.
- Productivity increased at an amazing rate over the last century, providing much more and better food, goods, and services for less.

All of these trends are important in building the Financial Time Machine, for they determine the four financial factors that comprise the vital components of the machine.

Many of the megatrends are interrelated. For example, living longer allows people to be single longer, get married later, and have children later. Another mega generational trend permeating this chapter is that each successive generation obtained more education than the previous one. A longer life allows for more education, not just in terms of formal degrees, but also in terms of life learning either for career advancement, career maintenance or for enrichment. Higher educational attainment leads to more innovations, including medical advancements like the analysis of the human genome, which in turn leads to longer lives.

Longer lives and higher education levels also lead to ever-improving productivity. Just look at the advancement of knowledge through the Internet. A major initial intent of the Internet in the early 70s was to speed knowledge sharing between researchers throughout American universities. Now, practically anything you wish to know is instantly available to you through your hand held device. No matter where you are, you can access the world's vastly accelerating knowledge base and then communicate it to all of your friends or associates. The instant knowledge flow itself increases knowledge acquisition.

In my earlier book, *2020 Web Vision*, I talked about how the number of web pages doubles every 6 months. When I wrote the book in the early 2000s it was surprising to see the law worked for over ten years. I jokingly call this "Oberst's Law," after the more laudable Moore's law, which predicts silicone chip circuit expansion. The law portrays how fast knowledge access is expanding.

Ten thousand years ago, the Mesopotamians in the Fertile Crescent, now Iraq, instituted agriculture. This freed some of their citizens of the constant quest for food so they could pursue other endeavors like building an army and conquering their neighbors. Having time not spent in hunting and gathering allowed Egyptians to build pyramids, Greeks to develop philosophy and democracy, the Italians to foster the Renaissance and discover the new world, the Persians, Alexander, and Romans to conquer the known world at the time, and the Americans to put a man on the moon.

Up until the late 19th Century, humans spent half of their time producing food. As agricultural productivity steadily improved, more people had time for other valuable pursuits like education, innovation, manufacturing, and the military. We learned how to make millions of different devices, which saved even more time, making life more enjoyable and less a struggle for survival. Manufacturing productivity also accelerated, so fewer people can now produce far more goods. The pace of manufacturing productivity now grows exponentially.

So where is all of this leading? There is a temptation to imagine a Camelot, a Great Society, or a Utopia like that of Sir Thomas More or

Rousseau. In effect, over the last 100 years, we created a service-based economy in the developed world, in which two out of 100 of us provides the food, one out of 10 produces goods, and the rest of us serve each other. The seven out of eight of us who serve each other provide education, security, customer service, medical care, fire protection, financial services, fast food, fine dining, entertainment, recreation, retail goods, transportation, energy, housing, travel, communications, maintenance, art, and innovations.

At the turn of the Twentieth Century, a typical workweek on the farm or in a factory was 60 hours. Children, after graduating from grade school, frequently started working full-time at 13. Today, thanks to productivity improvements including time off, the typical workweek is 35 -36 hours; and many young adults do not start working full-time until after college at age 22 or 23. Will continuing progress lead to substantially more leisure time?

Utopia?

Citizens in some Arab nations with vast oil riches receive free education through college, healthcare, social security, and payments from the government. For example, there are no taxes in Saudi Arabia yet the government provides free healthcare, education, and social security. In Saudi Arabia, foreigners supply over 90% of private labor, performing all the menial tasks. The vast majority of Saudis work in high paying government jobs. The Saudis have this type of society and may be happy but are still worried about high unemployment and are working to shift private sector jobs to Saudis, especially after the Arab Spring. Unemployment for 16 – 25 year olds is up to 40%, while nearly one-third of the population are foreign nationals. People need to feel they are contributing to their society and that their work is valuable. From the Saudi Royal Family's perspective, too much leisure time can be dangerous.*

Most European countries provide a vast array of social service to their citizens including national healthcare, social security, unemployment, welfare, education, and early retirement. Europeans have a least four weeks of mandatory vacation time. Spain has 38 days and the French take off the entire month of August. The French also experimented with 35-hour workweeks. Some Greek workers retire as early as 52 (as can many unionized Americans.) Facing severe national debt, the Eurozone is struggling to pay for promised benefits and must cut the social benefits. The U.S. faces a similar crisis due to an overwhelming federal debt of over $200,000 for an average family of four and climbing.

In reality, developed nations were able to pay for an unprecedented level of social benefits because of the War Boom Babies and reduced defense budgets. Up until the latter half of the last decade, the Boomers were in their peak earning years. They outnumbered the Silents who utilized retirement and healthcare benefits by nearly two to one. Now the Boomers are leaving the workplace and starting to receive the promised benefits, but there are fewer workers to support them.

Other generational megatrends also work against the developed nations' social systems. When the Greatests started their journey on this earth over one hundred years ago, the average woman had six children, but now the average in the U.S. is 2.03, less than the replacement rate of 2.10.   During the 70s and 80s when the Xers were children, the birthrate was even less than 2.0.* The Greatests grew up with numerous siblings who expected to have their parents live with them or adjacent to them on the farm, in the town, or in a city neighborhood. Duplexes were popular in the 1920s to 1960s, many of which contained parents in one unit and one of their children's families in the other.   But then the average life expectancy was in the 50s, so only a fraction of the elderly population lived beyond their working years, and, if they did, numerous family members shared their care. Now we assume society will provide care for the elderly.

Another megatrend is that the majority of single households also shifts the burden of care from the family to the state. Many people do not have children, so they will not have someone to take care of them in their old age.   Others are divorced and it would be difficult for the typical two children to take care of two elderly parents who do not even live together and may be in different cities. These megatrends taken together (Increased life expectancies, reduced birthrates, and a majority of single households) shift the burden of care for the elderly from a traditional family responsibility to a burden for society as a whole.

The retirement system may possess some social justice. In 1900, the typical agricultural family had 7 children who went to school until 13 and then started working on the farm full-time.   Before then, they spent much of their free time performing chores. If the parents lived much beyond 60, which was longer than most, their children took care of them. Now most kids don't start working until 18, or 22 if they go to college. Their parents support them into their 20s, expecting little in return. There are fewer children and they often do not live in the same community. Instead of working on the farm, each successive generation pays more into the Social Security system so that the state takes care of their parents, who gave them so much and expect so little in return. Therefore, even though they may not physically take care of their parents, they contribute to their care.

Quality of Life

To Socialists, the European model approaches Utopia. To conservatives and Ayn-Randian's like Allen Greenspan, this is a nightmare that stifles individual initiative, innovation, and responsibility. Although such a goal is a worthy one, it is not likely that we will reach a Utopia for some time for we will still likely have poverty, crime, and wars throughout the 21st century. Perhaps a better objective might be to increase our quality of life.

The United States is the most powerful nation on the Earth, but surprisingly does not rank highly on Quality of Life. It ranked 13th on the Economist's Intelligence Unit's index and 31st out of 137 nations on the Quality of Life Index by World Press.* *

Based largely objective measure like life expectancy infant mortality, and per capita GDP, the World Press index intends to reflect livability for average inhabitant. Stagnant blue-collar wages over the last three decades and an unusually high rate of poverty contribute to the U.S.'s lower performance. The lowest rating was for peace, which while fighting two wars, makes sense.

The quality of life improved for all developed nations over the last 50 years. From a worldwide perspective developed country wages languished, but over the last 10 years, wages in the rest of the world increased dramatically including: Eastern Europe, Spain, Ireland, Russia, Korea, Japan, China, India, Mexico, Indonesia, and Brazil. So the quality of life dramatically increased for most of the world's population largely due to the benefits of globalization, productivity improvements, and world trade. It is not so much that the quality of life in the United States declined, but that the quality of life in many other nations increased at a faster rate.

The developed nations who fought the Second World War will likely face a rough patch over the next decade due to the quadruple threat of the retiring Boomer wave, increased life expectancies, declining birthrates and single households, but this will be nothing compared to hardships of WWII 70 years ago. They are already adjusting their social benefits, since as their Boomers stretch their systems, they must become more budget conscious. The U.S. faces the same pressures.

Rapid productivity advancements will continue to improve manufacturing providing ever more goods per unit of labor, but commodities will periodically become more dear leading to higher prices for some goods. The numerous gains already achieved in service productivity will continue to accrue at an even faster rate, so that the service avocations nine out of ten of us will occupy will supply ever more value to our fellow citizens.

More nations will enter the ranks of the developed nations providing a higher standard of living to their citizens. Hopefully, the improved quality of lives in these nations will lead to fewer wars thereby reaping the benefits of peace realized in Europe and much of the developed world. Hopefully, the developed world will continue to find peaceful solutions to their conflicts.

There will be many challenges ahead like caring for the Boomers without bankrupting the developed nations of the world, but technology will offer numerous innovative solutions, sponsored by the continuing advancement of the digital generation - the Millennials.

4

Building the Financial Time Machine

In the first chapter, we introduced the concept of the Financial Life Cycle using the simple metaphor of a ruler to portray the stages of one's financial life up to 100 years. In the following two chapters, we explored the five twentieth century generations and the unfolding megatrends that influence the financial behaviors of each successive generation. To construct the Financial Time Machine we will now add a second component representing these generations.

The essence of generational economics' value as applied in this book consists of simulating each generation's passage through their Financial Life Cycle and examining the corresponding effects upon the macro economy.

Planning Ahead

Growing up as a Boomer in Cleveland Heights, our class sizes were large, with typically 30 to 40 kids crowded into rooms built for our Silent predecessors. No doubt, many suburban school systems struggled with the same population boom. The school system finally developed a plan to build additional schools costing millions of dollars each, but these schools were not finished until after the Boomers graduated. Then, with fewer Xers, many classrooms were empty, so they tore down some of the old schools, built to last another 40 years.

The obvious question is why they could not have seen that after the Boomers passed through the school system, the number of students in the system would decline. All they really needed to do was survey the births in the city to know about how many children would enroll in kindergarten in five years. With this information they could have planned for the number of classes and the resulting schools they would need.

The scenario applies to the United States, since we have known when the Boomers would retire for 50 years. Why couldn't our leadership have planned for this event? The purpose of the Financial Time Machine is to help plan for future events based on available current information.

As we progress, we will work through the steps used to build the time machine and then show how it operates. Though the model it is based on is complex, operating the machine is relatively easy, much like driving a car is fairly easy, although the engineering behind it is extremely complex.

Financial Life Cycle Ruler

Age
```
0.... l....10....l....20....l....30....l....40....l....50....l... 60....l....70....l....80....l....90....l..10(
 CHILDHOOD            | EARLY |  NEST  |  PEAK  |WEALTH |  DOWN- |   MID   |   LATE
                      CAREER  BUILDING EARNING  ACCUM.   SIZING  RETIREMENT  RETIREMENT
```

Here are the steps to assemble the Financial Time Machine:

1.   Add the generations
2.   Assemble the core of Financial Time Machine
3.   Incorporate the financial factors
4.   Assemble the full time machine
5.   Test the Financial Time Machine

Step 1. Add the Generations

As the diagram above displays, we fashioned the Financial Life Cycle by marking off the financial stages every ten years. Creating the Generational Ruler follows a similar pattern, marking off each of the individual generations in turn according to their length with a year equal to a tenth of an inch. The number of years each generation occupies, and the corresponding length on the ruler, is below.

Generation Measurements

Generation	Years	Inches
Millennial	25	2.5
Xer	15	1.5
Boomer	19	1.9
Silent	20	2.0
Greatest	25	2.5

Below is a box representing the Boomer generation.

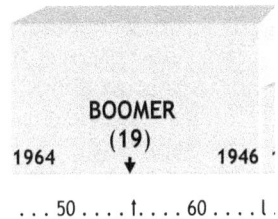

- Although the size may have been changed to fit on this page, the Boomer's box was originally 1.9 inches long to represent the 19 years the Boomers occupy.
- The bottom line displays ages for the Boomers. In 2011, they range in age from 46 to 65.
- The lower right corner of the box contains the first year of each generation with the lower left containing the last year. For instance, the Boomers were born between 1946 and 1964. These dates are in reverse order, which is essential for the smooth operation of the time machine, as we will observe in the final assembly. Each box also contains the number of years in the generation, located in the parentheses below the generation's name, for instance the **(19)** directly under "BOOMER."
- There is also an arrow in the middle of the generation. This represents the midpoint of a generation. For the Boomers, the midpoint occurred for those born in the summer of 1955.

Building a box for each generation and placing these on the Generational Ruler results in the diagram below. The picture contains the five generations in order starting with the youngest generation. Each generation's box represents the size of that generation. So, the Millennial box was originally 2.5 inches long corresponding to their 25 years.

Generational Ruler
2011
Original size: 1 year = 1/10th inch

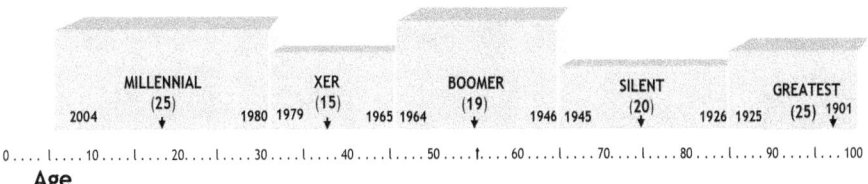

The size of the ruler reduced to fit onto the page.

Like the Financial Life Cycle ruler, the bottom line displays ages from 0 to 100. Therefore, in 2011 the Millennials rage in age from 6 to 31. Since one generation follows another, the five 20th century generations fit well on our 10-inch ruler, although about half the Greatest generation is now over 100 and therefore, not represented on the ruler.

There is one other characteristic you likely noticed regarding the Generational Ruler, namely that each generation's box differs in height. The height symbolizes the relative size of a generation.

Below is a table summarizing each generation's relative size among other characteristics portrayed on the Generational Ruler. The relative size compares each generation to the Boomers with the Boomers set at one. The Boomers are the focus generation, since of the five 20th-century generations they are the largest and they were born in the middle of the century. The Millennial box is close, but not quite as large as the Boomer's.

Generational Characteristics (in thousands)

Generation	Years	No. yrs	Ave. Births	Rel. Size	Low Births	Peak Births
Greatest	1901 - 25	25	2,900	.73	2,777	2,965
Silent	1926 – 45	20	2,535	.57	2,200	2,900
Boomer	1946 - 64	19	3,988	1.00	3,470	4,295
Xer	1965 - 79	15	3,420	.86	3,144	3,760
Millennial	1980 - 04	25	3,912	.98	3,612	4,112

The biggest difference is between the Silent generation, and the Boomers, whose box is **75%** larger than the Silent's. The size is extremely important. Ever since they were born, the Boomers have had an inordinate impact on the economy at each stage of their Financial Life Cycle. Even before they started their first jobs, their sheer numbers created demand for housing, roads, appliances, schools, food etc.

Step 2. Assemble the core of the Financial Time Machine

Now let's combine the two rulers by placing the Generational Ruler on top of the Financial Life Cycle Ruler, so that the generations line up with their current financial stages. The figure below shows this combination.

Financial Time Machine 1.0
Generational Ruler

With this version of the time machine, we can begin to see where each generation is in the Financial Life Cycle. The table below shows the median age of each generation, which is reflected by the arrow in each generation's box and the financial life cycle phase they occupy.

Generational Midpoints

	Age	Phase
Millennial	18 ½	Childhood
Xer	38	Nest Building
Boomer	55 ½	Wealth Accumulation
Silent	75	Mid Retirement
Greatest	97 ½	Late Retirement

If we look at the midpoint of each generation, we see that the midpoint Millennials' age is 18, at the end of their childhood. They are graduating from high school, about to enter college or start a job.

Taking a closer look at the Boomer box, we see that the late Boomers to the left of the box, those born in 1964, still occupy their peak earning phase while the early Boomers are already downsizing. In 2011, the first of the Boomers, Kathleen Casey-Kirchling, obtained Medicare at 65. In 2012, the first Boomers collected full Social Security at 66.

What we just created is very simply a Financial Time Machine. As we move the Generational Ruler to the right over the Financial Life Cycle Ruler, we move each generation through their Financial Life Cycle with each tenth of an inch representing a year in their financial life.

By moving the Generational ruler to the right, we will go forward in financial time. By moving to the left, we go back in financial time.

In the middle of the time machine is a dotted line separating the Generational ruler from the Life Cycle ruler. If you like, you could make your own Financial Time Machine. To do so, copy the diagram above and cut the copy on the dotted line in the middle. There is a larger version in the Appendix at the back of the book.

Step 3. Incorporate the Financial Factors

We need to add more substance to the Simple Time Machine 1.0 in order to make it more meaningful. Let's, therefore, look at the four key financial factors:

- Earnings
- Debt
- Spending
- Savings

Earnings are typically the money we receive in return for our labors - what we see in our paycheck whether paid on an hourly or salaried basis. Earnings also include interest, dividends, capital gains, rents, profits, etc. - the items that show up on your tax return, which comprise your total gross income.

Debt is what you owe, which might be your mortgage, home equity loan, car loans, credit card balances, or a loan you took out to start a small business like a pizza shop. It might include the money you borrowed from your friend Joe the carpenter to help start the shop.

Spending is what we use our income to buy, those things that show up in a monthly budget, or credit card statement, and also our impulse buys that do not show up on the budget, which we sometimes regret.

Savings include everything we put away including savings accounts, CDs, savings plans like 401(k)s, IRAs, investments, stocks, and the equity in our house or boat. A better term might be the added wealth we accumulate over time. It also includes the added value of our pension if we are fortunate enough to vest into one.

When we earn money, we can do two basic things with it after we pay our taxes: spend it or save it. If we want to spend more than we earn, as we do when we buy a house or car, we can borrow money with the promise to pay it back over time. Therefore:

Earnings + Added Debt = Spending + Savings

Basically the source of our funds either through earnings or debt equals what we use these funds for - spending or savings. By the time we enter our late thirties, most of us have items that fit into all of the four key financial factors listed above. Hopefully, even though we may have a high mortgage we have some savings for a rainy day like a layoff or at least some money in a defined contribution plan like a 401(k). These factors change over time.

Peaks

The following chart depicts the Financial Life Cycle with the peaks for each of the financial factors. These have value since they help us see where the generations are with respect to these key indicators.

Peak Financial Factors

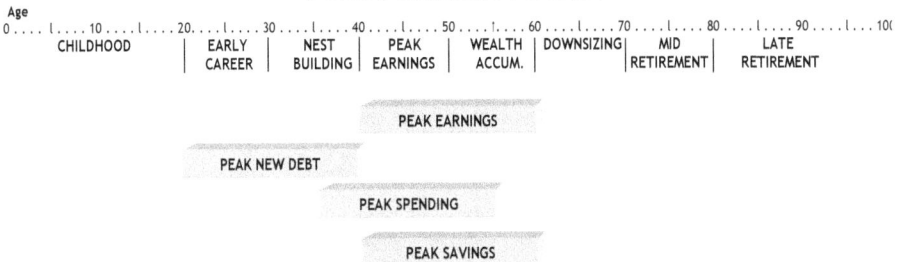

The boxes indicate the peak for each of the factors, and span 20 years. The first factor to peak is New Debt from ages 20 to 40 when people are going to school, building their careers, nesting and spending more than they earn.   Notice that this is new debt and not total accumulated debt. The next factor to peak is spending from 35 to 55 when we earn more and continue to build the nest and care for our children. Peak Earnings and Peak Savings both occur from 40 to 60 when we save for retirement in earnest.

Of course, everybody's financial profile varies.   The peaks are calculated based on the millions of people who occupy a generation and reflect their behavior on average. For simplification, each of the peaks occupies 20 years. Before moving on it might make sense to talk about how the peaks were calculated, but you can skip this section if you prefer.

Financial Life Cycle Propensities
(Optional Reading)

The propensities roughly represent the average economic effect each member of a generation supplies to the economy as a whole for each of the four financial factors. There are four propensities, one for each of the four financial factors:

- Earnings Propensity
- Debt Propensity
- Spending Propensity
- Savings Propensity

A propensity indicates how high or low a factor is during a particular 5-year period of time in the Financial Life Cycle. Propensities determine each economic factor's peak. For instance, earnings propensities are at or near the peak from ages 40 through 59.

For the purposes of Generational Economics, the actual propensity number is not as important as whether it is increasing, stable, or decreasing. Propensities are in approximately one thousand dollar increments, although due to inflation these numbers vary widely when each generation passes through its Financial Life Cycle.

The following chart shows the four key generational economic factor propensities in the five-year increments.

Propensities 15-55

Age Range	16-20	21-25	26-30	31-35	36-40	41-45	46-50	51-55
Earnings	3.5	20.4	31.4	38.3	45.7	49.7	54.2	59.0
Debt	1.4	2.7	3.6	4.6	2.7	1.3	0.5	0.1
Spending	5.0	23.0	32.0	37.0	39.0	41.0	41.5	41.5
Savings	-0.1	0.1	3.0	5.9	9.4	10.0	13.2	17.6

Propensities 56 -100

Age Range	56-60	61-65	66-70	71-75	76-80	81-85	86-90	91-95	100
Earnings	59.4	42.1	27.9	21.7	14.6	8.4	3.9	1.7	0
Debt	-2.5	-2.5	-3.0	-2.5	-2.0	-1.0	0	0	0
Spending	38.5	30.0	24.0	19.0	14.0	9.0	7.0	5.0	0
Savings	18.4	9.6	0.9	0.2	-1.4	-1.6	-3.1	-3.3	0

The propensities indicate where one expects to be in their Financial Life Cycle at a particular age relative to a particular economic factor like earnings. These are roughly in thousands of 2010 dollars. What is important to the model is the relative value of the propensities, regardless of the timeframe. The propensities will remain constant throughout time, although they may be adjusted conceptually based on generational or economic behaviors.

Of course, individual behaviors vary widely. An executive in an organization may earn 400 times what the janitor earns, even though they live in the same generation. One person realizing the multiplicative effect of early savings and investments may begin saving 8% of their paycheck when they graduate from college, whereas someone else may have no savings at 50. Therefore, the propensities represent the average of all of the members of a generation.

You may notice some propensities are bolded, which indicates when a particular propensity peaks. For consistency purposes, each peak period consists of 20 years, since the model is designed to detect long-term macroeconomic cycles, versus short-term changes.

You'll also notice that the first 15 years of the life cycle contain no propensities. Other than part-time jobs, children have little earning or spending potential until they start working at around 16, so propensities are not listed prior to this age.

As each member of a generation has different propensities, so too do the generations themselves exhibit different propensities. For instance, having lived through the deprivations of the Great Depression and World War II, the Greatest Generation's propensity to save was very high. After Wall Street crashed in 1929, many never bought a stock again.

People who go through rough times like wars, depression, and famine tend to save more, people like my Greatests generation father. My father excelled, competing as a world-class athlete in two sports, playing on a National Championship football team, blocking for the Four Horsemen at Notre Dame, and earning an Olympic Medal. As many star athletes did, he with the backing of his mentor, Knute Rockne, became a college coach.

Like many coaches, he moved with the fortunes of his teams -- to larger schools when they won and to smaller universities when they lost. His five children, my older siblings and I, were born in four different cities in four regions: the East, Midwest, South, and Mid Atlantic. After losing a position in Buffalo, he became a day trader in Philadelphia in 1929 and lost much of his substantial savings to margin calls. He never bought another stock again; instead rooting against what he thought was a corrupt marketplace. Because of his experience, he remained a careful spender and fierce saver.

Those who feel more secure save less. The Silents, who were born during the Depression and war, saw steady economic expansion throughout the rest of their working lives. The Boomers as a group never experienced severe economic hardships and therefore their propensity to save is less than the Silents. This helps to explain the financial behavior of U.S. citizens in the 90s and early 00s. However, those behaviors changed after the Great Recession. Before the Great Recession, the saving rate became negative ---insane considering the Boomers who were approaching retirement's gate.

After experiencing the Great Recession, the Xers and Millennials will hopefully adopt a more balanced approach. Many of their grandparents, like my father, did not invest their money, but rather posited it into savings and CDs and therefore missed reaping higher returns from a diversified portfolio. However, their grandparents did have pension funds from the companies they spent their careers with, who in effect invested in the markets for them, guaranteeing them a fixed payout for life. While young, there was no social Security or Medicare, so these provided a welcome benefit, into which they put less than they drew out. Unfortunately, few of the Xers and Millennials will have the luxury of spending their entire career in one company with a pension plan. They will have to fund much of their retirement themselves and will have to work longer to obtain Social Security.

Many people in the private and particularly the public sector retire during their fifties from positions such as teaching, police, fire, and the autoworkers. In these cases, individuals potentially work as little as one-third of their life (30 out of 90 years), with their retirement lasting longer than their working years, up to 40 years. Unfortunately, this is a reality we are just starting to face, but unless there are incredible productivity improvements, a generation cannot expect to go to school until 22, retire 30 years later at 52 and live until 90. As Greece discovered, the long-term resources are just not there.

So depending on the Earning, Debt, Spending, and Savings behaviors of each generation, the Financial Life Cycle can shift slightly to the right or left. In reality, as the expected lifespan expands, the Financial Life Cycle itself expands.

As mentioned before, for the propensities, Earnings + Debt = Spending + Savings. The supply of money equals the uses of money. What we take in, in terms of Earnings and Debt, equals what we pay out, in terms of Spending and Savings.

Let's take Bill as an example. Bill graduated from college two years ago and just received a healthy raise earning $50,000 in his new position as a Network Coordinator. He needs to replace his beater VW bug from college, because it is falling apart. So Bill decides to buy a new Prius costing $22,000, for which he will take out a $20,000 loan.

After putting $2,000 towards the car, Bill will save $2,000 this year, just in case there is an unexpected layoff. He will spend the rest, or $46,000 including taxes. Bill's Earnings + Debt = his Spending + Savings as shown below.

Incoming		Outgoing	
Earnings	$50,000	Normal Spending	$46,000
New Debt	$20,000	Car Spending	$22,000
		Savings	$ 2,000
Total	$70,000		$70,000

Generally, we can do two things with our earnings: spend it or save it. We can increase our spending if we add debt, as we do with our credit cards, and when we buy a car or house. Trading current spending against future earnings makes sense when incomes are increasing, a new family is starting to stock their lives, or in Bill's case, when buying the car after graduation.

It is important to note that the debt propensity consists of added debt and not total debt. We increase spending by taking on additional debt as Bill did when he took out a car loan. Once we have that debt, it becomes a deduction from savings. In Bill's case, the $20,000 loan reduces his net worth. Of course, the value of the Prius increases his net worth, but that value declines over time.

The interest we pay on the debt becomes an expense and in effect, limits available spending in the future. Depending upon the terms and interest rate Bill will pay up to $300/month on principle and interest, thereby reducing what he can spend on other purchases.

The following graph displays the four propensities over time.

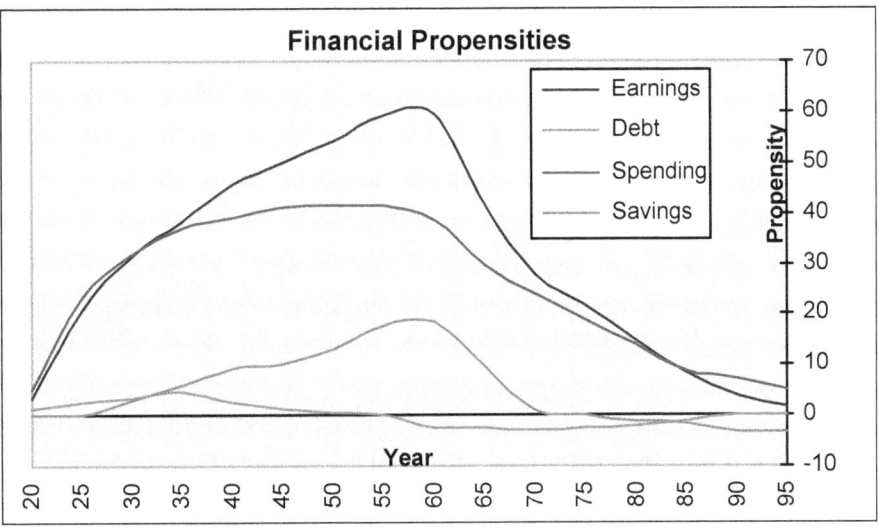

The propensities rely upon the quantum effect of the generation's members rather than each individual – the average effect is more significant. We earn little as children, and then earnings climb rapidly in our twenties and thirties. In their twenties, some members start to earn money at their jobs, while others are still going to school. Some members retire in their late fifties, while others work into their seventies, and still others semi-retire.

Although a few people continue to advance their careers, real salaries level off for most by their mid forties. **Earnings** peak at 60 and decline precipitously as the generation retires. The vast majority of corporations, but not all, organize on a pyramidal basis with fewer slots at each higher level, therefore the odds of progressing become ever more remote. However, other earnings such as Interest, dividends, and rents increase at this time, therefore total earnings still incline into the sixties. Most of the early Boomers I know retired in their late fifties or early sixties, due to generous pensions and long service within one organization.

People tend to add **Debt** through their twenties and thirties when their earnings are growing and their need to spend on school loans, housing, furniture, appliances, and cars is high. Their debt load is high in their forties and fifties, but at this time, they are not adding much new debt. By their late fifties and sixties, they reduce their debt - paying off mortgages, buying cars with cash, and paying down credit card balances, (their additional debt propensity is negative as the chart shows.)

Spending crests in the late thirties when people are in their peak acquisition years. This trend continues through the early fifties, supported by higher incomes, but average real spending does not change much over the 20-year period. By the time people are in their sixties and downsizing, they do not need to buy many new goods, but merely replace what they have. By the sixties, spending is rapidly decreasing, but part of the reduction is due to the dwindling number of members within a generation as they pass on. Their impact on the total economy therefore declines.

Savings are the same as added Net Worth or the additional wealth one accumulates over a lifetime minus the debts incurred. The returns on wealth (interest, dividends, appreciation etc.) add to our earnings, which we may, in turn, spend or save. Savings are also composed of the required added corporate savings in Pension funds funding future retirements. Once vested, we have guaranteed rights to those funds when we retire.

Prior to the Great Recession household wealth peaked at about $68 trillion. Due to falling stock and real estate values, it fell to $51 trillion during the recession. By the end of 2012 household wealth nearly recovered to its previous levels and was at $66 trillion.* Inheritances also add to wealth. Approximately $7.6 trillion will transfer to the Boomers from their predecessors. As the Boomers pass on they will transfer their wealth to their children and grandchildren.*

The time machine accounts for wealth transfers from the older to younger generations. It does not account for abnormal additions to wealth such as the unrealistic real estate valuations prior to the market crashing or the abnormal loss of value during the Great Recession. Instead, the time machine tends to smooth these out with a gradual increase over time for each generation.

Savings peak in the early sixties, then rapidly decline as a generation enters retirement. By the seventies, these are negative as people draw off their savings, which would occur earlier except that the wealthier members of a cohort who are still earning on investments push up the average. Much of the wealth of wealthier members of a generation is not spent by them, but passed to their children, taxed, or given to charity.

The calculation of the propensities is complex, based on research provided largely by the U.S. Government and economic publications.
Some of the factors included in the calculations include:

- Workforce size
- Part-time employment
- Average earnings by age
- Average debt by age
- Average spending by age
- Average net worth by age
- Pension earnings
- Retirement employment
- Retirement ages
- Singles
- Interest payments
- Wealth distribution
- Average saving rate
- Population changes
- Death rates

Step 4. Assembling the full time machine

The next page contains the fully assembled Financial Time Machine version 2.0.

The Financial Time Machine 2.0

Generations

It may be difficult to think of what is included on the previous page as a machine especially a "time machine" but please be patient. Later we will create something more exotic like the Delorean in "Back to the Future." This version is relatively simple and therefore relatively easy to digest, but surprisingly powerful, as you soon will experience.

The Financial Time Machine 2.0 possesses everything the earlier version contained with a couple of additions to the Life Cycle portion. First, we added the peak periods for each of the factors: earnings debt, spending, and savings. Second, there is now a dateline below the ages, represented in blue. If we are going to use our time machine to go forward and backwards in time, it would be nice to have something to indicate a date - all time machines have a date indicator. These dates correspond to the age of the midpoint Boomers. In the center of the machine at 2011, we see that the midpoint Boomers' age is 55 ½. In 2001, the midpoint Boomers' age was 45 ½, whereas in 2021 the age is 65 ½.

As we slide the Generational ruler back and forth, the Boomers' midpoint arrow points to the date. Therefore when looking at the Boomers, we will be able to see which date we are talking about without having to convert ages into dates. Even when we are examining other generations, the midpoint Boomer arrow will tell us the date.

Step 5. Testing the Financial Time Machine

Before we proceed any further, let's try a test run of our time machine. If you like, copy the previous page -- on the copy, cut along the doted line. There is another copy of the Financial Time Machine contained in the appendix that you can cut out or copy. Now you can move the Generational Ruler over the Life Cycle Ruler. Remember, if you move the Generational Ruler to the right, you go forward in financial time. If you move the Generational Ruler to the left, you go back in time. Imagine there is a click at midnight of New Year's Eve of each year as you go forward or backward.

Move just one click to the right. Now we see that the leading edge of the Boomer's box moved from 65 to 66. As mentioned before, in 2011 the first Boomers became eligible for Medicare. In 2012, the first Boomers became eligible for full Social Security.

Reset back to 2011, then slide the Generational ruler ten years to the right. The midpoint arrow should line up with 65 and 2021. The date gives us a convenient way to see what year it is as displayed below:

The Financial Time Machine 2.0
(In 2021)

Generations

	MILLENNIAL (25)		XER (15)		BOOMER (19)		SILENT (20)		GREAT (25)
2004		1980	1979	1965	1964	1946	1945	192(	

```
0....l....10....l....20....l....30....l....40....l....50....l....60....l....70....l....80....l....90....l...100
B.D. 1961      1971       1981       1991       2001       2011       2021       2031       2041       2051
```

CHILDHOOD	EARLY CAREER	NEST BUILDING	PEAK EARNINGS	WEALTH ACCUM.	DOWNSIZING	MID RETIREMENT	LATE RETIREMENT

PEAK EARNINGS

PEAK NEW DEBT

PEAK SPENDING

PEAK SAVINGS

Life Cycle

So now, we see that in 2021 half of the Boomers are over 65 and the youngest is 55. Most of the Boomers will be in the Downsizing stage at this time. Most Xers (aged 48) will be in their Peak Earning years, while the majority of Millennials (aged 28) will be in the Early Career or Nest Building stages.

You may already be thinking of the consequences of such moves, which is the topic of the next chapter, where we travel back in time and look at what transpired over the last 30 years for the Boomers.

Section Two

5

Taking the Time Machine Back in Time for the Boomers

Now that we have time machine, let's continue along our journey focusing on the Boomers to see how their generational economics led to the longest boom period in U.S. history. You may find the results intriguing.

In this chapter, we will test the accuracy of the time machine by traveling through time and testing the time machine's predictions versus the economic realities of each period. We will start in 1981, near the end of the period of stagflation in the 1970s then advance forward, stopping several times along the way until we arrive in 2004. As we approach the Great Recession, we will stop more frequently, increasing our observations before, during, and after this pivotal event.

Looking at the time machine and the economy might become tedious, so we will peer at each time slot through the eyes of two typical occupants of the period to see how the economic gyrations affect them. John Peters follows a blue-collar calling, whereas his best friend, Bob Ostrum, pursues a white-collar career.

With the midpoint arrows serving as the date dial on a Jules Verne's time machine, we may travel either backward or forward in economic time. These arrows represent roughly the center of the mass for each generation's population. Here is how the arrows work:

1. When an arrow crosses into the peak phase for a particular economic factor such as earnings, half of the generation has entered that phase.
2. As the arrow advances towards the middle of the phase, that phase is at its zenith for the generation with all or substantially all of its members in the phase.
3. Later when the leading edge of a generation passes out of the phase, the phase starts its descent with half of the generation already out of the phase.

Try it on your Financial Time Machine. A copy of which is included at the back of the book for you to cut out and operate if you like.

2011 Financial Time Machine

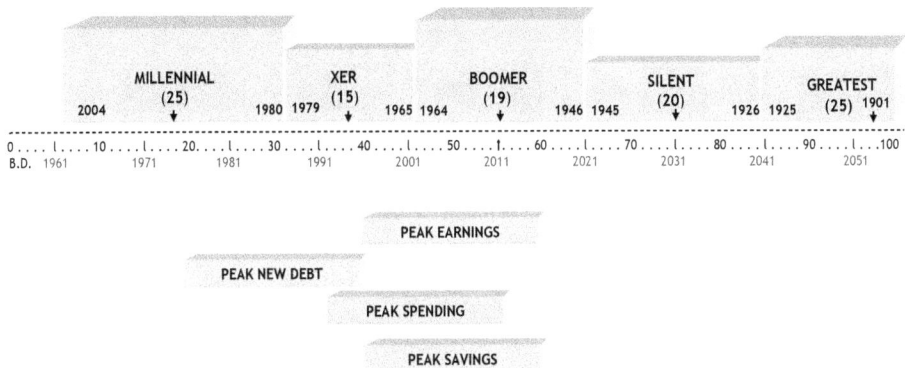

Note: We eliminated the line displaying the Financial Life Cycle to save space, which we will no longer need.

For instance, let's take a look at just earnings:

If we move the Boomer midpoint arrow to age 30, we see the leading edge of the Boomer's box is nearly 40. The Boomers are therefore just about to cross into the peak earnings box.

Age 30

As we continue to move the arrow to the right to age 50, as pictured below, we see all the Boomers are now in the peak earnings phase.

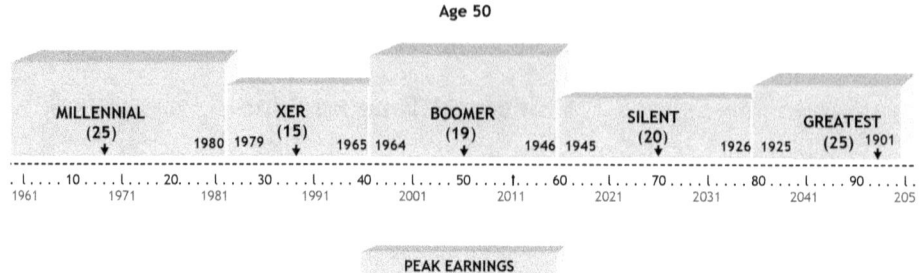

By age 60, half are still in their peak earnings phase and half are out of it.

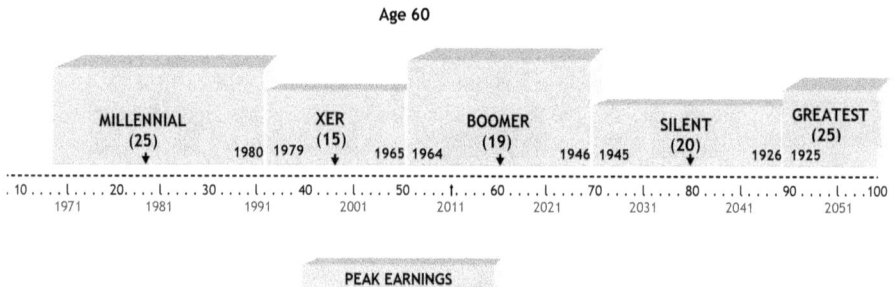

By age 70 in 2026, none of the Boomers are in peak earnings any longer.

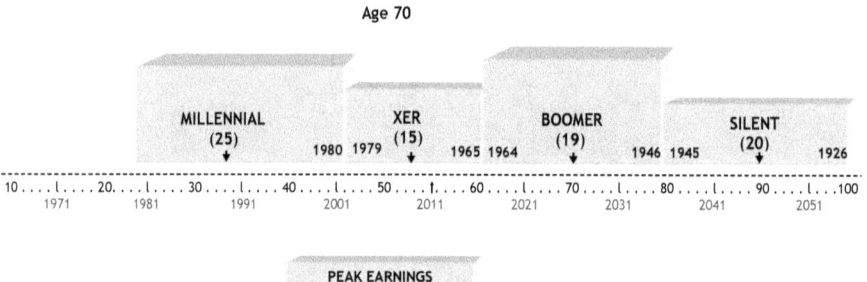

A generation's passage through its peak financial phases seems reminiscent of the moon's passage through its lunar phases. Initially we see no moon, and then if the night is clear, we see the first sliver of the new moon. Midway through the month the moon becomes full and bright, then gradually diminishes over the next fortnight, completing its cycle. So it is with a generation as it passes through its peak phases, with the maximum illumination occurring when it is full, contributing the generation's maximum power to the economy.

As each month's moon passes through the sky, each generation passes though the economy. Some generations are brighter than others are because of size. The Boomer "moon" happens to be 75% brighter than the Silent's.

1981

Let's take our simple Financial Time Machine 2.0 and go back in time with the Boomers – back thirty years to 1981 when the largest generation in American history commenced their financial journey. Imagine Michael J. Fox flooring his Delorean, screeching through the town square, and hitting the power line attached to the clock tower just as lightening strikes the tower. In our case, it is much safer - we simply line up the Boomer midpoint arrow on 1981 as shown in the diagram below.

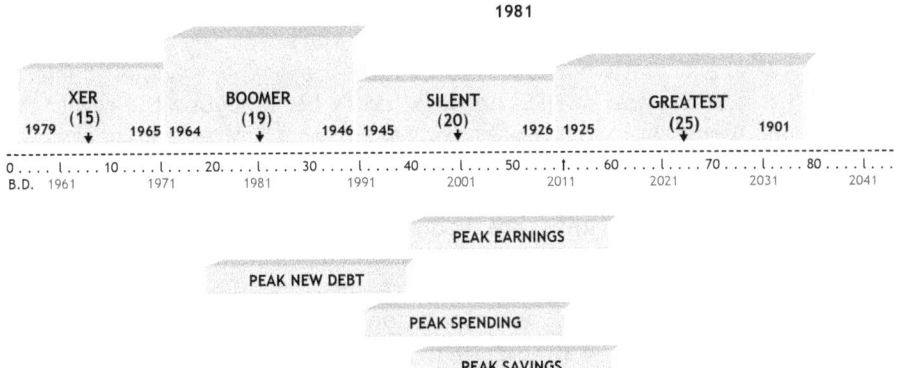

As we see, the midpoint boomer is now 25 years old and the boomers range in age from 15 to 34. Most are young adults starting their jobs and careers, having completed their high school or college education, but a few are in still in high school. The Boomers income is rapidly rising as inflation continues at double-digit pace, but the 70s have been a rough time to start a career. Kim Carnes' "Betty Davis Eyes" leads the charts followed closely by Olivia Newton John's "Physical" and Journey's "Don't Stop Believing." Harrison Ford in *Raiders of the Lost Ark* is the top grossing film, more than doubling the receipts of Henry and Jane Fonda's Academy Award winning *On Golden Pond*.

In 1981, the economy is already in its fourth recession in just 12 years. This one is particularly bad with unemployment at 10.8%, making it difficult for the massive number of Boomers to enter or advance in the workforce. The generational economic cause of these recessions is not due to the Boomers though; since they are in the early phase of their careers, they have had little economic impact over the last dozen years. As we will see later it is the Greatests who caused this rough patch.

According to the Financial Time Machine, the largest generation in U.S. history is about to enter their peak spending and in two years, by 1983, the series of recessions will end as the U.S. economy enters a period of sustained growth. The Boomers will supply the financial stimulus for this growth, initially through their high level of spending and debt. Their earnings and savings are also increasing at a rapid rate and by the middle of the decade, the first Boomers will enter their peak earning and savings phases too. From the viewpoint of the Financial Time Machine, the Boomers come to the rescue of the ailing U.S. economy with their record levels of spending and soon to be record earnings, and savings.

As we see above, most Boomers are in their peak new debt years. Since they cannot afford all of their purchases such as a new Datsun (Nissan) 280Z, they take out car loans. Despite the brief recessions, many early Boomers are starting families and buying that first house with a 30-year mortgage at 14%. They are more mobile than their parents are, so in a few years when they transfer, they will buy a new home. They have credit cards but the balances are reasonable. Some Boomers save a little in the new 401(k)s but most don't think beyond the company match and many don't even take advantage of that. After all, there is so much to spend on and retirement is a long way off. Following an almost Pavlovian response, they feel they must have what they see on TV.

The War Boom Babies are young and largely because of them, America transforms into a youth oriented culture. Even though they occupy fewer years than their predecessors do, they still comprise approximately one-third of the population. The median age in 1980 is only **30**. In 1970, it was less than **28**, which explains why Madison Avenue is proficient at churning out add campaigns aimed at Boomer wallets.*

Two Boomers

Let's take a look at two typical Boomers: John Peters and Bob Ostrum. We will follow them and their families throughout the time machine to see how its projections affect those living through each period in these shaded sidebars. John and Bob were both born in Orange County in the summer of '55 and have been best friends since 4th grade. Their parents migrated from the Midwest (Detroit and Cleveland) in the fifties. During their teen years in the late sixties, they hung out and surfed at Newport Beach. Both starred on their high school championship baseball team and dreamed of pro careers. John won every game that year as the team's pitcher and Bob with a .353 average led the league in batting. John played on an AAA team briefly, until he was injured and Bob played in college. Now they play ball on the same team two nights a week with some of their buddies.

John, who happened to have a strong resemblance to John Lennon, soon married a beautiful blond named Pat at 21 and had their first child shortly thereafter. Pat and John now have two children: a boy and a girl. After a couple of years in community college, John started working at a small local aerospace manufacturing plant as an expeditor to support his young family. He was laid off in a recent recession, but was hired back after only two months. Pat, a brilliant student, dropped out of UCLA to care for the toddlers, something her parents were disappointed in, but adjusted to, since her mother married at 19 too.

John just bought their first house for $98,000, a small 3-bedroom ranch with a hefty 14% mortgage. He makes a good wage of $19,000, but paying the monthly mortgage will be a stretch for a while. He doubled his hourly wage since he started working five years earlier but most of that is due to double-digit inflation. Pat plans to start work in a year when her oldest begins kindergarten. The added income will be necessary to pay all those new bills. The couple is currently purchasing the furniture and appliances needed for the house on credit cards.

Bob graduated from college a little over a year ago with a degree in Systems Analysis from USC and is now working as a consultant helping to install accounting software in local hospitals. As a nerd, Bob dated little in high school but does now. He enjoys backpacking in the High Sierras and traveling with plans to see every state and Europe. He is into the running craze and participates in numerous sports in addition to baseball, his favorite.

Bob grosses about $15,000 a year and will live with his parents until he pays off his college loans. He drives his dad's old Ford Galaxy that he acquired for $500.

1991

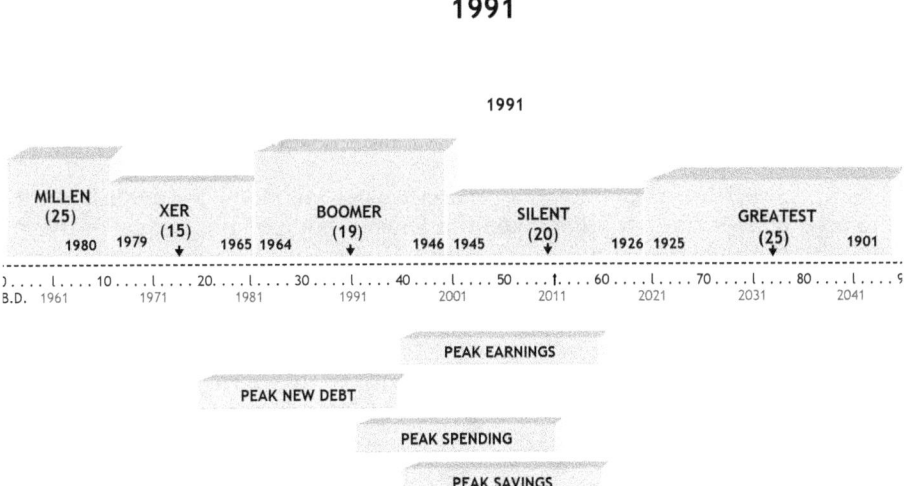

Now let's set our time machine forward ten years to the 90s and 1991

when the average Boomer is 35 and they range in age from 25 - 44. The Boomers earnings are steadily increasing while half the Boomers are in the heart of their peak spending phase. Most add debt but although their total debt load remains high, the early Boomers are not taking on as much new debt as before. Some are starting to save more, with about a third entering their peak saving phase.

Boomer spending powers the economy. Now, largely in their thirties and early forties, the Boomers are buying houses at a record pace. Unlike their parents, most have only two or three children; still, the early Boomers trade up for larger homes as their families expand and children age. They expect each child to have their own room unlike many of them who roomed with their same-sex siblings throughout their childhood.

According to the Financial Time Machine, with so many Boomers entering their peak financial factors, we expect this to be a boom period for the American economy. Sure enough, the 80s turn out to be the second longest period without a recession in U.S. history lasting 7 years and 8 months.

During the 1980s, the record number of Boomers enters their nest building years, which as expected leads to a housing boom, with mortgages supplied by the savings & loan industry. Housing prices soar, especially in Texas where these can be acquired with as little as 10% down, which feeds speculation. In addition, during the 1980s, there were several pieces of legislation that reduced regulation and oversight of the savings and loans.

By the end of the decade, the FED raised interest rates to stave off inflation, and the housing bubble burst. This along with widespread fraud, due to a lack of regulations, leads to the Savings and Loan Crisis. Seven Hundred and forty-seven S & Ls fail costing $160 billion largely funded by the American taxpayer. Many think the bailout led to a lack of moral hazard that would lead to further financial industry abuses. This crisis also results in a recession in 1991, which when compared to the others was relatively mild.*

In a sense, the Boomers' generational economics forecast the housing bubble that foreshadowed the Savings and Loan crisis, since they were in their nesting phase. Although it facilitated the bubble, resultant speculation, and eventual bursting, it did not directly lead to the deregulation and fraud that ensued, although any time we have these bubbles, there are those who commit fraud to profit from it. It is not until the bubble bursts that the true depth of their fraud is revealed. The bubble might obscure their actions, but once it bursts these become apparent.

During the 90s, the Baby Boomers are buying new appliances, new furnishings, electronics, toys, and clothes for their growing kids, their first PCs, and huge SUVs to ferry the kids around to endless activities and sports. Some now pay tuitions at parochial or private schools since they no longer trust public education while others move to pricier suburbs with higher taxes to pay for better schools. They expect to take family vacations. Many are divorced and now have two houses doubling the number of bedrooms, which they will not need when the kids go off to college. Even though their debt is high, as dutiful parents they save for the kids' education.

Large remodeling stores like Home Depot and Lowe's sprout up in every city and the thirty somethings start taking out new home equity loans with escalating rates to pay for the renewed home improvements - a new trend. Mortgage rates decline to a more reasonable 9%, so they refinance, thereby freeing up even more to spend.

Despite the nesting boom, a surprising number of Boomers live alone, especially the late boomers in their late twenties and early thirties who are concentrating on their careers and delaying families. This is especially true for women, who benefit from new career doors now open to them. Many others are married with dual incomes and delay having children, prompting the new acronym "DINKs," Dual Income No Kids. A record number will have their first babies in their late thirties and even early forties. Still others are divorced and living alone. These single Boomers expect to take exotic vacations to Alaska, Europe, Club Med, Costa Rico, China, Peru, China, etc.

Unlike their parents, Boomers expect to have their own toys too - pools, hot tubs, boats, motorcycles, video games, large screen TVs, PCs etc. When they grew up, meals were typically at the kitchen table and they rarely ate out. Now with both spouses working, they begin eating out in record numbers. All of which increases spending and credit card debt at rates up to 30%, so Madison Avenue is fat and happy.

The massive spending boom keeps the economy humming, especially since it constitutes the primary fuel for jobs in the U.S. Despite the mild recession in 1991, the high spending and highly educated Boomers facilitate a constantly improving economy.

John and Bob are now 35 years old. John and Pat sold their original home for $220,000 and with the added equity bought a new larger four-bedroom one with a pool for $320,000. This house is in a new development further out in what were the boondocks of Orange County. To build houses up the valley they scalp the top of the mesas into artificial plateaus, cover the 200 acres with black plastic, pop up houses, then fill with sod, plants and palm trees. The houses sell like hot cakes. When released, John and Pat had to bid on a house without knowing the specific one they would receive. Luckily, they obtained their second choice with a magnificent valley view. John now has an hour commute to his same job along a brand new freeway through the metamorphosing hills.

The house still requires finishing touches like landscaping and a deck, so John is a frequent visitor to the nearby Home Depot. John Jr. is a big help on Pat's seemingly never-ending list of projects. Pat and John together earn $60,000 which seems respectable, but they can never seem to save much other than putting away a couple thousand a year into the kids college fund and about 4% each to their 401(k)s.

Their kids, Suzy and Johnny, are now 13 and 11. John is very protective of Suzy because she is turning out to be as pretty as her mother and he does not want boys like him hanging around her. Feeling imprisoned, Suzy shows signs of rebellion. Johnny enjoys every sport and excels as a pitcher like his dad. The family just bought a SUV to ferry the kids around to their various events. Pat has been working for eight years as a teller in a nearby bank. Her extra income allowed them to buy the bigger house, but their credit card balances represent a persistent worry.

Bob is now working for his third company. He was putting in 80 hours a week as a Hospital Consultant, but he burned out and spent six months backpacking through Europe. He then acquired a lower position as a programmer at one of his hospitals and soon acquired the IT management position. After five years, feeling a lack of professional stimulation, he is now a project manager for the headquarters of a *Fortune 50* multi-Industry conglomerate developing their largest system.

Although he has dated several women, Bob is still not married, but is finally in a longer-term relationship. He attends USC's graduate school working towards an MBA. Between work, trips for work and study, Bob has little time, but still manages to play softball with John on Sundays. He enjoys get away vacations to Mexico and the Caribbean where he suns and enjoys numerous athletic activities. Bob receives a good salary of about $45,000 and now rents a small three-bedroom house. He has little time to spend on the house other than mowing the postage-stamp size lot. With no credit card debt, he paid off the Nissan 300Z he bought 2 years ago. He contributes 6 percent of his salary to a 401(k) and has $30,000 in savings he plans to use on a down payment for a house someday, but worries about rising house prices.

2000

As we move our Financial Time Machine forward (shift our generational ruler right) throughout the 1990s, more Boomers enter their peak earnings phase. This, the largest generation, also continues to be in its peak spending phase. Furthermore, most of the Boomers enter the peak saving phase. All of this is magnificent, something analogous to triple convergence, when three planets align. The 1990s constitute the sweet decade for generational economics. According to the time machine, with the financial factors at their peak for the peak generation, this should be one of the best decades in American History.

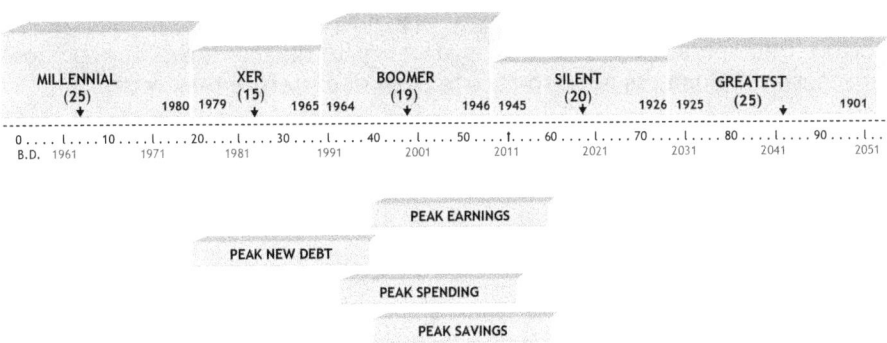

Indeed, it was the longest period of growth in American history, a decade of unprecedented economic expansion. In fact, there was only one mild recession in 17 years after 1991. Unemployment is low as the stock market climbs to unprecedented levels. Nearly everyone feels wealthy. By the end of the decade, President Bill Clinton and a Republican led Congress buoyed by the booming economy even balance the budget for four years, the first time since the mid 50s.

If we click our Financial Time Machine forward year by year, we see that up until 2002 three financial factors are increasing. Boomers start to pass out of their peak new debt phase, but this only means they are not adding more debt. Their debt level remains high and will not decline until the next decade. By looking at the time machine, with more Boomers entering the triple convergence, it is easy to see why the economy is in such good shape. As we enter the new Millennium, all of the Boomers enter their peak spending phase with most occupying both their peak earning and savings phases. From a generational economics perspective, this is as good as it gets. Of course, where the other generations are influences the economy too.

The previous peak generation, the Greatests, is now retired and most have passed away, so they no longer have much effect upon the economy. The Silents are either retired or retiring and therefore withdrawing their economic stimulus from the economy, but since they are the smallest 20th century generation this has less of an effect. The smaller Xers are just starting to enter their peak factors, so they offer little impact thus far. The Millennials are currently too young to influence the economy much. Therefore, the Boomers constitute the major economic force at this time due to their record numbers and their position in their Financial Life Cycle.

2004

As we proceed ever closer to the present, we will stop more frequently to examine what transpires. If we adjust the indicator arrow on our time machine to 2004, the picture changes. As you see, earnings still increase

- this is great. Savings propensity also increases – another marvelous sign. Debt passes its peak and is starting its decline – this is good too because the Boomers need to reduce their debt before they retire.

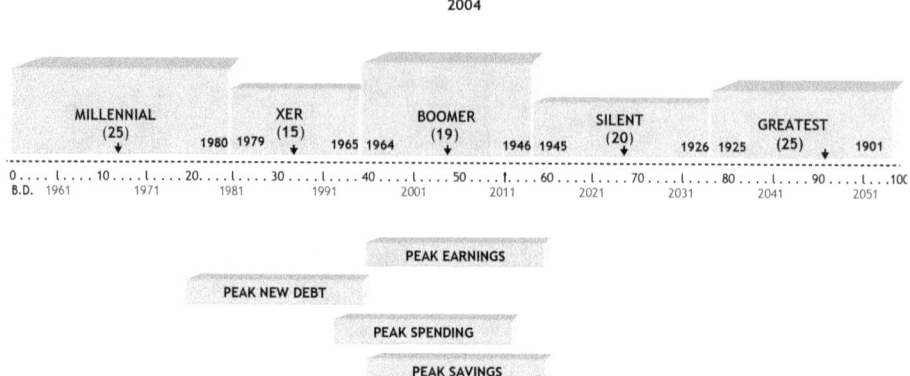

Notice for the first Boomers, spending starts to move out of its peak, suggesting that the generation's spending propensity is waning. For an economy addicted to consumer spending, this suggests an undetected yet disturbing trend - something like termites in the foundation. At first, you do not see them, but they slowly eat away your home, and they are only detected when disaster strikes. At this time, the Xers are moving into their peak financial factors, but the Xers are smaller than the Boomers, so the resultant economic stimulus will be substantially less. The Millennials are a large generation, but at the start of their careers, their economic stimulus is negligible.

As the Boomers reduce debt, they correspondingly increase savings in anticipation of pending retirements. Their investments, now at the peak, earn more as does their portion of a company's pension plan.

Starting in 2002 for the first time since the Boomers entered the economy 55 years ago, two of the indicators: debt and spending decline. The largest factor, earnings, continues its incline so it is not all bad news, but what happens when that too declines?

With three of the financial factors at or near their peak, according to the Financial Time Machine, we expect the early portion of the 2000s to return to the good times even if these are not as robust as before. The economy does pick up after the dot-com recession signified by the market's quick recovery of losses and subsequent new highs. Employment returns as the economy runs on all cylinders once again. The financial factors have been increasing for the Boomers since the mid 1980s when they first entered their peaks. The time machine predicts that this should be a stellar period for the U.S. economy. In reality, up until 2004 the longest period of expansion in U.S. history was interrupted only by a brief recession in 1991.

There is a sense that something is not quite right though. Examining the time machine, we see that although Boomers are in their peak, they will shortly leave their peak financial factors. What does this portend? We will examine the predicted decline in the next chapter where we look at the Great Recession through the lens of the Financial Time Machine.

John and Bob, now 49 and middle aged, still play slow pitch softball on Sundays, but their joints ache more. Like seemingly everyone, they talk about their stocks and picks regularly.

After 23 years with the same company, John suffered a "staff reduction," during the dot-com bust. Following a year of unemployment, he found a similar job, but the benefits are not as generous and the company has no pension plan. The commute expanded to an hour and a half, so John has little free time during the week; plus the cost of gas is a concern, especially for the second SUV. That was a tough year for the Peters when their savings depleted. They now earn $75,000, but considering inflation, it does not seem like much more. Earlier, John took out a $50,000 Home Equity loan to pay for the larger pool and spa, which is now a burden.

Daughter Suzy is 27 and quit college after three years when her dad became laid-off. She is waiting tables and modeling part-time. John Jr. was an accomplished student at UCLA majoring in Electrical Engineering, but due to the layoff the Peters could no longer afford it and Johnny left school. Johnny worked in the booming construction industry for a couple of years, saving all he could, and took out loans to attend nearby Cal State Fullerton. He will graduate this year and hopes to join a computer company in Silicon Valley.

Bob, finally married back in '96 to Jennifer and now has a lovely baby daughter, Christina. John stood beside him as his best man and Pat served as a bridesmaid. Bob left his aerospace job before a set of layoffs occurred and now manages a local consulting practice for a global firm. With his services in demand, he spends more time traveling the country. He would prefer to spend more time with his wife and daughter, who after an unusually long-spell away from home recently said, "Where Daddy -he live here anymore?"

Bob and Jennifer, currently a 39-year-old schoolteacher, earn about $180,000 a year. In 1999 they bought a $500,000, new 2,900 square foot four-bedroom, three and a half-bath house in Orange County, close to Bob's office. After a dip in area housing prices during the recession, the market ascended to new heights and the house is now worth over $1 million. The Ostrums save 8% per year; in addition, both have employer sponsored pension plans.

6

How the Financial Time Machine Predicted the Great Recession

In 2007, the stock market is soaring to new heights as housing values increase to unprecedented levels. With such high stock prices and housing values, the average American feels rich. Those in their 40s and 50s think they will be able to use the excess equity in their houses to retire. With housing values increasing so much, many invest in second and third houses in western and southern cities like Las Vegas, Phoenix, and Fort Meyers where prices are increasing by double digits. The construction industry is booming. Over the last 24 years, there have only been two brief recessions so they feel the risks are minor. It seems like the good times will continue forever and as usual few realize the bubble will soon burst.

By 2007, earnings and savings begin to decline for the first Boomers. Spending has fallen for 5-years and all of the Boomers are now out of their peak new debt phase indicating that demand for new debt should decrease in the overall economy. As they downsize while approaching retirement, the early boomers pay down their debts.

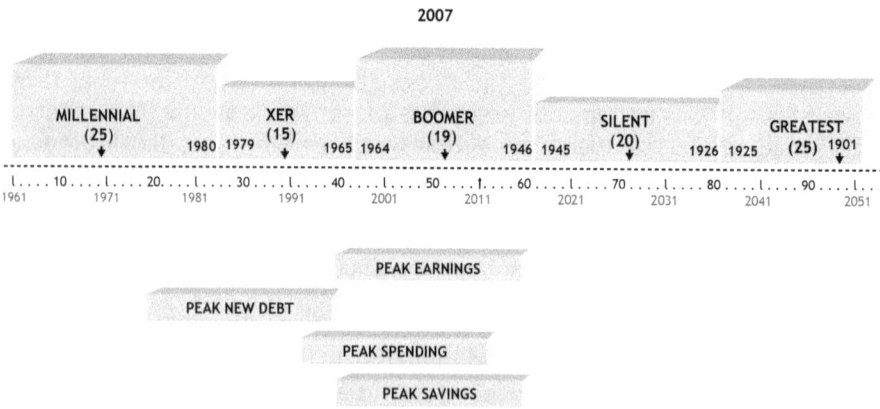

For the first time in 40 years, **all four financial factors are descending** for the Boomers depleting their long-term financial stimulus to the economy. While the factors are still at high levels, the fact that these are declining is not immediately obvious; like the blue skies and calm seas before a hurricane or the mild tremor that everyone dismisses prior to an earthquake or volcano. The economy continues to boom with the Dow rapidly approaching another milestone of 14,000 recovering all it lost since 2000 and more.

The Financial Time Machine predicts that the boom period is over and a decline is imminent. Even without the time machine, we intuitively sense that the largest generation in U.S. history is about to downsize, retire, and therefore withdraw their financial stimulus from the economy. Certainly such a shift with have economic consequences.

The housing bubble continues to inflate. The financial system, perhaps realizing the pending decline in loan demand, promotes two products to stimulate further lending: subprime and home equity loans. The flawed premise is that rapidly increasing housing prices will continue to rise and therefore equity will grow and even if a borrower cannot make their payments, the house will be worth even more. So they start selling loans to people who in the past could never qualify for a mortgage with a traditional bank having little or none of the previously required documentation. Since the repeal of Glass Steagall, which limited commercial bank securities activities and affiliations between commercial banks and securities firms, banks can now take on risks that had been illegal since the Great Depression. Banks are no longer traditional and the less diligent mortgage brokers currently issue most of the loans.

Investment banking firms who may now speculate on risky investments batch the loans into bundles of about a hundred and sell these as mortgage backed securities. Realizing immense profits and huge multi-million dollar yearly bonuses, they start multiplying profits with thirty to one margins so they can make even more money. Even though significant portions of their ingredients are rotten, the rating firms like the S&P who derive their fees from the investment banks obligingly mark these moth eaten bundles as AAA. Then they sell the risk laden assets to large investors looking for safe high returns such as the pension and 401(K)s funds rich with cash in anticipation of the pending Boomer retirements.*

The total value of home equity loans, based on the equity one accumulates in their house, skyrocket. In California, both John and Bob's houses are worth more than twice what they paid. John's home priced over $700,000, is now worth an extra **$400,000**. Bob's home now approaching a million and a half is worth an extra **$900,000**. Is it any wonder they and their compatriots feel wealthy?

At 52 during this stage of their financial lives, the midpoint Boomers like John and Bob should save furiously for their retirement. Instead, they feel rich and erroneously think their ever-increasing housing values will fund retirement. Some realize that if their kids can never afford to buy their house, housing values can't continue to rise because there will be fewer buyers. Naively early Boomers take out home equity loans to buy exotic sports cars, vacation homes, and investment properties. When savings should be at the peak, the saving rate is unfathomably negative.

Consumer spending composes 70% of the economy. Due to two long wars, the national debt climbs at an ever-increasing rate. Meanwhile, the first Boomers are retiring.

2010

Let's set the time machine forward another three years to 2010 to see what the Boomers financial world looks like then. Here we see that all of the four factors declined rapidly. Real earnings approach 2001 levels. Boomer debt decreased substantially and it is now apparent that as the first Boomers start to retire, savings too decline. Spending is down dramatically, which is devastating for an economy addicted to consumer spending, analogous to an economy going through withdrawal pains.

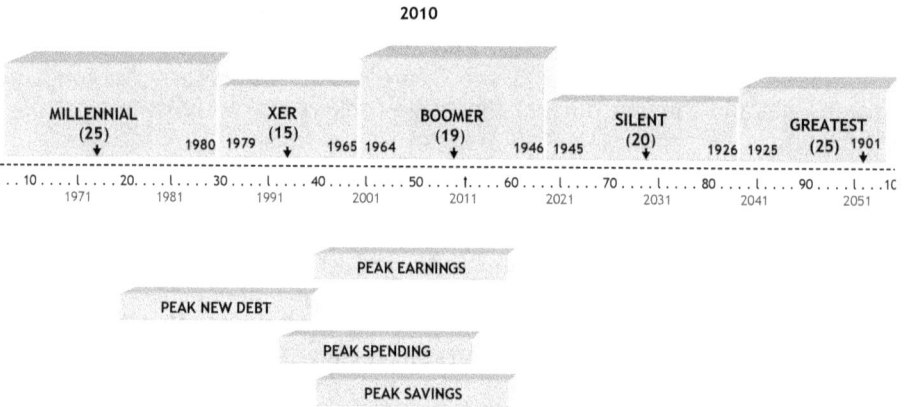

Comparing the last two periods of the time machine, we expect a severe reversal of fortunes to occur after 2007 and before 2010. We expect the boom period to end and an elongated period of decline to commence. What we expect is not just the normal short recession, but something far worse.

What happened?

The complete Financial Time Machine did not exist in 2001, but a rough model using many of the same generational economic principles predicted a severe recession or depression commencing in 2008, thereby advocating an exit of the market by then. The recession hit in December of 2007, but it was not until the summer of 2008 after Lehman Brothers bankruptcy that the economic picture rapidly deteriorated. Then, the mega-sized insurer AIG, along with many of the largest banks and investment houses, teetered on the brink of collapse. With thousands of stocks falling precipitously, the markets tumbled like avalanches. Not since the Great Depression did the world's economy look so dire. People, especially the Boomers who were already starting to retire, saw as much as half of their nest eggs - comprised of their homes and investments - evaporate. Fearing bank closures like 1928, many people actually stuck money into mattresses.

President Bush and Congress passed a $700 billion bank rescue plan called TARP, paid by the American taxpayer, which cost the average family of four $10,000 and they were livid. Those on Wall Street, who reaped multimillion dollar and even billion dollar bonuses for years playing exotic games of chance with people's pension funds, caused the crisis and now they received hundreds of billions of dollars to cover their bets, with little legal consequence or expense to themselves.

Representing the largest demographic segment of the population, the Boomer's peak earnings fueled the boom economy of the late 80s, 90s, and early 2000s. As they entered their fifties and sixties in increasing numbers, they needed to stop spending and borrowing so much and save for retirement. Shortly after the Millennium, a few wealthy and unionized Boomers were already retiring, drawing off their savings, investments, and company pensions, thereby reducing total Boomer earnings.

Up until that time, earnings were not the only fuel stoking the consumer-based economy; so were spending and debt. In anticipation of ever-increasing appreciation, consumers felt comfortable spending more than they earned by increasing their debt. For many, the only way they could afford a house in a place like California, where mortgage payments absorbed up to an unsustainable 35% of their income, was to hope earnings would continue to rise.

The federal government encouraged them to spend as did state and local governments, which were raking in record tax receipts from higher incomes and ever-escalating housing values. For over 25 years, government revenues and spending at all levels mushroomed to unsustainable levels that could not continue once earnings declined. Periodically, during recessions, government revenues tied to earnings, spending and property values fell, but all they needed to do was ratchet up tax rates a little to keep the money flowing in at an ever-higher rate. State spending that consumed 6.4% of GDP in 1985 consumed over 10% in 2010 - a 54% increase in spending in 25 years.* Not including extremely generous benefit packages, government wages used to be lower than public wages, but now the average government pay was 20% higher and Federal compensation was astoundingly 60% higher than private compensation. According to the Bureau of Economic Analysis, In 2010, the average compensation including benefits was $83,679 for Federal workers versus 51,986 for the private sector.*

Savings and investments soared to unprecedented levels largely due to the accumulation of Boomer savings and reserves in corporate and union pension funds. With the stock market at record levels, there was so much money sloshing around the system that there were not enough quality investments, so Wall Street created exotic innovations to attract the new money, promoting higher returns on products like mortgage backed securities and derivatives.

The Fed Chairman, Alan Greenspan, the SEC Chairmen Arthur Levitt, and the successive Treasury Secretaries, Robert Rubin, Larry Summers, and Henry Paulson, under both Clinton and Bush, all espoused deregulation of these newly minted complex products and the hedge funds who managed these, using dangerously low margins. (Previously, Rubin was the Co-Chairman and Paulson the CEO at Goldman Sacks.) As Greenspan had stated for the previous 20 years, the markets will regulate themselves.

One voice, that of Brooksley Born, Chair of the Commodity Futures Trading Commission, predicted the pending crisis, and was crushed by this all boys club who thwarted her efforts to regulate these potentially explosive products.*

The time machine predicted an unprecedented period of economic expansion from the mid-80s through the early 2000s, for as we saw in this last chapter this is when the largest generation occupied their peak financial factors providing immense stimulus to the economy. These leaders buoyed by seemingly endless economic success evidently did not recognize the possibility of the looming disaster -the tropical depression becoming a tropical storm. They thought their postulations favoring the market's self-corrective abilities actually led to the economic success. Unfortunately, these men in their exalted positions convinced the President and Congress to steer towards the rocks at high speed, instead of urging caution and a watchful eye. What might have been a major recession as predicted by the Financial Time Machine turned out to be much worse, because they ignored the lookout, Brooksley, who saw the rocks on the horizon. They left the new products and players in the market unregulated.

Of course, these new players with their exotic concoctions did what investment bankers and brokers have done for 200 years leading to financial crisis after financial crisis. They gamed the system thereby garnering hundreds of billions of dollars in bonuses, commissions, and investment profits. Manufacturing was no longer the largest industry, Finance was, and this was no longer the old-fashioned financial industry that provided value and money to help businesses grow. It became more and more speculative with less real added value.

One of the attributes that makes investing in the U.S. attractive to foreign capital is that it is a relatively fair game, because of the regulations. Many other world markets offer potentially large returns, but do not provide protection to those who invest there. Imagine pro football without rules and referees. Because of the high National Debt, the nation is dependent upon foreign purchase of our debt, of which the average American family's share is $200,000. Much of what caused the Great Recession was a lack of oversight and copious, unsupervised, questionable behavior.

After the crash, Alan Greenspan the longtime Fed Chair admitted he was wrong. Arthur Levitt said he admired Born for her courage and wished he had listened to her in time.*

The number of new offerings on the United States stock exchanges has steadily declined over the first decade of the 21st century, while those in other countries have increased, highlighting the world's distrust of our markets which sent the rest of the world into a serious recession too. The U.S. lost the AAA rating it held for decades. Of course, if we had a country version of the Financial Time Machine, we would see that others like Italy, Germany, Greece, Spain, and Japan were also sailing into rough waters whilst their own Baby Boomers started to retire, although some of their leaders knew this was about to occur and planned accordingly.

Once the Great Recession commenced, earnings drastically declined as unemployment skyrocketed for not only the Boomers, but also the Xers, and particularly the early Millennials. Unemployment five years afterward slowly recovered, the slowest since the Great Depression, so it will take time for real earnings to recover to the 2007 level.

One surprising consequence of the recession is that many Boomers were not able to retire as planned. They lost a substantial portion of their retirement portfolios, although if they followed the recommended guidelines most should not have been in risky stocks. Stocks have recovered but have a long way to go to reach pre-recession levels, plus the typical 8% expected return over the intervening years. Treasuries, CDs, and AAA bonds paid miniscule returns. Full Social Security payments will not accrue until Boomers are 66 or 67, which commenced January of 2012.

So now, all of the Boomer factors are declining. Similar to the scenario presented above with many Boomers retiring later, the peak earnings box will shift slightly to the left. The prolonged recession further exacerbates the situation by decreasing earnings even further due to high unemployment. So, the spending propensity should adjust lower too.

Why not Earlier?

So why didn't the Great Recession start immediately after 2002 as spending propensities began to decline instead of the end of 2007. The dot-com recession in 2001 vented the building pressure of the economic volcano about to blow. During the early 2000s, home equity loans artificially propped up consumer spending. Up until this time, housing prices had rapidly risen due to the record number of Boomers seeking homes, accentuated by high divorce rates and later marriages leading to dual domiciles. People felt richer than they really were and spent their irrational wealth on SUVs, home additions, home entertainment centers, vacations, and vacation homes, all paid for by home equity loans and illusionary home equity appreciation.

During this period, consumer spending rose to record levels as a percentage of GDP. The savings rate, at a time when it should have been at its zenith, became unfathomably negative. The national political leadership, including the president, encouraged this reckless behavior to keep the economy burning, but the fuel to stoke the bonfire would soon run out.

Even though spending propensity declined, earnings were still peaking until 2006 when the first Boomer became 60. Then, earnings and savings propensities began to decline too. According to generational economics, the forces that caused the recession smoldered underneath the surface, but were not yet visible. Fed Chairman, Alan Greenspan spoke of the looming housing bubble, but could not see all of the immense implications. In Michael Lewis's book the "Big Short," some people and hedge fund managers figured it out and bet millions on the looming crash. They made millions and even billions of dollars by doing so (five hedge fund managers garnered bonuses of over a billion dollars in crisis ridden 2008): their penny bets paid off in dollars by the American taxpayers rather than failed AIG, who booked most of the risky bets. The core cause of the recession were the subprime, unsecured home loans, whose Adjusted Rate Mortgages(ARMs) reset, throwing many into default.

So how did all of this happen? Below is a brief summary of the causes of the financial crisis.

1. The government, mortgage companies, banks, and investment houses encouraged subprime lending with little oversight of the required standard practices and procedures. People without jobs acquired loans they could not possibly afford. The mortgage suppliers thought that because of the rising housing market, when those people defaulted on their loans the eventual owner of the mortgage could make even more money by selling the foreclosed property.
2. In the past, a local bank or savings and loan closed the mortgage, and then administered it. Now, these institutions would sell the mortgage, pocketing the profits immediately. When the originator of the loan also administered the loan, they made sure the buyer could make the payments since the institution lost money if the buyer defaulted (buyers had to have jobs, a down payment, a good credit history and the payment had to be a reasonable percentage of their income - no more than 25% - 30%.) Since the mortgage originator was no longer directly responsible for the loan, the buyer/seller relationship was abrogated.

3. Previously, the Fed audited banks, savings and loans, and mortgage companies to ensure they were using proper lending practices, but Greenspan and the Fed refused to thoroughly audit banks thinking that the market would take care of itself - self-regulation. With few Fed audits, the mortgage industry became further emboldened.
4. Investment banks packaged the subprime loans along with other good loans into Mortgage-Backed Securities.
5. Despite the number of subprime loans in the package, the rating agencies (paid by the investment firms requesting the ratings) rated the Mortgage Backed Securities AAA.
6. The Mortgage Backed Securities then sold on Wall Street primarily to major investors like pension funds looking for and in many cases required to buy AAA rated securities. The demand for AAA rated bonds escalated, thereby creating a loop, in which more Mortgage Back Securities were needed, requiring the creation of even more loans. The mortgage market now resembled a manufacturing production line. Get more mortgages; pass them down the line where they are packaged into Mortgage Backed Securities, then sell the MBSs. Unlike a manufacturer, there was no real quality control.
7. The law required the original loan document to foreclose the property. The various appendages of the financial industry originated, transferred, packaged, and repackaged the mortgages so many times that the original mortgage documents were lost in the shuffle. So, financial institutions hired robo-signers to fake required signatures to millions of fake documents. Ten-dollar an hour clerks forged fictitious bank Vice Presidents' names to hundreds of thousands of mortgages. The false names were kept short, so they could sign more documents per hour.
8. Some members of the investment community looked inside the Mortgage Backed Securities and discovered these were junk, so they bought insurance from AIG even though they did not own the security. You could buy a billion dollars of insurance against default for 20 million bucks. Investment houses like Goldman Sacks facilitated this process and bought insurance themselves, while advising their investors of their "stellar" products.

Much of what the Financial Time Machine predicts parallels what occurred in the lead up to the crisis. If the FTM existed then and policy makers followed its projections, the crisis could have been mitigated. The Financial Time Machine shows that the demand for housing would eventually shift, but housing is a slow moving market and it takes time for it to ripple through the economy. The subprime mortgages exacerbated the process. If the government or the financial industry would have seen what was going to happen as they should have, or listened to those who saw it coming, there still would have been a dip and a recession, but it would have been less severe and not cost us three or four trillion dollars as some estimate.

Others estimated it as high as seven trillion, which is not that far-fetched considering the two trillion dollars in lost wages due to the excessively high unemployment thus far, TARP, the stimulus package, lost interest, and high commodity prices due to the Fed's zero interest policy.

The Time machine is not an exact model, but rather is concerned with large generational economic forces, so the margin of error is at least a year. In this case, a portion of the delayed reaction related to Boomer behavior. Many Boomers did not follow their financial life cycle. Fidelity produced ads showing a green line that if you followed, you would obtain your financial goals. Simply put, the Boomers strayed from their green line and instead bought that sports car when they really should have invested money for their retirement.

This was especially true in California, Arizona, Nevada, and Florida, where they assumed that their escalating housing values would fund their retirements and they could take out home equity loans to fund the sports car. (John had $400,000 of extra value while Bob had nearly $1,000,000.) When the houses dropped 50 -60% in value, one quarter to one half of the houses in those states sunk underwater and those Boomers, who did not follow their green lines, will have to work a few more years, especially if they went through a period of unemployment.

Each generation's financial behaviors affect their particular Financial Life Cycle. The Greatests and Silents were conservative, and if anything, could have left the green line more often, but they experienced the Great Depression and were therefore cautious about spending or gathering too much debt. Hopefully, the Xers and Millennials will learn from their parents' mistakes, their grandparents' good behaviors, and follow the Financial Life Cycle. As Suzie Orman says, they should, "stand in their truth." Thus far, the younger generations are doing better than their predecessors, and are cutting back on credit card debt. In 2002, 63% of those under 35 carried a balance, versus 45% in 2010.*

Let's look at the causal effects of the Great Recession a little closer in the context of the Financial Time Machine. So, this huge generation who increase their earning power for half a century, finally starts to reduce their earnings. As they are doing so, the Xers are increasing their earning power, but they have fewer members. The Millennials are also increasing their earning power, but their earning propensity is still very low and they do not have more members than the Boomers to counter the economy's lost income. The net effect is a significant reduction of financial stimulus to the economy.

Earlier, when the Silent's earning power decreased, it was not a problem, since the Boomers, even though they had lower earnings, had many more members to make up for Silents leaving the workforce. As the Earning and Spending dials recede for the large Boomer Generation, their contribution to the economy will diminish, greatly depleting a consumer dependent financial system.

The Greatests would have created a similar effect as they retired. The fewer Silents were not enough to make up for Greatests exiting the workforce and the Boomers, although large in number, were earning little having just started working. If the Time Machine is correct, there should have been some deeper recessions at this time. We will explore this in the next chapter. Later we will see if the Financial Time machine predicts the Great Depression.

In 2010, John and Bob are 54. John lost his job during the recession and has not found another yet with underemployment in the LA area hovering around 20%. The value of his house dropped 40%, but most of the mortgage is paid off, so John's family will not lose it if they can keep up with the payments. Unfortunately, they also took out a $75,000 home equity loan to finish the basement. Pat earned a promotion at her bank as a Loan Officer, but due to the crash, the bank went under and she is working reduced hours until the new bank decides which branches to close. The payments on their Home Equity Loan became ever more burdensome to pay.

Bob and Jennifer are doing OK. Bob's firm lost a significant portion of their management consulting business and he along with his team is working reduced hours. Jennifer still has her teaching position in the Irvine schools, but most communities are cutting teachers due to budgetary shortfalls. She has 20 years of service and because of her seniority is not likely to lose her position, but there is talk of cutting pension benefits, since CalPERS experienced severe losses during the crash and under current circumstance, it will be difficult to build the fund back up. The state faces severe budget shortfalls too and must cut back on education funding. Even with reduced hours and bonuses, they still earn a comfortable $140,000 a year.

The Ostrum's savings plan lost value, but they hope these will recover while they continue to contribute. Even if both lose their jobs, Bob and Jen have enough savings to last a year. Their house also lost 40% of its value, but it is a little above what they paid. Bob also took out a home equity loan for a finished basement, which they presently pay off at a faster rate, since interest on their CDs is practically zero.

Meanwhile, John and Pat planned to use the equity in their home to fund an early retirement, buying a two-bedroom condo near the beach. Pat dreamed of long walks along the beach listening to the crashing waves, and sipping wine while watching the sunset. John planned to ride his bike along the ocean's all-purpose trail and thought he might even try surfing again. But, that dream seems a long way off now, especially since their 401(k) lost half of its value too.

Johnny was let go from his software engineering job in Silicon Valley and moved home until he can find something else. Suzy is still waiting tables, but the modeling gigs ended. She broke up with her fiancée', Tad, a construction contractor, who has not worked fulltime for a year. Suzy hopes to complete college when the economy improves, although with escalating tuitions it will be a challenge.

Bob and John no longer play softball, but as life long best friends they still get together regularly to play a round of golf and complain about the economy. John works at the course part-time, so he gets their rounds for free, and Bob buys lunch and the beers.

Bob and Jen discussed the plight of their best friends and decided that whatever happens they will not allow them to lose their home. The only problem is that John is too proud to accept any financial help, so Jen mentions something to Pat; just letting her know that they are standing behind them. Pat broke down and cried in relief giving Jen a long hug. The recession and their daily financial problems take its toll on her.

7

The Greatest Generation and Parallelism

The Financial Time Machine shows how Boomers passing out of their peak financial factors led to the Great Recession. The previous large generation was the Greatests. If the Financial Time Machine truly predicted the downward cycle caused by the Boomer's, then it should predict a similar financial downturn when the Greatests begin to exit the economy. Did such an event really occur?

Now in their late eighties, nineties, and one hundreds, the heralded Greatest generation, who lived through such a pivotal era, slowly fades into history. When they started working in the 1920s and 30s, few Greatests thought of retirement, for most companies did not provide pension plans. Social Security and Medicare did not exist, and with a life expectancy of 60, most thought they would work until they dropped, or if they lasted that long, live with their large families. Currently they have little economic effect other than to pass on their remaining wealth to the Boomers.

A Comparable Arc

The Greatest generation led a financial life in many ways similar to their Boomer offspring. Since detailed records of nationwide births did not exist prior to 1909, it is difficult to discern exactly how many Greatests were born, but extrapolating available data shows there were approximately 70,000,000. In 1930, the U.S. population was 122 million, so allowing for some deaths like the flu pandemic in 1918 that killed over a half a million Americans, the Greatests constituted over half of the population. Due to their high numbers, the generational effects upon the economy resemble that of the Boomers.

There are 42 years between the midpoints of the Greatest in 1913 and the Boomer in 1955. By merely adjusting the yearly scale 42 years, we constructed the Greatest Time Machine displayed below with the year set to 1939. The Midpoint of the Greatests' box now determines the year.

1939 Greatest Financial Time Machine

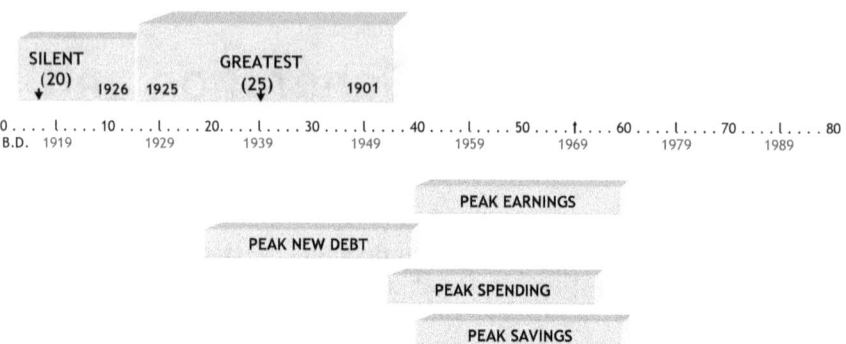

According to the picture above, the Greatests' ages vary between 13 and 38. They occupy their peak new dept phase: busy getting married, building nests, and having children, but this is the end of the Great Depression. Unemployment has been high, wages low, and it is tough to scrape by. For many, just putting food on the table is a struggle, so they have little thought of buying a house, new furniture or the latest laborsaving appliances like an automatic washing machine. Plus, with housing prices declining, real estate is not a particularly wise investment. Finally, they are beginning to get their feet back on the ground, but in two years, an all-consuming war will define this generation causing them to further delay nest building.

1959

Let's now go forward 20 years. With the booming economy of the 1940s and 1950s and a shortage of labor, the large industrial U.S. companies who dominate the world's economic landscape now offer pensions to retain trained workers. Many take advantage of the GI bill and for them opportunities abound as the only intact world economy roars. After the ravages of World War II, it will take three decades for the other economic powers with their greatly diminished industrial complexes and populations to catch up.

A major reason for the economic boom of the 50s and 60s is due to the record number of children the Greatests have as they nest. They move out of the farms and apartment buildings and into bungalows in newly hatched suburbs, where they now buy automobiles to commute to work. They need to clothe their children and provide for their educations so they became teachers and professors. New industries like television, aeronautics, and electronics take off, requiring thousands of workers and managers. They build a massive interstate system to transport the voluminous goods they require. Most of the Rosy Riveter moms stay home to care for their Boomer broods. For men, work scarce during the depression and directly after the war, becomes abundant, because there is just so much to build and do.

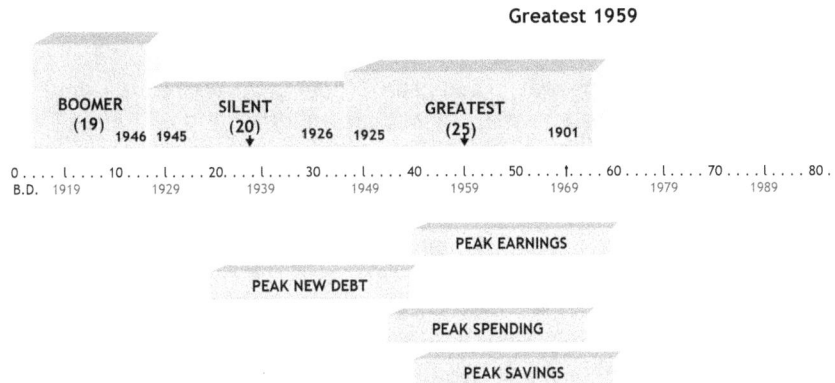

Greatest 1959

What we see in 1959 looks fantastic. From 1949 until now, all of the Greatests' financial indicators climb at a rapid rate, when most of the Greatests occupy their peak earning, spending, and saving phases. The only financial factor in decline is debt. A couple of mild recessions occur in the 1950s, largely due to Fed policy adjustments. Otherwise, the 1950s and 1960s prove to be an extraordinary period of prosperity, where the country's GDP expands from $300 Billion to $1,050 Billion, a 3 ½-fold increase.*

With the exception of the war, what we see thus far for the Greatests spans a similar arc to that of the Boomers. When this large generation hit their peak financial years from the fifties through sixties, the economy expands at a rapid rate, comparable to the 1980s and 1990s when the large Boomer generation was also in their peak financial cycle.

Greatest generation's Greg Ostrum

Bob Ostrum's father, Gregory, was born in 1914 in Cleveland near the midpoint of the Greatest generation. Shortly afterwards Cleveland became the fifth largest city in the nation. It was the second largest steel producer after Pittsburgh, the second largest auto producer after Detroit and the former home of J.D. Rockefeller's Standard Oil, the largest corporation in history. Greg starred as an all-state pitcher with a scorching fastball who dreamed of a pro career.

His father, Bob's grandfather, was a prominent banker, who lost most of his money during the crash of 1929, so the family had no money for Greg to attend college. At the time, it seemed everyone was poor, so Greg and his family, even though they had to scrape by, did not feel any worse for being poor. Fortunately, he received a partial scholarship to

Princeton for baseball.

Greg graduated with an engineering degree in 1936 and luckily during the depression, found a job with Thompson Products in Cleveland as an airplane designer. Two years later, he married Cathy Clark. By 1941, they had a boy and a girl.

Greg signed up for the war and fought on Omaha Beach in the D-Day invasion. Following the war, Thompson Products gave Greg his job back. He and Cathy then had another boy and girl in 1946, and 48. Seven years later Robert (Bob) arrived.

In 1959, Thompson Products merged with Ramo-Woodridge to form TRW and asked Greg to move to Los Angeles to be a project manager for their Saturn projects. Ramo-Woodridge led the development of ICBMs, Atlas, and Gemini rockets, which later sent the first astronauts into space and to the moon. In 1960, Congress, due to a perceived monopoly in the burgeoning aerospace industry by TRW, took half of TRW's engineers to form NASA. Greg was not part of this restructuring.*

He and Cathy bought a house in Orange County not far from TRW's sprawling college-like campus, Space Park, called, "the land of the light weight Einstein's," due to the thousands of rocket scientists like Greg who worked there. The house cost $28,000 which was a stretch, but Greg now earned $9,000 a year. The Ostrums led a great life, barbequing near the pool and watching their happy brood enjoy the wonderful California weather and all of their sports.

1970

Let's take a look at what was happening for the Greatests back in 1970 when they first retired. Like the Boomers, all of their propensities are in decline, but relatively high up until then. Since the Greatest generation is longer than the Boomers, the last cohort of the generation will extend the time they spend in their peak phases, but by 1970, the much smaller Silent generation occupies the four financial peaks, signaling a dramatic drop in economic stimulus.

This generation, however, was if anything too conservative with respect to savings, debt, and spending. In 1970, the economy was not addicted to consumer spending. The Greatests, who tended to work for the same company for 30 or 40 years while living in the same house, were paying that house off. They did not use credit cards much and many bought cars with cash. They remembered the Stock Market Crash of 1929 and justifiably did not trust banks or brokerages, so they resisted investing in the markets again. Fortunately, their abundant well-funded pension trusts invested on their behalf.

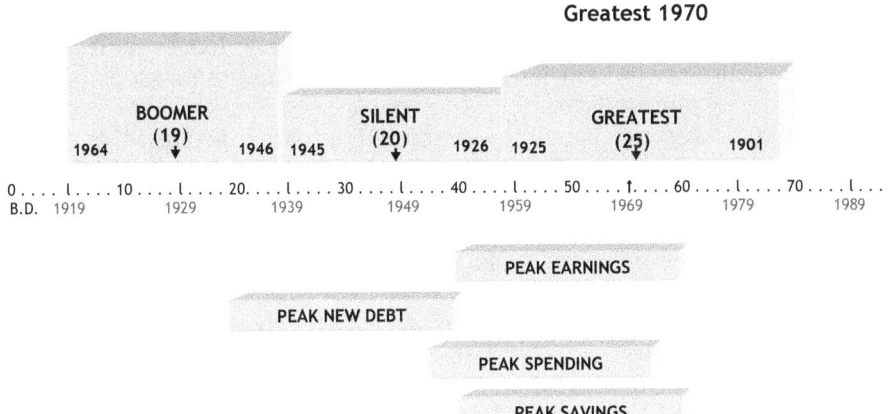

As we enter the 1970s and more of the Greatests retire, their Boomer children or grandchildren are still in school or just commencing jobs and careers, so they can not yet make up for the loss of income and spending. The 1970s and early 1980s prove to be a rough decade for the economy with high inflation, then stagflation, and for the first time in 30 years, competition from abroad, primarily from the Japanese auto and steel makers. Part of this phase of globalization results in the Arab Oil Embargo, when gas prices double and lines at stations wrap around the block - a rude awakening to the fact that we were no longer the only player in the world Monopoly game.

In December of 1969, the longest period of U.S. GDP expansion ends in a mild recession. Three years later in 1973 with unemployment of 9 %, the most severe recession since the Great Depression follows. Then in 1980 – 1982, there is an even more devastating double-dip recession with 10.8% unemployment, constituting the worst figures in 75 years.*

1970s Era Recessions

Recession	Length	Unemploy.	GDP Decline
December, 1969 - 70	11 mo.	6.1%	-.6%
November, 1973 - 75	1 yr., 4 mo.	9.0%	-3.2%
January, 1980 - 80	6 mo.	7.8%	-2.2%
July, 1981 - 82	1 yr, 4 mo.	10.8	-2.7%

The Greatest generation resembles the Boomers with their numbers similarly exceeding the Silents who follow. Earlier, some Greatests died in childhood, some in the 1918 Flu Epidemic, and others in WWII, but most survive and prosper until the 1970s when they retire. The Social Security Act of 1932 guaranteed them a decent retirement, the first full generation to have this, and the Medicare Act of 1965 guaranteed them healthcare just as they begin to retire when healthcare costs escalate.

With increased life expectancies, they enjoy longer and more lucrative retirements than their predecessors. They draw more out of Social Security and Medicare than they put in, but many of their Boomer sons and daughters are happy to subsidize their care. Besides, this is the Greatest Generation who lived through the Great Depression and won World War II on the beaches of Omaha and Iwo Jima. Who then went on to reconstruct Europe and in the factories of Detroit, Pittsburgh, and Cleveland, built an immense modern infrastructure for the United States.

These dads were not in touch with their feelings, because of the horrors they saw in Europe, Northern Africa and the South Pacific, and the way they were raised. These moms lived for their families. It seems poetic justice that a generation, who had it so tough in the beginning, did so much, and gave so much to their children and nation, should have a comfortable, well-earned retirement.

Stagflation

The four recessions above occur as they retire sapping their financial stimulus from the economy. The term typically applied to the 1970s' economy is stagflation – stagnant growth and high inflation. The period is not as bad as either the Great Recession or the Great Depression, but constitutes the worst in between these two, book-ended by four decades of unparalleled growth. **Malaise** well describes the 70s. A decade when America lost its first war, (Vietnam), was plagued by the OPEC oil embargo, lost its preeminence as the world's dominant auto manufacturer, faced the hostage crisis in Iran, and experienced double-digit inflation.

For 11 straight years beginning in 1971, U.S. investors withdrew more from stock funds than they invested, signaling the exit of the large Greatest generation from the economy. The Dow Jones Industrial average was practically the same in **1982** as it was in **1966**, seventeen years earlier, showing that it too, like the economy, stagnated.* If this same pattern held true for the Great Recession, we would not have expected the market to completely recover until 2024.

In 1970, the midpoint Greatest is 56, comparable to the midpoint Boomer at 52 in 2008. Their Financial Time Machines, although not exact, looks similar to the Boomers' with both generations' economic factors in decline. At first, this seems like a large variation, but there are 25 years of Greatests versus 19 years of Boomers, so even though more Greatests retire, there are still more Greatests in their peak phases to keep the economy humming. Plus, the Greatests retire later.

The Bureau of Labor statistics data reflects that the average retirement age for males was over 64 in 1970 versus 62 in the mid-2000s.* If we deduct the extra six years of Greatests, this provides an age of 63 when the malaise hits. This is a year earlier than their retirement age of 64. The first Boomers hit their average retirement age of 62 in 2008 at the start of the Great Recession; therefore, the two generations are highly comparable.

Both of these years, 1970 and 2008, represent the start of extended periods of economic stagnation. It is not just the leading edge of the generation, or the midpoint that defines the decline, but rather the generation's trailing edge. In 1970, the youngest Greatest is **45**. In 2008, the youngest Boomer is **44**. In 2008, many Boomers already retired, as had many of the Greatests in 1970. But, there were still Boomers and Greatests moving into their peak phases providing continuing stimulus to the economy. When the next, smaller generation moves into their peaks, the economy experiences a decline. Following this smaller generation is another peak generation, but since that generation is just starting to earn money, they do not yet offer enough economic stimuli to offset the decline. For example, in 1970 the mean Boomer was only 15-years old.

In the case of the Greatests, the much smaller Silents began entering their peak earning and savings phases in 1966. The Xers entered these peak phases in 2005. In both cases, generational stimulus fell three or four years before the decline commenced. The economy is more like a ship than a powerboat, taking time to turn from expansion to contraction.

These trailing generational edges symbolize the most dramatic drop in economic stimulus for the peak generations. The large generation of Greatests exiting the economy in the 1970s has an affect similar to that of the previous chapter's Boomer exit during the late 2000s and 2010s.

Parallelism and the peak generations

If we direct the Time Machine back even further in time to 1929, we see where the Greatest generation stood at the onset of the Great Depression.

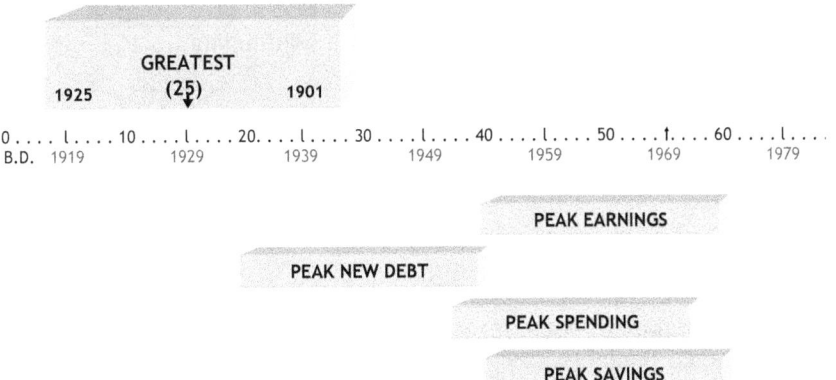

In 1929 with ages ranging between 3 and 28, the average Greatest was only **15** years old. The preceding period called the Roaring Twenties constituted a time of great expansion when the Greatests were in school and starting their working lives. Of course, not many of the Greatests went to college or even graduated from high school. Because a national child labor law did not pass until 1938, work might commence as early as 12 or 14. As their financial factors indicate, the Greatests have little effect upon the economy at this time other than through their parents creating a high demand for housing, goods, and employment.

After the 1920s, the next period of rapid GDP expansion occurred 40 years later during the 1960s when the Greatests were in their peaks. This constituted the longest period of expansion in U.S. history lasting nearly nine years without a recession. At this time, the Boomers were coincidently **15** years old.

Collapses followed each expansion. The Great Depression followed the Roaring Twenties and the 70s malaise followed the booming 60s. Of course, at 15, the Greatests in 1929 and the Boomers in 1970 could not cause the downturns because they were too young. They were the next peak generation about to enter the economy with a promise of better times to follow.

In the 1990s, we set another record for the longest expansion. Curiously, the new record for the longest expansion also preceded the Great Recession. Astoundingly, the midpoint Millennials turned **15** in 2008, the first full year of the Great Recession. Again, the Millennials did not cause the contraction, but rather their parents, the previous peak generation Boomers, did.

Midpoint ages at Collapse

Collapse	Expansion	Peak Generation	Next Peak Generation	Age at Collapse
Great Depression	Roaring 20s	?	Greatests	15
70s Malaise	8.8 yrs	Greatest	Boomers	15
Great Recession	10 yrs	Boomers	Millennials	15

To summarize:
- The Great Depression followed the booming Roaring Twenties.
- The 70s malaise followed the longest period of economic expansion in 180 years of U.S. economic history.
- The Great Recession followed the new longest period of economic expansion.
- The midpoints of each of next peak generations comprised of the Greatests, Boomers, and Millennials were each 15 at the onset of these financial crises.

Perhaps these are simply coincidences. After all, in each of these cases most of the young generations are still in their childhood, teens, and twenties when the contractions occur. Therefore, they have little effect upon the economy other than indirectly through their parents. So their parents would be buying houses, furniture, appliances, and all the things we spoke of earlier, while taking on their highest debt level. All of this would certainly be stimulative to the economy leading to high employment and explaining the parallel boom decades of the 1920s, 60s, and 90s.

But why do the worst recessions and the depression follow these boom periods? From a generational economic viewpoint, we saw how the Boomers passing out of their peak economic factors led to the Great Recession with the same scenario playing out with the Greatests passing out of their peak economic factors leading to the 70s' Malaise.

In the next chapter, we will examine the Great Depression to see if there is more to the parallelism we just uncovered. We will take the Financial Time Machine back even further to see if it explains a major factor causing the depression. Is there yet another peak generation that led to the Great Depression?

Greg Ostrum retires in 1975 at 61 years old. He headed up the Saturn 10 project, which was the first spacecraft to exit the solar system sending messages back to earth 32 years later. As a Project Director, he earned $26,000.

With a marvelous pension from TRW, Social Security and now Medicare, Greg retires with a full pension. He and Cathy plan to tour Europe and Asia for a full year, a life-long dream of hers. Then they want to buy an RV and tour U.S. parks while they are still young and able. One of Greg's goals is to drive the RV up scenic coastal route 1, visiting every beach along the way.

8

Generational Waves and the Civil War Generation

The Great Depression

What about the Great Depression? Was there a large generation passing out of the productive economy at that time? If there were, this would further support the Financial Time Machine's postulations. Unfortunately, we know little about the demographics of the generations in the 1800s that preceded the Greatests. With scant statistical evidence prior to 1909, it is difficult to fully reconstruct the preceding generations to see if there was a similar parallelism happening to the Greatests' predecessors in 1929. Indeed, the original scope of the book did not include this concept, but it seemed intriguing and inescapable. If generational economics explains the economic cycles since the Great Depression, could it also be a catalyst of the depression itself?

Let's look two generations prior to the Greatests to see what was happening then. Using average, 20-year generations, one spans 1861 - 1880 and the other spans 1881 - 1900. The Civil War ran from 1861 - 1865; so theoretically, there would have been a Civil War Baby Boom generation starting around 1866. Is there any evidence of such a generation?

During the Civil War, there were 620,000 deaths, as many as all other U.S. wars combined and over 1,000,000 casualties, roughly 3% of the population. Those casualties were largely constituted of those in their childbearing years. With so many young men killed or injured in the North and the South, it is questionable whether there was indeed a Civil War Baby Boom. However, up until the 1940s, there were more men than women in every age group, with one exception. The 1870 Census shows there were 99.2 men for every 100 women – not much of a difference. So, even after the devastating war, there were nearly as many men as women and since reproduction depends upon the number of women, there would have been plenty of couples to have children.*

Published in 1984, *Baby Boom 2*, by Michael Phillips, states that the non-immigration population jumped 48% after the war, comparable to the 47% jump after WWII.* This makes sense, because with so many men away at war for up to four years, birthrates during this time of stress would have been extraordinarily low. In addition, the civilian population in large sections of the country, particularly in the South, was under siege with only meager supplies. During periods of constrained food and materials, species naturally reproduce less. After the war, husbands would reunite with their wives and younger soldiers would marry their sweethearts and then reproduce.

The 1920s Census has a 90-year-old table (back to 1830) showing the number of people by age, every ten years when the census was taken. This table displays ages in 5-year increments. The analysis below shows a remarkable 48% increase for the Civil War generation compared to the preceding generation. During this time of rapid expansion each generation was approximately 30% larger than the preceding; therefore, a nearly 48% increase was still exceptional.*

Civil War Era Generations
(in millions)

	Post War of 1812	Pre Civil War	Civil War	Post Civil War	Greatest
Population of Generation[1]	13	17.2	26.5	34.1[2]	43.2
Increase		32%	48%	28%	27%
Total population	23[3]	39[3]	63[3]	76	106

Notes:
1. Twenty year generations, not including last five years of Greatests. This number is taken from successive censuses as close to birth, but also includes young immigrants.
2. Averaged over 15 years represented as 20 years.
3. Census 5 years after generation.

The economic expansion following the Civil War was, indeed, analogous to that following World War II. From 1869 to 1879, the real GDP grew at a blistering **6.8**%. The 1880s was the highest decade of real growth in nearly 150 years. While building the massive railroad and steel industries, capital investment also enlarged tremendously during the 1880s, increasing nearly **500%.**

By 1890, the USA leapt ahead of Britain for first place in manufacturing output. Inventions during this time of optimism include the telephone, phonograph, typewriter, electric light, and movie projector. Today we have the iPhone, iPod, iPad, LED light, and Netflix, but these are in a sense the latest evolution of devices invented prior to the 20th century. By the dawn of the 20th century, cars began to replace horse-drawn carriages.*

As World War II demarcated the generations of the 20th century, so too would the Civil War define the generations of the 19th century. Using the same lengths as the Boomers and Xers, we can reconstruct our theoretical generations from 1866 - 1884 for the Civil war boom generation; and 1885 – 1900 for the following generation (call these the 20th Century generation.) This gives a midpoint of 1875 for those born after the Civil War.

Granted this is a stretch but let's take our time machine back for the "Civil War Boom Babies" (Civil War Boomers.) These great, great grandparents were 80 years older than the Boomers. Here is their Financial Time Machine in 1929.

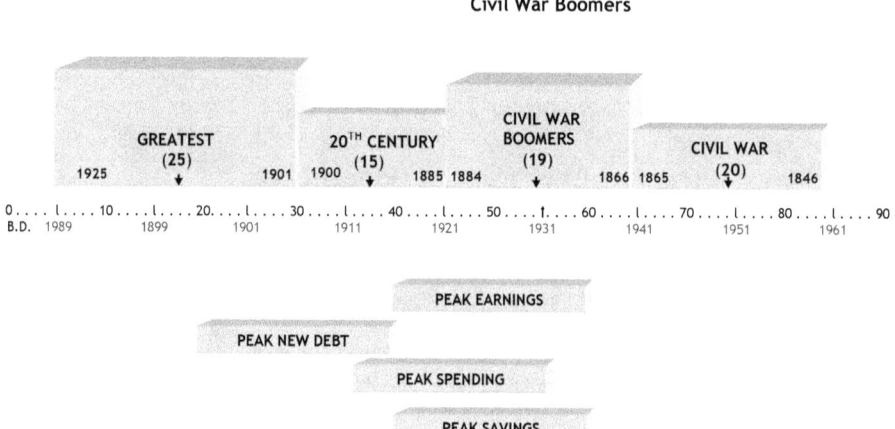

Note: Generations not drawn to scale.

What appears is very surprising - the Civil War Boomers picture with respect to their financial factors in 1929 is very similar to the Boomers in 2008. Like the Boomers, when the Civil War Boomers financial factors declined, thereby withdrawing their stimulus from the economy, we had the Great Depression.

The following table summarizes the three economic downturns.

Comparison of major U.S. downturns since 1900

Downturn	Years	Preceding Boom Period	Downturn Length	Peak Unemp.	GDP Loss
Great Depression	1929- 38	8 yrs	9 yrs	24.5%	-26.7%
70s Malaise	1970- 82	9 yrs	9 yrs	10.8%	-2.7%
Great Recession	2008 - ?	10 yrs	4 +? yrs	10.1, 17.4%	-5.1%

For the Great Recession, the 17.4% includes discouraged workers, not included in the unemployment number. These are the people who although they are unemployed have given up looking for work.*

The following table examines the ages of the various peak generations during the depression or the major recessionary periods. The similarity in the ages is astounding, especially considering that generational economics is not the only cause of these financial downturns, but merely a catalyst. Generational economics may set the stage for the play, but the actual timing of the events depends upon the actors and the script.

Peak Generational Ages

Financial Downturn	Older Gen	Midpoint Age	Last's Age	Younger Gen	Midpoint Age
Great Depression	Civil War Boomers	53	45	Greatest	15
70s Mailaise	Greatest	56	45	Boomer	15
Great Recession	Boomer	52	44	Millennial	15

The economy stepped out of the Depression in 1933 and did not return to another severe, although shorter, recession until four years later in 1937. People typically think of this entire period as the depression though. Likewise, the Great Recession technically ended in June of 2009, but with unemployment still above 7% in 2013, it is difficult to suppose we are truly out of the Great Recession. Recessions typically account for at least two quarters of negative GDP growth. Once the economy starts to experience positive growth, it may take years for it to recover all it lost especially in light of inflation.

The Malaise was not as bad as the Great Depression or Great Recession. The difference was that the economy still percolated. As the U.S. finally faced global competition, the much larger, highly educated Boomer generation entered the workforce providing a balancing force. We were also in a transition from a manufacturing economy to a digital economy driven by the educated Boomers. Just as the Greatests provided the momentum for the transition from an agrarian to a manufacturing economy, the Boomers powered the transition from manufacturing to the digital revolution.

Cycle

It would be presumptuous to assume that it applies in all cases, but there does seem to be a cycle operating here – an expansion/contraction cycle demonstrated by the previous list of economic downturns. Starting with the contraction lets examine the potential cycle a little closer. The peak generations are the Civils War Boomers, Greatests, Boomers, and Millennials. The lull generations are the Twentieth Centurys, the Silents, and the Xers.

Contraction

The contraction or bust phase of the cycle exhibits the following characteristics:

- An Older peak generation downsizing, retiring, and expiring, thereby reducing stimulus to the economy, drawing down accumulated wealth to fund retirement, leading to less available capital.
- A Lull generation in it's nesting phase with vastly reduced birthrates.
- Fewer housing starts, and less demand for appliances, furniture, food, clothing, and goods.
- Lower demand across multiple industries leading to downsizing.
- An increase in unemployment.
- The younger peak generation seeking employment leads to lower wages.
- Sustained low or negative GDP growth.

Expansion

- The peak generation is in nesting phase with higher birthrates.
- Increased housing starts, and demand for appliances, furniture, food, clothing, and goods.
- Higher demand across multiple industries leads to increased capacity.
- Higher employment.
- Higher wages.
- Sustained high GDP growth.

The successive generations create a wave pattern. What results is a sine wave, similar to what you might see with AC current, but this sounds too much like physics. Instead, imagine watching waves approaching a beach with successive crests and troughs. When you watch the waves hit the beach, you see the water rush up the shore as the crest crashes, then recede from the shore during the trough until the next crest. The generational waves provide an expansive force to the economy. When they recede, there is contraction. Like waves, each peak generation or lull generation is not the same height or width.

The following picture shows generational waves washing over the economy. These advance from the right to the left, the last of which is the Millennial wave. If you stood on the economy's beach to the right in the mid-18th century and peered out 150 years, this is what you would see approaching the shore.

Generational Waves
Expansions

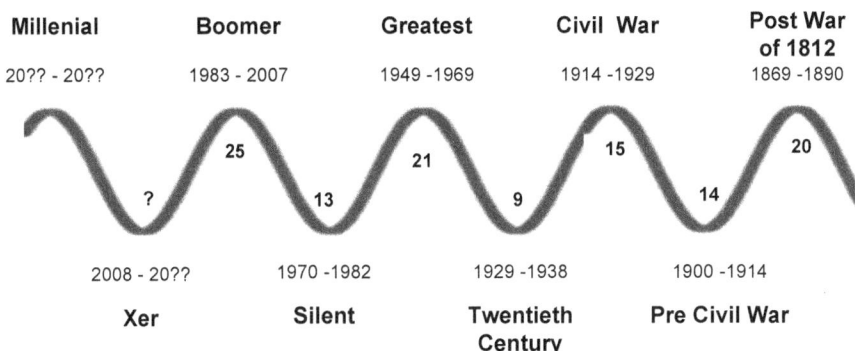

Millenial	Boomer	Greatest	Civil War	Post War of 1812
20?? - 20??	1983 - 2007	1949 -1969	1914 -1929	1869 -1890

25   21   15   20

?   13   9   14

2008 - 20??	1970 -1982	1929 -1938	1900 -1914
Xer	Silent	Twentieth Century	Pre Civil War

Contractions

The periods for each expansion and contraction are pictured above along with the dominate generation at the time, namely the generation who was in their peak economic factors. The numbers in the center of each phase of the cycle indicate the length of each generation.

So over the last 140 years we have a series of expansions and contractions synchronized with the peak generations. Each of the expansions lasts an average of 20 years, followed by a contraction averaging about 12 years. The Great Depression only lasted nine years, which World War II short-circuited when the nation's industries ran at full speed.

The period that includes the war is not included, since the war influenced economic results much more powerfully than generational economics when a record amount of public debt financed war production. The period from 1890 to 1900 is also not included, because it is a period of neither expansion nor contraction. Consider these transition periods.

Expansions and Contractions

Economic Cycle	Dates	Length (years)	Real GDP Growth	Avg.[1]
Expansion				
Civil War	1870-90	20	191%	9.5%
Roaring Twenties	1914-29	15	78%	5.2%
World War II	1949-69	21	139%	7.0%
Millennial	1983-07	25	124%	5.2%

Contraction				
Civil War	1900-14	14	31%	2.2%
Roaring Twenties	1929-38	9	1%	.1%
World War II	1970-82	13	35%	2.9%
Millennial	2007 -?	4 +	.1%	----

1. Non-compounded average
GDP figures from USGovernmentSpending.com.*

Cataclysmic events like wars, famine, and plagues can cause the cycle to reset, as did the Civil War and World War II, although these events also rmarkably tend to synchronize with the waves. Each century's major wars seem to follow a similar generational pattern. The distance between the start of the Revolutionary War and Civil War was 85 years and the distance between the Civil War and World War II was 80 years. Following the coincidental logic, the next major war would arrive in 2021 to 2026, which hopefully does not happen.

The cycles immediately following the wars have strong expansions and mild contractions. Conversely, the non-war cycles have slower expansions and severe contractions. The period following the Civil War resulted in real average growth of a remarkable 9.5% and that following World War II resulted in 7% growth. The subsequent contractions produced growths of 2.2% and 2.9%, which were not spectacular, but not terrible either.

The growth rates during the less robust Roaring Twenties and 1990s were both 5.2%, but the contractions that followed were dismal with near zero growth for extended periods of time. Although their characteristics are remarkably similar, the period and amplitudes of the waves vary.

The wave action produces an incredible effect, but this is not the only force acting upon the economy. The events of the time, policies, character of the people, and leadership also hold sway. That is why an analysis of each generation in light of these factors along with the time machine produces a more accurate picture.

The stock market, long thought to be a barometer of the economy, offers additional reinforcement to the time machine's cyclic prognosis. Thirteen years after the stock market crashed in 1929, it was still down 10%. This was the time when the Civil Wars were retiring.

A similar phenomenon occurred during the 70s malaise when the market plateaued for 17 years, from 1966 to 1971, as the Greatest generation traded in their stocks for cash and bonds. Then again, in the 2000s, after the Great Recession, it took the Dow Jones until 2011 to recover to the level it obtained ten years earlier in 2001. As further evidence, it turns out there was another market plateau from 1906 to 1916, during the Civil War contraction when the generation prior to and during the Civil War retired.

In each case, the markets dropped as the peak generations retired, cashing in investments to live on during retirement and for more secure bonds. Today, investments in bonds are escalating, while the money invested in stocks continues to decline even though bonds pay little and the stock market has doubled since 2009. As of October 2012, investors withdrew a net $138 billion from stocks, while investing a trillion dollars in bonds.*

Many gifted financial journalists, national financial advisors, and strategists seem surprised by the lack of equity investment and attribute the lack of stock investment to a lack of confidence in the markets, which is certainly true. But, I believe there is a larger force at work. There is a huge generation at or near retirement that is following the advice of financial advisors to switch investments from equities to bonds. For those who invest in retirement date funds, the funds automatically perform the switch. Pension funds too are following a similar path, converting stocks into cash payments for the increasing number of retirees. A huge number of pension funds froze their pensions, so they no longer need to buy equities, but only sell these.

The characteristic that most accurately predicts when expansions and contractions will occur directly relates to where the peak generations are in their Financial Life Cycle, which supports the postulations of the Financial Time Machine.

In the next chapters, we will observe the Silents and Xers, but before we do so, we will build a new and improved version of the time machine. Then it is off to the future.

9

The Revised Time Machine

Even though a little worn from our journey, our simple time machine served us well, helping to portray generational economics' application to the Financial Life Cycle. But now it is time to trade in the old model for a new improved version - something more like you expect a contemporary machine to look like. The current version illustrates how the dynamics between the generations and their Financial Life Cycles work together to produce both boom times and bust times, but it is a little cumbersome to operate. This model readily portrayed when a generation entered its peak financial factors along with the consequence of those occurrences. With the operating principles of the time machine firmly in place, let's update the Financial Time Machine's metaphor, so it is easier to work with.

Skipping over the Jules Verne 1890s version let's go directly to a *Back to the Future*, Delorean style Financial Time Machine as pictured below:

Financial Time Machine 3.0

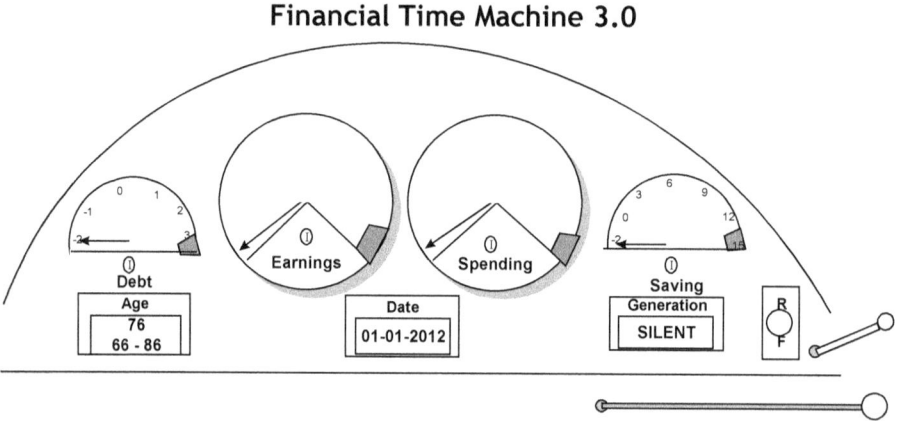

Having several dials, the new machine resembles an automobile dashboard with all of the information contained on the Financial Time Machine 2.0. The most noticeable difference is the dials at the top of the dash indicating the four financial factors. The lower displays provide information regarding the generation and dates. The concepts remain the same, but we replaced the slide rule with instruments. Operating it is similar to operating an automobile.

Financial Time Machine 3.0 Operating Instructions

1. Selecting the Generation: Below the dashboard to the right is a shifter. To choose a generation, we select a gear on the 5-speed transmission (Greatest, Silent, Boomer, Xer, or Millennial.) The selected generation shows up in the generation display on the right of the dashboard.

2. Selecting the Direction: A separate lever to the right of the dashboard above the shifter determines whether we go forward or in reverse (back in time.) From neutral, we move the lever down for forward or up for reverse.

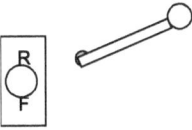

3. Driving through Time: Once we select the direction in time we wish to travel, we press the accelerator slowly to start moving through time. The faster we press the gas the faster we go. Please pay attention to the date display in the center of the dashboard. As we approach the desired date, we will need to slow down, because it's a hassle to stop, change direction and go backwards. There is a second display to the left of the date showing the age of the generation we are going back in time with. Below the age is the age range for the selected generation.

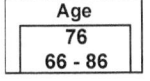   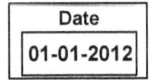

4. The Financial Result Display: On the top of the dashboard are four dials representing each of our key financial indicators: Debt, Earnings, Spending, and Savings. The red line tells us whether a particular factor is at its peak. Notice the circle towards the bottom of each dial. This tells us when the factor is inclining or declining. An "I" will appear if the factor is inclining, and a "D" will appear if it is declining.

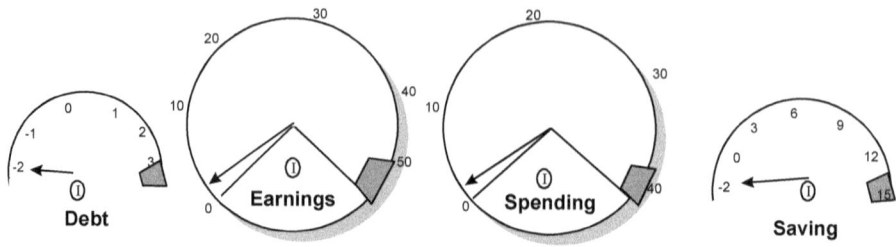

The higher the dial, the more that particular factor contributes to the economy. When a dial points straight up it is at half of its peak for that factor. The economic dials are analogous to dials on an actual automobile as explained below:

- **Earnings :** *Tach* – Tells us how fast our economic engine is running.
- **Spending:** *Speedometer* – How fast we are going through our money.
- **Debt:** *Temperature dial* – If the Debt dial goes too high, we are in danger of overheating our economic engine.
- **Saving:** *Gas gauge* – The more we save the further we will be able to go. We do not want to get dangerously low on savings.

This new time machine will help us better visualize the impact of a particular generation upon the economy at a particular point in time. We will test drive it on the Silent generation in the next chapter.

Section Three

10

Silents

Earlier, we used the time machine to examine the economic effects of the Boomer and Greatest's generations as they passed through their Financial Life Cycle. These two large generations led to record booms when they were in their peak financial factors followed by busts as these factors declined. Now we will shift our focus to the lull generations of the Silents and Xers. If our hypothesis is true, since they are smaller generations, we should not have booms when they are in their peaks; instead, we should have periods of decline, because the stimulus they offer to the economy declines relative to the previous generation. Let's see how this works out, initially for the Silents.

1955 Silent relief

Let's take the new time machine for a spin. We shift the Delorean's gears to Silents, put the direction lever in reverse to go back in time, and slowly press the gas. With a roar, the machine comes to life. Looking out the window, we see history unwind in front of our eyes. The months fly by, but if we press too hard on the accelerator, the machine shutters. As we approach 1955, we ease up on the gas little by little until we finally arrive at July 4th, 1955.

1955 Financial Time Machine 3.0 dash

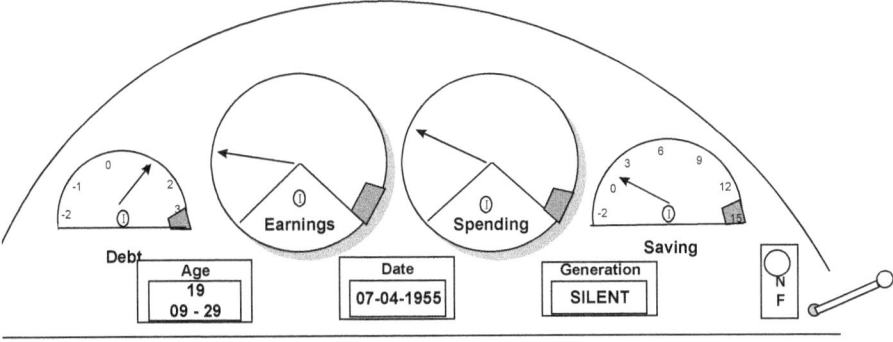

With our heads still reeling from the experience, we take a breath, then look at our dash and focus on the financial indicators. The only dial that is anywhere near the red line is debt. The others are still very low, but this makes sense when we look at the age dial - 19 years old for the midpoint Silent, with their ages ranging between 9 and 29. At this point, the generation is so young that they have little impact upon the economy, but all of the indicators are inclining as shown by the "I"s in each of the dials.

We do notice that Silents are past the middle of the debt dial. What does this mean? It means that the first of the Silents are approaching their peak debt phase, but the peak has yet to be reached.

The 1930s proved to be a rough time for the Silents and their parents who experienced unemployment of up to 25%. Even when their fathers got jobs, with everyone willing to accept any work, these jobs did not pay well. Nearly everyone was poor, so no one cared what clothes he or she wore to school. Meals were simple and cheap. For some, meat was an infrequent luxury. At Christmas, children considered themselves lucky to receive a single toy or a new pair of shoes. But since nearly everyone endured the same experience, the Silent kids did not know any better, which made it easier for all to bear.

When the war came, the Silents' men were too young to enlist, but some of their fathers did go off to war. During the war, they saved scrap metal and grew victory gardens. It was a time of extreme patriotism. The Silents' dads who were too old for the war or had a restriction like flat feet, now found it easy to obtain work. War plants hummed, and their moms got jobs too. The parents now made decent wages especially with the abundant overtime. The only problem was there was little to spend money on, since there was so much rationing to support the war effort, so they bought war bonds.

After the war, with so many GIs returning, it was difficult for the first Silents to secure a job. By 1955, over fifteen years after the Great Depression and ten years after the war, with low unemployment and higher wages, most families prospered. They cashed in their savings bonds for houses, leading to the post-war housing boom and construction jobs. The young Silents were fairing much better during this time of relative abundance. In the early 1950s with the draft still on, they went off to fight in Korea. When they returned two years later, they might go to college under the GI bill or start working in any of the abundant jobs earning ever-higher paychecks and nesting.

Silent generation's John Peters Senior

In 1955, we find John Peters Sr. in the LA County hospital's waiting room. His wife, Sue, is having a tough time delivering her first baby. John paces back and forth puffing on his second pack of Camels worried about his young wife and wanting to see her, but the hospital does not allow men in the delivery room.

Born in 1934 just before the midpoint of the Silents, John grew up in Detroit where his father worked for GM loving everything about cars. At 15, his dad bought him a broken down 1943 Buick for fifty bucks, which they restored. He and his friends loved driving through the drive-in burger joint listening to the super charged engine roar through its throaty chrome tailpipe.

With his intense interest in cars, John had little time for sports or school other than shop class, art class, and baseball, for which he took off his leather jacket and proudly donned his Detroit South uniform. John, a "bad boy," dated Sue Long, a cheerleader, throughout his Junior and Senior years. They married a year later as did nearly all of their friends.

John started working as an auto mechanic, at which he excelled. Then, in 1954 after being fired for arguing with his boss, he and Sue decided to try their luck in Los Angeles where they heard jobs were plentiful. Once in LA, John bought a small garage with a loan cosigned by his dad and started his repair business.

Back in the waiting room, while lighting the last cigarette in the second pack, John worried about how he would support his young family. Then, the nurse finally came into the waiting room announcing that John had a healthy 8 lb 3 oz. baby boy. He rushes into Sue's room to see the spent mother and new baby. They decided to name the baby John also, or John junior, from the Boomer chapter.

1966 Silent Boom

Without changing the generation, we slip the directional shifter into forward and push on the gas heading for 1966. The fifties and sixties fly by as we see the LA landscape dramatically change with roads, freeways, and housing developments sprouting up all around the city as the surrounding farms and orchards disappear. Schools also sprout up in newly minted communities. We see large strip centers and cars gathering around drive-in burger joints and drive-in theatres. We even see the first jets zipping into LAX. What we view is fascinating, but we manage a glimpse at our dials and see these slowly rise. As we slow, we see cars flying through all of the new freeways like blood cells through arteries. If we did not know better, we might think automobiles were now the dominant species of Los Angeles.

We focus on our indicators on the dash to see that debt is at the red line, nearly pegged. Earnings are high, passed the middle of the dial, as spending approaches the red line. Savings are just below the mid-point. At this point in time, the Silents financial factors are climbing, but up until now have had little effect upon the economy. The 1950s and 1960s are decades of rapid GDP growth (boom times), in which the GDP grew 283% from under $300 billion to over $1 trillion. But, this growth cannot be attributed to the Silents for they have yet to reach their peaks.

1966 Silents

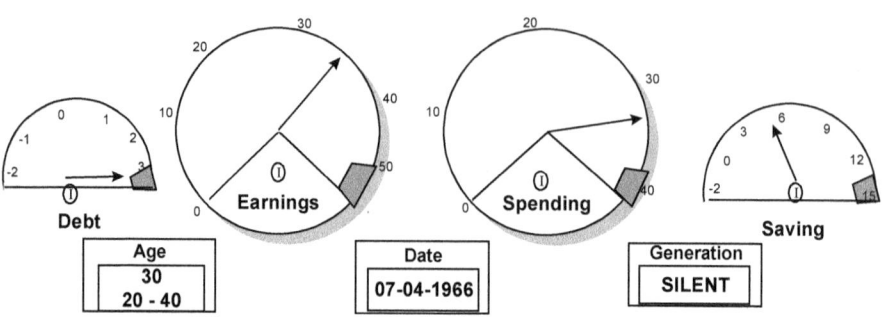

Age
30
20 - 40

Date
07-04-1966

Generation
SILENT

The Silents range in age from 20 to 40 with a mid-point of 30 and are in their early career or nest building phase.

As we saw earlier, this is a boom period, so jobs are plentiful particularly in construction, government, and the factories. Since the Silents are a lull generation, the boom is not so much due to their financial factors as much as that of their Greatest predecessors whose financial factors are peaking. The Greatests with their military induced, top-down, management style build large organizations and occupy the senior level positions, but as they move up, there is an abundance of lower level positions.

Likely due to the post-depression, post-war euphoria, the Silents nest earlier than any other generation before or after them, so spending and debt are higher than the average propensities. They have kids early and buy houses earlier too adding fuel to these optimistic times.

[Note: The numbers on the financial indicators derive from the propensities from earlier versions of the time machine and represent the average of the whole generation. The red area represents the peak 10 years.]

1986

Continuing forward in time, we drive rapidly as the 1970s fly by. We glance at the instruments and observe these are constantly rising. As we approach 1986, we slow to notice that Earnings, Spending, and Savings occupy the red zone for the Silents.

1986 Silents

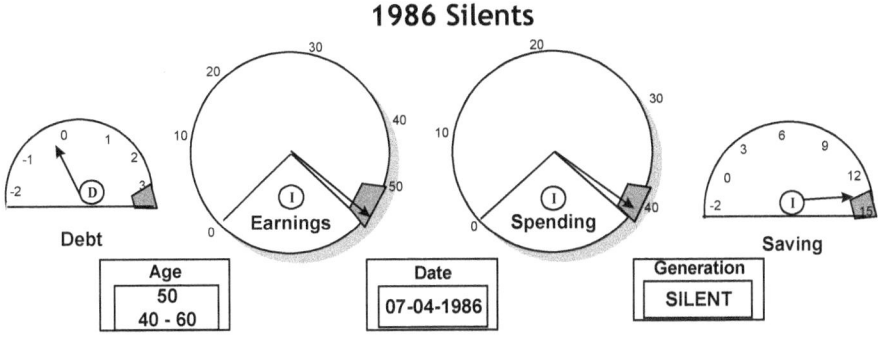

Debt is very low, indeed in negative territory, meaning the Silents are paying down those debts. With three factors at their peak, 1986 represents the peak for the Silents. Financially these are good times, but not because it is the peak of peaks for the Silents. The negative effects of the larger Greatest generation exiting the economy largely pass as the Boomers enter their peak phase. The 70s and early 80s are the period when the Silents are in their peak financial factors. If the Silents had a heavy sway upon the economy these should be good years. Instead, these are the trying years of the 70s Malaise, during which the economy experience four recessions. The last one in 1982 was the worst when the Silents were still peaking. This reality lends credence to the time machine's supposition that lull generations like the Silents do not lead to a booming economy.

Since we are with John's auto-oriented generation, let's floor the Financial Time Machine -errrrrich. The faster we go, the higher the Financial Time Machine hovers and what we see resembles a zooming, Google Map-like movie below. As the years fly by, we barely make out what is happening, but we see LA growing like an over zealous virus with constantly more freeways and developments devouring the orchards around LA accompanied by ever more strip centers, malls, and businesses. What used to be a coastline with bungalows now sports an array of multi-family dwellings and apartments. Then realizing we are losing control, we stomp on the brakes and after spinning a couple of times, discover the year 2001 on our indicator.

2001 The Golden Age of retirement

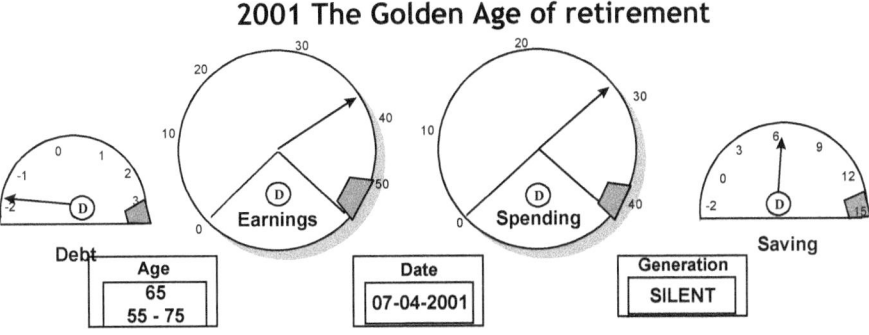

2001 Silents

The LCDs on each of the indicator dials display D indicating that the Silents ranging in age from 55 to 75 are, from the perspective of the economy, in decline. Earnings are still high since about a third of the Silents still work, but this is considerably lower than the peaks in 1986. Debt is negative.

As they downsize, their spending and savings dramatically decline. With less financial stimulus to the economy, why isn't there a serious recession in the 1990s? This is because the Silents are a lull generation. By this time, the Greatests' financial power is negligible and the Boomers, entering their peak financial years, have more than enough financial juice to make up for the Silents' withdrawal from the economy.

Most Silents retire during what will likely become the golden age of retirement. They now have Social Security, Medicare, pensions, and 401(k) plans. Since they grew up during the Depression, many Silents, unlike their Boomer antecedents, accumulate six figure savings accounts too. Plus, the stock and real estate markets are flying high, so they reap sizeable gains as they transition to safer investments prior to the looming crash.

When the Greatests left the economy in the 1970s, numerous mid and high-level positions opened up for the Silents who faced less competition for these spots. In the 1980s, the government passed legislation, protecting pension plans, which afterwards led to many companies termination of the now complex plans. Many in this generation faced the restructuring of the late 1980s and 90s, but by then had 30 to 40 years of service in their guaranteed pensions.

If they worked in the dwindling number of factories, which were not outsourced en masse to China until the late 1990s, they had seniority and, therefore, were the last to depart. Then, you saw an abundance of white hair while walking the factory floors. Even if asked to leave, they often received generous buyouts and could retire early or pocket the money and obtain a similar job in the booming 90s. If they had a government job, they might accumulate 30-35 years of service and retire with a full pension in their mid fifties. Some then worked part-time as security guards, substitute teachers or in another municipality, while they collected both a retirement check and paycheck.

Since the Boomers followed the Silents, there were plenty of workers to fund Social Security and Medicare. Forward thinking national leadership would have increased funding, cut benefits, or at least raised the retirement age, but instead they continued to raise benefits. (They did raise the rate and age for the Boomers and will likely raise it even higher for the Xers and Millennials) The Silents, especially those who worked for large corporations, the government, or unions also had retiree medical, which pays for their medical benefits after they retire even if they retire at 52, 13 years prior to their Medicare eligibility. This benefit is also rapidly disappearing for future generations, since the government protected it in the 1990s (required prospective funding under FAS 106.) Afterwards, companies thought these regulations and pre-funding requirements were too restrictive, so they stopped providing the benefit.

Growing up during the rough times of the 1930s and early 40s, there is a poetic balance for the Silents. They started off with practically nothing and generally ended up doing well financially, enjoying a well-earned retirement. Their only concern is that their children and grandchildren will likely not be able to enjoy the fruits of the American dream and rich retirement they enjoy.

John and Sue had two girls in 1957 and 1959, which made their two-bedroom Anaheim apartment cramped, so in 1960 they bought a 3-bedroom home in Orange county in one of those new large-scale planned communities for $19,000. The new house just happened to be across the street from the Ostrums where John Jr. will meet Bob.

In the seventies, "John's Auto-motion" garage fared remarkably well. He appreciated the lines, unibody design, disk brakes, high rev engines, and rack and pinion steering of the European models, so he started repairing these too. Driving the highly responsive cars was so much fun, but they tended to breakdown frequently, something fortuitous for John's garage. After the gas shortages, U.S. consumers, especially in California, bought Japanese cars. At first, he thought these were junk, but their quality consistently improved, so he started repairing these too and eventually employed 40 people in 3 garages.

John's business did well. With a swollen ego and perhaps because they married young, he wanted to "experience" life and asked Sue for a divorce. Even though none of their parents divorced, most of their friends did so in the 1970s. It seemed like some kind of California, free-living, sexual revolution induced, marriage plague. John leapt into the disco craze, making up for lost time in the dating world.

John longed for his family, so he begged Sue to take him back promising to reform. Sue initially refused, but after excessive wooing eventually relented.

John and Sue retired in 1996 after selling his garages for a sizeable profit, and then bought a house with an ocean view big enough for the grandchildren to sleep over and play on the beach nearby. John and Sue love retirement, taking long walks along the beach and becoming active in local charities, where they met many interesting people. John tells everyone he meets how much he loves retirement.

11

Generation X

The term Generation X sounds derogatory unless one thinks of X as standing for exceptional. Those in this "exceptional" generation following the Boomers were born from 1965 through 1979 and as a lull generation, exhibit many of the same characteristics of their Silent parents though the times were certainly different.

By looking at the relative height of each of the generations on the original Financial Time Machine, we see that their numbers do not differ as drastically as the Silents do, each sandwiched between two larger generations. There were about 60% more Boomers per year than Silents versus about 20% more Boomers than the Xers.

There are no catastrophic events for the Xers like the Depression and World War II leading to the sharp decline in births for the Silents. There are fewer Xers, primarily because most are the children of the smaller Silent generation -- an echo generation. As time extends onward from a cataclysmic event, the subsequent generational boundaries are more porous. In other words, early Boomers would have had Xer children, whereas later Boomers had Millennial children, so the boundary between the Xers and Millennials is less pronounced. Indeed, the number of births at the tail end of the Xers was not much different from those of the early Millennials.

The years the Xers were born, the late 1960s and 1970s were, as we saw earlier, rough financially. With the Viet Nam war loss, cold war, energy crisis, hostage crisis, rampant inflation and the first loss of American jobs overseas this became the worst decade since the Great Depression. As many of their parents lost their jobs during the four recessions of their childhood, the Xers innately sensed that they were less secure than the previous generation. During the 1970s, the first signs of an erosion of the middle class appeared. Their childhood would occupy the worst stage of the American economy over a 70-year period.

When the Boomers grew up, school systems strained to contend with the overwhelming enrollment increase, therefore classrooms were crowded with as many as 40 or 50 students. Besides the lack of facilities, there were not enough Silent teachers to go around. Therefore, Boomers grew up in a crowded world with little individual attention. When the Xers occupied these same schools, class sizes diminished, and there were plenty of newly minted Boomer teachers to supply the demand. Therefore, they experienced less crowding and potentially received more attention.

1990

We will not have to drive our time machine back far, since the Xers were not born long ago. Let's shift our gears on the Financial Time Machine 3.0 into Xer and put our directional lever into reverse, then hit the gas until we land at 1990.

1990 Xers

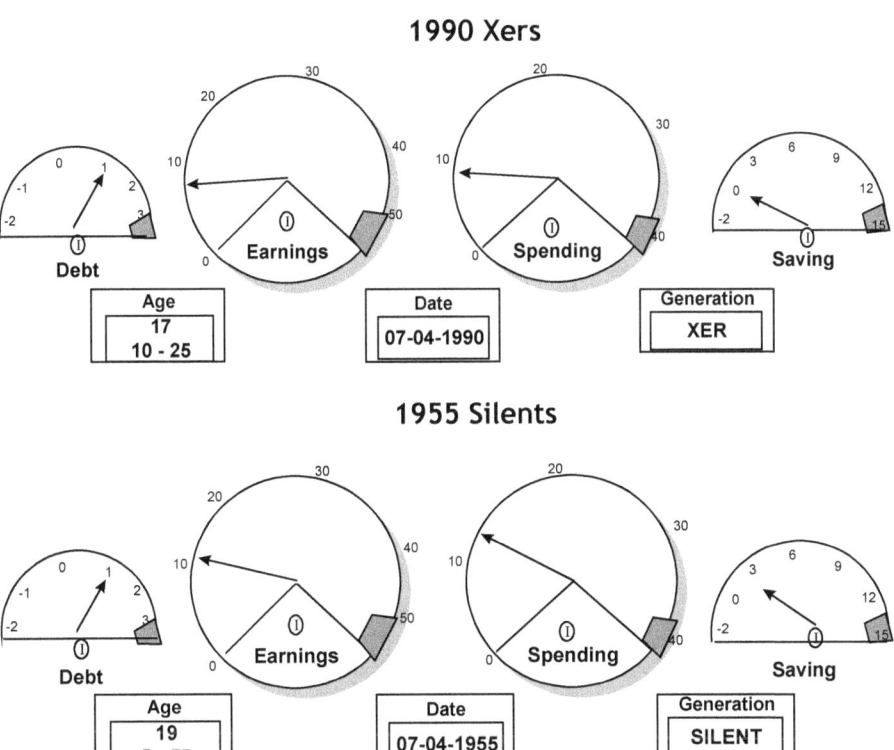

The dashboard above resembles that of the Silents in the early 1950s. The Xers range in age from 10 to 25 as they begin to enter the economy, so their indicator dials are naturally low. The first half of the Xers is either in college or at work. But since they follow the tail-end of the Boomers, it is more challenging to find jobs in their desired fields. With 70 million Boomers filling the prime entry-level positions over the previous 20 years, it is difficult for both the early Xers and the tail-end Boomers to enter the workforce. Indeed, during the late 1980s and early 1990s, it was hard for college graduates even with technical degrees to find immediate employment. I call this the tail-end phenomenon. The first Silents experienced the same phenomena when the Greatest Generation returned from the war, during which time there was a severe recession.

A brief recession started in 1990, ending one of the longest periods of continuous expansions in U.S. history. Lasting 8 months, with peak unemployment of 7.8%, this recession was not particularly severe. At the time, all the Boomers financial indicators ran in high gear providing tremendous momentum to the economy to power through this recession. A contributing factor of the recession proved to be the savings and loan (S&L) crisis, in which 1600 S&Ls insured by the Federal Deposit Insurance Corporation closed costing the American taxpayer $125 billon at the time. After deregulation, S&Ls took on riskier mortgages contributing to a real estate bubble, which eventually burst when sky-high interest rates eventually collapsed.*

Anyone who lived through the Great Recession might think this story sounds familiar. The precedent that the federal government bailed out the financial institutions who made enormous profits while taking undue risk established a moral hazard that many think led to the severity of the Great Recession. The Fed and Treasury Department after this point in time doubled down on deregulation, stating the markets could regulate themselves. In 1999, Washington repealed Glass-Steagall, thereby integrating banking and Wall Street.

Let's take our time machine forward in time to 2005 for the Xers.

2005 Xers

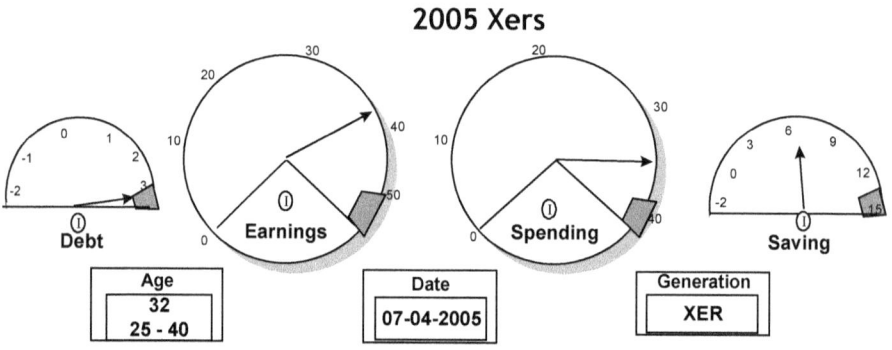

Age
32
25 - 40

Date
07-04-2005

Generation
XER

Here we see that the Xers range in age from 25 to 40 with most in the nesting phase of their Financial Life Cycle. We see that three of the financial indicators are high, but not yet at their peak for earnings, spending, and savings. One indicator is in the red line: debt. This is great period for the Xers. As we saw earlier, the decade up until 2001 was the longest period of expansion in U.S. history, interrupted only by the dot-com recession. This recession lasted only 8 months with unemployment of 6.3% and a GDP loss of only .3%. Overall, it was a minor recession except that it took unusually long for employment to rebound, and the high-tech dominated NASDAQ lost over half of its value but soon recovered.

By this time, the Xers found positions in their desired fields. The only industrial sector to lose significant employment was manufacturing, as the service and financial industries now dominated the employment landscape. Because of the loss of millions of well paying manufacturing jobs, salaries for those who did not attend college declined significantly, as they entered the service sector en masse. Spurned on by subprime and home equity loans, well paying construction jobs were plentiful.

Parallelism

Sandwiched between two large generations, the Silents and the Xers's, Financial Time Machine results resemble each other.

1. Both experienced financially rough times in their childhood.
2. Both found it difficult to obtain their first jobs
3. Both experienced extended boom cycles during their nesting phase.

Looking forward for the Xers

Will the Xers continue to experience a scenario similar to the Silents? With more Boomers leaving the workforce, more senior-level positions will open up for the Xers who face less competition for these slots. Indeed, with a decline in senior management and skilled human resources, salaries may finally escalate relative to inflation. As they enter their peak earnings phase, they will exert more force upon the economy.

The hallmark of the Silents was that they experienced the best time for retirement of any generation – an advantage accruing to a lull generation. If leadership does nothing to correct the funding problems of Social Security and Medicare, there will be fewer benefits to distribute to the Xers. The Social Security Administration projects they will run out of full funding by the early 2030s when the first Xers are retiring.

Instead of solving the Social Security crisis, Washington reduced Social Security funding just when the first Baby Boomers received full benefits in January of 2012. To stimulate the economy, they cut employee contributions to Social Security by a third in both 2011 and 2012. According to the Social Security Administration with this action and high unemployment from 2008 to 2012, the fund will run out of money approximately three years earlier - by 2033.*

With the extinction of most pension plans, pension benefits will not help provide for Xer retirements as it did the Silents. Xers have 401(k)s and have proven to be wiser savers than the Boomers, so they will hopefully do all right. The Xers will have to work longer than their Silent predecessors to receive the same level of benefits in their retirement.

Xers Johnny and Suzie

John and Pat Peters' children, Suzie and Johnny, are tail-end Xers. Actually, since both his father and grandfather's name was John, Johnny would be John the third. John the first was a Silent, John the second a Boomer, and John the third a Xer.

When their father, John Junior, lost his long-time position during the dot-com crash both children had to leave college. Suzie was in her junior year and Johnnie was a freshman. Suzie had good grades and meant to go back to school some day. Johnny worked hard to put himself through nearby Cal State Fullerton and obtain his engineering degree by sheer perseverance and then found a position in Silicon Valley.

While home, Johnny began dating one of Suzie's friends, Marilyn, who Pat and John adore. There are not many eligible women in Silicon Valley, and Johnny's coworkers are jealous, so Johnny and Marilyn designed an app and website to match Southern California girls with Silicon Valley geeks called CaliforniaGirls&Geeks.com. They do a personality match, and the site offers coaching for interacting between what seems like two different species.

Suzie finally started nursing school in northern California where she lives with her brother not far from Silicon Valley. They talk about the difficulties of their adult lives compared to their grandparents. Grandpa had his garage seemingly all of his life and it just got more profitable even though he had no degree. Their dad went nearly 25 years before the first real layoff and he still has a pension he will be able to draw off in retirement.

Many of their friends do not have fulltime jobs or toil at something they do not enjoy, generally do not make much money, and have been laid off multiple times. Johnny and Suzie do not think much about retirement, but realize they will probably have to work into their late sixties. There just does not seem to be any real security in the world any more, but they swear to each other that they will support each other and persevere.

12

Onward to the Future

Now to the fun part - using the Financial Time Machine to travel into the future – All Aboard! Up until this point, we employed the time machine to journey back in time. We not only discovered the machine correctly predicted the three significant downturns in the economy over the last 100 years, but that it also predicted the three boom periods too.

Booms and Declines

Peak Generation	Boom	Decline
Civil War	1920s	1930s
Greatest	1960s	1970s
Boomer	1990s	2000s

Until 2013, the current downturn lasted over five years. With unemployment still above 7% and repeated threats of another recession, people wonder when the current contraction will truly end. They wonder when we will again have sustained growth. Let's first travel into the future with the Boomers and then in the next chapter examine the evidence the Financial Time Machine supplies to predict this pivotal event.

What we found in our time travels is that the peak generations affect the economy as a full moon affects the tides. When the peak generation is economically at its zenith, it exerts the maximum pull upon the economy. Therefore, to understand where we are heading, we need to focus on the current peak generation once again. We also discovered when a peak generation's four financial factors peaked, we had an economic boom. At the point when the factors diminished, we had a decline.

When we left the Boomers in 2010, we saw their financial propensities were declining. So let's first step back into the Financial Time Machine, shift our gears into Boomer, slip our direction lever from neutral into forward, and push on the gas. The Delorean's sleek stainless steel body lurches forward and then settles smoothly into the future. Since this is our first trip into the unknown, we want to be a little cautious so let's go forward to 2016 to see what it looks like. Below is the dash of our Delorean, style time machine when we land in 2016 with the median boomer turning 61 and the oldest 70.

2016 Boomers

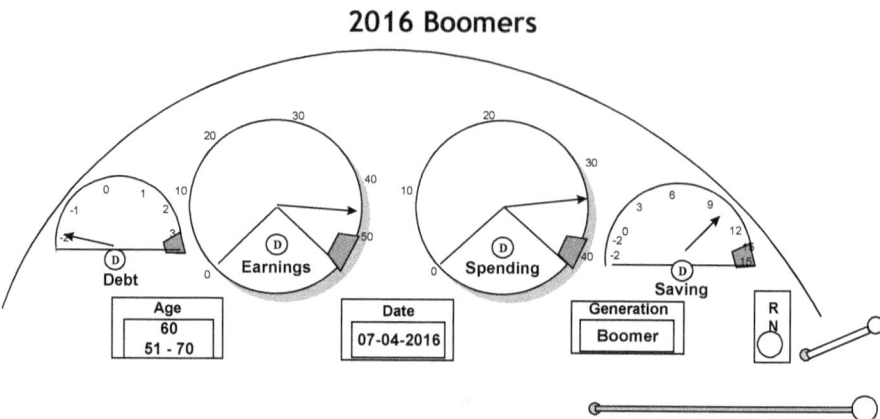

The earnings dial, although still high is no longer in the red zone and is in decline. Younger Boomers in their fifties are still in their peak earnings years, but nearly half of the Boomers retired. Even though they retired, the Boomers still receive earnings from their investments, especially while they are in the early portion of their retirements. Theoretically, they are still earning from their pension and Social Security funds too; since initially the funds are returning nearly as much from their portion of the funds as these pay out.

Debt is below zero, as the early Boomers continue to downsize and pay off their loans. Is it any wonder the housing and mortgage markets continue to struggle when the largest generation in U.S. history no longer desires additional housing or mortgages? The all-important spending dial is substantially below the red line too indicating deceleration for the consumption addicted economy.

Similar to earnings, savings are still high, but no longer in the red zone and declining. But wait, if two of the key factors are near their peak level, namely earnings and savings, why is there a problem? Shouldn't this still be a good thing for the economy? While it is true that these two factors are at near peak level for the boomers, for half the Boomers, both of these factors rapidly decrease.

The slope up to the peak is fairly mild, but the decline on the other side of the peak is steep. This makes sense for those Boomers who no longer earn money from employment and instead are living off their savings and investments.

The indictor light in each of the dials is (D) signifying that all of the dials are waning. The fact that the economic factors for largest generation in the history of the United States are all contracting does not bode well for the economy.

What we expect to see is flat to slow real growth from 2008 until 2016 with better than a 50% chance of another recession. Of course, generational economics is not the only cause of recessions. Usually banking/investment greed, business fraud, or the actions of the Fed are the direct cause of recessions. Generational economics merely sets the stage. Similar to a pump used to blow up a balloon, the economy's balloons will eventually blow up and burst, but banking, business, or Fed interventions serve as the pin that pops the balloon prematurely.

What we have seen over the last few years supports the Financial Time Machine's prognostication, since growth following the Great Recession has been sluggish at best with stubbornly high unemployment not seen since the Great Depression. In the first quarter of 2013, unemployment was still 7.9%. Over the five years from 2008 through 2012, real GDP growth averaged only two-thirds of one percent (.66%.) Even since the recovery started in the summer of 2008, GDP has averaged an anemic 1.58% growth rate.*

Typically, over the last 80 years, it took two quarters for employment to recover following a recession. Then with the 1982 and 1990 recessions, it elongated. By the 2001 recession, it took 48 months for unemployment to reach pre-recessionary levels. Sixty-eight months after the 2007 low unemployment rate of 4.4%, we were still at a whopping 3.5% above that rate. Even at twice the current pace, it would take 4 ½ more years to return to the previous levels.* *

2021 Boomers

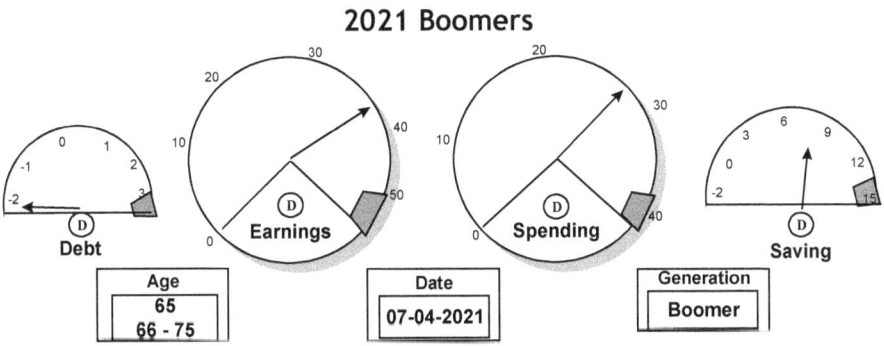

Age	Date	Generation
65		Boomer
66 - 75	07-04-2021	

Let's go forward another five years to 2021 when the median Boomer is 65 and they range in age from 56 to 75. Now with over half of the Boomers retired, earnings and savings drop precipitously. Spending, no longer high, is at levels not seen since the Boomers were in their mid-twenties. Debt is pegged and no longer a factor. There are two primary reasons for this situation:

1. Retired Boomers spend less on work related expenses like gas, mileage, parking, clothes, and lunches. The biggest reduction is that they no longer save a large portion of their earnings for retirement. Including the employer and employee social security, pension invest-ments and defined contribution plan contributions, total savings could be as high as 40% of their pay. Now, they are not paying any employment taxes and since their earnings are lower, they pay lower

state and federal taxes.   In addition, the vast majority of their mortgages and home equity payments should be long gone.   All of this adds up to vastly lower spending.

2.   Unfortunately, Boomers are starting to pass away, not at high rates while they are in their sixties and early seventies, but much higher than when they were in their fifties.   Fewer Boomers will therefore spend less.

Below is a chart showing how fast the financial factors fall once a generation reaches the retirement precipice.   Notice that up to 55, earnings, spending, and savings all rise at a moderate rate.   Then spending starts to fall, followed by an even more precipitous earnings and savings decent after 60.   The Financial Life Cycle provides a consistent source of stimulus to the economy, until it radically drops.   Is it any wonder we have such drastic financial downturns?

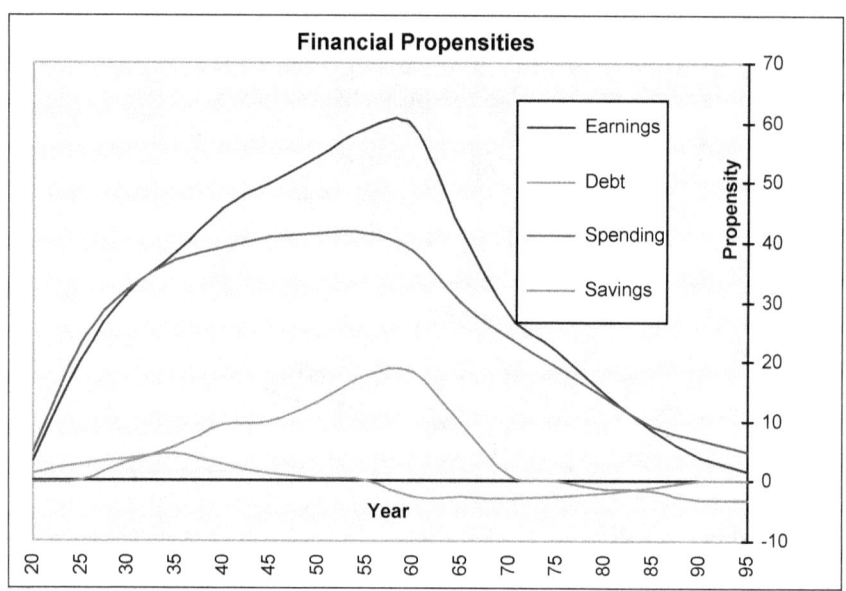

If we skip forward to 2026, we see, as expected, all of the dials went down significantly and are at levels not seen since the Boomers were in their twenties when they just started into the productive portion of their Financial Life Cycle.

The earliest Boomers are turning 80 with only the late Boomers in their sixties still working.   One unfortunate reason for the economic factors decline is the Boomers are dying at an increasing rate.   With average life expectancy at 78, unfortunately, over a quarter have already passed.   The surviving Boomers still spend nearly what they had five years earlier; and those with serious health problems or in nursing homes spend significantly more, but overall Boomer spending is down, because there are fewer of them.

2026 Boomers

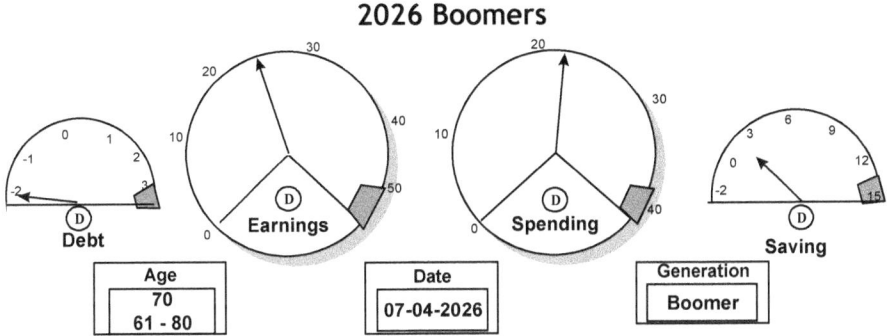

Age
70
61 - 80

Date
07-04-2026

Generation
Boomer

With savings negative for the first Boomers, they draw from their retirement investments.   Earnings are less than half of the peak. Spending too is nearly half its peak, which still helps the economy, but there are fewer earnings to back this up, since only the youngest Boomers are still working at their original careers.   The expenses for leading Boomers, now in their seventies, are increasing as they begin entering nursing homes largely funded by Medicaid.

We near the end of the long Boomer Financial Life Cycle saga, for as their numbers continue to decline, they will have a diminishing impact upon the economy.   Their estates will pass to the Xers and Millennials helping these burdened generations save for their retirements.   But it is not a sad story, for the Boomers had a long and prosperous life enlightened by amazing technologies they largely invented, unprecedented cultural, educational and travel opportunities, and for many, an enduring charitable generosity.

Although they hid under their desks to practice for a nuclear attack that never came, they grew up in the 1950s and 1960s during a time of rare optimism.   Patriotically, they launched careers in science so we could beat the Russians to the moon, which we did, and then applied that scientific knowledge to create the third-wave, digital revolution.   In the 1960s, they reveled in Rock and Roll, experimented with drugs, started the sexual revolution, died in Vietnam; and protested against the injustices of that war, race, sex, and sexual discrimination.   As hippies, they reveled at the "Summer of Love" in San Francisco and at Woodstock in upstate New York.

Partially due to the war and draft deferments, they graduated from college in unprecedented numbers.   In the 1970s and 80s, during the disco era, they became yuppies, formed families, became soccer moms, and worked brutally long hours at their professions.   Many thought them to be overly materialistic and narcissistic. Exercise, running, jazzercise, volleyball, racquetball, softball, backpacking, and healthy eating provided welcome antidotes to their claustrophobic factory, office, and cubicle existence, but caused their joints to wear out.

Many of their grandparents inhabited the abundant farm fields the Boomers visited as children. Many of their parents inhabited the blaring factories built during the first three-quarters of the 20th Century. Boomers largely inhabited the offices of the shinning towers and grass lined office parks, in which they designed and built the digital revolution and the global economy. As the factories started to disappear, they joined the service sector opening restaurants, manning customer service lines, and building homes.

Since 1992, three Presidents have been Boomers with another one or two possible. The Boomers fought in four wars including Vietnam, the Gulf War, and the post-9/11 wars in Afghanistan and Iraq. Three of these were the longest in U.S. history lasting over a total 30 years. General David Patraeus, who commanded the last two wars, is a Boomer. In addition, the Cold War spanned 43 years of their lives. Even though they protested for peace against the military-industrial-political complex, they enjoyed only 12 years of that longed-for peace.

They were the first Mouseketeers and the first to use a mouse, teenyboppers, disco dancers, hippies, nerds, day traders, DINKs, yuppies, soccer moms, and "hover" parents. When they were children, jet-setting became the province of the rich and famous. Then they were the first to fly routinely around the world en masse. Finally, they experienced the drudgery of flying on bankrupt airlines. They started off writing letters, calling on rotary phones, listening to 45 LP records and transistor radios, writing on paper tablets, and watching black & white TVs without remotes. Now they attach to smart phones, iPods, iPads, large screen 3D HD TVs, Facebook, and Twitter.

They spent more time with their children than their predecessors, some becoming "hover" parents. As a result, their children feel closer and more at ease with them than they did wit h their Greatests parents. In the 1990s, they enjoyed an unprecedented time of wealth and 3,500 square foot mc mansions. They invented the brave new world of digital technology, PCs, Cell phones, the Web and helped business to be immensely productive through their designs and software programs. They built some of the world's largest companies like Apple, and Microsoft.

Whereas their predecessors worked in the hierarchical structures that won the war, they learned to work with each other in teams. They broke the genetic code and developed hundreds of medical miracles that extended their lives.

Farewell Boomers!

As the Boomers Financial Life Cycle winds down along with their economic stimulus, we look for an economic revival in the next peak generation, the Millennials, who are the topic of the next chapter.

13

The Millennials to the Rescue?

We just observed how the tremendous mass of fiscal stimulus the Boomers transmitted to the economy led to the longest period of expansion in U.S. history, followed by the Great Recession when their stimulus faded. Eventually, as their numbers recede over the next 25 years, they will have less effect upon the economy, but we certainly do not want to wait that long for a sustained recovery and a boom. The offset to the Boomers decline is the Millennials' ascendance - the next generational wave to wash over the economy.

The Millennial wave is not as dramatic as the Boomers because the generations preceding and following the Millennials are not drastically different than they are; therefore, the generational wave action is not as pronounced. On average, they are 15% larger than the Xers. With the number of births declining in the four years following the Great Recession, the following generation is only 6% larger than the Millennials. Still, the Millennial wave represents a significant positive economic force, which other countries will envy as we will observe in later chapters.

In this chapter, we speculate that the large number of Millennials entering the economy will balance those Boomers leaving the economy. The critical question, is when? There are three ways to analyze the effect of the Millennials going forward in time.

1. The Financial Time Machine
2. Parallelism
3. Economic stimulus

We flew the time machine back in time for each of the preceding generations and will do so for the Millennials, but before we do, we might want to try some other techniques derived from the time machine's travels. We are familiar with parallelism, where we drew similarities between subsequent peak generations, such as the Boomers, Greatests, and Post Civil Wars. This along with generational economics performed extremely well in predicting the economic cycles over the last 140 years, so let's see what parallelism predicts over the next 20 years.

Another technique is to look at the economic stimulus each generation provides to the overall economy. We speculate the Millennials will provide a welcome countervailing economic stimulus that will eventually overcome the negative Boomer bias. Stimulus is a byproduct of the Financial Time Machine's financial factors that we will be readily able to analyze.

Since we are looking at the future, having three views will help us to triangulate just when the economy will truly recover and then thrive once again.

Parallelism

Back in Chapter 8, we explored the wave-like pattern of expansions and contractions that pass over the economy in-sync with the peak generations. Here is the chart that summarizes these, focusing on the core or the worst portion of the contractions.

Expansions and Contractions

Economic Cycle	Dates	Length (years)	Real GDP Growth	Avg.[1]
Expansions				
Civil War	1870-90	20	191%	9.5%
Roaring Twenties	1914-29	15	78%	5.2%
World War II	1949-69	20	139%	7.0%
Millennial	1983-07	24	124%	5.2%
Contractions				
Civil War	1900-14	14	31%	2.2%
Roaring Twenties	1929-38	9	1%	.1%
World War II	1970-82	12	35%	2.9%
Millennial	2007 -?	5 +	.1%	----

GDP figures from USGovernmentSpending.com

We see the contractions last from 9 to 14 years, with an average of 12 years. Three observations does not provide a highly reliable sample size, but if we assume the Great Recession will last 12 years, this results in the contraction ending in **2020**.

But, didn't the recession supposedly end in the middle of 2009? With unemployment for most of 2013, still over 7.5%, and real average GDP growth of only .1% through 2011, we were not out of the woods yet. There were two deep recessions during the Great Depression and four during the 70s Malaise, so it is reasonable to expect another recession or prolonged stagnation. In reality, we approached a recession in the summers of 2010, 2011, and 2012 with near zero GDP growth.

Let's proceed a little further with parallelism looking to see if there are any other lessons we can apply from the peak generations. We also saw some amazing similarities between the ages of the peak generations when the contractions hit as displayed below:

Peak Generational Ages
at the start of the contraction

Financial Downturn	Older Generation	Last's Age	Younger Generation	Midpoint Age
Great Depression	Civil War	45	Greatest	**15**
70s Mailaise	Greatest	45	Boomer	**15**
Great Recession	Boomer	44	Millennial	**15**

In each case, the age of the last members of the waning peak generation was 44 or 45. Even though the next peak generation does not cause the contraction, they astoundingly all averaged the same 15 years old.

What about the end point of the recessions? How old were the peak generations at that time? If there is such a high correlation at the start of the contraction perhaps there is at the end too.

Peak Generation Ages at end of Contraction

Contraction	End	Younger Generation	First's Age	Midpoint's Age
Great Depression	1939	Greatest	**38**	25
70s Mailaise	1983	Boomer	**37**	27
Great Recession	2017	Millennial	**?**	25

We see that the first Greatests were nearly the same age when the Great Depression ended as the Boomers were when the 70s Malaise ended – **37-38**. If we apply the same logic to the Great Recession, the first Millennials will become **37** in **2017**, or **38** in **2018**.

What is behind the similarities? In 1939, the first Greatests were **3** years into their peak spending phase. In 1983, the first Boomers were **2** years into their peak spending phase.

The Millennials will be **3** years into their peak spending phase in 2017. The significance of this is that spending by peak generations primes the economy's engine. After a contraction, you expect it would take time to get the flywheel moving again with at least 2 to 4 years of peak generation, peak spending. Think of it as pushing the bulb on a gas trimmer or lawnmower a few times to get gas to the cylinder to ignite the piston and start the engine roaring.

These generations were in their peak debt phase for at least 10 years prior to the time, but debt alone does not stimulate the economy. It stimulates the economy when you buy assets such as a car, appliances, furniture, or house, but afterwards you have debt payments that deflate your capability to spend money on additional assets. The key is spending. While in their twenties and thirties while new debt is high, spending still builds. Extending the analogy, debt compares to the choke of a garden machine engine -- you set the choke first then prime the engine. It will not start unless you perform both actions.

Economic Stimulus

When we introduced the four financial factors, we presented a simple equation:

Earnings + New Debt = Spending + Savings

The economic stimulus a particular generation exerts upon the economy also equals either side of this equation:

<u>Generational Economic Stimulus</u> = <u>Earnings + New Debt</u> = <u>Spending + Savings</u>

Let's look at the Generational Economic Stimulus (Stimulus) when the Boomers were at their peak at 55 years old. The earnings propensity listed below was 59.0 and the debt propensity was .1. The spending propensity was 41.5 and the savings propensity was 17.6.

Propensities from chapter 4 along with Stimulus.

Age Range	16-20	21-25	26-30	31-35	36-40	41-45	46-50	51-55
Earnings	3.5	20.4	31.4	38.3	45.7	49.7	54.2	59.0
Debt	1.4	2.7	3.6	4.6	2.7	1.3	0.5	0.1
Spending	5.0	23.0	32.0	37.0	39.0	41.0	41.5	41.5
Savings	-0.1	0.1	3.0	5.9	9.4	10.0	13.2	17.6
Stimulus	4.9	23.1	35.0	42.9	48.4	51.0	54.7	59.1

Age Range	56-60	61-65	66-70	71-75	76-80	81-85	86-90	91-95
Earnings	59.4	42.1	27.9	21.7	14.6	8.4	3.9	1.7
Debt	-2.5	-2.5	-3.0	-2.5	-2.0	-1.0	0	0
Spending	38.5	30.0	24.0	19.0	14.0	9.0	7.0	5.0
Savings	18.4	9.6	0.9	0.2	-1.4	-1.6	-3.1	-3.3
Stimulus	56.9	39.6	24.9	19.2	12.6	7.4	3.9	1.7

Earnings + Debt   = 59.0 + .1   = **59.1**
Spending + Savings = 41.5 + 17.6 = **59.1**

Both sides of the equation equal the same number - 59.1. Therefore, 59.1 represents the economic stimulus contributed by the Boomers or any generation when they are 55, since at 55 these are the same. Did you notice on the Financial Time Machine's dash, the readings on the dials always equal each other when a generation is the same age?

[In reality as discussed earlier, due to generational megatrends, and generational characteristics, these numbers may adjust slightly. For the purposes of this book, since it focuses on long-term trends, such variations are less important. The variations would be an interesting topic for another book though.]

When the median boomer was 55, they ranged in age between 46 and 65, so a few of the Boomers would retire early. The peak stimulus for all of the Boomers would have been in 2006, when the midpoint Boomer was 50, barely preceding the Great Recession.

Before we go any further, let's think how big this number really is. Let's say 50 million Boomers were working at that time and their average stimulus is $55,500. The total economic stimulus of the Boomers approaches three trillion dollars $2,775,000,000,000 ($55,500 x 50,000,000).

Imagine a massive scale with both the Boomers and Millennials' economic stimulus standing on it representing trillions of dollars of stimulus. Currently, the Boomers weight on the economies scale is declining rapidly, while the Millennials weight is inclining, but not yet rapidly enough to make up for the lost Boomer's weight. It is detrimental to the economy when the weight goes down, beneficial when it rises.

Following is a graph of the stimulus from the chart above:

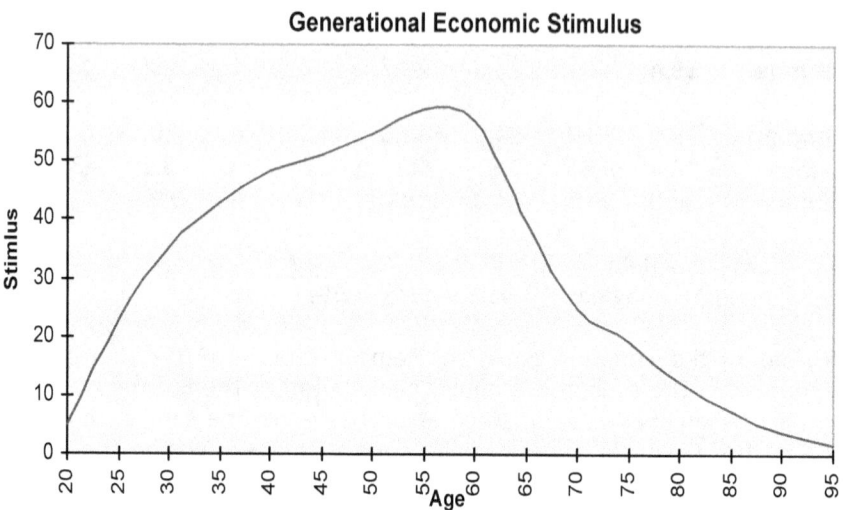

As expected, we see the stimulus rises steadily until retirement and then drops precipitously.

As the Boomers begin to leave the economy, Millennials take their place. The first appreciable number of Boomers retires in 2006, when they are 60. Certainly a few retire earlier if they: won the lottery, made millions in their business, or occupied a union. The focus should be on the leading edge of the generation, those leaving employment. In 2006, the leading edge of the Millennials is 27 years and entering the work force. These Millennials will in effect take the place of the retiring Boomers leaving the workforce. Since the number of Millennials is similar to the number of Boomers, an analysis of these two generations makes sense.

If we add the stimulus for the first Boomers and the first Millennials, we see how they balance out over time. The first cohort of Millennials enters the economy in 2001. This first cohort is between 16 and 21 and their average stimulus according to the propensity chart is 8.5. In 2001, the first cohort of Boomers is 50 to 55 and their average stimulus is 59.1. Together these add up to 68. If the value of the Boomers total economic stimulus at this time were $2.8 trillion, the Millennials' would only represent about $400 Billion of economic stimulus, but this is about to change.

Combined Stimulus for first Boomers and Millennials

Year	Combined Stimulus	Boomer Stimulus	Millennial Stimulus
2001	68	59	9
2006	82	57	25
2011	76	39	37
2016	69	25	44
2021	68	19	49

Here is a graph of the combined stimulus from above.

Combined Stimulus

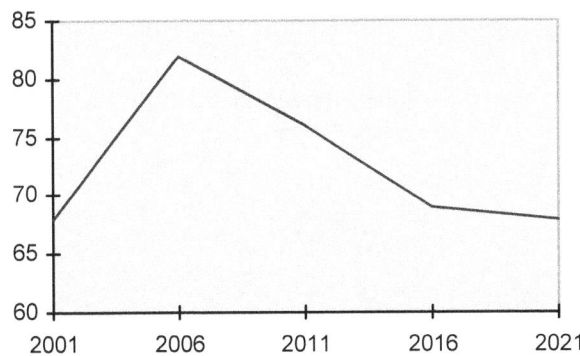

2001 to 2006: The first interesting thing we notice is the huge stimulus jump from 2001 to 2006, when the Boomers were near their peak and the first Millennials launched their careers. The Boomer stimulus does not change much, but there is a radical increase in the Millennials stimulus when this first cohort increases their spending and debt levels. No wonder the economy burned at the time.

2006 to 2011: We notice a large drop from 2006 to 2011, which explains the Great Recession (no wonder the bankers and investment houses missed this.) Up until 2006, the economy's engine roared on all 12 cylinders then there was an abrupt curve in the road. The increase in Millennial stimulus is, unfortunately, not enough to compensate for the larger loss of Boomer stimulus.

2011 to 2016: Here we see another large drop in combined stimulus, but by now everyone is well aware of what is happening. With stimulus still dwindling, we do not expect a full recovery prior to 2016.

2016 to 2021: By this time, the drop in stimulus levels off and we expect a mild recovery sometime within this period or shortly afterwards, although according to the combined stimulus it may not be spectacular. Now, the increase in Millennial stimulus is offsetting the loss of Boomer stimulus.

It is presumptuous to read too much into the stimulus analysis, because although it focuses on the peak generations it does not take into account the stimulus of the other generations or the size of the generations. These two generations represent approximately the same number of average births, so the analysis works well.

Time Machine and Millennials

Placing our directional lever in reverse, let's switch our gears now to Millennial and head back to 2005 where we see the median age is 13.

Millennials 2005

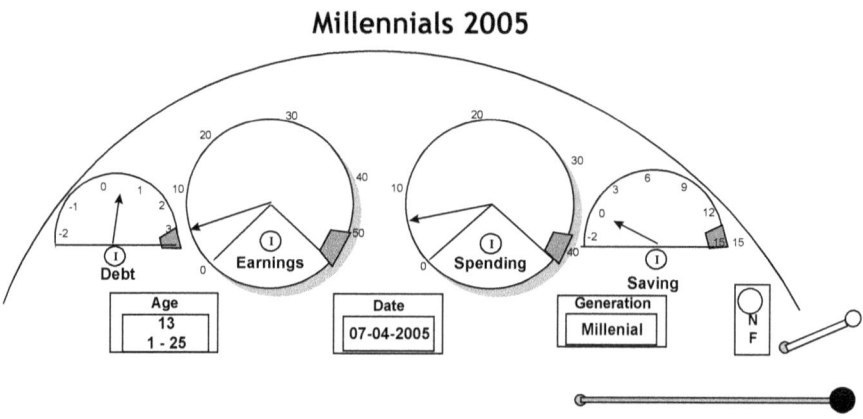

As we notice above the dials barely move. By 2005, the financial factors are still relatively minor for the Millennials, since most are in school and not producing much income other than through after school and summer jobs, although a few are in their early twenties and have regular jobs now.

Now, the early Boomers are starting to reduce their spending and debt. Up until 2005, Boomer income steadily inclined. The Millennials entering the workforce add steam to the booming economy.

Earlier, the small numbers of Xers who launched their careers replaced the even smaller numbers of Silents retiring. For the past few years, the large ranks of Millennials replace the Silents. The Boomers are not retiring in mass yet, so earnings are about as high as they will be for sometime.

Near peak Boomer spending declines slightly, but Millennial spending more than compensates for the loss. With Boomer spending in the red zone, our consumer spending addicted economy shifts into high gear. With so much to spend, employment is high and constrained assets like housing and land in demand.

Millennials 2010

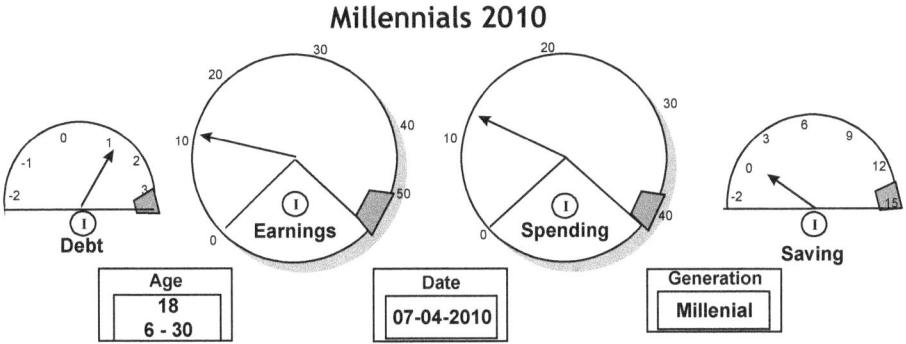

By 2010, we are picking up speed with the Millennials ranging in age from 6 to 30 with a midpoint of 18. Most are in school, but the first cohort commences their careers. They postpone marriage and childbearing, so they delay peak spending. Due to the escalating cost of college and high credit card debt, they enter peak debt earlier.

These first Millennials' earnings are not enough to make up for the huge drop by Boomers. Up until this time, earnings were growing at an accelerated pace, so the loss of net earnings will deprive the economy's engine of the torque it needs to move forward.

The leading edge Millennials make up what the leading edge Boomers lose in spending. But for an economy now addicted to consumer spending, it will not be enough. The investment and banking industry's activities artificially prop up spending with subprime and home equity loans avoiding the crash for a year or two, but like an addict, this is only a temporary fix for the economy.   Interest payments on these questionable loans later rob the economy of productive spending. By 2007, debt reaches record highs and unbelievably, savings are negative. When the economic engine seizes, the over inflated housing bubble bursts taking with it the subprime mortgages and mortgage-backed securities.

Unfortunately, the Great Recession hits this generation hard. Up until 2012, unemployment for those 16 to 25 is over 19% and the rate for 25 to 35 year olds is 1% higher than the national average. Those without high school or college educations have higher unemployment rates and even the college graduates find it hard to acquire a position in their chosen field.

Outsourcing adds to the lack of jobs. According to the Commerce Department, as reported by the Wall Street Journal, in the 1990s, U.S. multinationals created 2.9 million jobs in the U.S. while increasing employment oversees by 2.7 million. The most notable job transfers are of manufacturing jobs to China. In the 2000s, U.S. multinationals create

2.5 million jobs overseas, but sadly cut 2.9 million in the U.S. The most notable outsourcing was of service sector and information technology jobs to India.*

US Multinationals Job Creation

	U.S.	Foreign
1990s	2.9 million	2.7 million
2000s	-2.5 million	2.9 million

Congressional and administrative policy did little other than encourage outsourcing and pay lip service to improving the American jobs picture. They even imported over a million "temporary" programmers primarily from India, under Congress's H1-B program, as unpretentious American programmers and technicians faced repeated lay offs.

The Millennials who did not attend college find few of the high paying manufacturing jobs their parents had in the online want ads. Those that are still available in the rescued auto industry are at substantially lower wages. Even the Millennial college graduates find fewer available service-oriented, professional, managerial, and teaching positions.

The Financial Time Machine suggests that a turnaround could happen as early as 2017, but there are some concerns, which may cause adjustments, primarily the exceedingly high unemployment rate for the Millennials. This is affecting half of the Millennials without a college education especially hard, since their unemployment rate has been over 20%. Many of the Millennials who do have jobs work near the minimum wage, which provides little stimulus to the economy. So we can adjust the Millennials' earning and spending dials down a couple of notches, which will not provide enough stimuli to restart the economy, until the employment picture improves.

At this stage, the Millennials are not having a great impact upon the economy, not enough to offset the declining stimulus of their Boomer parents.

Millennials 2015

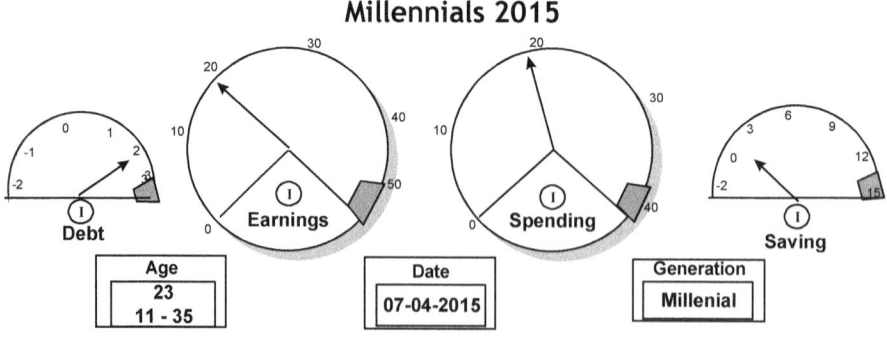

Let's drive our time machine forward 5 more years to 2015. Here we see all the propensities rise with debt nearing the red line and spending nearing the halfway point, as we add more speed. The most encouraging sign is that as more of the Millennials enter the workforce their earnings jump, although it is not enough to make up for the lost Boomers earning power. As a result of the Great Recession wealth loss, the Boomers work longer and the Millennials unfortunately still have a higher rate of unemployment, especially the uneducated. Earnings will adjust downward reducing Millennial gains.

Spending is up, nearly enough to make up for lost Boomer spending. The leading edge of the Millennials is just about to enter their peak spending phase. Spending, however, dampens since Millennials marry and reproduce later; a process further delayed by the recession, stagnant wage growth, and working class marriage rates under 50%.

The savings dial looks just as bad, for while the Boomers begin to draw down their savings, the Millennials are not yet saving much. Plus near zero interest rates offer little incentive to save. The good news is that the Xers are now in their peak financial factors, although their smaller numbers mute the effect.

2010 to 2015 looks like a stagnant first half of the decade. Since generational economics provides no major economic boost, these years will likely be subject to broad fluctuations. Major events such as a slowdown in Asia or a recession in Europe could cause this less resilient economy to falter into another recession. With declining savings, the financial industry will find fewer buyers for its products.

Millennials 2020

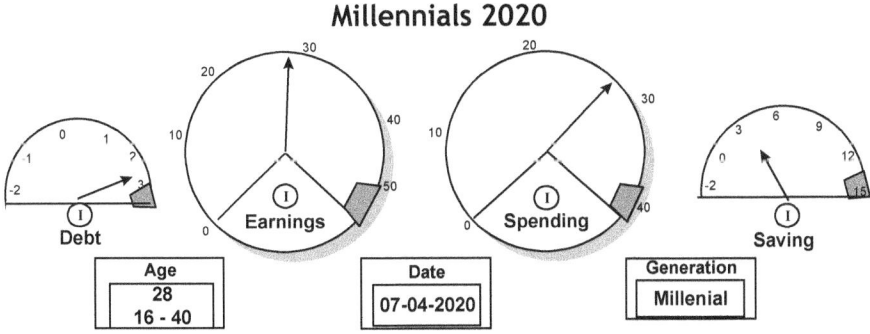

Let's proceed a little further to 2020. One of our dials is at the red line and three are above the mid-point indicating healthy economic stimuli, now we are rolling. Finally, the Millennials begin to drive the economy. Many of the Millennials, even though they marry and rear children later, are now in their thirties and start families. They buy houses, toys, clothes, appliances, decorations, and are remodeling. Over the last five years, houses begin selling at a brisk pace again.

The first Millennials enter their peak spending phase, bringing a powerful spending force to the economy. The first cohort is on the precipice of their peak earning and savings phases too.

If in the event the economy remains low until 2020 and Millennials continue to delay child bearing similar to the Great Depression, there will be a rebound effect. Over the first five years of the Great Recession, birthrates were below replacement levels and the number of births declined. Like the Greatests and the Boomers, the Millennials will have their own mini-baby boom, which will stimulate the economy.

One more factor occurs at this time. The Boomers ages range from 55 to 74, a period when although they need increasing healthcare. They are still highly mobile; but this is a time when their death rate starts to climb. By then, actuarial tables expect 22% of the Boomers to pass. These Boomers will hand their estates off to their Xers and Millennial children, which will in effect increase their earnings, spending, and savings and reduce their debt, thereby adjusting their dials higher and helping the economy. So by 2020 or shortly afterwards, we expect the economy to balance with the Millennials compensating for the Boomers losses.

Millennials 2025

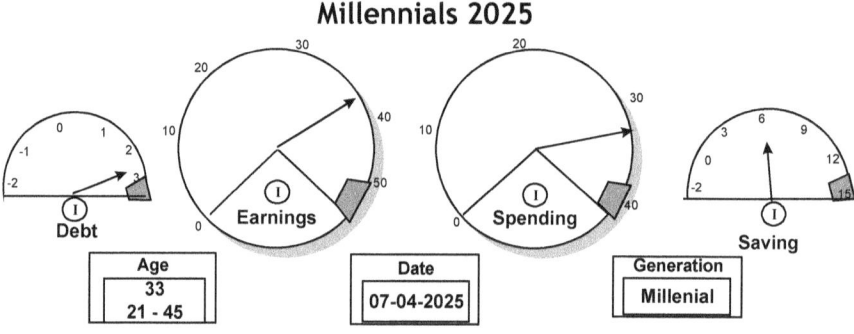

By 2025, all of the Millennials dials are running at full speed. The first cohort is in triple peak, and by now, the Millennials will drive the economy forward with their amazing innovations. The following Millennial cohorts are in their nesting and early career phases. Since the Boomers will largely be retired, the demand for Millennial workers will be high and therefore unemployment will be low with wages high. Companies will compete to attract scarce skilled resources. By now, 90% of the workforce will be in services with healthcare, technology, and robotics continuing as boom industries. As we will see later, Europe, China, and Japan's workforces will decrease, increasing the demand for skilled resources worldwide. This will provide an edge to the U.S. labor force, particularly to the Millennials in their most productive years.

By 2025, the Millennials will fulfill their role as the rescuers of the U.S. economy and by this time if not before, the economy should once again enter boom times. From this point onward, the Millennials will dominate the economy.

Triangulation

We applied Generational Economics to provide three views of the future:
1. Time Machine view
2. Parallelism view
3. Economic stimulus view

Geared to travel rapidly through time in five-year increments, the Financial Time Machine cannot give a precise year for the full recovery. It predicts the economy will likely improve by 2021 or shortly afterwards.

Using parallelism, we saw the major contractions over the last 100 years lasted about twelve years, thereby predicting a recovery in **2020**. We observed peak generation ages.   The recoveries for both the Greatests and Boomers started when they first turned 37 or 38. The first Millennials turn 38 in **2018**.

We then looked at the economic stimulus a generation contributes to the economy. This analysis also results in a recovery between **2016 and 2021**. Using the Financial Time Machine to travel through the future, confirms the 2016 – 2021 prediction. All four analyses point to a recovery between 2016 and 2021 with a more precise date of 2018.   The only concern is that none of the analyses predicts a sustained boom economy by then.

There is one concern though, namely that these analyses do not account for all of the generations simultaneously. They do account for the differences between the dominate Boomers and Millennials, but what about the Xers and the Silents. The next chapter will explore all of the generations simultaneously to see if this confirms our estimates and can provide a more exact date for the recovery.

Events

Of course, there could be many economic events that speed or slow the recovery, some of which appear below and are always possibilities. Think of these as interim effects, more like the periodic recessions that tend to come and go, but do not disturb long-term prospects. In most recessions, the GDP drops, climbs back within a year or so, and then continues to grow to new heights. In major contractions like the Great Recession, it takes longer.

- Black swan events such as the Japanese tsunami, nuclear disasters or periodic Middle East turmoil.
- Major wars
- Periodic global slowdowns such as those in Europe in the 2010s or Asia in the 1990s.
- Individual country debt problems – potential defaults in the PIGS (Portugal, Italy, Greece, and/or Spain.)

- Financial con games on Wall Street like:
    - o Oil Embargo and energy price fixing in the 1970s
    - o The Savings and Loan crisis of 1990
    - o Enron, WorldCom, Anderson and the dotcoms in 2001
    - o The subprime loan debacle in 2008

In the past, events in the U.S. swayed the global economy. The financial media frequently quipped, "When the U.S. sneezes the world catches a cold." But, the U.S. represents a smaller portion of the global economy with the EU and Asia now larger. Therefore, over the next ten years the interconnected global economy will influence the U.S. more – just look at commodity prices. Shortly, China's economy will exceed that of the U.S. The International Monetary Fund (IMF) estimates this will occur in 2016 with the U.S.'s share of the world economy dropping from 20% to 17.7%.*

Events like those above will tweak the adjusting knobs on the time machine, so that the large generational effects will change, but the generational effects, if initially muted, will more than make up for temporary setbacks. Similar to the long expansion after World War II until 2008, there were 11 recessions, which set the economy back. If you step back and look at the GDP over those 60 years, the overwhelming trend is upward with brief valleys.

While observing waves hitting a beach, you notice that some are larger than others are and go further up the beach. But the tide is a much larger force, so that even though one wave may not travel far, if the tide is rising, more waves will follow that climb much further up the beach. A larger concern is the failure of U.S. leadership to manage its budgets, deficits, and national debt, which will likely cause another major recession or rampant inflation similar to the 1970s with attendant stagflation.

Therefore, we do not expect a prolonged upturn until after 2016 and we expect a recession by then. Sometime between 2016 and 2021, we may see a sustained upward trend, perhaps starting as early as 2018, depending upon unemployment and when the next recession hits. Only once in 175 years have we gone 10 years without a recession and that was prior to the Great Recession. There were 38 recess-ions during that time -- on average, one every 4 ½ years. Bank failures and speculative bubbles bursting, similar to the causes of the Great Recession, led to most of these recessions. During this time in American financial history, there were numerous periods of rampant inflation and deflation.

Due to regulation and the actions of the Federal Reserve, our developed economy appears to be more stable, such that the dark forces causing most of the drastic financial calamities remain, to a large extent, in check. However, the hubris prior to the Great Recession demonstrates that our national leadership has not yet mastered the most dominant force affecting our economic prospects - generational tsunamis.

14

The Super Time Machine

The previous explorations portray how each individual generation impacts the economy. As expected, the largest generation caused the largest tidal effect, but to truly assess the consequences upon the economy, requires an examination of all of the generations simultaneously. What we need is a multi-generation version of the Financial Time Machine.

We took the Financial Time Machine back in time for all five of the twentieth century's generations. This examination shows how peak generations since the mid-19th century led to record booms and when they exited the workforce, disastrous busts including the Great Depression, the 70s malaise, and the Great Recession.

Hope for recovery from each economic downturn comes as the next peak generation rises. Therefore, we expect the Millennials to rescue the U.S. from the negative Boomer effect. There is however, a concern, namely that the Millennials are not much larger than the Xers and indeed are slightly smaller than the Boomers. The Millennials will eventually compensate for the Boomers, but not all of the Millennials have even entered the workforce. The Xers are entering their peak levels and perhaps could accelerate the recovery, but what about the Silents who are still drawing well-earned retirement income?

To understand how and when the economy will flourish again, we need to look at all of the generations concurrently and see how they all influence the economy at the same point in time. Doing this would be analogous to driving five time machines into the future simultaneously and comparing the results.

Imagine five Delorean time machines lined up at the starting line, each with a driver from one of the five generations: Greatest, Silent, Boomer, Xer, and Millennial. They set the generational lever to their generation, and patch out racing in time to see who will arrive first. When they arrive at say 2021, they record the four instrument readings from each dash and average these together to see how the economy fares at the time. In my family, there are four generations of Genes, my father, my oldest brother, his son, and his grandson. All were competitive athletes. Imagine the four of them plus a yet to be born Gene racing back in time in the five Deloreans.

Rather than driving five machines through time, recording 20 financial indicator readings and comparing these, let's build a single time machine that simplifies the process - The Super Time Machine, which will average these automatically. So instead of 20 instruments, we now have only four.

Let's add another radical improvement. From the last chapter you may recall that the stimulus equals the sum of the earnings and debt. It also equals spending plus saving, so the stimulus, in effect, represents all four factors. The stimulus is the force one generation exerts upon the economy. We can therefore summarize all four indicators, (or really 20 indicators) on one dial. The new time machine will present the total economic stimulus at a particular point in time that all of the generations provide, greatly simplifying the process. Here is the Super Time Machine.

The Super Time Machine

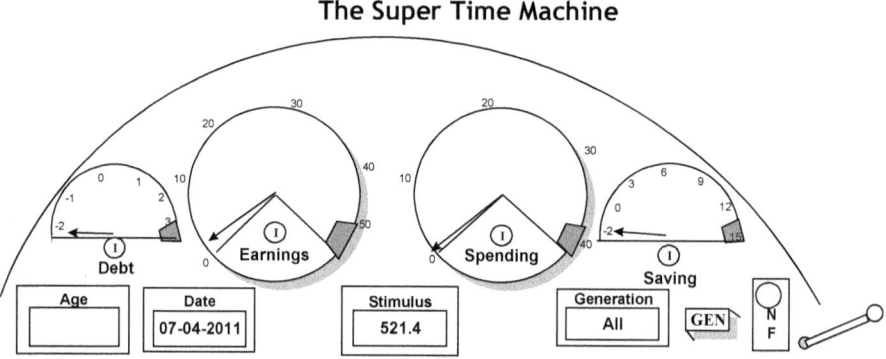

This time machine's display above looks similar to the earlier one with the addition of the stimulus indicator in the lower center. Since it represents all of the five generations, the generational shifter is gone, but there is a selection button, which can switch the display to show any of the generation's figures for a selected year. So at a particular time, you can still see the Boomer or Millennials readings if you like.

When the generational shifter points to **All** as above, the only reading the instruments display is the stimulus reading, since the others no longer register. The calculations also adjust for the relative size of each generation. Therefore, the only meaningful readings to consider are the date and stimulus level. If we selected Boomer on the Generation display, it would display the four readings for the Boomers in 2011.

The key figure on the Super Time Machine's dash is the stimulus reading – 521.4 in 2011. Rather than presenting the entire dash for each year, it is easier to present just the stimulus reading. If we went back to 1991, the stimulus reading would be 428.5. In 1996, it is 471.1. We could show the time machines for selected periods, but since the only reading that matters is the stimulus reading, I will drive the machine back and summarize the results in the following chart, saving you all of that driving and time, plus several pages of boring time machine displays. The following chart displays the machine's results back to 1991.

Super Financial Time Machine
Stimulus Readings

Year	1991	1996	2001	2006	2011
Stimulus	452.8	471.1	489.9	508.5	521.4
Difference		18.3	18.7	18.7	**12.9**
Change		4.0%	4.0%	3.8%	2.5%

The chart portrays the stimulus all of the generations contribute to the economy in a particular year - analogous to driving five Delorean's through time and adding each of their stimulus readings for each generation together. We also added a line for the difference from one period to the next along with the corresponding percentage change it represents.

During the 1990s and early 2000s, the differences in the stimulus grew at approximately 4% per 5-year period indicating a strong generational economic force. During this expansive portion of the cycle, the economy exhibited robust growth. Then after 2006, the stimulus dropped dramatically signaling the zenith of the economic expansion and the start of the contraction. Therefore, we would expect the economy to regress somewhere during this period, which it decidedly did.

Since the first Virginians in Jamestown and the Pilgrims in Provincetown, the U.S. economy has experienced steady and at times, exponential population expansions. Despite periodic recessions, the GDP generally continued its upward slope. Much of the increase accrued due to the rapidly expanding U.S. population, although it was also due to the constantly improving agricultural, industrial, and technological productivity. This pattern continues with the stimulus provided by the growing population of Boomers, Xers, and Millennials replacing the declining Greatests and Silents in the economy. However, the rate of population growth is slowing, reflected in the lower stimulus growth.

Now let's drive the Supper Financial Time Machine into the future where we see the following results in 2016.

Super Financial Time Machine
Stimulus Readings through 2016

Year	1991	1996	2001	2006	2011	2016
Stimulus	452.8	471.1	489.9	508.5	521.4	528.7
Difference		18.3	18.7	18.7	12.9	7.3
Change		4.0%	4.0%	3.8%	2.5%	1.4%

Here the added stimulus reading is even lower (1.4%) indicating that there will be no sustained recovery. With such a reading, we would expect to see periods of limited growth followed by near zero growth or a likely recession.

In the U.S. for much of the period from 2008 until 2016, the number of births slows below the replacement level to 1.9 for fertile female. As the birthrate continues to decline, by 2013, it still has not reached the 4.3 million-mark set in 2007. When there is high unemployment and even half of the college grads cannot find the jobs they desire, people delay marriage and child bearing until better times. Immigration slows as the number of new illegal immigrants declines. When there is a lack of jobs, especially like those in construction, there is little employment for undocumented workers.

Super Financial Time Machine
Stimulus Readings 2021

Year	1991	1996	2001	2006	2011	2016	2021
Stimulus	452.8	471.1	489.9	508.5	521.4	528.7	535.4
Difference		18.3	18.7	18.7	12.9	7.3	6.7
Change		4.0%	4.0%	3.8%	2.5%	1.4%	1.3%

Unfortunately, when we drive to a little further, the stimulus increase of 1.3% in 2021 looks about the same as in 2016, implying that the U.S. is still in a contraction now lasting 13 years. This contraction rivals those of the 1970s of 13 years and the Great Depression of 9 years. The economy still grows during the period, just at a very slow rate. As we will see later, this is not all bad news for there are other nations who experience even higher negative stimulus growth during the same period and will likely teeter on the edge of recessions for years.

A potentially positive aspect to the prolonged contraction is that people's expectations will likely adjust to the lower growth. In the mid-2000s prior to the crash, consumers, the government, and particularly the financial system expected continually rapid growth. They all bet on and leveraged the expected growth. Consumers bet on housing and growth investments expecting these to rise continuously at rapid rates. The government bet on rising GDP that would continuously reduce the relative size of the growing debt. And, the financial industry using margins of up to 30 to 1, bet on a variety of highly leveraged financial instruments that depended upon a booming economy. When the expansion finally tipped into contraction, the consumers, government, and financial industry lost their bets resulting in the Great Recession. The Great Recession would not have been as bad if people's expectations had adjusted prior to the inflection point.

Once the consumers, government, and financial industry adjust to lower growth, we should all be in better shape. Added to the chart below is a row portraying the rate, at which the stimulus is changing. Let's call this the growth expectation. So in 2021, even though stimulus growth is anemic, the rate of change stabilizes at -9%. This reflects people's potential expectations of change.

Super Financial Time Machine
Stimulus Readings 2021

Year	1991	1996	2001	2006	2011	2016	2021
Stimulus	452.8	471.1	489.9	508.5	521.4	528.7	535.4
Difference		18.3	18.7	18.7	12.9	7.3	6.7
Change		4.0%	4.0%	3.8%	2.5%	1.4%	1.3%
Expectation			-1.7%	-4.0%	-34%	-45%	-9%

Notice in that between 1991 and 2006 there was little change; therefore, people would continue to expect continued rapid growth, because they were had been conditioned to such growth. Throughout the last several centuries, people continuously expect boom periods to last and are constantly surprised when they burst.

In 2006 to 2016, people still tend to expect the economy to turn around, but they are disappointed by the rapidly diminishing stimulus growth. By 2021, stimulus growth begins to stabilize suggesting that people's expectations too should stabilize.

Will the U.S. economy turn around prior to 2021 and start into another expansion as our previous analyses portray? Let's drive a little further to 2026. The chart below adds the 2026 reading.

Super Financial Time Machine
Stimulus Readings 2026

Year	1996	2001	2006	2011	2016	2021	2026
Stimulus	471.1	489.9	508.5	521.4	528.7	535.4	538.3
Difference	18.3	18.7	18.7	12.9	7.3	6.7	2.9
Change	4.0%	4.0%	3.8%	2.5%	1.4%	1.3%	0.5%
Expectation		-1.7%	-4.0%	-34%	-45%	-9%	**-58%**

Whoa! - with the largest drop in stimulus growth yet, 2026 looks abysmal. By then, added generational economic stimulus approaches zero. At -58% the expectations too are vastly out of sync. People will grow accustomed to stagnant growth, but the lack of new generational stimulus will likely be shocking. Expect another, possibly severe, recession between 2021 and 2026.

The large expected drop is mostly due to the Boomers. Switching the generational lever to "Boomer" on the Super Time Machine presents the following image. In 2026, the Boomers range in age from 61 to 80. Nearly all of the Boomers are retired and over the last ten years, their stimulus drops like a rock. The Boomer component of the total stimulus declines by over 33%, the largest drop in history for any 20th century generation. The debt dial is pinned. The earnings dial is below the halfway point composed largely of pension and savings plan payments. The savings dial is just above zero. The spending dial is still slightly above the midway point, but most of this spending is comprised of Boomers drawing from the economy for retirement, medical expenses and extended care.

Boomers 2026

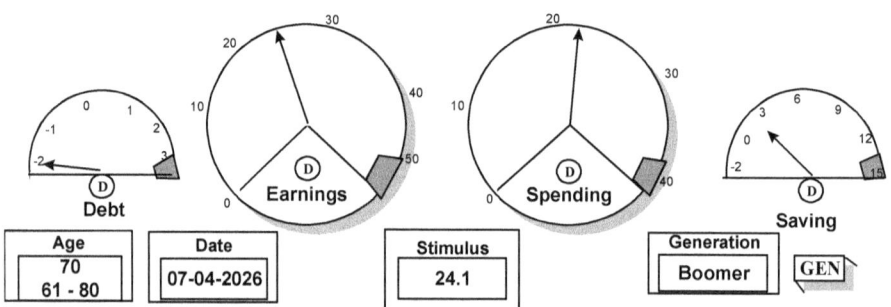

Age	Date	Stimulus	Generation	
70	07-04-2026	24.1	Boomer	GEN
61 - 80				

This reading was really a surprise. Is there no hope for the economy? Will the U.S. experience over two decades of stagnant growth like Japan?

Year	1991	1996	2001	2006	2011
Stimulus	452.8	471.1	489.9	508.5	521.4
Difference		18.3	18.7	18.7	12.9
Change		4.0%	4.0%	3.8%	2.5%
Expectation			-1.7%	-4.0%	-34%

Year	2016	2021	2026	2031	2036
Stimulus	528.7	535.4	538.3	545.1	553.6
Difference	7.3	6.7	2.9	6.8	8.4
Change	1.4%	1.3%	0.5%	1.3%	1.5%
Expectation	-45%	-9%	-58%	**136%**	22%

Being depressed by the results and apprehensive about proceeding further, we reluctantly drove the Super Time Machine into the future once again. Above are the readings we recorded for 2031 and 2036. The stimulus reading for 2031, thankfully, shows a rapid rise and an expected incline of **136%** - woo woo! This welcome news indicates an inflection point prior to 2026. The contraction should end prior to then commencing the long awaited and welcome expansion. These growth rates are not spectacular and indeed mirror those of 2016 and 2021, but they are heading in the right direction, which is the key to identify the much sought after turning point.

Let's assume a relatively severe recession ends in 2023 clearing the way for expansion (it could be 2022 or 2024 depending on events at the time.) Therefore, the contraction ends in 2023 meaning that it lasts 15 years. This is similar to the previous two contractions, and to the 14-year contraction 100 years earlier at the start of the 20th century. These contractions typically last 13 – 15 years with one exception, the Great Depression, which only lasted nine years. World War II short-circuited this contraction as the nation's industries ran at full speed.

The Super Financial Time Machine (FTM) completes the picture below, which displays the generational waves and troughs washing over the economy since the mid-19th century. Imagine that you are on the eastern shore in say Virginia Beach, to the right, looking out at the incoming waves. What you see is one wave after another approaching the shore, the last of which is the Millennial wave.

The Boomer expansion ends at the end of 2007 when the contraction commences. According to the Super FTM, this contraction point will continue to approximately 2023 when the cycle will restart once again. The FTM predicts a relatively long contraction because for the first time in U.S. history, the current peak generation, the Millennials, is not larger than the previous peak generation, the Boomers.

Generational Waves Washing Over the Economy
Expansions

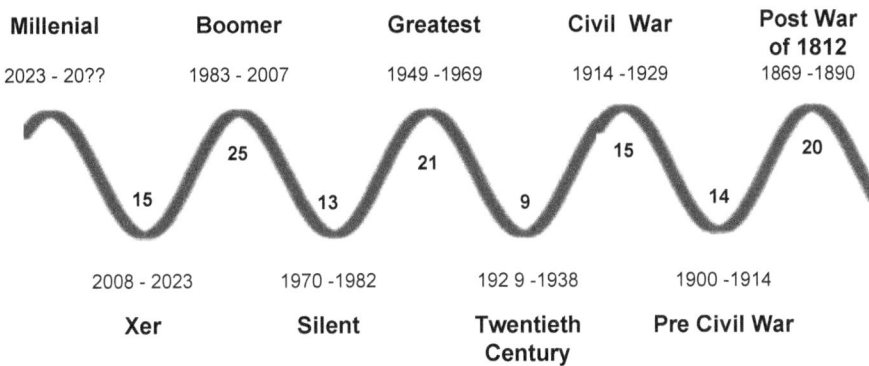

Millenial	Boomer	Greatest	Civil War	Post War of 1812
2023 - 20??	1983 - 2007	1949 -1969	1914 -1929	1869 -1890

25   21   15   20

15   13   9   14

2008 - 2023	1970 -1982	192 9 -1938	1900 -1914
Xer	Silent	Twentieth Century	Pre Civil War

Contractions

A couple of positive notes apply to the discouraging scenario above. First, even though the stimulus is low, it is still growing. As discussed later, other nations will experience negative stimulus growth during the same period, so this is not all bad. Expectations for stagnant growth will take time to adjust to for a country addicted to 200 years of generally robust growth. Even though the generational economic stimulus is low, other factors are involved such as national leadership and productivity. Productivity can add a percent or two to GDP growth, although during the prolonged contractions, productivity will likely falter.

Leadership also provides a key difference. In the 1990s, Washington faced mounting deficits and heroically balanced the budget. In the 2000s just before the Boomers retired, they foolishly reduced revenue and increased spending resulting in a doubling of the national debt, in a sense crashing the ship of state upon the economic rocks, resulting in the Great Recession. Will they recognize the current stagnant expectations for the economy and steer a prudent course?

Summary

Here is what the generational economics analysis projects:

1. The amount of generational economic stimulus should constantly increase, since the U.S. population is increasing.
2. Through 2006, stimulus increased at an extremely high rate averaging 3.9%, which predicts rapid growth.
3. From 2006 to 2011, growth slows dramatically, indicating a sharp reversal.
4. From 2011 to 2016, the contraction continues, although there will still be slow growth with a high likelihood of a recession.
5. Following the expected recession, from 2016 to 2021, the economy should improve slightly and then linger in stagnation.
6. The period from 2021 to 2026 is a surprise. The economic outlook worsens; and therefore, the Super FTM expects another recession.
7. By 2026, expect a sustained period of growth, not as good as the 1990s, but still robust. The FTM predicts this period will last until the 2040s, provided U.S. leadership puts its economic house in order and there are no major calamities.

After constructing the Super Financial Time Machine and peering into the future, what are the implications of this analysis? The next section examines such implications.

The scenario presented is, regrettably, not an optimistic one and as mentioned, much depends upon the quality of leadership over the next decade, so a couple of chapters are dedicated to leadership and policy implications. The section concludes with some recommendations for leadership based on the FTM's projections.*

Section Four

15

Future Implications

The Financial Time Machine does not predict the precise date when the economy will fully recover or when we will have the next boom. It shows we will likely have a recession by 2016. The specific date depends upon the events occurring at the time. The financial system (including banking, brokerages, and the Fed) caused most of the dozens of recessions over the last 200 years while generational economics sets the stage or serves as the catalyst for the inevitable downturn. However, cataclysmic events like war, bubbles bursting, or massive fraud accelerate this timing.

Can we avoid recessions? Yes! The time machine indicates downward phases, during which the risk of a recession is high. The decisions made by institutions, individuals and the government can delay or mollify a recession, or conversely, exacerbate its severity. During the 70s downturn, we had four recessions, but there could just as easily have been three. Fed policy, institutional greed, and governmental policy made the Great Recession worse than it had to be. Consumer spending and the corresponding high debt load delayed the inevitable recession, but contributed to making it more severe. The time machine predicts we are in a period of economic hardship lasting at least a decade, but the first recession during the period could have been less severe, if policy decisions were more enlightened.

There is a temptation to think that the severity of the recession does not matter - if it is deeper than expected, we will make up for it with higher subsequent growth. This is true for the relatively mild recessions we experienced over the last half of the 20th Century. But, with severe downturns such as the Great Depression and Recession, there is a downward spiral of unemployment and idle productive capacity that is self-perpetuating and difficult to reverse. Therefore, policy decisions at the national, institutional, and individual level do make a difference.

For instance, since the Great Recession, entrepreneurial activity and investment is down with new investment concentrated in one area - Silicon Valley. The number of new businesses, the engine of growth and jobs is also drastically down. Part of the reason for this is due to the banks reluctance to lend to new and small businesses, but another reason is the severe recession, which made everyone including those who might start a new business more cautious and risk adverse.

Layers

When you look at many charts, such as a particular stock's price, you can select the time period to display its results in years, months, weeks, days, or even by the minute. If you view a particular stock's annual chart, what you might see is a steady climb. But when you then select a weekly view, what at first seems to be a steady rise is composed of numerous smaller peaks and valleys with a generally upward trend. So it is with the national economy having many vicissitudes within a larger trend. The Financial Time Machine looks at the economy on a large scale - every 5 years. Within that period, there will be many fluctuations, with the time machine predicting the larger, smoother trend line.

The time machine's predilections will prove to be valuable for long-term investment. Financial advisers counsel clients to think about long-term goals, retirement, or the children's education, and not to worry about market fluctuations and timing. Some mutual funds require long-term investment commitments with stiff penalties for early withdrawal. Many treasury, corporate and municipal bonds have five, ten, or even twenty-year durations.   When deciding between multiple long-term investment vehicles it is wise to consider future cycles, for this is where the true returns accrue.

Corroboration for the FTM predictions

The FTM's predictions over the 2010 decade appear pessimistic, considering typical past economic growth rates of 3 to 4%. Indeed, U.S. real GDP growth averaged 3.25% from 1947 to 2012.* For the first 15 quarters of the recovery following the Great Recession, the economy averaged only 2.1% GDP growth rate. Following the double dip recession of 1980 - 1982 at the end of the 70s malaise, it averaged 5.3% over the same 15 quarters.

Are there others who support such an analysis? The Congressional Budget Office projects the GDP will average 2.4% growth from 2013 to 2022, above the FTM's forecast.

Bill, "the Bond King" Gross and Mohamed El-Erian, co-chief investment officers of the highly successful PIMCO, think the U.S. will not have growth beyond 2% anytime soon. PIMCO manages nearly $2 trillion in its funds with its principal Total Return Fund outperforming its category consistently for five years. As a surfer, Bill Gross believes in long-term economic waves. According to their staff's analyses, 2% growth rates might become the new norm not for a couple of years, but for a couple of decades.* This analysis concurs with the Financial Time Machine analysis, although the FTM predicts a sustained recovery within a decade and a half.

Forecast

Over the last 60 years, we saw short periodic recessions followed by rapid growth and renewed prosperity. Unfortunately, this will not be the case for the approximately 15 years commencing in 2008.

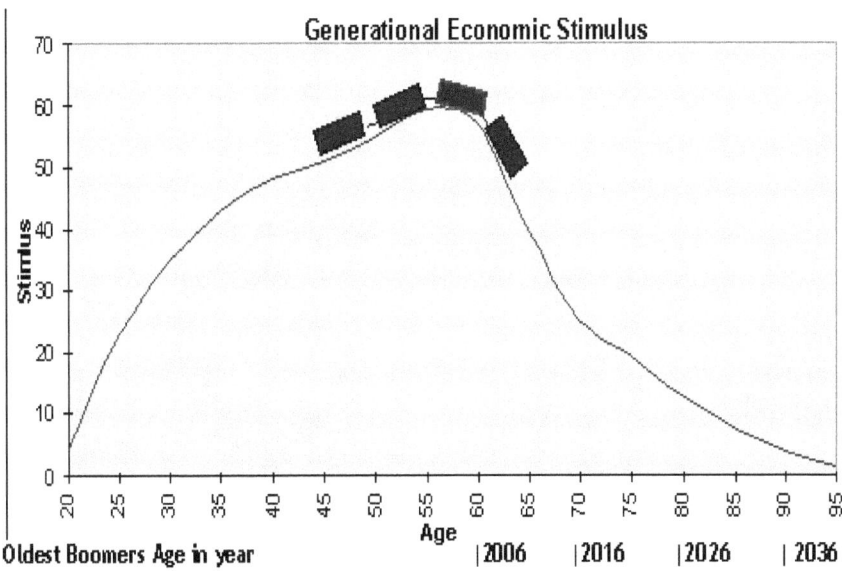

Above is a summary of first or oldest Boomer's stimulus. The chart shows the first Boomers age with the corresponding year listed below (in 2011, the first Boomer turned 65.) Notice that the stimulus chart resembles a roller coaster track. Think of the Boomers occupying 19 rows (years) of seats, one for each year of the Boomer generation. As the coaster's first Boomers edge over the precipice in 2006, the coaster moves slowly, then as more Boomers slide over, the coaster quickly picks up speed.

Imagine four roller coaster cars (five rows per car) full of Boomers careening over a steep 2000-foot summit, slowly at first, then after the last car races over the hump, ever faster until they approach 100 miles an hour. As they speed downward, the stimulus, represented by the track, rapidly declines.

Following the Boomers is another train with three cars of Xers, but some of the seats in these 15 rows are empty, since there are fewer of them. So, when the last Boomer tips over the edge of the precipice, the Xers are at the top of stimulus mountain, but because of their fewer numbers they just do not have enough financial mass to make up for the careening Boomers.

In the meantime, a third coaster is climbing, clicking steadily up the manmade mountain with five carloads of Millennials. Their stimulus is steadily increasing and all of the seats are full. The stimulus the Millennials gain as they rise higher will surely offset the stimulus the Boomers lose. Each click on the upward slope represents a year or one row on our roller coaster ride. As we saw in the last chapter, this should occur somewhere between 2021 and 2026.

Stimulus and GDP

Let's take another look at the change in stimulus from the combined stimulus chart. This is the chart that looks at all the generations' entire stimulus simultaneously. Intuitively, it seems there should be a relationship between GDP and stimulus.

Stimulus and GDP

Year	1996	2001	06	11	16	21	26	31	36
Stimulus Change %	4.0	4.0	3.8	2.5	1.4	1.3	0.5	1.3	1.5
Average Real GDP%	3.3	3.8	2.8	0.1	?	?	?	?	?

GDP figures from FRED, the St. Louis Federal Reserve.

When the rate of stimulus change is high as it is from 1991 until 2006, we had the longest period of expansion in history. When it began to slow after 2006, we had the Great Recession.

Interestingly, as we see above, the stimulus change mirrors real GDP growth. When we had high generational stimulus, we had high GDP growth. When the generational stimulus was lower, as it was from 2006 to 2011, we had extremely low growth – near **zero**.

The stimulus from 2006 to 2011 was still relatively high. Examining this period more closely, we expect the stimulus to be high through 2007 and decline rapidly until 2011. The GDP numbers presented average high and low values over the five-year period, which were negative at times.

GDP growth and stimulus growth are in percents. GDP is an annual figure, whereas stimulus spans five years so even though they resemble each other, other factors are relevant, most notably productivity. According to Paul Ashworth of the forecasting firm Capital Economics, productivity has been growing at about 1% recently.* So, approximately 1% of GDP growth is attributable to productivity. Therefore, we do not expect GDP to match stimulus, but rather to correlate to stimulus. When stimulus growth declines, we expect GDP to slow. When stimulus growth increases, we expect GDP to increase. Generational stimulus is a powerful leading indicator, perhaps the most powerful.

The Financial Time Machine (FTM) predicts the period from 2011 to

2016 will be one of continued slow growth, much slower than the mid 1980s to mid 2000s. It is likely we will see yet another recession by 2016 followed by continued slow growth from 2016 to 2021.

Let's look at the GDP data thus far to see how the FTM performs.

Recent GDP Growth

Year	07	08	09	2011	2012	2013#
GDP	2.1	-3.2	-.1	2.3	2.0	2.0	1.8

#Projected*

Thus far, the years since the Great Recession have been ones of slow growth averaging 2.0%, consistent with the FTM's predictions.

The period from 2021 to 2026 produces the lowest added stimulus in 50 years. At first, it seems we were climbing out of the contraction, but the .5% stimulus growth looks menacing indicating real GDP growth likely to be barely above 1%. With such slow growth prospects, expect yet another recession between 2019 and 2026. After that recession, say by 2024, we expect a sustained economic expansion lasting into the mid 2040s, although not as pronounced as in the past.

If we continue with the roller coaster analogy, the economy will slide down the track rapidly from 2008 until about 2018. Then it will climb a short hill until the early 2020s when it drops again and then starts to rise by the mid-2020s.

The time machine predicts that we will likely experience a stagnant economy until the early to mid 2020s. Since much depends upon the actions of Washington, the financial industry, and the global economy, it is difficult to project exactly when we might experience recessions. For anyone interested in better managing their portfolios, it would be nice to know when such reversals might occur. Of course, this version of the time machine cannot exact dates of such occurrences, but we can provide probabilities of when recessions are likely to occur. We can, therefore, represent the Financial Time Machine's forecast similar to a weather forecast.

25 YEAR ECONOMIC FORECAST				
2011-16	2016-21	2021-26	2026-31	2031-36
Stormy High Economic Head Winds	Partly Cloudy Bursting Bond Bubble Stagflation	Severe Storms Stagflation PM Clearing	Sunny Warm Clear Skies	Sunny Warm Clear Skies
80%	50%	70%	20%	30%

- **2011-16**: Turbulent markets, high economic head winds, severe economic storms likely - chance of recession 70%
- **2016-21**: Chance of recession 50%.
- **2021-26**: Stagflation continues, cool, severe economic storms - chance of recession 70%, PM clearing.
- **2026-31**: Sunny, warm, clear skies - chance of recession 20%.
- **2031-36**: Sunny warm, clear skies - chance of recession 30%.

Similar to a weather forecast, there is a probability of ill economic activity (a recession) associated with each period.

The likelihood of a recession by 2016 is high. Proactive Washington leadership and a lack of Wall Street mischief could avert this recession, but currently that seems unlikely. Notice that there is also a less likely chance of a recession from 2016 to 2021. We expect extreme bond inflation to occur around 2018, which will cause stress to the markets explained in the next chapter. With effective leadership, there is a chance this bubble can be averted. Then, in the early 2020s, we expect a relatively severe recession. Notice the extremely low stimulus change from 2021 to 2026 portending extremely low or negative growth during the period.

If you add up the chance of recessions over the first three periods, it equals 190%. Therefore, the FTM predicts two recessions over 15 years.

This prognosis sounds unusually pessimistic, but remember there has been on average one recession every four or five years. There were only two recessions over the last 20 years, but the FTM predicted this to be the best period in U.S. financial history and we are no longer in the upward portion of that cycle.

When my wife and I lived in San Diego, the weather was predictable - morning fog lifting by noon, then sunny with a high of 72 and a low of 60. The same forecast could go on every day for weeks or even months. Being a weather forecaster seemed like such a boring occupation. The one variation was that the weather inland was always warmer than the coast (90s), cooler in the mountains (60s), and much hotter in the desserts (100s), but the weather in these other zones of San Diego County could be the same for months too. San Diego weather resembles where the economy has been for the 25 years preceding the Great Recession, after which the climate changed.

In the Midwest and in particular Cleveland, the weather constantly changes - 40s one day and raining, 80s the next. During one particularly cold February day, all the weather announcers predicted no snow because of a frozen Lake Erie so therefore, the infamous snow machine was off. The snow machine begins when a dominant northwest wind picks up the warmer lake's moisture, chills it, and then dumps it onto the city. When the lake freezes, there is no lake moisture to pick up; therefore, there is no snow.

Unexpectedly, a low front pummeled the area with two to three feet of snow in just 12 hours, shutting the city down. Some people did not arrive home from work for five hours. The fierce storm stranded hundreds of travelers in the cold and deep snow on Interstates 80 and 90.

Unbeknownst to the weathermen and ladies, there was a portion of the lake near Toledo that was still unfrozen and the Northwest winds carried moisture directly from there to the city. So it is with the time machine – unforeseen events can cause unexpected results, but when it is February the Midwest expect lots of snow. Analogously, the time machine cannot predict a severe economic downturn on a particular day, but can indicate when to expect a downturn during the period.

We learned that distant global conditions like warm waters in the Western Pacific (El Nino) affect weather patterns throughout the U.S. with cooler and wetter winters in California and dryer, warmer winters in the Midwest. The effects of these patterns can last for months, so that although normally "it never rains in sunny California," under the influence of El Nino it might pour every day. El Nino affects the jet stream and the jet stream affects regional weather patterns.

The current economic conditions highlighted by the FTM are similar to an El Nino. We will be under the influence of an economic jet stream producing an inordinate number of lows over a decade.

Corollary to Change

Early in my career, before smartphones, I had a circular calendar with a day per page that you flipped over. Each day there was a saying under the date, which I enjoyed reading. Inspired by these brief words of wisdom, I wrote a maxim on the base that applied well to what I did

"The only thing that is constant is change!"

The maxim pertains to the last 50 years of digital transformation, as it did to my role in management consulting, system design and organizational transformation. It also applies to the last 100+ years of innovation in every industry including most notably agriculture, and manufacturing.

Later, after managing a particularly demanding project, I saw the maxim and wrote a corollary to this maxim on the calendar base:

"The result of constant change is consistency."

To varying degrees, we all crave consistency in our lives. We crave change too, but If we experience too much change, we cannot wait for a calm spell. San Diego weather is a testimony to consistency.

After the horrors of the Great Depression and World War II, the nation craved the consistency the 1950s provided. Then jobs, family, and friendships were secure. People did not want to rock the boat and welcomed hierarchical order, civility, and prosperity. With low crime, low divorce rates, high unemployment, high moral fiber, and censorship, the 1950s epitomized an ideal world, if you were white and not poor. By the mid-1960s, the protected children of the post-war era wanted to leave their comfortable nests, experience change, and challenge the system, parts of which deserved reformation.

From the perspective of the largely Greatest, elder generation, who experienced such tragedy, struggled mightily, and worked hard to provide their children a bright new world, the rebellious young Boomers were difficult to endure. In a sense, the rebellion was unkind to the parents when all they craved was consistency and well deserved peace.

The large Boomer generation, by virtue of its record numbers and relatively secure childhood thrived on change. The Millennials are not much larger than the Xers and the post millennials are approximately the same size as their predecessors. Indeed, the number of births since the Great Recession is down with the population only growing .7% in 2012 or 2.3 million, the lowest rate since 1940s.* The births will eventually increase, but this new generation with a continuously declining birthrate will still not be appreciably larger than the Millennials. Therefore, population growth is relatively flat - like a calm sea with no population waves on the horizon. With the exception of immigration, we will likely have a slow-growing population for 30 years or more.

Immigration

Based upon the number births, the current version of the Financial Time Machine does not include immigrants, because of the lack of precise data. As we will see, when we later observe other nations, immigration can be an important balancing factor to aging populations. Fortunately, the U.S. has had continuing immigration and nearly all of us, or our predecessors, were immigrants at sometime.

Prior to the 2000 census, undocumented workers were not fully accounted for. In 2010, some Hispanic groups urged their people not to fill out census forms, so the data is incomplete, and these census records do not fully account for illegal immigrants.

The 10-year censuses contain information on foreign-born populations though. These records provide input about when immigration occurred, which tend to reinforce the peak generations. The highest percentages of foreign born, primarily from Europe, was 14.4% in 1870, 14.8% in 1890, and 14.7% in 1910. The first two correspond to the economic expansions in 1870 - 1890.

During the contraction from 1929 - 1950 the foreign-born population dramatically declined from 11.6% of the population to 6.9%. Then during the expansion from 1950 to 1970, it rose slightly. This was not enough to offset the aging of earlier immigrants who added to the Greatest generation.

Since 1970, the foreign-born population has steadily risen. During the 70s malaise, it rose and then continued to rise throughout the 1983 – 2007 expansion. Since the Great Recession, there has been a reduction of foreign-born residents.

There is a high correlation, although not 100%, between immigration waves and generational waves, such that the immigration waves tend to reinforce the generational waves. In 1997, the foreign-born population represented about 10% of the U.S. population or 25 million. The 2010 census shows over 12% foreign-born. Those in their prime working and reproductive years, between 25 and 45, represent 43% of this population.

It is logical that more immigration would occur during expansions when there is an abundance of work and less immigration during contractions when there is higher unemployment. Since not all immigrants are included, it is difficult to assign foreign-born people to generations. It is likely most new immigrants would be younger and of working age, thereby adding to the number of people in their most productive years and peak financial factors. Immigrants, who are not yet citizens, are also younger with a lower medium age of 36.2.

Without commenting upon the political aspects of undocumented workers, immigration will help mollify the effects of the aging of America, since new immigrants tend to be younger and have higher birthrates. Without these higher births, U.S. birthrates would be below replacement levels. In fact, the white population in the U.S. is actually declining with more deaths than births. As we will see later, U.S. immigration is a primary reason our aging crisis will be less severe than Europe's or Japan's.* * *

The waves of peak generations like the Greatests, Boomers, and Millennials moving through the economy will be calm for decades. Therefore, the generational economic effect will slow. The waves that caused the three longest booms and three longest busts over the last 100 years will mollify. The Boomer and Millennial waves are still approaching the economic shore and will impact the economy until the 2030s, but after that time, expect relative calm at least from the perspective of the FTM. Using our weather analogy – we will have San Diego-like economic weather.

It is difficult to project exactly what the U.S. economy will be like in the late 2030s and 2040s, but baring any cataclysmic events, expect a period of economic calm with markets less buffeted by unexpected headwinds. Recessions should be mild and less frequent. GDP growth should be fairly steady, but not spectacular, generally in the 1 - 4% range with productivity and technological improvements continuing to add to GDP growth. Employment should be consistently high in the 4 – 6% range, especially with the large number of Boomers out of the employment picture. By then, 90% of us will work in service related industries. Scarce resources may periodically present economic problems, but technology will likely provide solutions to solve these problems at least until 2050. With smaller generational wave variation, economic bubbles and bursts should be less likely especially those related to housing, provided there are effective controls over deviant Wall Street behaviors. By then, the politicians should solve the debt crisis and consumer expectations should be more inline with reality.

By the 2030s, new data will enhance the Financial Time Machine model. Since generational economics provides a mountain top view and long-term economic indicator, it will help assess the economy's prospects from then on within the context of the then current generational megatrends. Periodic refreshing of the model will help provide course corrections.

Certainly, massive tragedies like another world war, pandemic, or a massive, unforeseen, cataclysmic event could cause storms of population change that reset the FTM's cycle. Something will happen. It always does.

The Boomer wave passing through the economy led to an immense amount of change. We did well harnessing this energy. But, the force of that wave is abating. The Millennials will provide additional positive force, but not as much. They are only 15% larger than the Xers, whereas the Boomers were 60% larger than the Silents. In some ways, we overestimated the power of the Boomer wave thinking that the growth of the late 1980s, 90s, and early 2000s would continue forever. So, we leveraged the expected power with irrational consumer and governmental spending. This is human nature, a mistake we manage to repeat continuously over the millennia. But, perhaps we can learn.

Retirement Implications

The largest societal challenge facing the United States, and, as we will see later, the rest of the developed world, are retirement expenses for the Boomers. The combination of longer life expectancies, decreasing birth rates, declining worker to retiree ratios, smaller family sizes, increasing number of single households, and increasing social funding proves to be challenging for the world economy. Indeed, this is the usual context of generational economics - funding for promised retirement benefits of the large Boomer Generation by the smaller subsequent generations.

Before the 1950s, very few people could afford to retire and even afterwards, only 47% of men over 65 retired. Prior to 1950, very few women worked outside of the home. Social Security did not go into effect until 1935. Earlier, only the wealthy could afford the leisure life, while the rest worked until they could no longer physically do so and then lived with their large families. By 2000, the retirement picture dramatically changed with only **17.5%** of people working past 65.

The Changing Retirement Picture

Year	Male Retirements over 65
1900	26%
1950	47%
2000	82%

How can society afford so many retirees? Well, in 1990, per capita real GDP was eight times higher than in 1890. Higher earnings at both the individual and corporate level facilitate people and their companies' savings, making mass retirement now feasible.*

The Financial Life Cycle portrays eight phases that we pass through in our lives. We could just as easily summarize these into five 20-year stages as listed below:

1.   0-20: Childhood
2.   21-40: Early Career and Nest Building
3.   41-60: Peak Earnings and Wealth Creation
4.   61-80: Down Sizing and Mid Retirement
5. 81-100: Late Retirement

In only two of the five stages, do we contribute financially to society: from roughly 21 - 60. In the other three stages, society largely supports us during our childhood and then later in our retirement. Granted, most people do not live beyond 80 and we are not saying people above 60 do not work or contribute to society. Still, we only work for about half of our lives (40 out of 80 years.)

Even during our working lives, most work about 40 hours of the 168 available hours available each week (less than a quarter.) If we include time off, we work a little over a **fifth** of the time and that is if we occupy a full-time position.

The early 2000s are a far cry from the early 1900s when the typical workweek was 60 hours. How is this possible? --- **productivity improvements.** It seems amazing that In approximately 40 years of working 40 hours a week we earn enough to raise our children, send them to college until they are 22 or 23, and retire on-average at 62, then live on-average to 78. Sounds like the good life.

Since they did not contribute to Social Security for their entire working careers and their contribution rates were much lower, the Greatests received more from Social Security than they deposited into it. They were also able to take advantage of pension plans, many of which began in the 1950s.

The Silents also contributed less to Social Security than they receive, had lucrative pension benefits, but unlike their predecessors the government protects these benefits. Earlier, companies would lay off older workers to avoid paying their pensions. My oldest brother worked for a major grocery chain as a meat cutter. One of the fellows he worked with was let go with nearly 30 years of service, just before he was eligible for the pension. The company saved the expense, but was heartless. Disgusted with the company, my brother became a math teacher at half the pay.

Passed in 1986, TRA 86 required that once workers attained 5 years of service, they acquired a pension benefit and they would continue to acquire additional benefits for each year of service after that time. This law also required separate funding for pension benefits that could not be used by the corporation. As a result, pension retirements became more secure. The Silents could also take advantage of newly instituted 401(k) plans making their retirements the richest up until now.

Unfortunately, for the Boomers, the number of company pension plans dwindled rapidly in the 1990s, so many do not have pensions, or their pensions were reduced, or frozen. Plus, the tacit guaranteed lifetime employment many companies professed in the 1950s through 1970s, when the labor supply was low, started to erode in the 1980s as we faced stiff global competition. Many Boomers could not accumulate 30 to 40 years of service with one employer, as their Greatest and Silent coworkers had.

There are several factors leading towards less lucrative retirements for the Boomers. The most notable is that the Great Recession led to declining home values, declining investment values and near zero rates of return on fixed assets. So just when the Boomers should be acculturating wealth at the most rapid rate, their wealth shrunk. The high cost of college educations, rising at twice the rate of inflation, also depleted Boomer retirement accounts. In addition, their parents are living longer than expected, thereby further depleting their retirement funds. Some of the Boomers parents will depend upon them for resources or will leave little in inheritances, which the Boomers could use to fund their own retirements.

Boomers also have to wait longer before they can receive full Social Security benefits – up to 67 for those born after 1960 versus 65. Unlike the Greatests, the Boomers contributed to Social Security their entire working lives. The average Greatest contributed 5% of their salary, and the average Silent 11%. The Boomers will contribute nearly 15% or three times the Greatests' contribution rate and nearly 50% more than the Silents'. The Xers and Millennials will contribute substantially more. Also, unlike their predecessors who contributed little or nothing to Medicare, the Boomers contributed for most of their careers.

In a series of laws, most notably TRA 86 passed in 1986, the government required prospective funding of private pension plans. Companies with pension plans were therefore required to pay pensions for employees with 5 or 7 years of service and calculate their liabilities for future payments to retirees each year. They also had to fund the pensions in accounts separate from the company's balance sheet. If a company went out of business or was an acquisition, which happens to most corporations at some time, the pension funds up until that point would remain intact.

Previously, companies used pension funds to finance their operations, which Washington no longer allows. When General Motors faced bankruptcy in 2008, they had nearly $100 Billion in pension assets. Certainly, they would have liked to tap into these funds to save the company, but Washington would not allow them to do so. Unlike GM, the government never followed its own rules and instead used its pension funds (Social Security) to finance its excessive spending, thereby radically increasing the national debt. In effect, Washington wrote IOUs to the Social Security fund.

Most of us pay more to Social Security and Medicare than for all of the other governmental programs combined. Employers and employees together contribute **15.3%** to Social Security and Medicare, whereas most taxpayers (80%) pay an average of only **14.7%** in federal taxes. No wonder Washington wanted to tap into this lucrative reservoir.

An irresponsible President Obama, Republican House, and Democratic Senate cut funding to the Social Security fund by over a third just when the first Boomers began to receive the benefit in 2010. The reason they lowered the payroll tax was to stimulate the economy, which was likely a good idea, but they could have just as easily lowered the income tax rate or provided a tax rebate. Instead of heading off the looming crisis, they made it worse. Prior to their actions, Social Security would run out of funds in 2036. By 2012, it would run out by 2033. (The full rate was restored in 2013.)

On January 1st 2008, the first Boomers received reduced Social Security payments at 62, the average retirement age. Then, on January 1st 2011, they received Medicare and in 2012, received full Social Security payments. They and their employers contributed up to 15% of their salaries into Social Security and Medicare since 1962.

The problem with Social Security is not funding. Employees and employers have been contributing to the fund for over 75 years. The problem is that Congress irresponsibly spent the money particularly over the last dozen critical years. Some politicians want to cut back benefits or do away with Social Security altogether.

Washington spends more on defense than any other program, substantially more than on Social Security. Spending on defense over the last ten years was over **7.6 trillion dollars**, or half the national debt. Over the same period, Social Security spending constituted $6.16 trillion.

Retirees are extremely conscientious voters who vote in much larger percentages than their children do. The Boomers will constitute the largest voting block in history with unparalleled political power. Imagine all of these former workaholics; former protesters having nothing better to do than vote.   Fortunately or unfortunately, it will be politically difficult to cut back drastically on benefits promised to them, especially for those nearing or in retirement.   Today, politicians risk their seat anytime they mention Social Security.   Imagine what it will be like in ten years when the retiree voter block is 50% larger.   The time to start funding the obligations was ten years ago when the budget was balanced.

The Bill is due

The bill for the excess is due.   Who does Washington owe the $16,750,000,000,000(September, 2013) and growing debt too?

Who Owns U.S. Debt

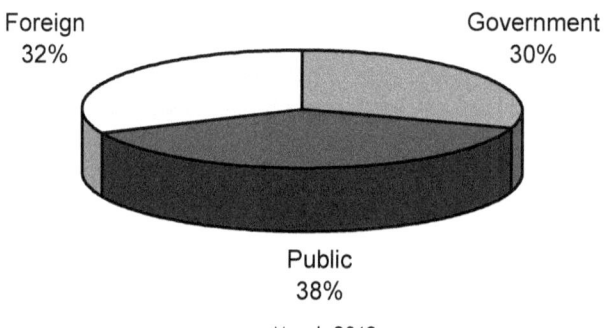

Foreign
32%

Government
30%

Public
38%

March 2012

- The government owns **30%** of the national debt largely due to Social Security, but as this obligation matures, Washington must find a source of funds to pay back this portion of the debt.
- The public owns **38%** of the debt primarily through treasuries.
- Foreign governments own **32%**, of which China and Japan hold approximately 8% each.

So retirees, the public and foreign governments each hold about 1/3rd of the debt.

Oddly, the Boomers, in effect, own much of that bill. About half of the government's portion of the debt is owed to Social Security largely accruing to the Boomers.   Treasuries secure the public portion of the debt. The largest buyers of treasuries are pension funds, 401(k)s, mutual funds, and investors saving for retirement, all of whom are now buying treasuries primarily to fund Boomer retirements.   A rough calculation shows that approximately **43%** of the debt is owed to Boomers through various vehicles used to help fund their nearly $30 trillion retirement.

(13 yr average retirement x $35,000 per yr, including SS and Medicare, x 65 million Boomers)

Business Implications

S&P 500 businesses, unlike consumers, the financial industry and all levels of government, typically manage their financial house well. With two trillion dollars in cash reserves in 2013, they demonstrated with the help of their Enterprise Resource Planning Systems that they can respond quickly to financial downturns. Up until now, business leadership has been conspicuously absent from the debate. Jamie Diamond of Chase (the same person criticized regarding multi- billion dollar derivative losses) convened a group of business execs to promote deficit curbs. Business has much to lose if we experience another serious downturn and are not able to manage our finances better, not to mention the loss of executive stock option values if the market should crash again. Diamond raised some interesting points in his Sunday May 12th, 2012 interview with David Gregory on *Meet the Press*.

- He called Washington and Wall Street the epicenter of the financial crisis.
- He favors higher progressive taxes on wealthy Americans including higher taxes on capital gains, since they benefit most from the stability and prosperity the U.S. offers.
- He favors Simpson Bowles, which he thinks is a fabulous road map to solving our financial problems. Simpson Bowles represented a bipartisan commission authorized by President Obama. Their plan contained a well-reasoned and balanced mix of budgetary cuts and revenue enhancements.
- He agrees with 80% of Dodd Frank and believes banks should be accountable including repeal of "Too big to fail." If a bank gambles and fails, they should be broken up. (Although Chase spends more money lobbying against Dodd Frank than any other.)
- Derivatives should be regulated (to a degree).

Sandy Weill the former CEO of Citi Bank favors splitting up the banks. While at Citi, he was credited as the major force for smashing the Glass-Stegall act, passed after the Great Depression that separated banks from investment houses. Many think the repeal led directly to the Great Recession, because banks were allowed to gamble with investors funds. Since they were too big to fail, taxpayers picked up the tab. On July 25th, 2012 Weill told CNBC, "What we should probably do is go and split up investment banking from banking, have banks be deposit takers, have banks make commercial loans and real estate loans, and have banks do something that's not going to risk the taxpayer dollars, that's not going to be too big to fail."

Weill added that he thought the banks would be more profitable if they were broken up and that the markets would function better.

Before the Great Depression back to 1792, major financial calamities occurred every 15 – 20 years. After the passage of Glass Steagall, we went nearly 50 years before another banking crisis; until the 70s malaise when once again thousands of banks failed, leading to the supposition that the reform actually worked. Still, we did not have another banking crisis until after its repeal.

The immense Boomers wealth is switching to a risk off mode - exchanging growth stocks, for value stocks, corporate and government bonds. Dividend paying stocks, out of favor during the boom, will be in demand; therefore, corporations will need to increase their dividends to stem the tide of investment leaving their stocks.

Growth stocks will find it increasingly difficult to obtain funds leading to less investment and a slower rate of change, since growth stocks by definition lead the way to innovation. None of this will happen overnight and there are countervailing Xer and Millennial forces, plus as the Boomers pass their estates to their younger postagentur, their heirs will invest in riskier alternatives. Still, the predominance of force in the market for sometime will be conservative.

Wall Street

Charles Ferguson in "Predator Nation," shows that even though Wall Streeters violated several laws such as Sarbanes-Oxley, no one has been prosecuted in the five years since the infractions.

PBS's Frontline featured a report regarding the lack of Wall Street prosecutions and convictions on January 22, 2013. Prior to the financial crisis there was widespread mortgage fraud spurred on by Wall Street firm's ravenous appetite to acquire all the mortgages they could to build their security bundles. Numerous due diligence underwriters, such as Tom Leonard said they were told to pass through obviously "fraudulent" mortgages for those who did not have jobs, or income. According to Richard Bowen, senior VP and chief underwriter for Citibank, 60% of the mortgages Citi held did not meet their own criteria. Yet, no Wall Street executives were convicted of fraud.

With no moral hazard, driven by greed and with a dysfunctional, captive Washington, Wall Street may cause yet another financial crisis likely by 2016. The later this happens the worse it will be. Think of a volcano building pressure about to erupt or a fault line about to quake. There are some leaders who could avoid this crisis, but it is doubtful their voices will overcome bi-partisan opposition. The financial downturn, driven by possibly **one-quadrillion** dollars of shadow derivatives by then, could be nearly as bad as the last time. This time, however, if the crash is severe, the public outcry will be deafening with a symbolic lynch mob demanding Wall Street and Washington heads. As in the 1930s, a galvanized public will demand pervasive reformation. Realizing the kind of actions that could occur, it would be in Wall Street's best interest to cooperate in avoiding such a calamity, something they have not yet been able to do.

According to the Social Security Administration's (SSA) 2012 Trustees Report, since 2010, the fund takes in less than it pays out, due to reduced tax rates.* Washington spent excess Social Security (SS) receipts, promising to pay these back in the future. The future is here and Washington must now pay the SS fund back, so SSA can make its promised payments. Initially, it will pay the interest out but starting in 2020, it will have to pay principle too. Instead of spending excess funds as it has up until now, Washington will have to find additional funding for its debt to SSA, likely by selling more treasury bonds if it can.

Since aging Boomers around the world are exchanging stocks for bonds, the government will initially find buyers for this added debt. Soon, the Boomers will start cashing in those bonds to provide for their retirement expenses. Expect this to happen around 2018 when half of the Boomers are retired and draw off annuities, pensions, 401(k)s, and bond funds heavily invested in treasuries to fund retirement expenses. By then, if not before, the market for treasuries will reverse. Since there will be a declining demand for treasuries, interest rates on treasury bills and bonds will escalate. Think of the stimulus roller coaster. 2018 will be the point where the coaster accelerates quickly.

Once the Boomers start selling their treasury bonds, we should be able to go to China to ask them to purchase these - right?

China

China has been a consistent source for buying U.S. debt. When the Boomers and pension plans start cashing in their treasury Bonds to pay for retirement expenses, will Washington be able to sell more treasuries to China? The boom in Chinese manufacturing in the 1990s and 2000s provided China with more revenue than they could possibly invest or spend, so they bought vast sums of the safest investments they could find at the time- U.S. treasuries, which now earn little, when considering inflation and future dollar depreciation.

Buying U.S. treasuries offers an additional political advantage to China, who in 2011 had a nearly $300 billon trade surplus with the U.S., 3 ½ times that of 2001. Up until the passage of the income tax in 1913, funding for the federal government came from tariffs. Washington could have enacted legislation to impose tariffs on unfair Chinese trade practices and an undervalued yuan. China might have retaliated by imposing tariffs on U.S. goods, but the preponderance of trade was in their favor, so a trade war would have hurt China and surprisingly helped U.S. finances and employment. Losing those approximately five million highly paid, largely manufacturing jobs cost Washington about **$100**

billion in annual tax revenues from those employees or a $1 trillion in 10 years, coincidently about what we owe China.

Free trade makes sense, but Washington could have instituted a fairer game by making it a little difficult for millions of manufacturing jobs to flow to factories in China effectively slowing the rate of departure as they did in protecting U.S. agriculture. Up until 30 years ago, it made sense to protect agriculture as the source of our food supply. Similarly, it makes sense to protect our manufacturing base as the source of our military supplies.

Imagine that we relied on Asian manufactures for our auto and aviation industries as we now do for our steel and electronics. All of these are components of defense products. In the unlikely event that we entered a war with China over the South China Sea or Korea we could not go to China to supply us with the goods we need to furnish our war effort. Since there is no peace accord, technically, we are still at war with North Korea and China their ally, the last major power we fought in the 1950s.

In the 1990s, China spent millions of dollars on lobbying and funding for U.S. political campaigns. China helped Washington finance its excessive spending habits by using a portion of its profits from U.S. trade in the 2000s. Now, China has leverage over U.S. policy. If the U.S. threatens to enact severe trade restrictions, China can threaten to sell massive amounts of treasuries, hampering Washington's ability to fund excess spending. Therefore, China and the U.S. have a codependent relationship.

As the second largest and soon to be largest economy in the world, China in its own best interest must foresee better investment alternatives. Enduring thousands of protests, civil unrest plagues communist China and it must appease its justifiably restless populous with higher pay, higher employment, momentous building, and infrastructure projects. China now has a larger middle class than all of the U.S.'s population, who demand more consumer goods, which require exhaustive supplies of raw materials China cannot supply itself. Surprisingly for a Communist society, according to the Boston Consulting Group, the top 1% of households control more than 70% of the nation's private financial wealth.* As an example, China now buys more cars than the U.S. They have an insatiable demand for iron ore, rice, wheat, corn, beef, oil, pork, copper, silver, gold, seafood, lumber, old computers, etc.

Wisely, they are investing in Africa and South America to supply the escalating number of resources they need to feed the demand of their burgeoning middle class and factories. After unsuccessful initial entrees into developed markets, similar to Japan in the 1980s, China is starting to buy strategic stakes in U.S. and European companies too. China also promotes a multi-national common currency versus the dollar, which to the degree this movement eventually succeeds, it will certainly diminish the dollar's added value as the world's currency.

China is very aware of our leadership's dysfunctional inability to solve our debt problems and our lowered credit ratings. They see what is happening in Europe and in their immense trading partner California. Indeed tens of thousands of Chinese expatriates live in Orange County, to the extent that many signs are in both English and Mandarin. Like any investor, they do not want to see the value of their investment in U.S. treasuries devalued. It would be politically unwise to sell massive quantities of treasuries, which will drive down the value of that investment. But, it may also be unwise to buy large additional positions, which will lose value when interest rates climb.

Unlike the U.S., China's political leadership is composed of engineers and quantitative businessmen who likely created models to see what will happen to U.S. debt over the next decade. They know the laws of supply and demand; what will happen to U.S. interest rates; and the marketability of treasuries over the next decade.

Soon China will find higher paying sources for investment other than treasuries and will not purchase additional hundreds of billions of dollars of U.S. debt. With ever-higher wages and a growing appetite for raw materials and goods, China is rapidly becoming a consumer-based economy both on the individual and national level. In this pseudo-communist nation, the poor clamor to have a piece of the pie and as China's economy cools, the poor will demand more employment and social services that will reduce China's surplus and available cash to invest in U.S. debt. Besides, China will continue to find more productive uses for surpluses other than receiving low real interest for potentially risky treasuries.

China's Chief Investment Officer for its $3.4 trillion of foreign reserves is Zhu Changhong, who spent 20 years in the U.S. starting with studying quantum physics at the University of Chicago. He was CEO, Bill Gross's right hand man at PIMCO, the huge U.S. investment firm. Zhu favors investing in diverse worldwide assets including U.S. bonds, equities, and real estate rather than just treasuries.*

Europe may recover and their debt will be more marketable than U.S. debt. Even if Europe does not recover, their debt will be on more of a par with U.S. debt as we will see in the next chapters. The Boomers will soon be cashing in treasuries. Therefore, a triple convergence appears on the horizon, in which European debt becomes more marketable, Boomers sell instead of buy U.S. debt, and China is no longer interested in the debt. Along with an unrestrained deficit and increasing interest rates, Washington faces a challenging future.

Hopefully, the U.S. will find the strength of leadership to avert another looming crisis otherwise we face an extended period of stagflation likely worse that the 70s malaise.

16

Leadership Implications

The Financial Time Machine presents a picture of stagnant U.S. economy until the 2020s. This picture will likely be composed of periods of moderate GDP growth followed by near zero growth or recessions. Exactly how this scenario plays out depends upon national leadership, which will influence the severity of the periodic downturns, and when we will finally reach robust growth again. In the next section, we will see some examples from Europe and Japan of how they have dealt with their similar generational economically induced, economic downward cycle. Since the Great Recession, some European countries have experienced triple dip recessions, while Japan has had two decades of deflation and stagnation. There are many similarities between the U.S. and these nations, such that we could a face similar fate. Whether we experience this fate or not depends upon the quality and character of our leadership - the topic of this chapter.

In the spring of 2012, I attended a presentation by David Walker, the former Comptroller General of the United States, who spoke about the pending U.S. financial crisis. He persistently advocates for fiscal responsibility, pointing out that our national debt as a percentage of GDP approaches that of many of the troubled Euro nations, such as Greece.

Below is a chart displaying the Debt to GDP ratio for the PIIGS nations (Portugal, Italy, Ireland, Greece, and Spain) that are the most troubled and in danger of default. The U.S.'s ratio is also included for comparison. Spain, one of the most troubled European nations has a debt ratio less than ours.

2011 PIIGS Debt to GDP ratios with U.S.

	Country	Debt/GDP
1.	Greece	178.9%
2.	Italy	122.0%
3.	Portugal	121.6%
4.	Ireland	112.2%
5.	U.S.	97.9%[1]
6.	Spain	77.1%

2013 U.S. ranking among PIIGS

	Country	Debt/GDP
1.	Greece	183.7%
2.	Italy	143.6%
4.	Portugal	142.8%
5.	Ireland	129.3%
3.	U.S.	106.5%[1]
6.	Spain	97.8%

PIIGS ratios from OECD, June 13, 2013
PIIGS figures include all Government debt,
1. U.S figures include only Federal Debt

The first chart contains 2011 figures, which for the U.S. were still under 100%. USGovernmentSpending.com shows the Federal Gross Debt/GDP ratio in 2012 was **103.3%**, rising above 100% for the first time in decades. In 2013, they project our ratio to be **106.5%**, still above that of Spain.

Including state and local governments' debts, our Gross Public debt ratio is **125%** in 2013, which is more comparable to the PIIGS total public debt ratios. Notice that this ratio is above all except Greece's in 2011, leading to the supposition that we may be only two years behind them. The lower Federal number is the one we typically focus on. Of course, all of these nations introduced measures to reduce their spending, which unfortunately did not result in a lowering of the PIIGS debt ratio, highlighting how difficult it is to reverse a high ratio once it exceeds 90%.

The accepted and well-documented wisdom is that up until your debt as a percentage of GDP reaches 90% you are OK; beyond that point, growth slows and there is a much higher possibility of default, which is playing out in Europe.

Harvard professors Carmen Reinhart and Ken Rogoff conducted a much-quoted study of world economies from 1790 through 2009. Their findings show that when the GDP/Debt ratio was lower than 90%, developed economies grew in excess of 3% on average. It mattered little whether the ratio was below 30%, 30-60%, or 60-90%. When the ratio exceeded 90%, however, the economies grew at less than 2%.

Interestingly, the U.S.'s rate averaged 2.67% prior to the Great Recession and .5% since, further supporting their results. Our debt exceeded 90% in 2010 for the first time since 1949, just after WW II.*

Reinhart and Rogoff performed extensive research on dozens of countries over centuries to compile their data, but there is intuitive logic to what they say. As your personal debt rises, you pay a higher percentage of your income to interest payments, and you are less able to invest those funds for the future growth. Many of us have seen this principle at work with respect to credit cards. When we overload our cards, the interest payments eventually become so large we can no longer contribute to our 401(k).

A University of Massachusetts grad student recently found some errors in Reinhart and Rogoff's calculations, but their case is still compelling as the following simple analysis portrays.

Following is a chart displaying Reinhart and Rogoff's growth rates for three different Debt/GDP ratios.

Debt/GDP	Growth
80%	3.1%
90%	2.8%
100%	1.9%

If we apply their analysis to the U.S. using the 2011 GDP figures of $15 billion, we see what the debt will be at each of the Debt/GDP ratios.

Debt/GDP Effects
(In Billions)

Debt/GDP	Growth	Debt
80%	3.1%	$12,000
90%	2.8%	$13,500
100%	1.9%	$15,000

Assume real GDP = $15,000 billion

As Debt/GDP grows, creditors become less confident in the debtor's ability to pay and interest rates tend to grow. The credit rating will be lower as happened to the U.S., which usually results in higher rates. The PIIGS nations pay substantially higher interest rates (2-5%) than Germany with its lower Debt/GDP ratio. Those who have high credit card balances typically pay much higher interest rates on their cards and on their mortgages, because of their lower credit rating. In the example below, the real interest rate rises as the Debt/GDP rises. In reality, the rise may be steeper as is the case in Europe.

Debt/GDP Effects
(In Billions)

Debt/GDP	Growth	Debt	Interest Rate	Interest
80%	3.1%	$12,000	3%	$360
90%	2.8%	$13,500	3.5%	$472
100%	1.9%	$15,000	4%	$600

To the previous chart, we added an escalating interest rate based on a declining credit rating. The spread on these rates would likely be higher.

The next column shows the corresponding Interest (Debt x Interest Rate.)

Debt/GDP Effects
(In Billions)

Debt/ GDP	Growth	Debt	Interest Rate	Interest	Added GDP
80%	3.1%	$12,000	3%	$360	$465
90%	2.8%	$13,500	3.5%	$472	$420
100%	1.9%	$15,000	4%	$600	$285

The last column contains the amount added to GDP according to each of Reinhart and Rogoff's growth rates using a $15 trillion GDP (Added GDP = $15 trilllion x Growth Rate.)

Now let's compare the Interest to the Added GDP. Notice that at the 80% Debt/GDP level, the added GDP exceeds the interest payments. Therefore, the economy is still performing well.

At 90%, the two are about equal, but at the 100% level, the interest payment is more than twice the added GDP. With substantially more revenue going into interest payments, it becomes harder to invest in programs to grow the economy, such as infrastructure, research, or education. This is a Catch 22, because with lower growth, it becomes progressively harder to make the payments. According to Reinhart and Rogoff, such a cycle can last for 10 to 20 years as it did in Japan and in numerous other countries over the last 200 years.

A National Bureau of Economic Research paper studied advanced economies since 1900 finding 21 cases where the Debt/GDP exceeded 90%. These periods of high Debt/GDP lasted an average of **14** years.* Interestingly, the FTM arrives at the same conclusion from a different perspective. Therefore, the analyses by Reinhart and Rogoff and National Bureau of Economic Research corroborate the conclusions of the Financial Time Machine.

The Deficit

Under the Bush and Obama administrations, the deficit tripled primarily due to the seven factors listed below.

1. Two expensive wars
2. Tax breaks for all
3. The Great Recession
4. Bank bailouts under TARP
5. Stimulus spending
6. Social spending
7. High unemployment

Thanks to historically low interest rates, the interest on the debt was only around $225 billion a year in 2012. However, when interest rates go up to more traditional levels of 5.5%, the interest will be around **one trillion** dollars, which is **$13,000** for the average American family per year (just for interest.) Even though S&P lowered the U.S. credit rating for the first time since 1917, we still do not have a difficult time finding buyers for our debt, although this situation will change. (The only thing that is constant is change.)

A major reason the U.S. can still obtain buyers for its debt is due to the economic difficulties in Europe, whose bonds are presently riskier than the U.S.'s. Once their economy improves and they solve their financial problems, their debt will become relatively more marketable and the focus will shift to the U.S.

China also realized that the long-term U.S. picture is unsustainable and started to diversify its investments in itself, the U.S., Europe, Asia, the Middle East, South America, Africa, and even Canada. Western Canada now exports more oil to China than the U.S. Much of China's investments buy infrastructure and equipment to harvest commodities such as oil, minerals, and timber in South America and Africa, but they are also starting to buy large portions of U.S. corporations like a U.S. bank and the fracking company Chesapeake, who is buying up rich Eastern Ohio oil shale rights. So, in effect, China now owns a portion of energy mineral rights to Ohio land.

When the return on downgraded U.S. government debt is only 2%; why not buy higher returning assets? The China Investment Corporation, a Chinese sovereign wealth fund, underweighted its investments in European bonds, due to expected low returns and high risks, indicating it would do the same with U.S. treasuries if these were no longer a wise investment. Plus the consumer side of China's economy is growing at a record pace, such that China's balance of trade with the world is more equal (some months they import more from developing countries than they export to the rest of the world).*

Eventually these two factors - China's declining U.S. debt investment and the end of Europe's financial crisis will lead to serious problems for growing U.S. debt. It is doubtful the two factors will hold off for longer than five years. Think of hurricane Sandy, which ravaged the Northeast coast in late 2012. Although, it was only a category 1 hurricane, the jet stream, and a full moon tide combined to magnify its deadly storm surge.

Both the Republican and Democratic leadership in Congress and Presidents Bush and Obama have been ineffective in solving a problem obvious for at least 20 years. Few think we will avoid the PIIGS fate of increased taxes, decreased public expenditures, and high unemployment. All we have to do is look in our own backyard, at the budget struggles and cutbacks of most American states and municipalities. California as the 9th largest economy in the world might be the 800-pound canary in the coalmine, as the state continually struggles to manage its budget ($16 billion deficit and 11% unemployment in 2012.)*

States

For over 40 years, the states continually increased their budgets through two mechanisms. Most states receive revenue from property, income, and/or sales tax. In good times, property values, income, and sales rise, so the states receive more money that they find ways to spend. In bad times, the states merely raise taxes to fund their operations. As a result, state budgets grew at a nearly constant rate of 7.5% per year for 30 years - over an eight-fold increase growing from 6% to **10%** of U.S. GDP.*

Despite five recessions, state spending never waned. Even after the Great Recession started in 2007 - pumped up by Federal funding for teachers, police, fire, and construction projects - state budgets still grew until 2011. It used to be that government employees received less pay than their private employee counterparts, which seemed somewhat justified with their added job security and benefits. Now, government employees earn 20% more than private employees and still have unrivaled benefits such as early, unreduced retirement pensions, although layoffs are now more common.

Pensions represent a nearly $1 trillion spending gap for the states. Since 2009, 45 states cut benefits trimming $100 billion from their budgets.*   These cuts do not include local guarantees for municipalities and counties, which are likely even higher. Several cities, particularly in California, such as Stockton, went bankrupt, although Detroit is the largest. The cost of funding state and local pension contributions has risen rapidly from 6% of their budgets in 2001 to 16% in 2012.*

The states must balance their budgets; but when housing prices crashed, their property tax revenue plummeted.   The federal government does not have the same balanced budget mandate. When their revenues go down, they continue to spend, sometimes even more. In FY 2012, Washington spent **35%** more than they took in. Even though states continually increased budgets through a combination of escalating property values and higher taxes, the states eventually faced a wall of expense they could not easily climb over, but instead had to chip away at. Without any effective checks and balances, Washington has been able to avoid the debt wall, but the wall has grown disproportionately large and will be much more difficult to surmount.

How bad is the current downturn?

Although it is debatable, most economists believe the Great Recession would have been far worse without three to four trillion dollars of bank and spending stimulus support from Washington. Normally, such a huge sum would have brought us out of a typical recession and back to traditional levels of employment and growth, yet five years afterwards, we still struggle with anemic growth and high unemployment. The Congressional Budget Office predicted we would enter another recession at the start of 2013 if the stimulus ends, leading to an approximately 3% drop in GDP. Their analysis supports the conclusion that the continued stimulus avoided an even more severe recession or depression. Why is this recession different from every other recession over the last 70 years?

Generational economics provides the answer. The record setting stimulus the Boomer wave provided the economy is depleting and we are in a new economic paradigm, in which the correction machinery of the last 70 years no longer operates well. Just look at the nearly powerless Fed. They have a set of tools that worked in the old paradigm, but in the new paradigm, these tools are largely ineffective. The Fed's typical tool of lowering interest rates can go no lower than zero and the bond buyback strategies of Quantitative Easing (QE) I, II, and III may hurt the economy as much as these help by raising commodity prices and increasing inflation. In an interview with CNBC's Maria Bartiromo on June 30th, 2011, long-term former Fed chair, Alan Greenspan said he did not think QE I & II helped the economy much.

> "Let me tell you why. Not only QE2 but QE1 has not been spent. A trillion and a half dollars, which is excess reserves have, to my estimation, not been spent. The way you can tell that is that the money multiplier, a ratio of the expansion of credit in the commercial banks and the monetary base, which reflects the expansion of the federal reserve balance sheet, that has changed not at all. You can see it in the fact C&I loans are rarely moving. Mortgages, if anything, are weakening in numbers and consumer credit is very dull, so that there is no evidence that huge inflow of money into the system basically worked."

For nearly 240 years, a rapidly increasing population provided ever-expanding stimulus to the economy. Our industrial and governmental institutions were in a sense addicted to this stimulus and continuously planned on more of it. Just look at the increase in federal and state spending over the last 60 years. Business also grew addicted to an ever-increasing marketplace with consistently more consumers spending continuously more. They faced competition, but at least their potential market grew.

The odd aspect is that the potential stimulus is still growing just at a much lower pace. Business, which is accustomed to periodic cycles, adjusts rapidly. By transferring hundreds of billions of dollars to local and state governments, Washington insulated them from adjustments for three years, but now they also experienced stimulus withdrawal pains. Eventually, Washington will have to adjust to less external stimulus. The longer it waits the more painful it will be. Like other businesses, Wall Street too will have to adjust to lower economic stimulus levels as the

Boomers cash in their myriad retirement vehicles. They may go to Washington to supply them with another round of artificial government manufactured stimulus, but Washington's ability to do so will steadily diminish.

Everyone realizes that the Great Recession is the worst since the Great Depression. At this time, we do not know how long this trying period will last, just as in the 1930s they did not know how long the Great Depression would last. Many economists blame President Hoover's policies for worsening the recession. By the mid 1930s, it appeared we were climbing out of the Depression, but in 1937, another severe recession sent unemployment back up to 19%. Many attribute this recession to either an attempt to balance the budget after the New Deal or tight Fed monetary policy. The history lesson there is that the quality of leadership can extend the current financial downturn or lead to better times.

The other point is that like the 1930s, no one knows how long the downturn will last. By the classic definition of two consecutive declining quarters, the recession ended in the summer of 2009, but each year growth slows and by summer, the market swoons as the possibility of recession looms. In the 4th quarter of 2012, five years after the start of the Great Recession, the economy declined by .1%. The average growth for the first 3 years following a recession has been averaged 4.23%, but this time it was only 2.07% or less than half the historical level.*

The Financial Time Machine predicts the economy will be stagnant until the early 2020s. This seems like an extremely long period - 15 or more years. For the Boomers and subsequent generations, downturns represented by recessions did not last longer than a year or two before GDP growth and unemployment returned to normal levels.

If we look at the economy from 30,000 feet versus 2,000 feet, we see a broader picture emerging beyond mere recessions. The 70s malaise with four recessions lasted 13 years. During that time, the individual recessions did not last longer than two years, but unemployment reached 10.8%.

After the 70s malaise, when the Boomers were at their peak stimulus level, we had a boom period that lasted a remarkable 25 years, with only two relatively mild recessions of 8 months and no more than 8% unemployment. There had been a similar boom period from the late 1940s through 60s, when the Greatest were at their peak that lasted 24 years. Below is the 30,000-foot view of the economy gleaned from the Financial Time Machine's analysis.

Economic Cycles

Economic Period	Dominant Generation	Years	Length	Reces-sions	Max Decline	Max Unemp
Great Depression & WWII	20th Century Millennials	1929-45	16 yrs.	3	-26.7%	24.9%
50s/60s Boom	Greatest	1945-69	24 yrs.	4	-3.7%	7.9%
70s Malaise	Silents	1970-82	13 yrs.	4	-3.2%	10.8%
80s/90s Boom	Boomers	1983-07	25 yrs.	2	-1.4%	7.8%
Great Recession	Xers	2008-23 ?	15 yrs?	3	-5.1%	10%

In the chart above, the busts occupy the darker sections, whereas the lighter sections contain the boom periods. When we look at the economy from this higher vantage point, the projected 15-year length of the Great Recession downturn does not seem unusual. The other impression we observe is that the economic cycles composed of a bust and boom last about 40 years, the length of two generations.

The two previous downturns lasted 13 and 16 years, so 15 years for the Great Recession seems in line, especially when considering it is already worse than the 70s malaise with little real GDP growth in nearly 5 years. Fifteen years is also the length of the dominant generation, in their peak at this time – the Xers.

As we saw earlier, the economic cycles extend back to at least the 1840s, creating a wave pattern of cycles over 180 years with four expansion waves occurring when the larger generations are in their peaks and four contraction troughs when the smaller generations are in their peaks.

Stimulus

It is difficult to estimate the value of stimulus spending, but the much discussed fiscal cliff analyses by numerous reliable sources provides a reasonable accounting of the stimulus's contribution to GDP growth. The unbiased Congressional Budget Office (CBO) conducted an assessment of the drag upon the economy of the Fiscal Cliff in May of 2012. The Fiscal Cliff refers to several events that would have occurred on January 1, 2013 including:

Expiration of the Bush tax cuts,
Expiration of emergency unemployment compensation,
Expiration of employee payroll tax reduction, and

Implementation of the Budget Control Act of 2011.

[It took until January 2013 when Congress reconvened to reach a compromise and narrowly avoid the fiscal cliff.]

Even though these actions increase the budget, they also stimulate the economy. The focus of the fiscal cliff discussion was upon how much the expiration of each of these measures decrease the GDP when the economy is barely recovering. Various interested parties quantified the drag on the economy for each measure, which interestingly gives us an accounting of the value of the stimulus. Prior to the cliff there was no such accounting, but when these were about to expire there was.

The CBO estimates the cliff's effect would produce a -.8 to -4.4% drag upon GDP, enough to send the U.S. into a mild recession in the first half of 2013.* Others project a 2-3% GDP reduction. The Fiscal Cliff is the kind of crisis Congress pays attention to, but it still took them to the New Year to address it.

Eighty percent of the components of the Fiscal Cliff are due to taxes and stimulus expirations. The CBO's analysis postulates that these factors contribute on average nearly **2%** to GDP growth. In the first half of 2011, the economy only grew at 1.3% and in the first half of 2012, it grew at about 2%. **Therefore, the absence of stimulus and increased taxes would have sent us into a recession in either 2011 or 2012.**

Nobel Prize winner Paul Krugman and Keynesian economics argue that we need even more stimulus to revise the economy. Economists think Keynesian tools worked well during the Great Depression, and the Bush and Obama stimulus spending did help to avoid a more calamitous recession, but the approach is dated. In a digital age when stocks are traded in microseconds, we need a more advanced economic toolbox and philosophy. It was not obvious in the 1930s what would work and what would not work. Many argued against stimulus as they do today. Programs like unemployment insurance, social security insurance, workers compensation, federal deposit insurance, and social security emerged then. The low national debt provided more room to maneuver.

Now, largely due to these progressive programs, our debt is high and there is less room to maneuver. We need new thinking, new strategies, and new ideas that the current political environment does not seem capable of spawning. Whether you agree with these or not, Bush's TARP plan, Obama's stimulus program, and the auto bailout were bold ideas conceived and implemented rapidly under extreme pressure. Do we have to have another crisis before leadership acts?

AIG constituted the largest recipient of TARP money garnering $182 billion. Recently the U.S. sold its remaining interest in AIG receiving a previously unfathomable profit of $22.7 billion for their AIG stock. As of December 2012, they recovered 90% of the $418 billion in TARP funds.*

Financing the debt - when will the bond bubble burst

Despite the dire circumstances, the current environment is ideal for growing U.S. debt: the sun is shining, it's hot, and we have plenty of water, but a cold wind is blowing as economic winter approaches. Due to the worldwide Boomer generation's ongoing retirement, there likely are over a **hundred trillion** dollars in the developed world's pension, social security, investment, and savings accounts steadily switching to fixed income investments. In some cases, funds mandate investing in AAA bonds. These funds currently invest in U.S. debt because of reduced European credit ratings and riskier emerging market debt.

Think of the now popular retirement date accounts, which automatically switch the client's balance from equities to bonds as the participant approaches the stated retirement date. For instance, take a 2020 retirement account of $100,000. In 2000, only 30% is in fixed assets, but by 2020 70% is. Each year the fund manager transfers 5% ($5,000) from stocks to bonds. This same effect is occurring for hundreds of millions of Boomers throughout the developed world.

There is one primary factor still supporting U.S. debt - namely the Boomers continued trading of equity for safer investments. As they approach retirement and retire, they will convert more of their stocks to bonds, annuities, CDs, and cash. According to AON Hewitt, the portion allocated to stocks in 401(k)s fell from 70% in 2007 to 61% in 2012, supporting our analysis.* A large portion of these investments are in treasury bonds and bills.

According to Liz Ann Sonders, Chief Investment Officer of Schwab, from 2007 until the middle of 2012, investors took $500 billion out of stocks and invested $800 billion into bonds.* By 2013, investors had invested $1 trillion more in bonds than equity, according to Bryon Olson, President of Windhaven Investment funds.* Initially, investors left equities because of the drastic downturn, but despite the market's rise since the recession ended and low bond returns, investors did not return. The Financial Time Machine predicted this result.

As Boomers retire, they will start using these investments to fund their retirement - they will sell treasury bills and bonds. Since only early Boomers have retired thus far, more Boomers are converting to bonds than depleting bonds, but this will soon change. The situation applies not only to individual, but also to pension funds, who according to Olson, for the first time in financial history, have more invested in fixed income than equities. Of course, the primary reason is that these funds will fund record boomer payouts, which for many closed plans is their last.

From 2003 until 2013, the demand for bonds has increased at a rapid pace. After 2013, the demand will slow as it approaches its peak. In 2018, the mid-point of the Boomers will reach the average retirement age. Up until that point, more Boomers will buy bonds then sell. After then, the cashing in of bonds will progress at a break neck pace.

The Generational Economic model supports the analysis as the following chart displaying the sum of Boomer savings propensities shows.

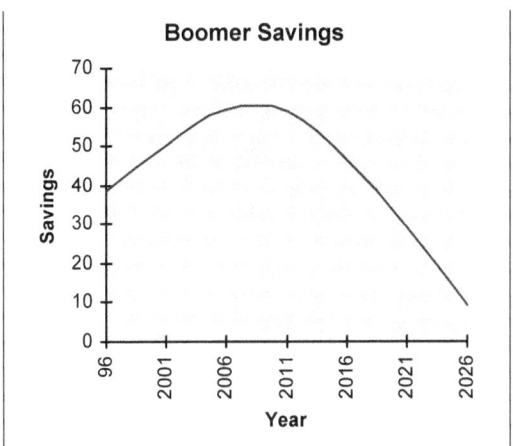

Sum of 5-year savings for all the Boomers.

Boomer savings peaked in 2006, declining only slightly until 2011. Notice how fast Boomer savings decline after 2011. Boomer investment in stocks started to decline in 2008, since they were transferring investment from stocks to bonds in anticipation of retirement.

Here is the Boomer investment scenario:

1. Boomer savings increased steadily until early 2000s.
2. As Boomers get close to retirement and retire, they convert stocks to bonds.
3. Demand for bonds increases until approximately 2018.
4. Boomers sell bonds to finance retirements.
5. After 2018, demand for bonds decreases.
6. With a lower demand, bond interest rates climb rapidly.

Boomer investment, particularly related to savings, is one of four mega-legs supporting U.S. deficits and mounting debt noted below:

1. Record Boomer savings
2. Boomer conversion from stocks to fixed assets, primarily treasuries
3. Downgrading of European debt relative to U.S. debt
4. Foreign investment in U.S. debt primarily by China and Japan, but also by other nations.

There are several implications of this fortunate or unfortunate quadruple convergence. Fortunate, because there are currently plenty of buyers for U.S. debt. Unfortunate, because U.S. leadership does not have to focus on the debt problems until these factors are that much worse.

Implications

1. Demand for U.S. debt is high leading to extremely low rates. The Feds monetary policy is also keeping rates low, but generational economics plays a large role in the policy working. If there were no market for U.S. debt, rates would be much higher.
2. Boomers will start selling treasuries to finance their retirement expenses at an ever increasing pace starting in about 2018.
3. Eventually Europe will climb out of its current financial morass and its debt will be more marketable versus the U.S.'s.
4. As U.S. debt becomes relatively more risky, China and other nations owning U.S. debt will reduce their relative stakes in U.S. debt.
5. Interest rates on treasuries will rise at a rapid pace.
6. Higher interest payments will make it more difficult for the U.S. to pay off debt or expand its budget.

The Euro crisis has gone on for four years and continues to flog the stock market. The Weatherhead Business School of Case Western Reserve University sponsors a semiannual Economic Forecast Luncheon attended by hundreds of financial managers and executives. Dr Samuel Thomas conducts the forecast, which I attended for several years. In 2008, before the scope of Europe's financial problems were known; he predicted that they would struggle until the banks fully disclosed the scope of their troubled loans. He said, because of their multi-national constituency, it might take years.

Sure enough, his predictions have come true. Periodically it seems like we know everything about the crisis and action is taken to end it, but then we learn of yet another problem. The latest revelation involves Spain's troubled banks, which will likely require tens if not hundreds of billions of euros to bandage. Spain has done a remarkable job of denying the depth of the troubled housing loans. To our credit, the U.S. realized the full extent of the banking problems and applied massive amounts of stimulus, which weathered the storm. Europe's approach has been to address a small part of the problem at a time, hoping it will just go away.

In reality, what we see is an inflating debt bubble with the Boomers, and Europe supporting the bubble. By 2018, the bubble will burst, and interest rates will climb. Depending upon Europe, China, and the perception of the safety of U.S. debt, the bubble could easily burst before that time. Much depends upon U.S. leadership and what they do to manage deficits, the debt, and perceptions. If they do nothing meaningful before the bubble pops, we face renewed high unemployment, rapid inflation, and slow or negative growth - stagflation like we saw in the 70s malaise, or worse.

The situation is a little like someone with high cholesterol and blood pressure at risk for a heart attack. If they exercise more and watch their diet, they will be fine. But, they ignore their doctor's advice, continue to eat salty, fatty foods, and seldom exercise. Plaque continues to build in their arteries and eventually when the artery clogs, they have a massive heart attack and must undergo bypass surgery. The surgery is extremely invasive, painful and expensive, but by that time unavoidable. If only they would have heeded their doctor's advice.

So it is with the U.S. debt. Relatively minor changes, fiscal dieting, and budget exercising now can avoid a massive collapse at an unknown future time. If we wait too long, the remedy will be very painful, invasive, and costly.

Stocks

The Financial Time Machine (FTM) stimulus chart shows Boomer savings starting to decline after 2006. At first only slightly until 2011, but since Boomers, their pension funds and 401(k) funds are switching from stocks to bonds this will grow ever faster. As mentioned earlier, investors withdrew $500 billion from stocks and invested $800 billion in bonds up until 2012, despite historically low rates. The same phenomenon is true internationally with hardly any net investment in global stock markets versus the investment in fixed assets. The DOW peaked at 14,164 on October 9, 2007 and did not achieve that level until the five and a half years later. With even a modest growth rate of 5% the Dow should have been approaching 19,000 by the end of 2013.

Companies will continue to create value and most S&P 500 companies have significant overseas investments in developing markets, so the value of these companies should increase and be reflected in their stock prices. However, the price to earnings ratio will continue to be relatively low, since the demand for equity investments will continue to decline. The price to earnings ratio averaged 16.8% throughout the last 20 years and in 2012 was only about 12%, further supporting the FTMs long-term stock exodus thesis.

As developing nations' middle and upper classes grow and their sovereign wealth funds grow, they will invest a portion of their savings in U.S. equity markets. These investments are small, but will eventually support higher equity values.

A few years ago, Dr. Thomas also spoke of how there is a huge amount of capital in the world looking for investment opportunities, but that there are not enough quality triple-A investments in the developed nations. As a result, he expected there to be more investment in lower rated foreign investment opportunities. His projections have largely come true with many developing markets like China, India, and Brazil growing at rapid rates.

The fact that in 2013 large companies are holding over two trillion dollars of cash says that they are not finding good opportunities in which to invest. A major reason to sit on the cash is economic uncertainty in the U.S. and Europe. But, they could expand in the U.S., since with the aid of their Enterprise Resource Planning systems they are able to downsize quickly should the economy decline. Most of these companies are global, so despite burgeoning developing markets, they still do not find enough in which to invest.

The 2018 bond crunch will present a problem for equities. As fixed income vehicles rates rapidly rise, investing in fixed assets will become more advantageous than investing in equities. Over the current 2013 - 2023 decade, there will be more pressure upon companies to increase dividends, especially with two to three trillion dollars of reserves sitting on the sidelines. Even tech companies like Apple and Dell now pay dividends. Those equities that pay higher dividends will attract more investment.

Over the last decade, the Dow lost 9.5 %, much more if you account for inflation. Will the 2010s be another lost decade for the stock markets? It likely will be. Certainly, there will be wide swings particularly before and after recessions. Millennial investments in stocks will add impetus to the markets, but the first Millennial will not enter their peak earning and savings years until 2020. The next decade, 2020s, however, should be a good decade for the markets. By then, Millennials will be earning more and investing a lion's share of their savings in stocks. Emerging market, upper, and middle classes will be established and investing in stocks. Some Boomers will pass away and their Millennial heirs will reinvest a portion of their inheritances in stocks.

Bill Gross of PIMPCO supports the FTM's analysis of the current decade, 2010s. He expects we will be lucky to obtain 3% real returns on stocks.

Banks

As portrayed earlier, the major reason the Great Recession was long and deep was because of the inordinate risks the banking industry took on derivatives, which are now ten times larger than the world's economy and climbing. The FTM shows we are in a contraction, but the severity, to a large extent, depends upon the actions of the investment banking industry.

President Obama had an opportunity to rein in the banking system when he bailed out the nearly bankrupt large banks so that the risks of another great recession would be minimal. Indeed, many of the heads of institutions like Citi and Bank of America expected conditions to be attached to the tens of billions in overt loans and trillions of dollars in toxic loan buybacks and under the radar loans, they received. They certainly understood the moral hazard they faced because of the high-risk bets they made and lost.

Many in the administration including Larry Summer, the chairman of the Economic Advisors, recommended attaching conditions or at least breaking up one of the largest banks.   They could have made renegotiating home loans a condition.   They could have made loaning to high-potential, small businesses a condition, since small business always lead us out of recessions and back to full employment.   Instead, President Obama followed the advice of his treasury secretary Timothy Geithner, former chair of the New York Fed.   (The members of the Feds are primarily bankers, elected by the banks they serve.)   Geithner favored a policy of "do no harm" with respect to the banks, which is exactly what Obama did.   There was certainly good reason to favor the banks during that time of extreme danger, but it was a lost opportunity. Perhaps Obama thought he could better manage the banks through regulation – another miscalculation.

After the repeal of Glass Steagall in the 1990s, in the years leading up to the crash, Wall Street made unprecedented profits and bonuses by betting on risky deals previously not allowed.   As they had in the past, the government did not regulate these questionable activities. Eventually the banks lost three to four trillion dollars on risky bets, and when faced with bankruptcy and dismemberment, the U.S. government bailed them out, lending them money at near zero interest rates, assuming their toxic assets, and paying 100% on their essentially worthless insurance claims.   The government did not require any conditions as Congress considered regulation.   Wall Street then invaded Washington, effectively bribing Congress and thwarting any real efforts to inhibit their lucrative, risky activities in the future.

Unlike the Great Depression, most of the causes of the Great Recession still fester in the unregulated, undisclosed, shadow banking system.   Congress passed the Dodd Frank bill, which most analysts think is mild and fails to address the major causes of the Great Recession, like "too big to fail," derivative trading, and the Glass Steagall repeal.   Wall Street sent an army of lobbyists and lawyers to Washington to thwart efforts to control their business.   By 2009, there were 1,537 financial lobbyists – about three Wall Street lobbyists for every member of Congress.

According to Johnson and Kwak "from 1998 to 2008, the Financial Sector spent $1.7 billon on campaign contributions and $3.4 billion on lobbying expenses."* Thus far, they have been highly successful in stopping the implementation of the watered down regulatory bill.   By the end of 2012 only a third of the 398 rules required by the act were finalized.   Over half the deadlines for rules have been missed.*   Some of the delayed rules include those to define standards for qualified mortgages and proxy access for stockholders.*   In May of 2012, the relatively conservative JP Morgan admitted it lost over $6 billion on failed derivative trades indicating that the casino game continues.

The Financial Time Machine postulates that we will have another recession by 2016. Exceptional leadership, like that of Teddy Roosevelt or the Republican Congress and Bill Clinton in the 1990s could avoid this fate, but there is little to suggest such a scenario will occur. Balancing the budget took a great deal of commitment, courage, cooperation, and compromise (the four Cs.) But, that was during the longest boom period in U.S. history. The longer we wait, the less time there will be to act, and as the Financial Time Machine indicates, we are in a sustained contraction, which makes it that much more difficult.

The essence of the leadership crisis lies with our current distended political system that provides ever-extended entitlement benefits and corporate welfare. This "bribery" system grew disproportionately during the extensive expansion phase, but can no longer flourish during the contraction.

To see the future, all we have to do is look at Greece, Ireland, Spain, Italy, Britain, and France. All of these governments faced with growing untenable deficits and high national debts, as a percentage of GDP, enacted severe cutbacks, consisting of:

- reduced retirement payments,
- increased retirement ages,
- vastly reduced government salaries,
- reduced government employees, and defense cuts.

The problem is that these measures led to a widespread European recession and unemployment reaching over 20% in some nations. Stimulus spending might have saved the Euro economy, but the reserves were spent. Does Europe now face a prolonged period of stagnation akin to Japan? With few reserves and growing debts is this the U.S.'s fate too?

Indeed, these are the same actions our troubled states and municipalities utilized. At the local level, defense cuts correspond to cutting police and fire forces. Such actions at the federal level are inevitable. It is more a question of when this will occur rather than if it will occur.

The Corruption of Congress

The typically labeled culprits of an overextended budget are a lack of revenue, high entitlement spending and, to a lesser extent, defense spending. According to former National Security Advisor Zbigniew Brzezinski, as a total budget including indirect expenditures of over $900 billion, our defense spending is more than the rest of the world's nearly 200 nation's combined, three times that of our Eurozone allies, and eight times the second nation, China. Defense spending over the ten years from 2003 through 2012 alone accounts for half of the deficit at **$7.625 trillion.**

Although not as large as defense, another major problem is the Social Security benefits owed to the Boomers from which the government has borrowed. Medicare, which is only partially funded, presents an even larger concern. The situation is like a ticking time bomb and the tick occurs as each month's Boomers retire, applying for Medicare and Social Security.

Two powerful lobbies protect the expenditures on defense and retirement benefits, accounting for **58%** of the federal budget: the defense industry and the AARP. To a large extent, our government is no longer responsible to the electorate, but to the lobbies who pay for their expensive campaigns. Since most of the funding needed to gain re-election no longer flows from their constituents, but from lobbies and super PACs, Congress feels less loyal to their districts and more loyal to the special interests, who they work with daily. [In the interest of full disclosure, many of my favorite clients were large defense contractors. I also worked for the corporate HQ for one of the largest, TRW, now Northrop Grumman.]

It is illegal to solicit bribes for legislation, but the current system encourages a mafia-like favor system. For example, one can imagine the following:

> "I will organize a fundraiser, which will raise $300,000 from the energy industry I represent to fund your campaign. At some later date, as the chairman of the energy committee, since we have a good relationship, I might visit your office to explain why extending certain allowances and deductions is such a good idea. At that time, we will even conduct the research and write the legislation for you if you like."

Even if it is not explicit, there is an implied quid-pro-quo. I will provide this gift for you, but I expect you will give me a gift later. If you do not support my legislation, I may not be able to raise the funds from my industry, lobby companies you need for your re-election. This example used energy, but you could substitute any industry and legislation.

In 1974, the average House campaign cost $56,000; whereas, in 2010 it was $1.3 million.* Part of the implied quid-pro-quo is that many Congressmen and staffers will find lucrative jobs in the industries they serve. There are a staggering 5,400 lobbyists who were former staffers.* Staffers who earn a mere $30,000 - $60,000 can expect to earn three to ten times as much as seasoned lobbyists, lobbying the same people they formerly worked with, who also will likely become lobbyists too.

The deal is much sweeter for Congressmen who earn $160,000, but can expect to earn up to $1.5 million as a lobbyist. And, there are plenty of jobs to be had. In 2009, there were 13,700 registered lobbyists spending $3.5 billion, twice what they spent in 2002. Between 1998 and 2004, over **50**% of Senators and over **40**% of House members became lobbyists. By 2009, 70 former Congressional members lobbied on behalf of the financial industry alone.*

On average, every $800,000 spent on lobbying results in $5 – $16 million of tax benefits.* The pharmacy lobby pressed Congress hard for Medicare Part D, which increased drug company revenue by $100 billion a year. In addition, the pharmacy crafted bill made it illegal for a strapped Medicare system to seek volume discounts in the U.S. or Canada.

The question is what will finally cause our dysfunctional government to act? The threat of default led Greece, Ireland, and Portugal to change their extravagant spending ways and introduce severe austerity measures, which led to riots and changes in governments. Italy, Spain, Britain, and much of the rest of Europe, realizing they were not far away from default also introduced austerity measures. Most of our states faced this eventuality and drastically cut services. Eventually, the U.S. must face the reality. Unlike Eurozone countries such as Greece, we will have no one to help us. China partially enabled our frivolous spending spree thus far, but in their best interest will not always want to invest in declining assets, unless they receive something in return.

The worst factor in the scenario is that we will no longer be able to afford our huge defense budget and be forced to drastically cut back on defense spending, which in 2011 was over 2 ½ times what it was ten years earlier under the balanced budget. Despite the end of the Iraq War, the defense budget declined by only 6% in 2012. This is nothing unusual, for every empire has experienced a similar scenario. Persia, Rome, Spain, France, Britain, Turkey, and Russia spent immense amounts of treasure on their armies and navies fighting wars throughout their empires until they eventually went broke and their empires collapsed under the weight of debt.

Perhaps the solution lies with the nearly 40% of voting independents who will decide the elections. In 2000, Tim Russert wrote on his mini white board the three factors that would determine that election – "Florida, Florida, Florida." In 2004, he wrote "Ohio, Ohio, Ohio." Now, although sadly Tim is no longer with us, it is "Independents, Independents, Independents."

The Tea Party surprised the pundits with how fast they were able to influence politics. They applied leverage to the Republican Party, such that a relatively small number could leverage the party who in turn leveraged Congress. The Occupy movement was also a surprise, but did not directly affect elections. The Internet is a tremendous lever that can greatly magnify a resonant message. It is difficult to see what it might be, but there just might be a way for an independent movement to lead us to responsible solutions.

How to Skirt Anti-lobbying Laws

Naturally, lobbyists are always looking for ways to circumvent legislation intended to thwart their influence with politicians. One particularly effective effort is the American Legislative Exchange Council or ALEC, a non-profit funded by large U.S. corporations such as Exxon, Pfizer, PhRMA, Koch, AT&T, and American Electric Power. Nearly 2,000 state legislators belong to ALEC approaching a majority in some states. Whereas membership for public legislators is $50 per year, the corporate lobbyists pay $7,000 to $25,000. ALEC holds regular meetings and conferences. These lavish events, paid for by the corporations, give the lobbyists an opportunity to wine, dine, and entertain legislators, in a manner, which might be illegal otherwise.

Interest groups comprised of both the lobbyists and legislators meet to draft "model" bills, which will be introduced in state houses and senates throughout the country. Hundreds of such bills have been brought before the state's lawmakers with a large percentage passed into law, the language often lifted directly from the model bill. Some of the successful bills include Right to Work laws, Conceal and Carry gun legislation, Environmental Protection Repeals, and Voter ID laws.

ALEC has been remarkably successful. The lobbyists are able to inject favorable legislation into potentially every state, while legislators are able to meet dozens of potential campaign contributors, who could be invaluable should they run for higher state or national office. **

The Second Constitutional Convention?

Congress refused to support a Balanced Budget Amendment, but our founders recognizing the potential for corruption, gave us another powerful tool. The Constitution allows the states to convene a constitutional convention. Two thirds of the states are required to support such a gathering, the primary purpose of which might be to pass a Balanced Budget Amendment, but they could vote on other changes as well. (The balanced budget requirements of other nations allow exceeding the budget during wars or severe economic hardships.)

Up until 2008, thirty-two states voted for the constitutional convention, just two short of the number needed to convene the convention. In 2008, Ohio almost became the 33rd, but declined to do so and since then some states withdrew their petition. A concerted effort in just two states like Ohio and Wisconsin could lead the way to the convention. The Balanced Budget Amendment was the main reason for the convention, but other causes, such as a line-item veto, term limits, Wall Street reform, or lobby reform could induce broader support in the needed two states.

It is not clear what might happen, but with good leadership and after much discord - like the first convention that produced our constitution- the second convention could lead to a more productive and incorruptible government. It seems that this is something we should do every 200+ years anyway. Such an endeavor composed of patriotic citizens, whose jobs do not depend upon their actions, just might cure our current dysfunctional, stagnated, vitriolic, political environment.

Congress defines how to organize the convention. When the second Constitutional Convention seemed inevitable in 1985, Senator Hatch drafted legislation to organize the event - SB 40. He stipulated that no members of Congress would be delegates.

Others suggest state elected delegates be composed of ordinary citizens who would be paid their regular salary and guaranteed their job when they return from their service. It should not be held in Washington or New York, but rather in a remote and inspiring location. It should be comprised of intelligent, passionate, yet reasonable, diverse citizens. They also suggest holding shadow conventions in universities and other locations to hash out preliminary state-oriented positions, general procedures, and guidelines.

Some might characterize the Second Constitutional Convention as "We the People" wrestling the fulcrum of power from the current bipolar Washington/Wall Street influence, but, in reality, like the first convention there would be a myriad of diverse interests. Their goal would not be to bargain for projects for their district, tax exemptions for their industry, or to snare contributions for their next campaign, but to ensure the nation's continued greater good. Hopefully, they, like our founding fathers, would focus on what is best for the nation in the spirit of the ideals encapsulated in the Constitution.

It seems odd that neither the Tea Party nor the Occupy Wall Street movement seized the opportunity to campaign for the Second Constitutional Convention for it would have been a relatively affordable way for them, as independent movements, to magnify their political impact. The Balanced Budget Amendment fits well into the Tea Party's objectives. The amendment likely does not fit the Occupy's objectives although the convention matches their style and if they were to garner the two additional states needed for the convention, they may be able to influence the outcome. Some, like Congress, may fear the results of such a convention, but ¾ of the state legislatures would still have to approve any amendments, ensuring the fiduciary responsibility of the conference.

In the next chapter, we will examine the policy implications of the Financial Time Machine's forecast, looking more closely at the dynamics of our current situation and how proactive leadership can avoid a potentially debilitating fate.

Summary

- Our Debt/GDP ratio is now one of the highest in the developed world and in 2013 ranked among the troubled PIIGS nations.
- As Rogoff and Reinhardt prove, when the Debt/GDP ratio exceeds 90%, growth slows dramatically below 2%.
- The major reason our Debt/GDP ratio is so high is that the national debt tripled over the last dozen years, outstripping the economy's ability to absorb it.
- State budgets have increased eight-fold over the last 30 years, but they must balance their budgets annually, and therefore have adopted a variety of austerity measures.
- As in our previous economic cycles, generational economics shows we will be in this downward cycle until the early 2020s.
- Without the stimulus spending accounted for by the fiscal cliff decisions, we would have been back in a recession in 2011 or 2012.
- Due to a rare and unsustainable quadruple convergence, the interest rates on our debt are historically low, but these will climb rapidly by 2018 at the latest.
- Due generational economics, stock prices will also languish throughout the decade.
- With unregulated derivatives amounting to ten times the world GDP, and no moral hazard, Washington has done little to prevent another cataclysmic financial event.
- Due to the current lobby-infested, dysfunctional political system, it is extremely difficult to initiate actions that will effectively prevent future financial crisis.
- One viable solution is to convene a Second Constitutional Convention and seize the fulcrum of power from the dysfunctional political environment.

17

Policy Implications

Before delving into policy implications, let's recap where we have been. We currently find ourselves in a contractive portion of the economic cycle caused by the receding Boomer wave's withdrawal of stimulus from the economy. This cycle is the last of at least four economic cycles stretching back to the 1850s, in which the contractions typically last between 13 and 16 years. Each economic cycle is composed of a trough and wave lasting about 40 years - the length of two generations.

The last wave crested in 2007 as it crashed upon the economy's shore and then receded. By late 2007, the Great Recession commenced with equity investments towed downward by the rapidly retreating wave. Since then, the economy has vacillated between a feckless recovery and a double-dip recession. Government manufactured stimulus averted repeated skirmishes with recession, but a mild recession by 2016 is inevitable without courageous leadership or continuing stimulus that will increase an overburdened national debt.

Due to record budget-busting spending over the last dozen years, the national debt tripled. This spending includes tax breaks, record government spending, two wars, TARP, and increased Social Spending on programs like Social Security, Medicare, and unemployment. The combination of low GDP growth and high spending leads to an unsustainable GDP/Debt ratio hovering above 100%, which will sap the economy's potential future growth. The following chart summarizes this scenario.

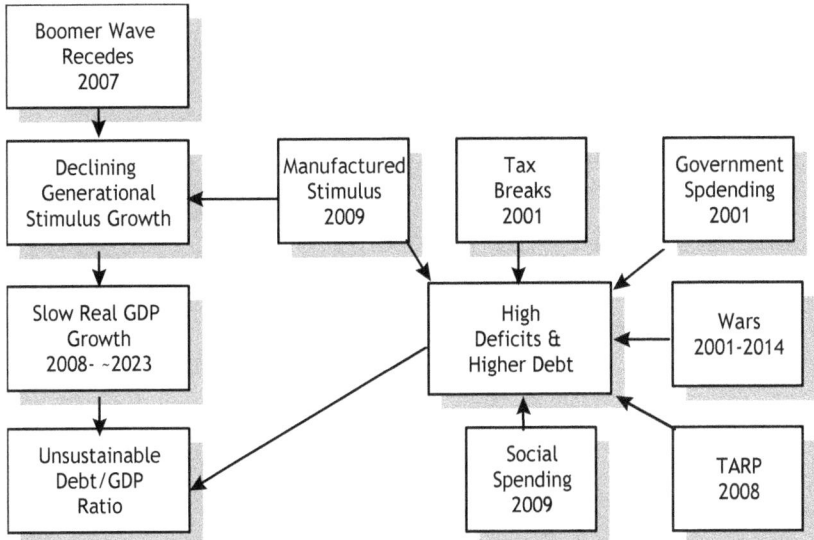

A combination of European financial troubles, record Boomer fixed asset investment, and foreign investment primarily from China and Japan supports the massive debt like an overloaded three-legged stool. In approximately 2018, early Boomers, then dependent upon fixed assets, will start cashing in their savings, thereby withdrawing support for the national debt. Confidence in European debt markets may hasten the bursting of the U.S. debt bubble. Once the decline commences, foreign investors such as China will divest U.S. debt. Even if they do not cut U.S. debt investments, they will not support future U.S. deficits and debt as they had in the past, which will make such spending unsustainable.

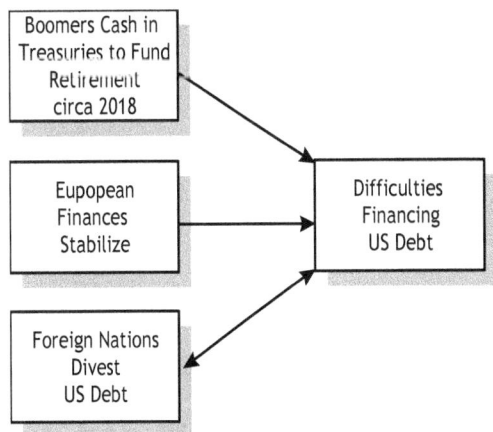

Following is a diagram of the summary thus far including the two diagrams from above.

U.S. Political Economic Model

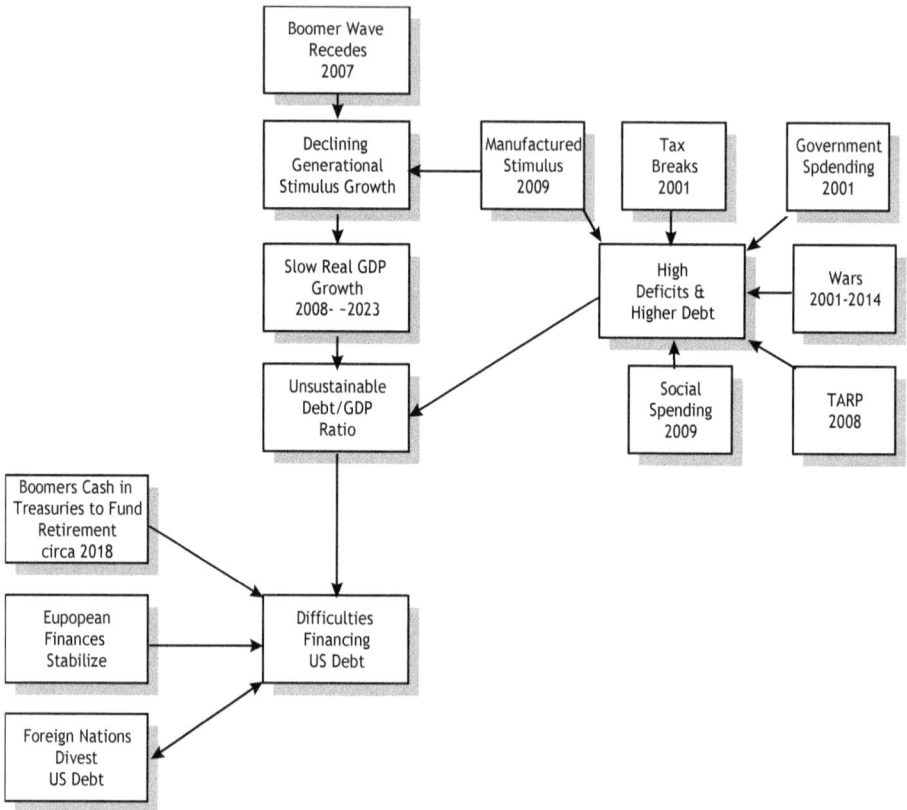

There are two components to the Debt/GDP ratio: Debt and GDP. During the boom period, excessive deficits did not appear as onerous because the GDP, as the Financial Time Machine expected, was extremely high. But by 2008, GDP growth declined. Excessive spending and bailouts used to prop up the failing economy led to even higher Debt. These two factors comprise an unsustainable Debt/GDP ratio. Fortunately, the three-legged stool supports the debt, but it will collapse once any one of the legs breaks.

Once U.S. debt support declines, interest rates will rise, increasing payments on debt and limiting other national investments. Without effective leadership, a destructive spiral will ensue leading towards broad austerity measures including slashing government payrolls, projects, defense budgets, and social support spending, such as Medicare, Medicaid, Social Security, and unemployment insurance. The picture below builds upon the previous one showing how austerity enters the picture. It also portrays how a spiral of escalating interest rates leads to stagnation.

U.S. Political Economic Model

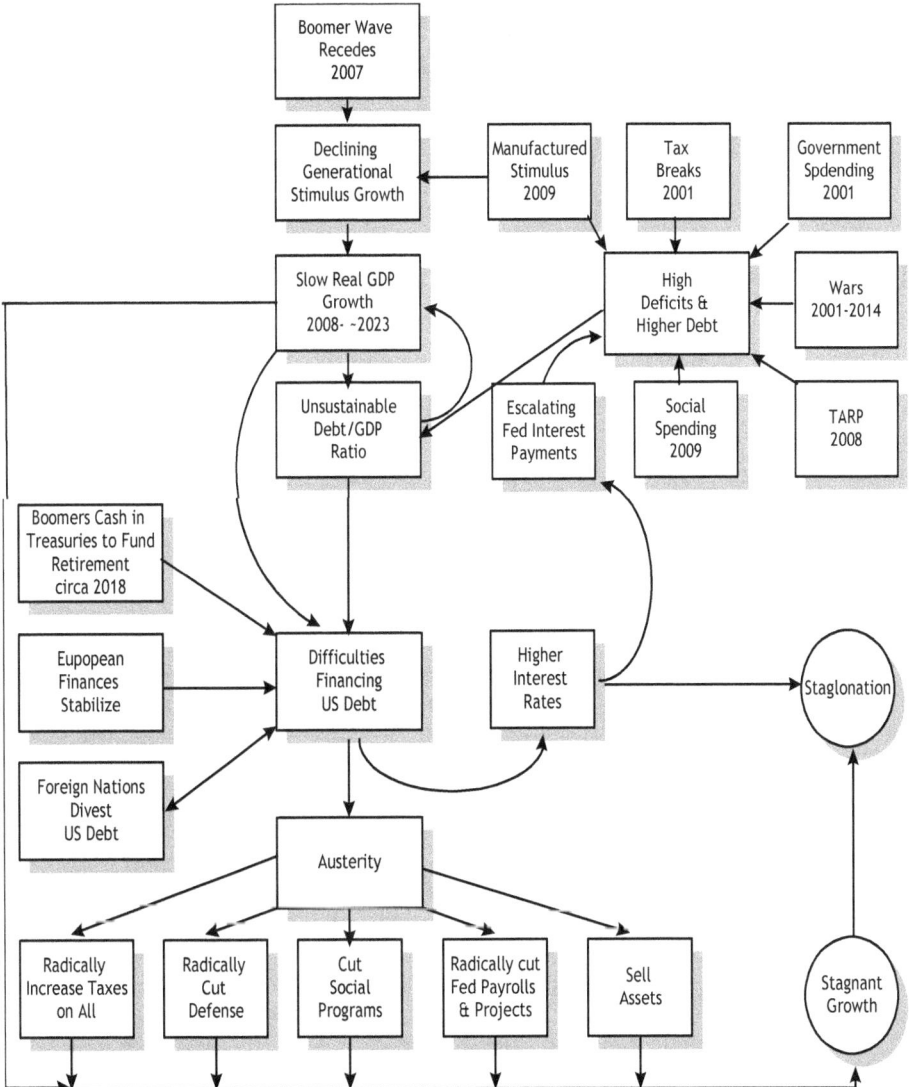

The austerity measures will lead to stagnant growth, comparable to what many European countries now endure. Increased taxes will reduce the amount of money consumers have to spend, save, and invest. Radically reduced defense budgets will decrease employment and our ability to project power globally. Cuts in social programs will reduce consumer spending further and increase hardship upon the poor and elderly.

It is unclear what, if any, assets the U.S. might sell or privatize. Greece may sell publicly owned utilities and ports, or real estate on some of its Mediterranean Islands. Certainly, the U.S. is not going to sell

Alaska back to Russia or Hawaii to China or Japan, but we might sell
military bases to host countries or domestic bases to developers, many of
which occupy ideal beachfront locations. It would be better if these
could be reserved for parks or future reassignment.

A spiral may ensue, in which radically increasing interest payments
keep deficits high. In the spiral, difficulties financing the national debt
lead to higher interest rates,

- which lead to escalating interest payments,
- which lead to additional deficits and higher debt,
- which leads to a higher debt to GDP ratio,
- which in turn lead to further difficulties financing the debt and
  slow GDP growth.

Once started, the cycle can repeat for years becoming a deadly spiral.
As the demand shifts by 2018 and the bond bubble bursts, governments
will have to pay competitive rates to attract buyers. Higher government
bond rates lead to higher loan rates and then to higher costs of capital
and therefore to higher costs of goods sold. Prices will rise
correspondingly and inflation may finally become a factor.

By 2021, the Financial Time Machine predicts relatively constant low
generational stimulus followed by even lower stimulus afterwards.
Sometime by 2026, the stimulus will pick up.

Here is where the story becomes critical. We already expect
stagnant growth because of low generational stimulus. According to
Reinhart and Rogoff, due to higher interest payments on the growing
national debt already slow growth will become even slower,- call this
stagnant growth squared or **(stagnant growth)**^{2}. If austerity becomes
necessary this too will lead to even slower growth due to massive cuts in
government jobs, spending, and support payments or stagnant growth to
the third power, **(stagnant growth)** ^{3}. With all of these headwinds,
instead of stagnant growth we will likely have negative growth and a
severe recession in the early 2020s if not earlier.

Our situation is similar to our European allies. Let's take a look at
the PIIGS versus other major European nations. The big three European
economies of the UK, France and Germany are included as a separate
column in the chart below to distinguish between the PIIGS influenced
European numbers. The PIIGS make the European numbers look worse,
whereas the big three are not so bad.

Key European Economic Indicators
(August 2013 from Trading Economics)

	PIIGS	Europe	UK,Fr, Ger
Debt/GDP	122%	90.6%	87.7%
GDP Growth	-2.5%	-1.1%	0.1%
Inflation	1.1%	1.6%	1.7%
Bond Rate	11.5%	---	2.0%
Unemployment	19.2%	12.1%	8.0%

The first thing we notice is that the PIIGS Debt/GDP is substantially above 100%, whereas Europe's at 90.6% is barely above the Reinhart and Rogoff's 90% mark. The PIIGS GDP is declining (-2.5%) whereas Europe's including the PIIGS is down less at -1.1%.

The inflation rates are surprisingly similar at 1+%, but the PIIGS bond rates are much higher. With the exception of Greece at 27%, the other PIIGS rates are 6 to 9% versus the big three's 2%. The most depressing statistic is that the unemployment rate for the PIIGS is over twice that of the big three's at a disheartening 19.2%.

The relatively high government bond rates paid by PIIGS countries have not led to high rates of inflation. Why is inflation so low when the bond rates are so high? You would expect that the higher borrowing rates would ripple through the economy causing higher prices.

There are two likely reasons higher government debt payments did not lead to inflation. In the middle of 2009, Europe had deflation due to the economic downturn. The U.S. also worried about deflation as housing and commodity prices tumbled. The PIIGS economies have high unemployment and negative GDP growth; therefore, they are not far from deflation. Europe as a whole has 12.1% unemployment and -1.1% growth, so they are not likely to experience inflation until conditions improve. With high unemployment, there is no pressure to raise wages and since PIIGS's housing is also declining, inflation is not likely.

Another likely reason is that with the glut of Boomers throughout the world approaching retirement, the demand for safe investments is at a record high, and therefore, the relatively solid sovereign debtors pay extraordinarily low interest rates.

Now let's add the U.S. to the chart. Our GDP growth rate and unemployment rates are all slightly better than the big three at this time. Our Debt/GDP approaches that of the PIIGS at 106%. A year ago our inflation and bond rates were lower, but now these are slightly higher. We are at a critical decision point.

Key Economic Indicators
August 2013

	PIIGS	Europe	UK,Fr, Ger	U.S.
Debt/GDP	122%	90.6%	87.7%	106%
GDP Growth	-2.5%	-1.1%	0.1%	1.4%
Inflation	1.1%	1.6%	1.7%	1.8%
Bond Rate	11.5%	---	2.2%	2.6%
Unemployment	19.2%	12.1%	8.0%	7.2%

We already face Stagnant Growth[2]. If we do not take appropriate action, we face Stagnant Growth[3,] a spiral of higher interest rates, austerity, social distress, severe recession, and unemployment similar to our PIIGS friends.

Imagine the situation in say 2017, when Europe finally cleans up its banking mess and its credit ratings rise. The U.S. has done little to balance its budget and the Debt/GDP is still above 100%. The early Boomers are cashing in bonds and there is little demand for U.S. treasuries. The S&P lowers the U.S.'s credit rating once more; China, and Japan along with other countries start divesting themselves of the now more risky treasuries. Since there is little demand for U.S. debt, rates escalate along with interest payments leaving less for other programs, such as the crumbling infrastructure. The economy slows even more and Washington finally realizes it must slash its budget immediately or risk default.

The treasury starts printing dollars, but because of the continually devaluing dollar, China, Japan, Russia and the EU press for the long-discussed basket of currencies to replace the dollar as the standard world currency, which reduces dollar demand and increases devaluation.

Washington drastically cuts the defense budget and DC payrolls, along with newly retired Boomer Social Security and Medicare payments. Then it cuts unemployment benefits, Medicaid, and food stamps to subsistence levels. As in Europe, the retirees, the growing roles of underemployed, and the swelling ranks of poor become incensed and unruly. Imagine hoards retired Boomers marching on Washington like the 1960s demanding full Social Security and Medicare payments.

Staglonation

During the mid 1970s through early 1980s, we entered a period of stagnant growth along with double-digit inflation known as stagflation. Inflation ranged between 5% and 15%, while GDP growth rates vacillated between an unsettling -7% and 17%. Real GDP growth averaged nearly 2%, so the growth was not as stagnant as the five years through 2012 with a .5% growth rate. Generational economics would say that the 1970s were not as bad as the 2010s will be.

Because of the low growth rates predicted by the Financial Time Machine over the next decade and the danger of deflation, we will not likely experience the run away, prolonged, double-digit inflation present in stagflation. Still government debt rates will escalate, as will the corresponding rates on savings and loans. Stagnant growth and inflating loan rates coins the word staglonation. (There may be a better word, but this will do for now.) The PIIGS are experiencing this phenomenon and it is where the U.S. heads. As the previous table demonstrates they have low rates of inflation (1.1%) with high debt interest (11.5 %.)

Because of high Debt/GDP, we do not see high debt rates leading to run away inflation. With low growth, and increasing energy sources, commodity prices will remain low. Due to the prolific natural gas and oil deposits in the Utica and Marsalis shale, the U.S. should be the largest world energy producer by 2020, surpassing Saudi Arabia and Russia. U.S. oil production grew from 6.4 million barrels in 2011 to 7.8 million barrels in 2012 and is expected to be 9.0 million in 2013, an astounding 40% increase in just two years.*

Because of reduced growth, corporations will not need to borrow heavily; therefore, the cost of goods sold will not reflect escalating corporate rates. Companies will not find abundant U.S. investment opportunities. Plus, they are flush with cash and do not need to borrow so they will not require much added capital. In addition, AAA corporate bonds will be on par with downgraded government debt, so they will find it relatively easy to acquire any capital they need.

Staglonation will be bad for small business, the engine of growth, due to high loan rates and low growth opportunities. But, staglonation oddly will be good for retirees, who will find higher CD and annuity rates along with relatively low inflation. Recently, retirees receive negative returns on their CDs relative to inflation, so the higher real returns will be welcome to Boomers and Silents.

Unlike staglonation, stagflation is a remote possibility (stagnant growth +inflation.) The U.S. economy represents approximately 1/5 of the world's economy, which will continue to decline. If Europe, China, Asia, and the rest of the world grow at a higher rate, they will demand more of the world's limited supply of commodities like rare earth metals. Commodity prices will rise, raising the cost of U.S. goods. Unlike the Eurozone, we do not have a common currency, so the treasury can continue to print money to pay our debts, which will devalue our currency and raise our prices further. The treasury has already flooded the currency market with a record amount of dollars. Under stagnant growth, it is doubtful we will experience double-digit inflation, but a more moderate form of stagflation is possible.

With our record deficits and debt, along with our high social support and defense expenditures, many people and even investment firms like PIMCO and Goldman Sachs expected interest rates to escalate by now. According to Liz Ann Sonders, Senior Vice President Chief Investment Strategist for Schwab & Co., we do not currently expect inflation for three reason:*

1. With high unemployment and plenty of people looking for jobs, there is little pressure to raise wages. If fact, the average wage for men from 25 to 65 is down 16% over the last decade - <u>wage inflation is unlikely</u>.
2. We have excess manufacturing capacity, meaning that the potential supply of goods is greater than demand; therefore, there is no pressure to raise the price of goods other than to reflect increased commodity prices - <u>goods inflation is unlikely</u>.
3. The velocity of money is extremely low, such that even with near zero interest rates, money too is not in demand. If more people and businesses wanted money, the rate would rise, but there is plenty of money in the system - <u>interest rate inflation is unlikely in the short-term</u>.

In effect, the risk of deflation offsets the risk of stagflation. Unlike Japan who has flirted with deflation for 20 years, the Financial Time Machine predicts slow growth, which under normal circumstances should stave off deflation. Mismanagement like that in the late 1930s or another financial industry fiasco could tilt us once again towards deflation, but the medium course of staglonation is the more likely scenario.

So, there are four possible scenarios over the next decade:

- Normal growth - not likely
- Deflation - not likely
- Stagflation - not likely
- Staglonation - highly likely

The Financial Time Machine (FTM) shows that there is very little chance we will experience normal growth soon, although, as in the other contractions, we will have brief periods of growth (a year or two.) Stagflation and deflation are possibilities, just not likely, which Washington and the Fed should be able to avoid. Although their tools are not omnipotent, they can provide steering to avoid these types of obstacles. Perhaps they can avoid staglonation, but not with the current toolbox.

To summarize, there are three causes of stagnant growth over the next decade:

1. Extremely low generational stimulus
2. Escalating national debt interest payments
3. Drastic austerity measure needed to reduce deficits

We cannot do anything about the first cause. As the FTM shows it is inevitable, but we can do something about the other two.

Working Down Our Debt

After 2018, if not before, there will be fewer buyers for U.S. debt and if our Debt/GDP is still high, our credit rating will naturally be lower, leading to higher interest rates. This might occur in a couple of years if Europe cleans up their financial mess and large buyers overweight European Bonds. Therefore, we need to lower our deficits, soon, very soon.

If we do nothing about the budget before the interest rates spiral, we face drastic austerity measures, which will surely lead to an elongated recession and sustained unemployment similar to the PIIGS of 10 - 15%. We need to reduce the deficits now to avoid drastic cuts later.

Once unemployment decreases more, it seems that it should be fairly easy to grow our way out of our high Debt/GDP ratio. After all, it did not take us long to go above the 100% pinnacle. This may be more difficult than it initially appears to be.

The U.S. debt was 2012 is $16.4 trillion. If the economy grows at a robust real rate of 3% and the debt remained the same, this would lower the Debt/GDP from 103% to approximately 100% in one year. At this rate, we could reach the 90% level in 5 years and a healthy 80% Debt/GDP in about nine years.

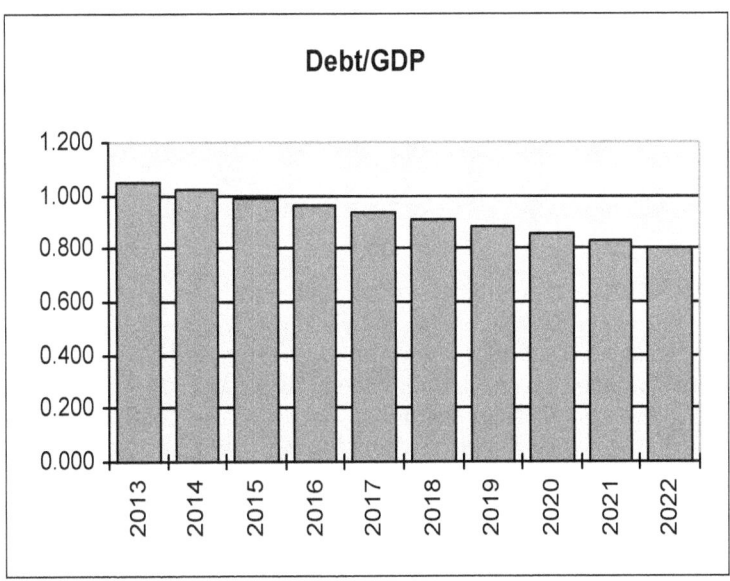

This assumes that a zero-deficit federal budget grows at only the inflation rate, currently 1.7%. But, the FTM predicts slower growth because of one and likely two recessions within those 9 years, which will require deficit spending for stimulus. Even with a balanced budget, it will take longer to reach a desirable Debt/GDP.

To save the economy we need to work on the debt side of the Debt/GDP ratio too. We must decrease the national debt, which means creating surpluses. In the last three years of the Clinton administration, the budget surplus averaged 1.5% of Debt/GDP. If Washington were serious, they could lead us to a similar surplus, which would result in an 80% Debt/GDP ratio in a little over five years, possibly before the bond bubble bursts. Since Washington has exhibited the symptoms of ADD (it lacks long-term focus), five years is a more attainable goal.

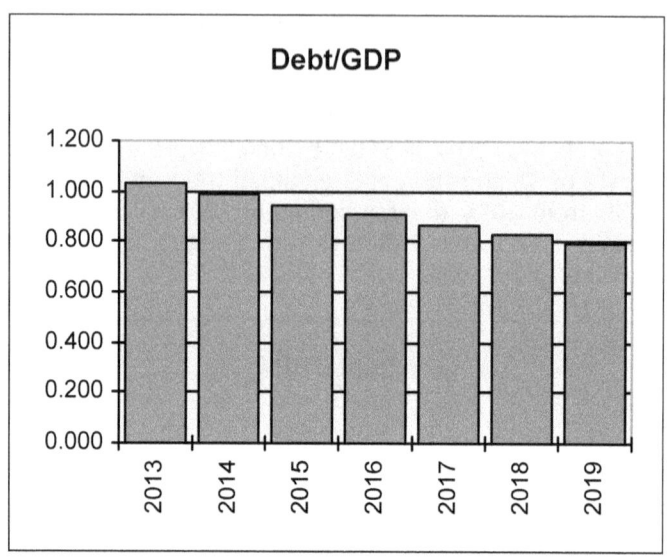

Because of an expected mild recession, it may take a little longer, but there are many related benefits. As we lower the deficit, we break the inflationary spiral, leading to lower interest rates and payments, which in turn make it easier to create additional surpluses, thereby eliminating (stagnant growth)[2]. Most importantly, we avoid the debilitating austerity measures of (stagnant growth)[3]. Employment will be higher along with higher consumption, which lowers unemployment, food stamps, and Medicaid payments. All of this adds additional tax revenues, which further add to surpluses.

Much depends upon Washington's leadership. Budget controls like those recommended by Simpson Bowles could go a long way in easing the contraction period, but the clock is ticking, little has been done and little time remains.

Relatively minor adjustment now to defense budgets, social spending, tax rates, government payrolls, and projects could save radical adjustments later. It seems silly to argue about whether the top marginal tax rate should be 35% or 39%, when during times of extreme financial distress it has been over 90% in the past and 70% or above for decades (1936 – 1980). If we do not manage the problem soon, we face rates similar to those in the past, something we would all like to avoid, since it was not just the top rate, but all of the rates that were high.

Cutting bloated federal staffs, projects, and payrolls by 10% now is much easier to digest than a 25% cut in five years. The administration could accomplish such a small cut through retirements and attrition over a couple of years. Cutting defense spending back to the balanced budget period prior to the two wars plus inflation, is much easier than cutting it by two-thirds later and risk being attacked by terrorists, or having our national interests bled somewhere in the world where we can no longer afford to defend ourselves. Carrying a Debt/GDP ratio of 100%+ makes it nearly impossible to finance a major war, because like all the empires of the past, we will eventually have little credit to fund such wars. Therefore, it is in the best interest our nation's defense to reduce defense funding now, so we have the credit reserves necessary to fight or discourage a war in the future. But it is not just about defense, it's about cutting or keeping level all budget categories.

Having been on a feeding frenzy for over ten years, Washington is morbidly obese. The signs of diabetes and coronary heart disease are obvious. It needs to go on a financial diet and start fiscal exercise or risk a heart attack, and massively invasive bypass surgery, such as a Constitutional Convention. A Constitutional Convention may be more analogous to gastric bypass surgery though, where we restrict the amount resources Washington consumes, since it seems to lack self-control.

Goal Programming

While consulting for dozens of multinational companies, we strove to improve their operations, systems, processes, and organization. It takes continuous effort and investment, but these companies are now highly productive, competitive, and profitable (not because of me, but because of their continuous improvement attitude.)   With discipline, the government can follow business' lead improving its operations and productivity like every other American industry over time.   Intelligent choices maximize resource utilization and minimize costs.   They did it before and they can do it again, but this time it will be even more challenging, because we are no longer in a boom cycle.

An example is Goal Programming, in which executives maximize various goals given competing resource availability. The goals might be to maximize GDP growth, or minimize issues like: unemployment, social pain, inflation, budget deficits, and provide national defense.   What level of spending on what budget items best accomplish the goals? Does spending on a payroll tax cut or extended unemployment maximize our goals? How does spending on earmarks or healthcare do with respect to our goals? Would spending an added $100 billon on defense or Medicare benefits be more productive with respect to our goals? Once the leaders define the goals and resource requirements, then the goal program will recommend optimal solutions along with alternatives.   The model is iterative, so they can try various scenarios seeking the best results. Such a scenario sounds techno-idealistic, since it ignores the political environment, but the political environment could also be expressed as constraints.

The current contractionary period should end by 2023.   With good stewardship, the second recession could be mild and short-lived or possibly non-existent. With do-little leadership, the current cycle will last longer than projected eliciting a protracted downward spiral of staglonation similar to the 1970s, but worse, since this generational contraction is more severe.

The hope for recovery lies with the Millennials, but the unemployment rates for blue-collar Millennials have been twice the national average. Through 2012, 50% of Millennial college graduates could not find jobs in their chosen professions. The longer it takes for this capable generation of promise to enter the mainstream, the longer it will take for the economy to recover. Through their efforts and investments, they are the ones who will lead the U.S. out of contraction.

Corporations

One wonders where the corporations will be with respect to the upcoming fiscal crisis. Is their responsibility only to themselves, their industry and their shareholders, or do they feel a sense of citizenship? The dictionary defines a corporation as, "A company or group of people authorized to act as a **single entity** (legally a **person**) and recognized as such in law." In 2010, the Supreme Court reaffirmed their individual treatment by ruling that corporations have the same First Amendment, free speech rights as individuals with respect to campaign financing. Like any citizen, rights infer responsibility.

Many corporations and industries conspire to lobby for favorable tax treatment and laws from Washington and as a result, the average corporate tax rate is about 12.5%. Now, through unlimited PACs they can spend whatever they like on Presidential, state, local, and Congressional campaigns to protect their interests. Granted, many corporations are civic minded and perform invaluable services for their local communities. But, is this environment really in their best interests when they have much to lose in a protracted downturn?

When you work for the corporation as an executive, you feel a dual citizenship to both the corporation and your nation. Sometimes corporate management faces conflict within this matrix. For example, when they must relocate a facility to another nation. They know once the plant closes, people will be out of jobs and the city and state will lose related tax revenue, to say nothing of the hardships those loyal employees will endure. [Nearly all of the S&P 500 companies I consulted too had foreign operations, but so did the medium sized ones.]

Corporations in the past have run countries - for example the East India Company in India, De Beers in Rhodesia, and United Fruit in Guatemala and Columbia. Companies today do not wish to run countries, but they naturally want influence.

As companies sell more of their products and operate more of their facilities overseas, they become less nationalistic and more global. To be successful in foreign markets requires an intimate understanding and adaptation to those markets and culture, thereby becoming less influenced by your country of origin's thinking.

In a downturn, with the help of their Enterprise Resource Planning Systems (ERPs) companies are able to sense and respond quickly, ordering fewer resources, cutting production and laying off human resources. Many companies recovered rapidly from the Great Recession resulting in high profits and capital reserves. Many others did not do as well, including real estate brokerages and construction firms. Hundreds of banks went out of business, as did thousands of small businesses. Once the largest company in the world, GM was practically bankrupt closing hundreds of dealerships and threatening hundreds of automotive suppliers.

During the Great Recession, millions of unemployed people received food stamps, Medicaid and extended unemployment benefits. Wall Street banks, the auto industry, public teachers, police, and fire fighters also received what amounts to corporate welfare.

It is in a corporation's best interest to be a corporate citizen and support the common good, because a sustained downturn or national default will greatly impact their bottom-line too. It is arguable that since corporations operate in a global environment, they need not be interested in the welfare of their host country, because they can always move to another. Halliburton, the largest contractor in Iraq, opened a Dubai headquarters after its dealings with Iran were found to be illegal, since Iran supplied opposition forces in Iraq.

This nomadic approach to corporate operations is flawed, because the global economy is so interrelated, negative impacts ripple throughout corporate operations. Most U.S. multi-nationals have a significant portion of their facilities and revenue in Europe. When Europe suffers, their bottom line suffers. China Inc. is extremely dependent upon Europe and their exports decline when Europe enters a recession. What affects Europe and China, affects the U.S., the rest of Asia and South America. To the degree a corporation exposes itself to individual players in the global economy; they should be concerned about those nations.

There is a parent child relationship between corporate America and Washington, in which the corporation operates like the child. The government sets the rules and punishes the corporation when it is bad, because it seems like the corporations are always trying to get away with something. A teenager may lobby their parents for an increased allowance, money to buy something, more independence, special treatment or fewer chores. Similarly, corporations lobby Washington for allowances, money for contracts, independence from regulation, special treatment, and lower tax responsibilities. When a child does not get what they want from one parent, they go to the other. When corporations, such as investment banks, do not get what they want from one party (Democratic), they go to the other party (Republican).

Washington, for its part, is seen as a too restrictive parent under the Democrats giving corporations too little trust and too many rules. While under Republican administrations, they are seen as too laissez faire, letting corporations run wild without discipline. It would help the relationship if Washington itself were more consistent.

It would also be helpful if there were a healthy adult-to-adult relationship between Washington and corporations. It would be better if the corporations thought of themselves as members of the national family, took on more responsibility, and tried to help out. The government could certainly use the help and in return offer clear consistent rules, support, and trust.

Corporations, therefore, should not only lobby just for what is advantageous for their bottom line, they should also lobby for what is best for the nation. Take for example the nation's crumbling infrastructure. Corporations depend upon the roads, bridges, and waterways to obtain their supplies and ship their finished products. If roads are closed or bridges are down, they face expensive delays. They depend upon utilities to power their operations and communication networks around the world to manage their facilities and process orders. The relative peace the defense department provides for U.S. multinationals facilitates smooth transactions around the globe that widespread war threatens to destroy.

The connection between the national infrastructure and corporations is easy to see, but there are other, less clear connections, like to the national debt. If we enter a sustained period of low or negative growth, corporate earnings will decline precipitously, since there will be less consumer spending on their products. Plus, their stock prices will plummet and executive bonuses based on stock options will be worthless. It would be in a corporation's best interest to have a lower tax rate and do away with all of the exemptions and supports. This will lead to reduced deficits and higher growth, but there must be prohibitions on lobbying for similar allowances in the future, or else we will end up in the same place a few years later. It implies that the government treats all corporations equally, versus favoring some over others. From the corporation's perspective, it is a fair game for all and all pay lower rates. Plus they save on lobbying expenses. High interest rates due to overleveraged national debt and inflationary devalued currency slow capital investment and eat away at profits.

We face one of the critical junctures in American history when the direction our leaders choose encompasses serious consequences for our future as a nation, testing the core of our political system's viability. These decisions, put off too long, will provide few viable remaining options. Within the framework of the Financial Time Machine, the next chapter offers several recommendations.

18

Recommendations

This section examines the current dysfunctional economic model constructed in the last chapter, searching for improvement opportunities. Before analyzing the model, consider the regulations that enabled the current situation.

Regulation

Following the Great Depression in the 1930s, Congress passed legislation regulating the markets that lead to the recession. Before then, the government did not track GDP or unemployment, but instead measured business activity. Many of the recessions prior to the Great Depression resulted in 20% or 30% reductions in business activity and we rarely went more than 3 years without a recession. After the regulations, the GDP never lost more than 4% and unemployment rarely exceeded 9%. Regulating the markets led to much less trauma and risk for business and individuals. Without fear of constant financial calamities, business could plan for sustained growth and individuals could build financial security.

In the 1990s, the nation enjoyed an unprecedented period of economic growth, which many, attribute to deregulation. However, with Boomers in their peak earning years, the Financial Time Machine predicts this would happen with or without regulation.

One wonders why we never seem to learn from the lessons of history. The U.S. markets, previously thought of as the fairest in the world, drew a huge amount of domestic and foreign investment to fuel growth. In effect, fair regulations became a competitive advantage in the world's capital market. Regulating the markets resembles refereeing sporting events. Imagine how brutal football would be without referees. Think about the broken legs, broken backs, and serious concussions the rules protect players from such as: roughing the quarterback, unnecessary roughness, clipping, and head tackles, etc. Sure, there are still infractions and the referees miss calls, but because of the rules, it is a much fairer game. The same applies to any contact sport: basketball, soccer, baseball, hockey, wrestling, or boxing. The rules reduce serious injuries, deaths, and ensure fair play.

My dad, Gene Oberst, played football at Notre Dame under his mentor and coach Knute Rockne. Knute is still the winningest football coach in major college history with 6 national championships in 13 years and a .900 record. During his senior year, Gene played every minute of every game blocking for the legendary Four Horsemen despite a broken nose and ribs. He thought the blood made him look fiercer. Personified by the thin leather helmets, the equipment of the time offered little protection, but the football players were much smaller too. At 6' 5" and 205 lbs, Gene was the largest man on the team. The Four Horsemen averaged a little over 160 lbs. yet many considered them the best backfield of the decade or perhaps the 20th century.   Then, student athletes went to college for an education and athletics, although significant, were secondary.   Today, most high school lines and backfields are bigger than those Notre Dame National Championship teams.   The game today is faster and the hits are harder, but the equipment and rules are more refined.

Similar to the way that intensive nutrition and weightlifting programs produce lightning fast 300 lb. high school linemen, computer-ization of the financial markets has greatly expanded its power. The hit that a lineman delivers produces much more impact than my dad could, but thankfully, there are rules to protect players with concussions that did not exist then.

Similarly, it makes sense for there to be fair rules to protect investors, pension funds, 401(k)s, and bank deposits. Prior to the Great Depression, the U.S. experienced a major financial breakdown about every 20 years (1797, 1819, 1837, 1857, 1873, 1907, and 1929.) After Glass-Steagall passed in 1933, the U.S. had only one banking crisis in nearly **80 years** (the Savings and Loan crisis, circa 1990.)* Since 1790, when the U.S. experienced 16 such crises caused by the financial and banking systems, Canada experienced none, not even the Great Depression. Why, because, their banks are not allowed to speculate in the markets; instead, they act like banks, a prudent approach.

In 1980, U.S. agencies regulated close to 100% of financial instrument trades.   By 2008, they regulated only 10% of these instruments, composed largely of derivatives.*   The estimated size of the derivatives market is currently **750 trillion** dollars and climbing significantly exposing the markets, investors, and the taxpayers to financial risk.

Recently, JP Morgan Chase lost over $6 billion in derivatives trading. Chairman Jamie Diamond thought this was stupid, apologized to investors, wonders how much exposure other banks have to such potential losses, and evidently favors some regulations. The banks' risky proprietary trades initially affect only their funds, but at up to a 30 to 1 margin, another collapse could bankrupt one or more of the largest banks. Then through federal deposit insurance, the American taxpayer is on the hook once again.   During the Great Recession, Bear Sterns, Lehman Brothers, and National City the fifth largest bank went down, although it is still a mystery why the government picked on National City when others were in worse shape.

With thousands of lobbyists and lawyers and billions of dollars of political and PAC contributions, Wall Street successfully watered down Dodd Frank and delayed regulation. Five years later little was in place to regulate hedge funds effectively or the soon-to-be **quadrillion** dollars of shadow banking derivatives, which even Wall Street executives admit neither they nor anyone truly understands. (As of Nov 1, 2012, nearly five years after the start of the Great Recession, only a third of the 398 Dodd Frank rules were finalized.)*

So, there is this unknown, undisclosed, complex, shadowy force, created by scientists and mathematicians, equal to ten times the world's economy that someday may destroy the world's economy. Meanwhile, investment firms and hedge funds, who caused the worst financial disaster in 80 years, bribe the world's developed nations to ignore the situation.

The Financial Time Machine predicts periodic rough weather until at least 2016. Some Boomers delayed retirement due to the crash, so even more Boomers will retire by then. According to a report by the Conference Board, 62% of those 45 to 60 are planning to postpone retirement.* They will divest themselves of stocks and move into safer bonds, cash, annuities etc. Given the massive political power of Wall Street, there is little chance anything will be done to protect the economy from another recession. The Financial Time Machine predicts a relatively minor recession, but complex betting could cause a severe one.

There will always be people and companies who cook up schemes to enrich themselves. Thousands of brokers and bankers over the last 100 years searched for angles to swindle the investor. These people comprise a Financiers' Rogues Gallery, some of whom are below.

Financier's Rogue Gallery

Birney Madoff	MF Global
Michael Milken	AIG
Joe Kennedy	City Bank
Lehman Brothers	Enron
Countrywide	WorldCom
Goldman Saks	Barclays
Bear Stearns	S&P
Tyco	Anderson.

There need to be rules and sophisticated refs to enforce the rules protecting the common investor, pension funds, and national economy. The debt caused by TARP, mortgage buybacks, and the stimulus plan, in addition to lost wages and lost taxes, jeopardizes national security.

Despite Simpson Bowles' joint taskforce recommendations, neither the Republicans nor Democrats have been willing to compromise their principles (or disappoint their lobbies who fund their elections), leaving the independent majority disgusted. Hopefully, they will be able to break the deadlock and solve the problem, but most pundits think this is unlikely.

Financial Time Machine Based Recommendations

Starting in 1990s, I worked with many large companies, such as BP America, Kraft, GE, JP Morgan Chase, Kaiser, and Blue Cross to improve their operations. One of the tools we utilized was process mapping. I would work in front of a white board and walk through a key process with the managers and staff responsible for it, charting each step as we proceeded. The end result produced something similar to a flowchart.

After detailing the process, while it was still fresh in their minds, I would ask them to brainstorm improvement opportunities. Afterwards we would spend days working on the processes seeking to streamline them, but the best ideas typically came during that brief review, sometimes accounting for a 30% - 50% reduction in time and cost. Sometimes the ideas were so great, we did not wait until the entire study was completed to implement them, but did so immediately. We even found unnecessary or duplicate processes that were immediately obliterated.

Borrowing from this technique, let's look at the chart from the preceding chapter and brainstorm for improvement opportunities. We know from the Financial Time Machine (FTM), that the economy will be in a period of sluggish growth until approximately 2023. We also know the national debt hovers at an unsustainable level. We are nearing a precipice where escalating interest rates will lead to an inflationary spiral, and stagnant growth. If we continue upon this course, the full recovery may not arrive until the late 2020s. We need something better.

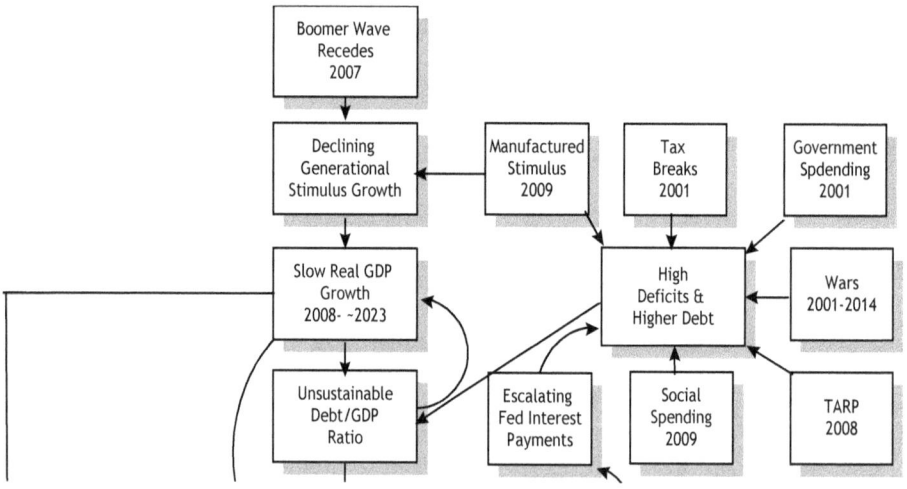

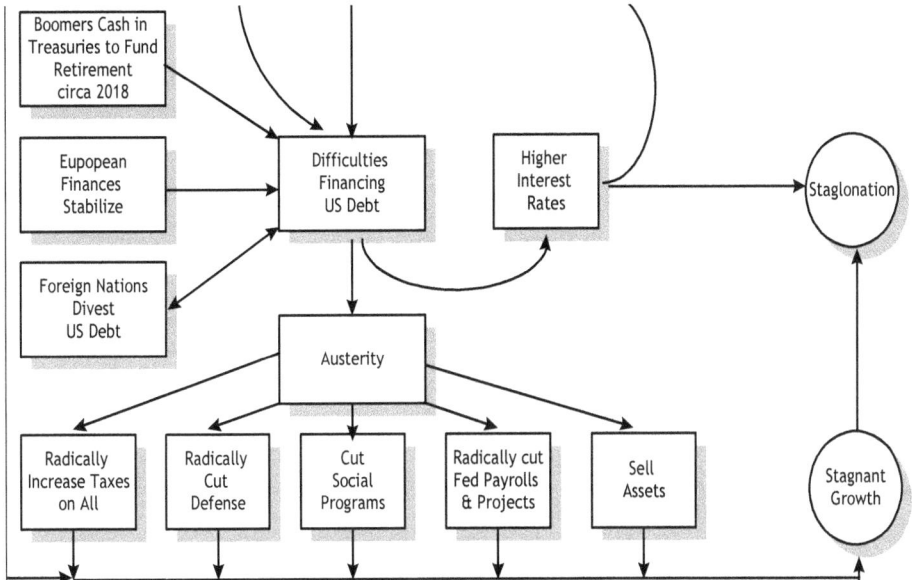

There is not much we can do about the Boomer wave receding, it's already happening and we squandered many earlier saving opportunities. Nor is there anything we can do about the three-legged stool supporting U.S. debt off to the left. The Boomers will cash in treasuries, Europe will eventually obtain financial security, and when either of these occurs, foreign investors will divest themselves of U.S. debt or at least decline to supply the immense needed future funds.

The Fed can try to keep interest rates artificially low, but like many European countries that now pay 5 -8%, eventually the price for our less than AAA rated debt will climb and we will have inflated loan rates. The goal is to limit this inflation, maximize GDP growth, and avoid staglonation.

There is only one prudent course left for the U.S., which is to operate on the causes of our high debt now before only the most drastic options remain. Those causes lie on the upper right of the chart. If we reduce the deficit, we correspondingly reduce the Debt/GDP ratio and increase future GDP growth. If we fail to do so, we risk inducing an inflationary spiral and staglonation.

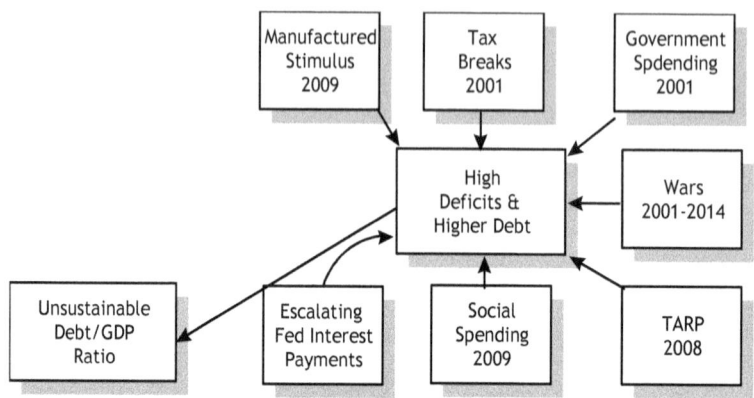

The boxes above represent the major contributors to the high deficits over the last decade. If we succeed as a nation in reducing these expenses, we can deflate the Debt/GDP ratio,

> thereby avoiding financing higher levels of U.S. debt,
> reduce interest rate inflation,
> avoid austerity,
> avert Reinhart, Rogoff stagnation,
> and avoid staglonation.

A huge economic storm approaches, which will lead to a 100-year economic flood similar to that of the Great Depression. We want to shore up the levies and lower the dam, because if it breaks it will destroy the low-lying towns and lives below. If we pull together and head off the calamity, we will experience higher growth, employment, and continuing productivity improvements.

Below are some brainstorming suggestions related to each area, which are generally consistent with Simpson Bowles. Admittedly, these may seem biased, but they are merely some straw man suggestions, from one person's perspective. You, hopefully, have others. These are in the order according to when they started adding to the deficit following the balanced budget of 2001.

1. Government Spending (2001) - Cut federal payrolls and projects. Reduce bloated government employment and contracting expenditures by 10% to 15%.

- During the recession until September of 2011 federal employment grew 13% to 250,000, so there is room for savings.*
- The average federal wage with benefits is $107,000, twice the average taxpayer's wage.
- Federal wages rose 48% over the last decade versus 28% for the private sector.*

- Over the last decade, the federal spending doubled from $1.79 trillion to $3.46 trillion.
- Over the five years since the Great Depression started, federal spending inclined by 39%. This can be somewhat justified by high unemployment payments, lower taxes and various stimulus actions, but most of these expired.*
- The DC housing market was the first to recover fully from the downturn with prices in April of 2012 nearly what they were prior to the Great Recession.
- The richest counties in the country surround DC, who surpassed Silicon Valley as the best-paid area in the nation.
- In August of 2012, unemployment in DC was 5.5%, far below the national average of 8.2% at the time.
- Thanks to the massive outsourcing over the last 20 years, the government spends twice as much on contractors as it does on employees. So it is not just about the number of federal employees.
- Most European countries, Canada and nearly every state, county, and city in the country faced stiff budget cutbacks, why not Washington?
- Nearly every *Fortune 500* company must cut back during downturns, why not Washington?

2. **Tax Cuts (2001, June)** – After reducing spending and after the economy recovers, raise the tax rate for a specified period of time. The danger is that if we wait too long, we may enter a crisis comparable to that of the Great Depression or World War II. These were the last times our Debt/GDP was this high, because we needed to spend heavily to stimulate the economy and protect the nation from German and Japanese invasion. Then, we ran up a huge debt comparable to today's. To pay the mountain of debt, the top marginal tax rate averaged over **87% for nearly three decades** (1936 until 1964) and taxes were high on everyone. These rates were ridiculously excessive. Such rates would greatly reduce spending, growth, and incentives if there is no other recourse due to delayed action.

- To protect against a recession, raise rates initially on the wealthy, who up until 2013 paid half what the average middle class citizen paid, since most of their tax payments derive from capital gains at 15%. (Due to social security, Medicare, city and state taxes, the average two-income middle class family pays over 30%.) Hopefully, it is not too late to raise the rates a little now and avoid devastating future rates like those of the 1930s through 1960s for all income groups. [In January of 2013, rates increased for the top .5 % of taxpayers, but this will not add much revenue especially considering the addition of over $60 billion of pork barrel spending needed to pass the bill.]

- Once the economy recovers, raise the tax rates slightly on all others for a specified period of time, such as five years with possible two-year extensions, so that Washington does not overspend when the economy prospers. Raising taxes on the middle and lower classes now will lower spending thus dampening a recovery. Even low-income earners should pay some taxes.
- Do away with allowances and payments (corporate welfare) to the oil industry, agribusiness, defense industry, drug industry, financial industry, hedge funds, unions, and other special interests. Decrease the top rate on business to be more competitive with other nations, which can be more than paid for by eliminating industrial welfare.

3. Defense (2001, Oct 7) -- Cut defense spending by 40% over 5 years ($400 billion savings per year = $4 trillion savings over 10 years.) This seems excessive, but at $600 billion, the defense budget would still be 50% higher than in the balanced budget of 2001 and more than make up for inflation. Well-respected former National Security Adviser, Zbigniew Brzezinski, said recently on the Morning Joe show that the U.S.'s spending on defense exceeds that of all the nearly 200 countries in the world combined. The Iraq war ended; Afghanistan is winding down, so why can't we return to the balanced defense budget? Plus, thanks to oil and gas discoveries in the U.S., we will not be as dependent on Persian Gulf oil and will not need trillion dollar defense expenditures in this region, which collaterally could reduce jihadist's interest in harming the U.S. and perhaps reduce our local security costs. Many of them want us out of the region. Not that we should leave because they want us out, but if we are not there, they lose a vital recruiting inducement.

Europe spends less than half of what we spend per capita on defense, enough to pay for their universal healthcare. We no longer need all the bases we have in Japan, Germany, Arabia, and Europe. Let those countries fund their defense.

- We should **not** cut military personnel because this spending represents only 9% of the defense budget. Therefore, **91%** of the defense budget goes to contractors, civilians, defense suppliers and other nations.
- The fall of every empire throughout history traces back to overextended spending on their military.
- Eisenhower, the most powerful general in world history, warned against the buildup of the military industrial complex.
- At a $600 billion funding level, ours would still be the most powerful military, more than four times that of the second nation, China.
- We will still be able to defend ourselves, but as George W. Bush ironically said, we should not be the world's peacekeepers engaging in wars that are not in our broad interest, and nation

building with unclear objectives and no exit strategy. Why not build the U.S. infrastructure necessary to support business activity instead of other nation's infrastructure.

- In peacetime, every country lowers their defense spending, although with terrorist threats we may not be totally at peace.
- Nobody feels we get much bang for our buck with an inefficient defense budget. A lower budget will increase credibility, productivity, and return on investment by forcing those in charge to select only the best, high priority projects.
- We just can't afford it any longer and at the current critical time, reducing current spending does more to protect us against future threats than continuously running aimless bloated defense deficits until we are broke.

Similar to reducing government expenditures, there is a fallacy that reducing defense expenditures will drastically cut employment and hurt the economy. In the short term, this is valid, but overstated in the long term. Most of the larger defense corporations occupy a number of project-based industries in addition to defense. They can transfer resources from one area to another and back to defense when needed.

Like the swords into plowshares analogy, defense technology can transfer to civilian applications and visa versa. There are hundreds of examples, many from the corporation I worked for, such as: fighter jets into domestic jet liners, the Internet, satellites, software, robotics, atomic energy, drones, surveillance cameras, global positioning, mapping, and microelectronics. In the Boomer chapter, we saw how laid off aeronautics engineers provided the brain capacity to jump-start the digital revolution in Boston, Seattle and Silicon Valley. Turning our defense engineers towards domestic applications leads to even more employment and future defense application potential. In addition, spending on defense applications is less cost effective than market based applications where the purity of market competition demands efficiency.

[In the interest of disclosure, I am not anti-military. My father directed a navy training program during WWII. My brother was an Army Captain and my other brother a Sergeant in the 101st Airborne. His wife worked for the Navy for 15 years. I was in ROTC. We have relatives who served in every war back to the Revolution.]

4. TARP (2008, Oct 3) - With $700 trillion in derivatives (ten times the World's $75 trillion combined GDP) another derivative driven crisis could send the world into a depression, especially considering the generational economics, reduced stimulus and depleted reserves. Invented by mathematicians and physicists, little understood derivatives are like atoms with the potential to collide, leading to a global financial winter. The U.S. in particular, needs to gain control over this potential conflagration and despite powerful Wall Street's influence, find a way to understand, monitor, and control such dangerous elements. The government should reinstate Glass Steagall so that banks are no longer gambling houses.   Greenspan realized that he was wrong regarding regulation - why can't Washington? As previously quoted, Sandy Weill, the Chairman of Citi Bank, credited with dismantling Glass Steagall, recognizing how it led to the Great Depression, wants it reinstated.

Have the investment houses and hedge funds that caused the Great Depression to be so deep, become indemnified?   Just like deposit Insurance (FDIC) and pension insurance (PBGC), financial companies should pay insurance to insulate the taxpayer from their repeated shenanigans over the last 200 years, so that taxpayers and investors are not continually debilitated by greed, dishonesty, and avarice. If they bore the prepaid cost of financial industry induced calamities, they would have more interest in eliminating such risks throughout the industry.

5. Stimulus Spending (2009, Feb 7) – Be judicious with stimulus spending. Washington can manufacture stimulus as it has over the last five years, but since any such stimulus is inefficient, it increases the debt more than it increases GDP, which is not a long-term solution. Extended unemployment payments make sense to a point, but these can become demotivating to potential job hunters. The length of our payments have been two times Germany's, three times Italy's and nearly four times the UK's.* Payroll tax relief is fairly efficient, but employees often save these extra dollars rather than spend the money to kick-start the economy. When the economic propensity to save is at its peak as it is now, tax rebates provide less benefit.   Many government stimulus programs result in inflated government employment to oversee contracts and wasteful spending that in the end may cost several hundred thousand dollars per job created.

6. Social Spending(2009) In 2009, Medicare's expenses exceeded its revenue.

- Increase the age for Social Security slightly over time – The average life expectancy in the U.S. is 78. When Social Security passed, it was 62. The economy cannot expect to fund long-term retirements. If someone wishes to retire early, he/she can save enough to do so.   For those in physically demanding jobs, preserve age-62 reduced Social Security benefits.
- Medicare is largely unfunded. Increase the Medicare tax slightly. The well-to-do should get what they put into Medicare, but not more.
- Clamp down on Medicare and Medicaid fraud. Any provider who gets Medicare or Medicaid payments should go through an audit on a regular basis and pay for the audit. Providers should be fairly compensated for their service.
- Repeal the $5 – 7 trillion-dollar Medicare part D and fix or negotiate Medicare drug payments as every other developed

country has at close to half the U.S. cost. By doing this, the current cost to seniors will be about the same and future prices will be lower. We just cannot afford this benefit for the hugely profitable drug industry any longer. Although the industry claims large profits fund research, the government pays for most medical research anyway - continue government funding for this breakthrough research.

- Introduce market-based healthcare, which will lead to productive, quality healthcare at a lower cost, releasing the same productive power that vastly improved the quality of and affordability of agricultural and manufactured goods. The current fee for service-based system does not have the types of incentives to reduce costs and charges, since the laws of supply and demand do not apply to it. The Obama plan, single payer plan, Ryan plan, and current insurance-based, pay-for-service plans are not productive market-based strategies.

    Low cost competitive healthcare is achievable over time through the Web by displaying provider prices versus quality ratings, industry certifications, and reviews, similar to buying goods on Amazon. Such a healthcare mechanism unleashes market and productive forces that will gradually reduce costs. An example of market-based healthcare is Laser surgery. Laser Surgery is not covered by insurance plans, but now costs about one quarter of its initial fees with a dramatic increase in quality.

We face stagnant stimulus growth over the next ten years. The GDP will still grow, but at a slow rate. The only meaningful lever we have to reduce the Debt/GDP ratio is to limit debt through measures like those suggested above. We can avoid significantly more drastic austerity measures if we take such actions immediately.

By limiting debt, the Debt/GDP ratio will fall to more sustainable levels. It will be easier for the government to finance its debt if it accomplishes the goal by the time Europe reaches financial stability, or prior to when the Boomers shed treasuries. The government will then pay lower interest rates and less interest. Inflation will be lower and the inflationary spiral will dampen.

Additional Suggestions

With moderate cuts, the U.S. can avoid stagnant growth, rampant inflation, and corresponding stagflation. If Washington cannot exert the leadership necessary to avoid the looming long-term financial crisis, perhaps citizens need to seek alternatives. Here are some additional suggestions.

- Campaign to enlist two more states to pass the Balanced Budget Amendment and hold a Constitutional Convention (assuming Alabama reinstates its petition.) Our current lobby-pleasing, two-party political system does not appear to be able to solve our fiscal problems in time. Washington and Wall Street are just too wealthy and influential. One more state's passage of the amendment, as in the 1990s, may give them the incentive towards fiscal responsibility. It could be either Ohio or Wisconsin.

- Support independents, and movements like the Tea Party and Occupy Wall Street, but perhaps less radical, which undermine the current pseudo-bribery system and leverage the political system.
- Like Canada, eliminate excessive TV political ads over the public airways. Each candidate receives a prescribed number of minutes on the public airways to communicate their message. Declare PAC TV ads illegal during campaigns. This will greatly reduce the funds Congress needs to raise from donors, reducing lobbyists' Rasputin-like hold on them and their quid pro quo overtures.
- Ensure that any investments by the government or military have a financially justified return-on-investment; this includes social spending with a corresponding social good - similar to the accomplishments of the 1990s.

Strategic Leadership

Following is a picture from U.S. Government Spending showing the Debt/GDP over the last 30 years. Notice how fast the Debt/GDP ratio grew after the Great Recession, from 64% to an estimated 106% in only 6 years. Prior to the recession, the Debt/GDP exceeded 60% only twice. The first time was following World War II when our national existence was on the line and the second was during the early 1990s. Then, Washington worked diligently to reduce the debt and the Debt/GDP dropped below 60% once more.

Washington did not continue to exercise fiscal restraint during the 2000s. From 2001 until 2009, the debt more than doubled. As a result, the Debt/GDP steadily inclined above 60% once more. Vice President Dick Cheney, when asked about doubling the federal debt famously said in 2002, "Regan proved deficits don't matter." What is important is the Debt/GDP ratio, which was not that high with the economy running in 5th gear. But by the end of the Bush-Chaney administration, the Debt/GDP ratio was the highest since the 1940s. The Debt/GDP grew by more than 50% during the Bush-Cheney years to 85.2%, dangerously close to the Reinhart/Rogoff economic stall speed.

Federal Debt to GDP Ratio

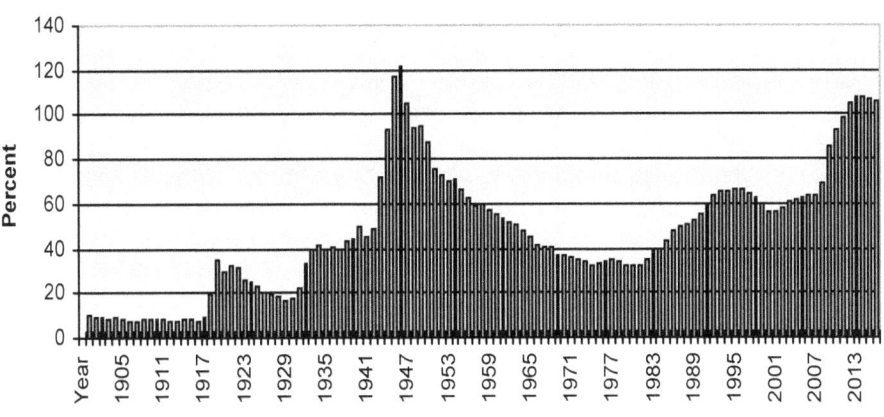

The Financial Time Machine (FTM) predicted that the period from the mid-1980s through mid-2000s would be the best economic times in history. Washington should have known the exceptional financial conditions would end. Borrowing the analogy of Joseph in Egypt from the Bible, the good years should have been a time to build reserves, not to squander the largess. (Joseph stored grain for seven good years that fed the Egyptians during the seven following bad years.) Granted, Washington did not have the benefit of the FTM, but history shows that we rarely go more than seven years without a recession.

During major wars, the Debt/GDP naturally increases. The highest Debt to GDP ratio followed World War II. We were able to effectively lower the ratio following the war, but then the top tax rate exceeded 90%, which few would like to see again and from a generational economic perspective, we were in an extended economic expansion.

Although it was extremely tough for the personnel who faced numerous long deployments, our involvement in Afghanistan and Iraq was relatively minor compared to the past major wars the U.S. fought, especially in terms of the number of military personnel involved. With no credible evidence of weapons of mass destruction, some such as Defense Secretary and Vietnam vet Chuck Hagel questioned whether we should have started a preemptive war in Iraq.

George H. W. Bush wrote a book about why occupying Iraq was a poor idea. In the first Gulf War against Iraq, the annual defense budget was about **one-third** of the second Gulf War's, 12 years later. George H. W. Bush founded a coalition of nations to fund the first Gulf war and instead of lowering taxes, raised taxes to pay for the war - a courageous stand, one that probably cost him a second term.

Each President has a ten-year plan to balance the budget, but this rarely comes to fruition. One obvious reason is that a ten-year plan is beyond their eight-year term.   Another is that there are always unforeseen circumstances that dissolve the political resolve.   State governments do not devise 10-year plans to balance the budget, because they must do so every year. A CEO who has a losing year does not devise a 10-year plan to balance the budget.   He slashes costs immediately otherwise he loses his job. In the mid 1990s when Clinton and Congress were serious about balancing the budget, it only took them three years to reach surpluses.

Like Joseph, corporations, states, and insurance companies build reserves for the bad times. These reserves help them to weather the storms they know are coming. Washington runs the government like someone living from paycheck to paycheck with no reserve or budget.

Members of Congress and the administration should adopt a longer-term view, rather than trying to game the system for themselves, their staffs, their corporate donors, and their districts. Part of their shared responsibility should be to plan and save for future contingencies. They should clean up the White House, House, and Senate, and leave their ancestors, future generations, and nation better, not worse, than they found it. To do so requires some wisdom, and a historical perspective.

In performing process reengineering, businesses rely on benchmarks to plan and improve their operations. Here are a few that apply:

1. We have a recession on average every four or five years.
2. Severe national disasters occur one to three times a decade.
3. We average only 10.5 years between wars, and spend 38% of the time in wars.
4. Generational economics predicts when boom times and bust times occur.

Save during the good times for the bad times – that is responsible leadership.
Recognize this. Plan on it. Save for it

A strategic solution

Every large business makes thousands of critical decisions every year that affect its bottom line and prospects. If government applied the same level of analytical thinking to their decision processes as they demonstrated in the late 1990s, they too would be able to make decisions that minimize spending, while maximizing returns.

During the 90s, I was a Regional Practice Manager for Watson Wyatt, now Towers Watson, a $3 billion global consulting firm. Our HQ was in Washington D.C., and since much of our consulting depended upon legislation, we kept close tabs on Congress and the administration with numerous offices throughout the area including the infamous K Street, where I traveled weekly for a time. Our delightful watchdog talked about how any bill had to be cost justified first, before it left committee.

As a result, few bills made it through, earmarks evaporated, and with strict discipline from both parties government actually shrank.

For instance, if the defense department lined up all of its projects based on Return on Investment (ROI - bang for the buck) the first one might have a return of 200% and the last one perhaps 1%. That means for every $billion we spend on the first project we get a two billion dollar benefit, whereas for every $billion we spend on the last one we only get a 10 million dollar benefit. Benefits can be intangible and tangible, such as social good or the ability to defend ourselves. If it does not generate much benefit, don't do it, which likely applies to half of the projects. When there is a seemingly limitless supply of funds, costs rise exponentially and benefits fall precipitously.

Many of the companies I consulted for ranked their IT projects according to value to the company as judged by the executives from highest to lowest. Then, based on funding they would draw a line on the project list with those below being funded and those below not funded. This ensured that the most valuable projects for the corporation were completed, while less valuable ones were not.

Few Congregational representatives think like business people. Instead, they judge a tax break or an investment of taxpayer funds by whether it will benefit their constituency, ideology, or the industries that support their campaigns. They do not judge it based on the nation's best interests versus other possible investments. "This bridge may cost a half billion dollars, which is only worth $100 million worth of time spent in traffic over 50 years, but it creates 500 jobs over two years in my district, rewards a key election city, and the construction firms who financed my last campaign." This is an example of one of the thousands of decisions Congress makes every year, but during the late 1990s, they asked the critical questions.

The 2012 tax rates were the lowest in nearly a century with the possible exception of a few of the Reagan years, even lower than under the recent Bush administration. Like stimulus, tax cuts are appropriate measures to pump up the economy during the typical short downturns of the last 60 years. But, this is not a short-term downturn. It is long-term and as such requires long-term management skills and solutions.

Working retirees

Since the core of the economic concern facing the United States is the number of aging Boomers, their extended life expectancies and the promises made to them, an obvious solution is to raise the retirement age, which many EU nations are doing and the U.S. is considering. Full governmental or union employee retirements in their fifties are unsustainable, when the retiree can expect to live longer than they worked. In addition, as the Boomers leave the workforce, there will be fewer workers to fill their open positions. For many, it becomes difficult to work full-time beyond 65, so society should find ways to encourage massive part-time employment opportunities in local communities and over the Internet. Part of the problem is that the mainstream working world thinks in terms of full-time positions. What if, instead, employers thought in terms of 20-hour positions, too; not just, ad hoc, part-time jobs, but regular positions. Some people work one position per week whereas others work two or in some cases three.

A retiree, a mother caring for children, or a person caring for an elderly parent, might occupy a 20-hour position. Retirees do not need full benefits like vacation, sick days, health-care, workers comp, unemployment, or retirement. With full benefits representing 25-35% of a person's total compensation, employers would pay substantially less for a retiree's 20-hour position. Supplemental Medicare insurance is a benefit retirees would appreciate, but one that is much cheaper than standard healthcare. The retiree and employer could split its cost.

The most obvious indicator of the aging crisis is the worker to retiree ratio projected to be 3 to 1 by 2030. As the Boomers age, they will need more people to care for them, which with such a constrained workforce will be difficult to supply. If people work longer before retiring or work part-time, the number of workers increases and the number of retirees decreases. Therefore, the ratio rises – in other words, more workers per retiree.

The first place to look for jobs is for retirees to care for other retirees. Many retirees help their older or disabled friends, but surely this can expand and there should be a website to facilitate it. Younger, more able retirees helping older and disabled retirees save younger workers' time, which will become a rarer commodity.

Millions of retirees are bored and yearn to contribute to society again, but lack a mechanism to do so. There is no reliable on-line employment site for retirees, but there should be. AARP could supply such a facility, but theirs is thus far anemic. Monster, Career Board, and other job sites focus on full-time jobs and therefore, have few part-time positions. Maybe there should be a new one or maybe one of these major sites can build such a site as a service to the nation, while obtaining fees from employers, because as we will soon see, this is a powerful, potential cost saver for them and source of soon rare skilled resources.

The key is the employers, one of those being the governments who also tend to think in terms of full-time positions. Hiring part-timers offers significant employer cost savings. There should be no unemployment, worker's compensation, Social Security, or Medicare tax paid by an employer for a retired worker. None of these applies to them, since they are already retired. Together these taxes represent nearly 20% of pay. If an employer paid the same rate to the retiree as they do to a full-time employee, they would effectively receive a 20% reduction (including the retiree's SSA they pocket.) Full medical insurance, paid time off, and retirement benefits typically represent another 15 -20% savings. So at the low end of the savings, an employer paying $30 of total compensation to a full-time employee can hire an equivalent retiree for $19.50/hr. A fulltime employee costs over 50% more than a part-time employee per hour.

If the retiree is less productive, they should receive less than the person in a full-time position is, but in many cases, this will not be the case. Older workers have a fierce work ethic and an immense amount of experience to draw upon. In many ways, they are more productive than a younger worker still learning the ropes.

Whether it is the morning, mid-day or afternoon, most workers experience biorhythms when their productivity wanes. A retiree will work 20 fresh hrs, since they have the rest of the time to themselves. They may not be as productive as they were when they were 40, but for most the differences will not be substantial and the workforce is aging, so employers will not have as many younger workers to draw upon anyway. With a reduced labor supply, the cost of labor will begin to rise dramatically in the latter half of this decade rewarding those organizations who successfully apply such a strategy.

There are many jobs that a retiree may no longer be able to perform such as heavy manufacturing, fire fighting, police work, construction, or stressful management jobs. But with the service sector now comprising 80% of the workforce, there are many more jobs they can perform like teaching, call center representative, retail clerk, programming, analysis, postal delivery, waiting tables, childcare, bartending, accounting, and general office work. A full-time assembly job may be too much for someone at 67, but a halftime job might be ideal.

Outsourcing then makes less sense, especially since Chinese wages are rising rapidly, their quality is low, and they now have a problem finding skilled resources. Due to their one-child policy, China's labor force will shrink dramatically providing less available skilled resources globally.

The financial incentive is a powerful one for business. The businesses that catch on will gain a powerful cost and quality advantage over their competitors. Let's take an example of a skilled COBOL programmer who is about to retire. Young employees do not want to learn ancient languages like COBOL (the Latin of programming), but there are billions of lines of COBOL still performing a valuable, more efficient role particularly in large enterprise systems.

Wally has 30 years of experience with an old, but still, vital language and the company's complex proprietary systems. It would take two years to train someone to become nearly as proficient as Wally. Wally's manager says that it will take 2 years before a new hire is even half as effective as Wally, and that 20 hours of Wally's time is worth 40 hours of a raw recruit's. Wally is tired of the hour-long commute and wants to spend more time sailing and with the grandkids, but he would not mind working part-time from home, contributing, and earning enough to afford a larger boat. Plus, he would like to see and socialize with his co-workers during coordinating meetings with the office.

Most medium to large IT departments are responsible for a variety of maintenance and development projects each year. With dozens of needed skilled workers, they allocate resources on a periodic basis and many projects call for only a portion of a skilled human resource's time. Therefore, it is relatively easy to accommodate part-time workers in IT. Plus, the older workers would maintain the older systems, freeing up the newer workers with more current skills to work on new, more desirable development projects. This will make recruiting young talent easier too.

Wally's total compensation including benefits and company paid taxes is $84,000 per year. Subtracting what Wally and the company save on unnecessary benefits and taxes results in an equivalent wage of $60,000, or $30,000 for a part-time position. Wally would earn the same amount he was previously paid for 20 hours, plus he saves 10 hours of commuting time and the associated expense per week. The company saves $14,000 per year, plus $75,000 in training and recruiting costs, and they are confident they are getting a proven, loyal, quality worker. This is a win-win situation. [Recruiting and training costs for a software engineer are on average $75,000 - $100,000.*]

From the business perspective, in the developed nations, there will not be as many workers in the future. Even though unemployment figures are unfathomably high now, the situation will soon shift. Currently, business has 3 million open positions, which they are slow to fill, because there is a lack of needed skills, skills their retirees have. Until recently, only a small percentage of Boomers have retired largely due to the following factors:

- Declining home values reducing their perceived wealth and retirement funds
- Equity market losses reducing retirement funds
- Near zero real fixed asset returns reducing retirement fund growth
- Reduced income
- Layoffs
- Lower company sponsored retirement benefits
- Higher Social Security age requirements

Some members of my team built retirement calculators for many large corporations like Goodyear, Blue Cross, Timken, Chase, and Ernst and Young. Plugging these factors into a revised calculator, intuitively results in a year or two added to their target retirement age.

The first Boomers to receive full Social Security benefits retired in January of 2012. All of these factors produce a spring like affect. Many Boomers who saw their wealth drop precipitously delayed retirement, but not for long. The housing market is finally staging a recovery and stock prices exceeded their 2007 highs.   By 2018, the returns on fixed assets will rise rapidly, finally supplying retirees with more income.   As time progresses, they will retire in ever larger numbers rapidly depleting the labor pool of highly skilled experienced workers.

At the same time, unemployment for the 20-30 year old Millennials (who will take the Boomers' place in the labor market) has been substantially higher than the national average, such that these vital human resources are not acquiring the needed skills to immediately take over.   Uneducated Millennials have the worst unemployment statistics and the education system has not prepared them well, so it will be difficult to replace the skills of the highly educated and experienced Boomers.   As we saw in chapter 1 unemployment in 2010 for those without a high school diploma was 14.9% versus 5.4% for those with a degree.   Many Boomers, who did not go to college, did graduate from high school where they received excellent vocational training that is rarely available today with repeatedly reduced school budgets. Unemployment for those with an associate's degree, which some vocational education programs were the equivalent of, was 7.1%

Over the last 60 years, people have bought into the retirement dream, heavily marketed by the financial industry that makes hundreds of billions of dollars from selling and managing pensions, 401(k)s, and mutual funds.   Before then, for most, retirement was not a plausible option.   In the 1950s, manufacturing companies facing a dearth of factory workers to perform menial tasks promoted the retirement dream - "Work for us for 35 years and you can retire to Florida or do whatever you like for the rest of your life."

Few Employers currently support defined benefit pension plans, retiree medical plans, or lifetime employment: those benefits that nourish the dream.   Still, the workplace continues to support the retirement dream.   They offer retirement counseling, planning, awards and parties.   There is nothing wrong with retirement or planning, it just needs adjustment   Employers should instead promote two options:

1) the typical retirement path,
2) another part-time path with incentives.

In the past, retirement was a way to reduce costs and renew human resources, but with the number of skilled resources soon diminishing and the average age inclining, the imperative changes.

See Appendix B to see what Government can do to encourage 20-hr positions.

This chapter completes the Implications Section of the Financial Time Machine.   The next section also builds upon the concepts of the FTM to see if these apply to other world economies too.   Such a premise seems improbable, but the results turn out to be surprising, as you will soon discover.

Section Five

19

Global Implications - Europe

This section expands upon the concepts applied to the United States to see if generational economics applies to other nations including those in Europe, Japan, Brazil, Russia, and China. If the concepts do apply, it lends additional support to the path posed by the Financial Time Machine (FTM) for the United States.

As we will also observe, some of these nations, due to their current generational economic state, predict what lays ahead for the U.S. - that they currently experience what the United States will experience in the over the next decade. The comparisons are striking, but must be ascertained with a comparative analysis of their individual economies.

Earlier we spoke of how similarly the U.S.'s financial situation compares to the troubled PIIGS nations of Portugal, Ireland, Italy, Greece, and Spain. The major, although not only, cause of the U.S.'s prolonged downturn is due to generational economics, as the Boomers' economic wave withdraws peak stimulus from the economy. Therefore, a question presents itself - does generational economics also apply to the PIIGS? If it applies to the PIIGS, could it possibly apply to the rest of Europe? If it applies to Europe, what are the implications for the U.S.?

The Boomer wave arose out of World War II. As the war raged in Europe, it consumed most of the continent. Within the PIIGS, Greece and Italy were heavily involved in the war, whereas Ireland, Spain, and Portugal fought to a lesser extent. The big three European nations comprised of France, Great Britain, and Germany had daunting roles in the war, losing a large proportion of their populations. So, we expect similar Boomer waves to transpire in the major combatant countries of World War II. Indeed, the top 16 countries with the oldest median age are nations who fought in World War II, supporting a possible linkage.

Following is the median age for the U.S. over time. As we see, the age declined until about 1970 and then inclines steadily until 2035. The lower medium age stems from the War Boom Baby births flooding the population. The median age begins to rise when the Xers enter the U.S. population in the late 1960s.

The median age graphs supplied by the United Nations (UN) provide an early indicator of future financial strain. A declining median age indicates a baby boom with a workforce that will expand in the future. An inclining age, approaching 40, indicates an aging workforce implying concerns.

Median Age of U.S. Population
From 1950 until 2100

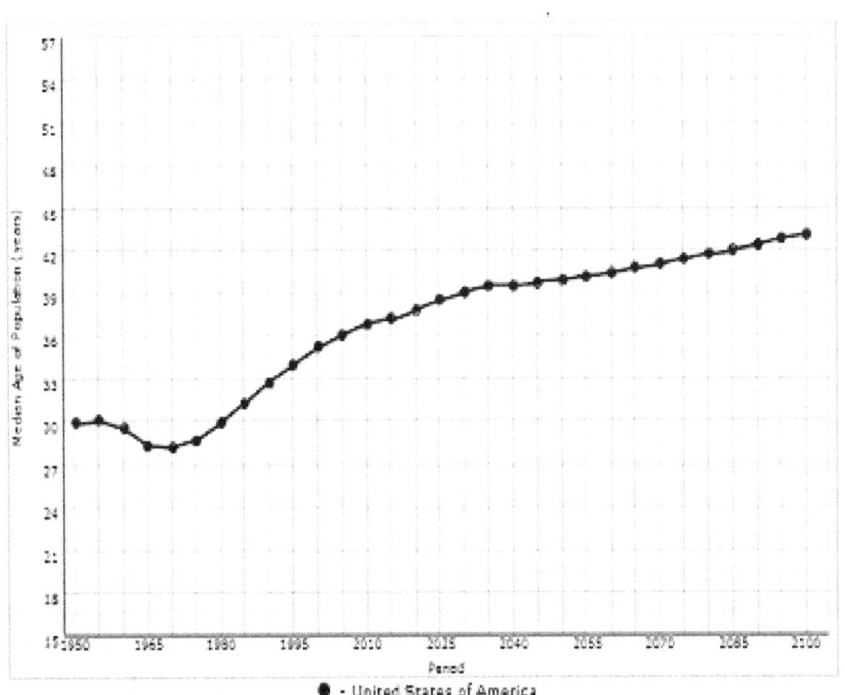

During the time the Boomers were born in the 1950s and 60s, the median age drops to 28 and then steadily rises. In the middle 2010s, it is around 37. By 2030, it levels off at 39 before climbing again in 2050.

Let's examine the big three along with the U.S. to see if a population wave exists for them after the war. As we observe in the following chart, they too display a similar trend. All exhibited a decrease in median age until 1970 or 1975 when the ages started to incline, indicating the expected war boom in these countries too. Interestingly, the UK's age levels off by 2015, whereas Germany's continues to increase until 2040.

Median Age or Population for
Germany, UK, France & U.S.

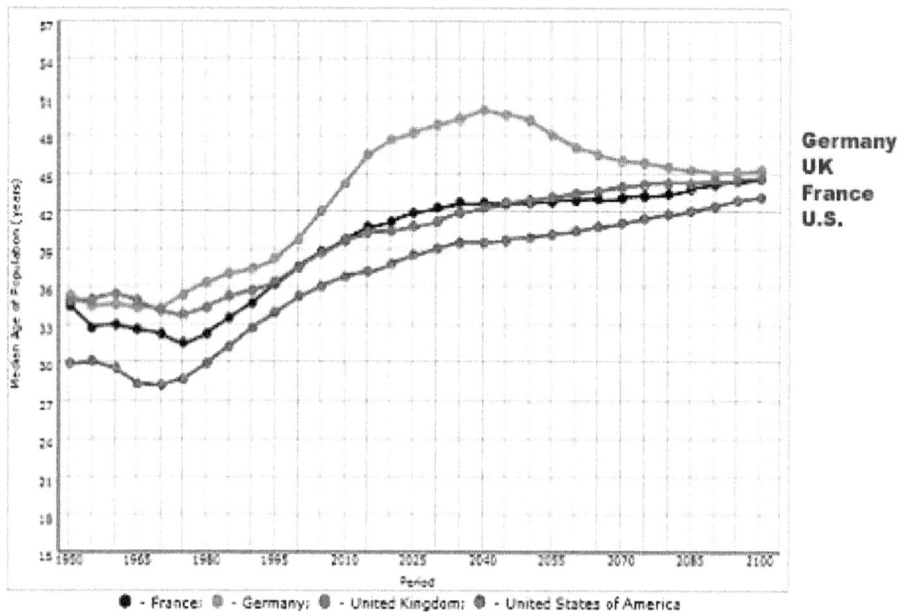

Germany
UK
France
U.S.

● - France; ● - Germany; ● - United Kingdom; ● - United States of America

The reason the UK's age stabilizes from 2015 to 2025 is there has been a significant amount of immigration since 2000 adding needed young adults and children to their population thereby leveling the average age. The birthrate for UK born women is 1.9% versus 2.3% for foreign-born women. By 2050, Eurostat expects the UK to pass France and Germany as the largest European nation.* England's population increased by 7% over the first decade of the 21st century, whereas Germany's declined.

Let's look at the populations of the PIIGS to see if a population wave existed for them as a result of the war. Greece, Ireland, Spain, and Portugal displayed a similar leveling of the population between 1970 and 1980, but Italy did not, suggesting a more severe aging crisis is in store for Italy. All of the countries median ages will continue to rise until at least 2030. Except for Italy, the PIIGS did not have major roles during the war, but they reveal a similar post-war population phenomena.*

Median Age of Population for the PIIGS

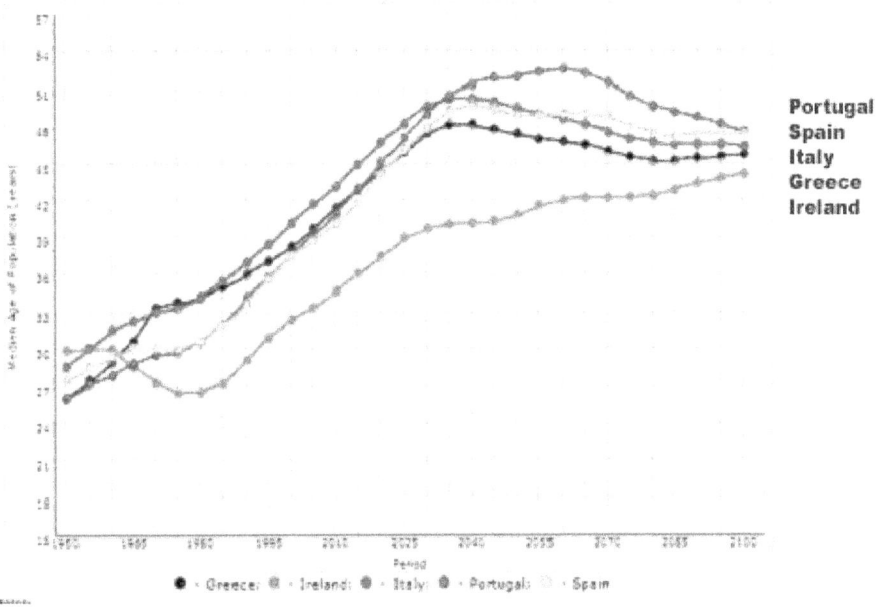

As a whole, Europe's birth rate increased up until 1965, signaling the Boomer population boom. Then it declined as their Xers were born.

Examination of the UN's birth records by country confirms the presence of the post-war population wave. The big three exhibit a population wave similar to the U.S.'s that increased until the period ending in 1965. Some of the PIIGS continued to increase until as late as 1975.

Population Waves by country

Nation	Increasing Births up to (Boomer endpoint)	Increasing Again (Millenial start-point)
U.S.	1965	1985
France	1965	1985
Germany	1965	1985
UK	1965	1985
Portugal	1965	None
Italy	1970	2005
Ireland	1975	2000

Greece	1970	2005
Spain	1975	2005
Japan	1975	None

The other interesting characteristic is when the births started to increase a second time indicating the presence of a Millennial boomlet like that of the United States. The previous chart summarizes when this occurs for the studied nations. The UN lists births in 5-year increments ending on the dates displayed, so changes might have occurred anytime during the periods.

The U.S. Millennials began to arrive in 1985, comparable to the big three. The PIIGS' Millennials arrived 15 to 20 years later. Portugal does not show a boomlet, instead their population continued to decline throughout the early 2000s. Japan is added to the analysis, since they were also a major WWII combatant and we will examine their economy in the next chapter. They too do not portray a Millennial boomlet. The fact that the PIIGS do not exhibit a significant Millennial population wave represents a problem for these economies from the FTM's perspective.

Early Warning Signs in Population Shapes

Watson Wyatt (now Towers Watson) researched the coming retirement crisis during the 1990. Based on the UN Population Division's World Population Prospects 2000 report, they produced profiles for most of the largest countries highlighting the looming future problems.

[Towers Watson is the World's oldest and largest actuarial and human resource consulting firm with revenues in excess of $3 billion. (I worked for Watson Wyatt as a Senior Consultant, local, and Regional Practice Manager in the 1980s and 90s.]

One of the depictions they utilized to emphasize the gravity of the problem were charts showing each country's population structure over time, as shown for Germany.

Germany's Population Structure in 1950

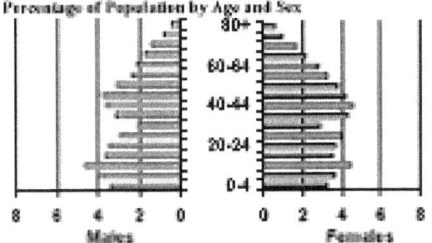

Germany's Population Structure in 2000

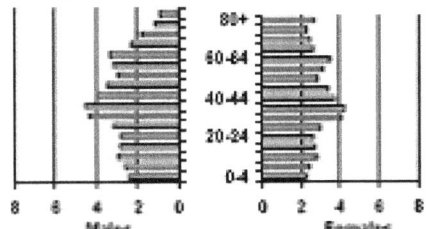

Germany's Population Structure in 2030

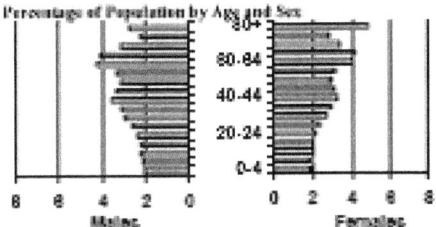

Source: UN Population Division, World Population Prospects (The 2000 Revision).

In 1950, Germany's population structure resembled a Christmas tree with a hollowed out section for those between 15 and 45, reflecting their severe war losses. By 2000, the population structure showed a bulge in the middle for those between 40 and 60 reflecting the German War Boom Babies commencing in 1950. Then by 2050, the structure will resemble an inverted pyramid with nearly all of the German Boomers in retirement.

Germany's post war baby boom passes through the years like a wave. Applying generational economics, we expect an economy to boom when the structure resembles a bulging column with a large portion of the population in their most productive years. We expect the economy to decline when it resembles an inverted pyramid having a large portion of the population retired. It is interesting to note that the German baby boom commences in the early 1950s, approximately five years after the

United States' does. A cursory generational economic analysis suggests that their economy will remain relatively strong until approximately 2013. Thus far, it has, but it is recently showing signs of strain.

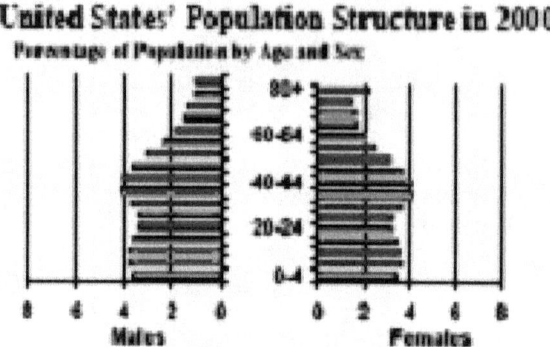

The U.S. had a large, curvaceous shape in 2000 with both large Boomer and Millennial bulges. Then the Boomers were in their peak financial factors implying a prolonged expansion

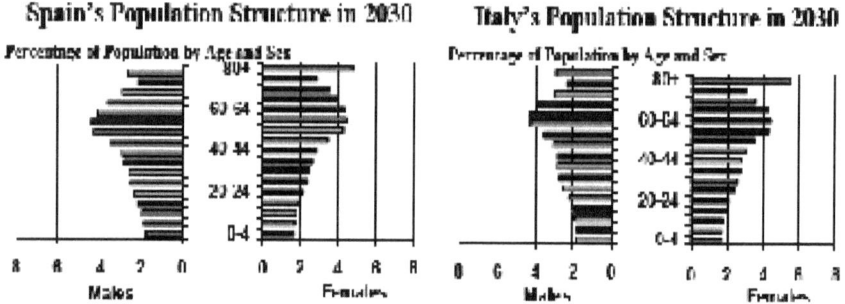

Most of the developed nations Watson Wyatt studied exhibit similar characteristics. Spain and Italy will look like an inverted pyramid in 2030, similar to Germany. By then, they too will have a large portion of their population in retirement.

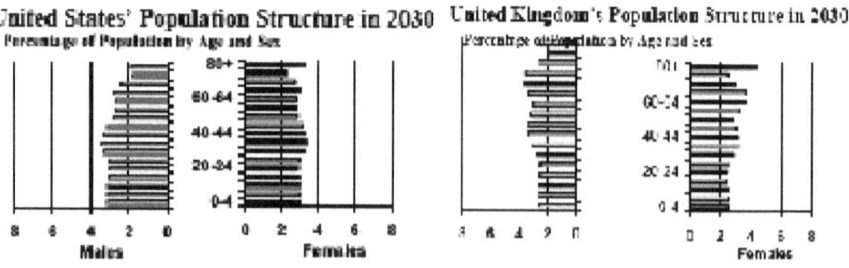

France's Population Structure in 2030

Percentage of Population by Age and Sex

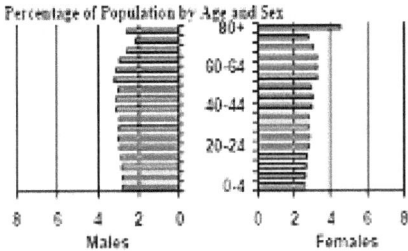

In 2030, the U.S. will look slim with minor bulges at the top for the Boomers and in the middle due to the Millennials who, at that time, occupy their peak financial years when the FTM predicts an expansion. The UK will resemble a slimmer version of the U.S.'s with a larger Boomer and expansion inducing Millennial bulges. France will look like a top-heavy pillar symbolizing few FTM related concerns. All of the countries exhibit a push of the population towards the later years, indicating potential problems supporting retirees.

The UN provided the population structures Watson Wyatt analyzed in their prophetic reports. The express purpose of these was to warn these client nations of the pending retirement crises, so they could plan to reduce the severity. Some nations heeded the warnings whereas others did not and are currently dealing with the consequences. Perhaps the U.S. put forth the best effort: first with the retirement act of 1986 and then with the balanced budget of the late 1990s. However, these worthy efforts were squandered by Washington in the 2000s just as the category 5 financial hurricanes bore down upon the nation.

Worker to retiree ratio

A fourth key indicator of the looming crisis consists of the worker to retiree ratio. In other words, how many workers support each retiree in the economy? When the worldwide Boomers were in their peak earning years, there was an abnormally large number of workers supporting the relatively smaller number of retiring Silents and retired Greatests. Now with declining birthrates and increasing life expectancies, there are more retirees per worker in the developed world, a trend that will only worsen over the next 20 years.

Workers per Retiree

Country	2000	2030	Drop
France	4.0	2.6	35%
Germany	4.2	2.1	50%
UK	4.2	2.9	31%

U.S.	5.3	3.0	43%
Japan	4.0	1.9	53%
Average	4.3	2.5	42%
Portugal	3.7	2.5	32%
Italy	3.2	2.3	28%
Ireland	5.9	3.6	39%
Greece	3.6	2.7	25%
Spain	4.0	2.7	33%
Average	4.1	2.8	31%

*Calculations based on data provided by the Population Division of the Department of Economic and Social Affairs of the United Nations Secretariat, These figures represent those over 65 versus those between 20 and 64.

We chose to represent the year 2000 since it is in the midst of the Boomer boom period. The choice of 2030 is when nearly all of the Boomers will be retired.

Notice that in 2000 all of the countries had three or more workers per retiree. By 2030, the ratio will drop significantly, 25% or more for all of the nations. The ratio for Japan and Germany falls by half indicating severe problems ahead. Ireland won't have this concern and the U.S. will be in surprisingly better shape than its European allies with a ratio of 3 to 1, despite a huge 43% drop off.

Europe's Prospects

In summary, generational economics **does** apply to Europe and the PIIGS. Since most of World War II was fought in Europe, they too experienced a baby boom followed by a Xer trough. Most of the nations' births start to grow modestly again by 2005, although it will take time before those newborns begin working and benefit their economies. Currently the fertility rate for continental Europe is 1.5%, far below the 2.1% replacement level. The average age for all of the listed countries will continue to rise until at least 2030.

Germany and Japan's median ages rise continuously from 1970 to 2040 representing significant challenges to these economies. Germany's median age peaks at an astounding 50 and Japan's at 53, whereas by comparison the U.S.'s will peak at 40 in 2035.

With dramatically fewer workers per retiree and generous public retirement programs, generational economics predicts a fate similar to the U.S.'s, but likely worse. Europe too will experience flat or negative growth prospects well into the 2020s and perhaps beyond. The population profiles for each nation differ, influencing their prospects. Much depends upon the quality of their leadership, the character of their people, and the legitimacy of their financial and banking systems.

Due to similar, although not identical generational economic profiles, Europe's experiences and future prospects are akin to the

U.S.'s. When the European Boomers were in their peak earning and spending years, Europe experienced an unprecedented boom period lasting for 15 years from 1993 until 2008. The U.S. also had its longest expansion, interrupted only by the dot-com recession of 2001.

Let's put this into perspective. We have all of these large, developed nations who experienced the largest population increase in their history after the war. Simultaneously, the life expectancies in all of these nations are expanding, while they provide increasingly more generous retirement benefits to their elderly. In addition, there is no war among these nations for over 50 years, a wonderful occurrence, which allows them to continuously increase national and personal wealth without depleting financial resources to fund such wars and rebuiding. As a result, there was an unprecedented accumulation of wealth saved for the developed world's Boomers' searching for "safe" retirement investments, of which there could not have been enough.

Like the U.S., the European Boomers were retiring by 2008 and starting to downsize. Spurned on by the same demand for AAA investments to finance Boomer retirements, mortgage backed securities grew rapidly. Housing values especially in the PIIGS nations grew at exponential rates. Similar to the U.S., their banking systems experienced severe stress when the housing markets collapsed and like in the U.S., one wonders why they could not see this coming, when the population structures supporting their economies were overburdened.

Portugal, Italy, Greece, and Spain along with Germany all have rapidly aging populations with a median age over 47 by 2030. Ireland is the exception with a median age of 40 by then and from a generational economic viewpoint does not fit entirely with the other PIIGS. Therefore, let's coin another term for the PIIGS minus Ireland or simply PIGS. Ireland is similar to the other PIIGS in that it too had rampant land speculation and a faulty banking system, but it does not have a generational economic component at this time.

Following the bursting of the real estate bubble and near bankruptcy of most major American banks, Europe too spun into a recession in 2008 - 2009. The U.S. barely avoided recessions in 2010 and 2011, but Europe succumbed to a double dip recession in 2012, when their GDP fell .3%. France and Germany still grew .9%, but this is still stunted.* After three quarters of negative growth and one quarter of positive growth, the UK's GDP shrunk 1.2% in the last quarter of 2012.* Granted, this is only a minor recession that did not affect all of its nations, but it underscores the depth of the problems Europe faces. In 2013, much of Europe finds itself in a triple dip recession.

I attend an annual economic forecast presented by Dr. Samuel Thomas of the Weatherhead School of Case Western Reserve University, which attracts up to 1000 financial and banking professionals. In late 2008 when the U.S. financial crisis was full-blown, he predicted that Europe's newer crisis would fester until all of the banks "confessed their sins." (In other words, their true losses) He predicted that due to their multi-national decision process, they would not take dramatic TARP-like action and therefore, would be mired in a financial quagmire until they did. For nearly every quarter of the last four years, Europe has faced yet another flashpoint that thrashes the U.S. and world markets. Five years later, his predictions still hold true as Europe is again in a recession.

Nearly all of the European nations' aging profiles exceed the United States' with many European nations having earlier average retirement ages. For instance, France's early retirement age was 59.4, Greece's 60, and Italy's 60.4. [In 2012 France extended their retirement age to 62, which many feel cost Sarkozy the Presidency after millions protested this change.]* The average EU retirement age was 60.9 in 2007 when the average U.S. retirement age was 62.* Then, why did these nations not succumb to a recession earlier?

A large part of the reason is that the PIIGS are part of the 17 member Eurozone, which all use the common Euro currency. In some ways, the Eurozone and EU are comparable to the United States. These two developed economies are of similar size, both are composed of multiple states, and approximately 2/3rds of the EU nations, as members of the Eurozone, use the same currency. But, here the similarities diverge. The U.S. has one federal government, one Federal Reserve and one national budget, where as the EU has 27. So, coordinating monetary policy becomes easier in the U.S.

The PIIGS ran up large deficits and since all in the Eurozone use the same currency, it became a shared problem. In the past, Greece simply would have defaulted and the drachma would be devalued. Now, Greece's excessive spending and huge deficits become a Eurozone problem.

In the United States, most states mandate a balanced budget, which became a significant problem to manage after the Great Recession, but one that would be much worse if they had piled up large deficits prior to the recession. Each nation in the Eurozone has large or very large national debts and is supposed to manage their deficits within limits, but there was no effective oversight or penalty for going over the limits. So, the PIIGS, in effect, took advantage of the situation, running up their debts with the idea that the 15-year boom period would last forever. As in the United States, there were millions of Boomers in their peak financial factors throughout the Eurozone and the rest of the developed world, searching for investments, so the PIIGS' debt attracted plenty of buyers.

Similar to the U.S., the Great Recession led to extremely high unemployment throughout the PIIGS, resulting in high unemployment payments. With falling real estate values and business revenues, there was less tax revenue to pay interest on the high national debts. Since all of the PIIGS face potential default, interest rates on their sovereign debt rose making it that much harder to pay down the debt. Banks throughout

Europe, and to a lesser extent the rest of the developed world, had funds invested in the PIIGS debt.   If these nations defaulted, it could bring down the European economy and likely lead to a worldwide depression. All of these circumstances are similar to what the U.S. faced in 2008.

As in the U.S., the pain is not the same throughout Europe. While states such as: Texas, Virginia, Iowa, and North Dakota barely noticed the Great Recession with low unemployment, others like California, Michigan, Ohio, Arizona, New York, and Wisconsin faced stiff challenges. Thanks to TARP, the auto bailout, fracking, and the stimulus plan Michigan, Ohio, Wisconsin, and New York are fairing well now. So it is with the EU. The big three faired better than the PIIGS.

From a Generational Economic viewpoint, the future does not look bright for the EU, largely because their population is older and they are economically more socialistic.   With the exception of two relatively smaller states, Ireland and Cyprus, all of the 27 EU nations are older than the U.S. As we saw earlier, this is particularly true for the big three and the PIIGS.

What Led to Europe's Economic Crisis

The increase in life expectancy is more dramatic in many EU nations as the table below indicates.   Two thirds of the EU nations and a vast majority of their population have life expectancies exceeding that of the U.S.

Life Expectancy at Birth
(focus nations in bold)

Rank	Country	Avg.	Male	Female
1	Japan	82.7	79.3	86.1
2	Switzerland	81.7	79.3	84.1
3	China, Hong Kong	81.7	79.0	84.3
4	Australia	81.5	79.1	83.8
5	Iceland	81.3	79.5	83.1
6	**Italy**	81.3	78.6	84.0
7	**France**	80.9	77.5	84.3
8	Sweden	80.9	78.8	82.9
9	Israel	80.7	78.4	82.9
10	Singapore	80.6	78.5	82.7
11	Canada	80.5	78.2	82.8
12	**Spain**	80.5	77.2	83.8
20	**Germany**	79.8	77.2	82.4
21	Belgium	79.8	77.0	82.5
22	**Ireland**	79.7	77.3	82.0
23	**United Kingdom**	79.6	77.4	81.7
24	**Greece**	79.5	77.0	82.0

| 35 | **Portugal** | 78.6 | 75.3 | 81.8 |
| 38 | **United States** | 78.0 | 75.4 | 80.5 |

Source: United Nations, Department of Economic and Social Affairs, Population Division (2011): World Population Prospects: The 2010 Revision. New York (Updated: 4 May 2011)

As in the U.S., productivity improvements over the 20th Century enabled developed EU economies to provide more wealth to their citizens thereby making widespread retirements plausible. The vast productivity improvements that apply to agriculture, manufacturing, and finally the service sector also reduced the amount of upkeep in homes, enabling women to work outside of the home throughout Europe, further increasing personal and national wealth.

Women Freed from Housework

PBS presented a series called "1900 House" portraying a London family living as they would in 1900 Victorian England with none of the modern conveniences. The wife's role was overwhelmingly difficult, requiring over 60 hours per week to clean, shop and cook for the family of five. Shortly into the experiment, she hired a servant to help with the load. There was no time to work outside the home. As women entered the workforce en masse starting in the 1960s, the percentage of working adults soared to nearly 70%, allowing families and society to save for retirement and also to consume more.* These added workers provided even more stimulus to the economy.

As observed earlier, consistent with generational economics, Towers Watson's reports in the early 1990s warned of the looming calamite. As in the U.S., the European Boomer wave peaked in the newly hatched European Union in the mid 1980s through mid 2000s bringing an unparalleled level of prosperity. When the Boomer wave receded, the EU faced prospects more drastic than those in the U.S.

European Millennials to the Rescue?

Due to the war, the EU had comparable Boomer and Xer generations, but did not have a large Millennial generation to ride to its financial rescue. In the U.S., the Millennial births are nearly as large as the Boomers. Here is a chart of EU births along with the corresponding U.S. Generations:

European Births by Generations

Generation	Period	Births#	Relative Size	U.S. Size
Boomer	1946-67	7.7 mil	100%	100%
Xer +	1968-90	6.0 mil	78%	86%
Millennial	1991-04	5.2 mil	68%	98%
Post Millennials	2005-	5.2 mil	67%	

#Births represent those at the end of the period per year.*
+ The Xer generation was extended, since the births continued at the same level

It is evident that the EU nations initially experienced something extraordinarily similar to the Boomer and Xer generations in the U.S., but then the stories diverge. The EU Boomers represent a large increase in births, followed by a similar Xer trough. In the U.S., the Millennials were as voluminous as their Boomers parents were, but in the EU, there was no Millennial bump. One possible explanation is a lack of immigration into Europe. In addition to the Boomers, the U.S. experienced rapid growth of foreign-born people from the 1970 to 2007. Since new immigrants tend to be younger and have more children, they would add to the Millennial births. At first from 1983-1990, the births held their own in Europe, but then from 1991 to 2004 there was a precipitous drop in births. By the new millennium in the U.S., the annual births are close to those of the Boomer generation, whereas in the EU they are a third lower.

The dramatic difference in the EU's Millennials story reveals the potential depth of the EU crisis. In the EU, there will be no large Millennial cavalry to ride to the rescue with their peak earnings, spending, savings, and borrowing. Instead, a smaller working generation will support their much larger Boomer parents.

The U.S. Millennials will get a break in terms of the number of retirees to support when the less voluminous Xers start retiring in the mid 2020s. However, the EU Xers also outnumber EU Millennials, so there will be no such break for them. This situation looks very challenging for the EU nations. Their Debt/GDP was 90% and they are working to keep this down, but doing so will be a tough slog as each year brings another round of Boomer retirees to support.

Social Expenditures

As expected, social expenditures in the EU, traditionally much higher than those in the U.S., represent a strong, bitterly cold, headwind facing the European Union too. Below is a table summarizing social expenditures for our focus nations.

Social Expenditures as a percent of GDP
2007

Country	Social Expenditures
France	31%
Germany	28%
Italy	27%
Greece	25%
Portugal	24%
UK	23%
Spain	21%
Ireland	19%
Japan	19%
EU	26%
U.S.	16%
OECD Average	19%

* *

The EU's social spending was 60% higher than the U.S.'s in 2007 prior to the Great Recession. As expected, considering the number of people receiving unemployment, food stamps, and medical care, total social spending would escalate during the Great Recession. In the U.S. in 2011, such spending accounted for 18.5% of GDP.* But, social spending in the EU with even higher unemployment would ratchet upwards too.

Overall, the picture for the EU nations looks bleaker than that of the U.S.

1. Their average life expectancy is higher than the U.S.'s
2. The average retirement age is slightly lower.
3. There will be fewer younger workers to provide for the large number of retiring Boomers.
4. The EU spends approximately 60% more on social spending than the U.S.
5. At 90% in 2013, the EUs current Debt/GDP is high, but below the U.S.'s.

The 1980s through 2007 when the Boomers were in their peaks was a boom period for Europe too, even longer than that of the U.S.'s. Like the U.S., they likely ignored the approaching crisis and failed to take significant action in time. Granted, some countries like Germany and the UK did display financial prudence, but many did not, driving up Debt/GDP at a time when they should have been driving it downward. Since the Great Recession, the European nations have taken numerous measures to correct their financial problems.

Without a huge multi-generational economic model, similar to the

FTM, specifically built for the EU nations, it is difficult to predict the precise course ahead for Europe, perhaps the topic of another book. If we tweak the U.S. Financial Time Machine a little and assume that European peak financial propensities are similar to the U.S.'s, we arrive at the version of the machine below the U.S's. Both of these charts include only the later three, focal generations: Boomers, Xers, and Millennials.*

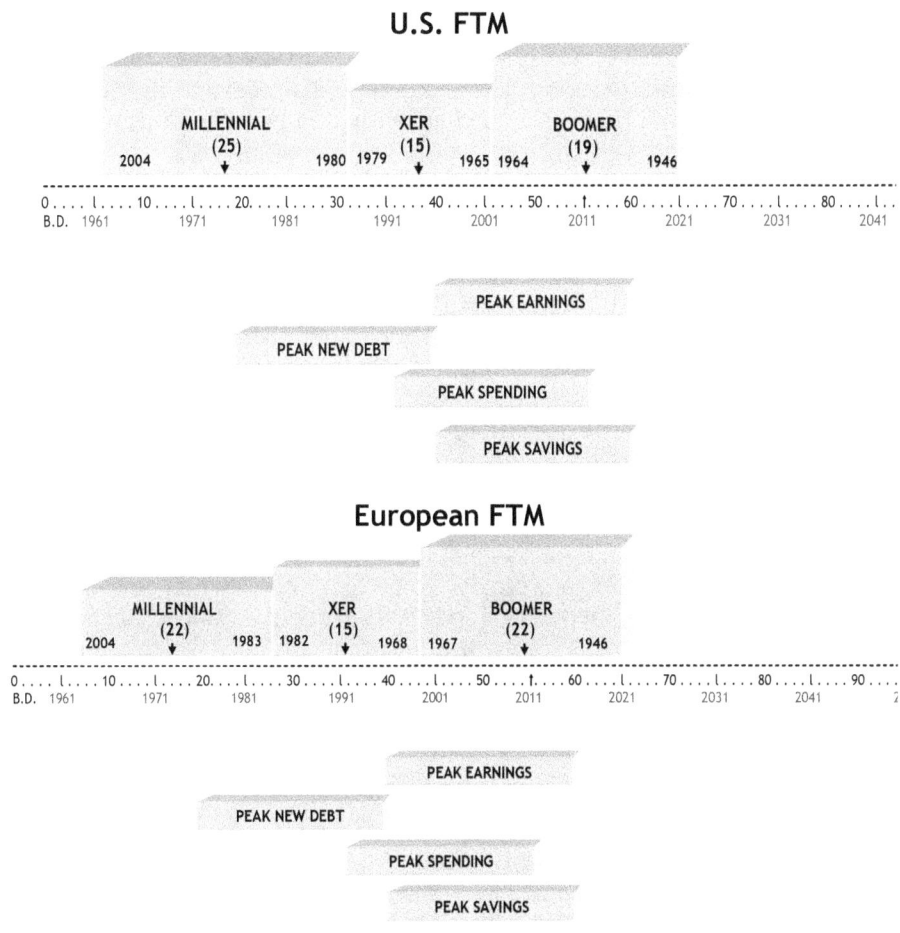

The U.S.'s version displays peak generations followed by trough generations. It is likely that the Greatest and Silent generations were even smaller in Europe due to the massive number of deaths there, but we did not project these, since we are no longer peering into the past. In the European model, there is no Millennial peak generation, instead we see a step down from Boomers to Xers, and once again from Xers to Millennials representing a dramatic difference.

We expect to see an expansion from the 1980s through late 2000s when the European Boomers pass out of their peak financial factors. Then, we expect a large recession. Both of these FTM predicted events happened, adding validity to the rough model.

Without performing the detailed calculations, combined generational economic stimulus will decline continuously until the Post Millennials start to reach their peak spending, sadly not until 2040. By then, the midpoint EU Boomer will be in their mid eighties and their drain upon the economy will greatly diminish. Up until then, the EU will likely face repeated recessions like the double dip recession they entered in 2012. For an area that went 15 years without a recession this has been a rough adjustment.

The Europeans, recognizing the looming crisis some time ago, published an aging report in 2009.* During their ongoing economic crisis, they introduced numerous cutbacks. In some European nations, like in the U.S., public workers were able to retire in their early fifties. Many EU nations extended the retirement age while upping their equivalent Social Security age. Such actions will increase the number of workers, while decreasing the number of retirees and hopefully provide a measure of relief to these beleaguered economies.

Each of the European nations possesses varied demographic and economic profiles; therefore, their prospects vary, like U.S. states. From the FTM perspective, Ireland, France, and the UK possess more optimistic prospects than Germany, Italy, and Spain. How they fare over the next 20 years largely depends upon their political systems and their policy decisions, which thus far, are proving to be extremely challenging.

The International Monetary Fund (IMF) expects advanced economies to grow around 1% in 2013 with the Eurozone at **.2%,** which generally resembles the European Commissions Autumn 2012 forecast.

European GDP Growth (%)

Year	2007	08	09	10	11	12	13	14
GDP Growth	3.2	.3	-4.3	2.1	1.5	-.3	.1#	1.6

European Commissions Autumn Economic Forecast 2012 *
#January, 2013 revised estimate

These figures substantiate the Financial Time Machine's projections for Europe thus far, showing an average growth of .5% over the 8-year period. Without developing a European model of the Super Financial Time Machine, we expect growth to remain sluggish for the foreseeable future. Given the stagnant growth expectations for the United States and the lack of a large Millennial generation to stimulate the economy, we expect the EU's forecast to be worse than the U.S.'s from the FTM viewpoint (sub 2% average growth with higher recession risks.)

With a large Boomer generation followed by two progressively smaller generations, a combined model would likely predict negative growth over the next 20 years or so.   However, productivity improvements can offset such dismal prospects.   Also, prudent policy decisions regarding deficits and spending can offset such a scenario. Generational economics is a powerful indicator, but it is not the only factor.

Such a forecast seems depressing, but perhaps an adjustment of expectations is in order.   We have grown accustomed to near zero interest rates, which considering inflation are actually negative in real terms.   Instead, we hunt for rates that might be .25% higher.   Therefore, the Europeans and we will likely grow accustomed to GDP growth rates under 2.0%.

Solutions

What should the EU do to manage its generational economic related debt crisis? This is the $10 trillion Euro question and beyond the scope of this book.   As in the U.S., European conservatives want to cut taxes, social spending and cut the deficits.   Liberals want to raise taxes and apply Keynesian stimulus to jump-start the economy.   The U.S. and various European countries tried both approaches and both largely failed with the possible exceptions of the UK, and Germany, and outside Europe, Canada.

Most European nations are cutting government employment roles and pay, as have most U.S. states and localities.   European governments have applied austerity measures such as raising the retirement age, slashing budgets, privatizing public companies, selling public assets, cutting government projects, and changing work rules.

One should recognize that this is a long-term problem; that leaders cannot solve by pressing a stimulus bulb thereby priming the economic engine so it starts humming again.   For many nations, the contraction will not end until the 2030s, when their Boomers are a lesser financial drain.   To truly minimize the economic pain requires a broad based approach similar to Gramm-Rudman, including intelligent tax reform, and spending cuts.   Productivity improvements will gradually help, but not enough and expectations need to line up with reality. Spending wildly on government programs may make it seem better for a while, but it will only worsen the future.

Europe may well enter a long-term contraction similar to Japan's last two decades, whose FTM profile resembles Europe's 15 years earlier. The next chapter examines Japan in light of the FTM to see if there are similarities to the European and United States' prospects.   If there are such similarities, what can be done to avoid Japan's fate?

20

Global Implications – Japan

Without developing detailed models for each of the major European economies, we applied the principles of the Financial Time Machine (FTM) to these nations finding that the FTM performed extraordinarily well predicting past and recent European economic cycles. It postulates that under the current generational economic conditions this and the next decade will be challenging ones for the EU.

Since Japan was a major combatant in the Second World War with a likely War Boom Baby generation, the Financial Time Machine may also apply to them as well. After the U.S. and China, Japan is the third largest economy. From a generational economic perspective, we will soon see that Japan's economy leads the U.S. and Europe by about 15 -20 years. Are there lessons to learn from Japan for Europe and the United States?

While collecting statistics regarding the EU's evolving financial crisis, I also collected data on Japan and was surprised to see the severity of their financial situation.

- Their median age is the highest of all the nations at over 44.
- Their median age peaks at 53 in 2040, the highest level for any nation in history.
- Their life expectancy is the highest at 82.7.
- Their average retirement age was 68.5 in 2009 – the highest.
- Their fertility rate is an extremely low 1.39.
- Their number of births has continuously fallen.
- By 2030, they will have only 1.9 workers per retiree, the worst ratio.
- The Debt/GDP ratio was 212% in 2013, but is largely owned internally.
- Their social expenditures are not much higher than the U.S.'s at 18.7% of GDP including national health care.

Here are some other economic factors:

Annual GDP growth rate	.4%
Inflation	.2%
Interest rate	.0%
Unemployment	3.9%

From Trading Economics, August 2013

The Federal Reserve would be pleased if they were able to have 3.9% unemployment and no inflation, although they would be concerned about the low rate of growth.   Japan's economy slowed in 2012 due to territorial disputes with China, but this appeared to be temporary. Will Japan finally succeed in exiting their elongated period of contraction or do more challenges remain? What does the FTM predict in this regard?

Japan too had a relatively severe recession in 2008 followed shortly by another less severe one from the end of 2010 to the beginning of 2011, due to the tsunami and resultant nuclear crisis.   By the end of 2012, they entered a triple dip recession with growth again slowing slightly.*

The 1980s were a period of robust growth for the Japanese, who did not experience a recession until 1993-1994, followed by others in 1998 and shortly afterwards in 2002. In less than 20 years, Japan weathered **six** recessions.   The 1990s were the "lost decade"; obviously, a misnomer, since the period of economic stress has now lasted two decades, in other words, the lost score.   From 1991 through 2012, Japan's growth averaged only 1.03%.* Japan is experiencing a period of prolonged deflation, in which wages fell by 7% with housing down over 50% over the lost score.*

The causes of this lost score sound familiar. Since World War II, the government encouraged people to save, creating an immense amount of wealth to invest.   By the late 1980s, with so much excess capital, opportunities became more speculative as housing, equity, and bond prices rose sharply.   Subprime loans and credit became easy to obtain with prime Tokyo property fetching up to $38,000 per square foot.

Eventually, the real estate and stock market bubbles burst.   Then the government began subsidizing failing banks and businesses.   As a result, from December of 1990 to 2003, the Nikkei index lost over 80% of its value.

With such dramatic losses, the Japanese experienced deflation from the early 1990s until 2013.   In response, the government initiated quantitative easing and reduced interest rates to nearly zero, which did not succeed in stimulating the economy. Similar to what we see in the U.S. and Europe, the banks had numerous bad real estate investments that they did not recognize, hoping these would eventually turn around. As a result, there was less money to fund businesses and homes. Instead of putting money into banks, people, afraid the banks would collapse, bought gold and U.S. and Japanese Treasury bonds.*

The Japanese scenario sounds frighteningly familiar, when compared to what is unfolding in the U.S. and Europe.   The excess capital, high stock prices, easy credit, subprime loans, real estate bubble, and stingy bank loans are analogous to U.S. financial conditions 15 years later. The solutions, using near zero interest rates, quantitative easing and auto bailouts, also sound familiar. One important difference is TARP, in which the U.S. bailed out the financial industry immediately, rather than letting its bad loans fester for years, as Japan and Europe did.

In 2013, reversing their previous low interest rate program, Japan's new Prime Minister, Shinzo Abe, commenced a program to jumpstart the economy by targeting a 2% inflation rate. The plan is to buy Trillions of yen worth of bonds to lower the value of the yen on the world market. This strategy should make their exports more competitive in the world markets.* With a Debt/GDP ratio over 200% this strategy could be risky though, since the interest payments on their debt will increase, but since nothing has worked in over a score, they feel it is worth a try.*

Thus far, Japan has experienced two decades of tough economic times and deflation. For over five years, the U.S. economy has struggled on the edge of a double dip recession. Will these troubles persist and do we face a fate similar to Japan's with frequent recessions? Let's look at Japan from a generational economic perspective to see if there are similarities or if these problems are just unique to Japan.

Generational Economic Parallel?

Japanese Births

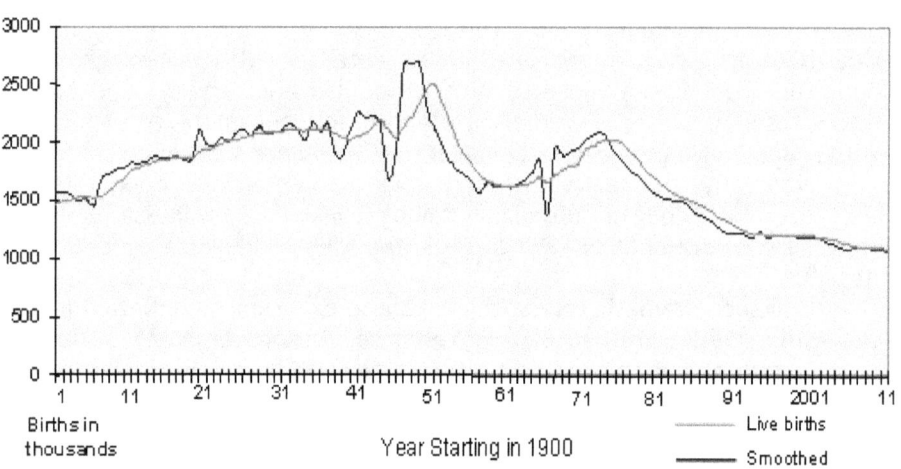

Above is a history of Japanese births. The red (lighter) line is smoothed by a 5-year moving average because it takes time for generational shifts to affect the economy. What we see from a macro perspective is a wave building for 50-years. There were brief declines in the late 1930s and end of the war, but these were of short duration. There was also a 5-year baby boom following the war, but this too was short compared to the U.S.'s 19-year, multi-child baby boom.

Essentially, a hundred plus years of Japanese birth history can be summarized as a long wave, followed by a shorter wave and then a long trough.

The population wave started to recede in 1952 until it built again through mid 1970s. Then, throughout the last four decades, the number of births steadily declined until 2007 when the deaths exceeded births. Now the population itself is receding, with the births about half of what they were in the twenties, thirties, and forties.

We certainly observe a distinct wave pattern, implying two economic cycles. At first, it appears Japan's wave pattern does not match that of the U.S. except for one calamitous factor - the war. The Japanese' equivalent of the Greatest generation suffered severe losses during World War II, losing 4 % of their population (2.6 to 3.1 million people.) Any loss is tragic, but by comparison, the U.S. only lost .32% or one tenth as many people. Most of the approximately 75 million worldwide war deaths were civilian, but in Japan's case, 70 - 80% were military. These losses would have largely been males between the ages of 18 and 40 in their prime nesting phase.

Japan's Population Structure in 1950

Percentage of Population by Age and Sex

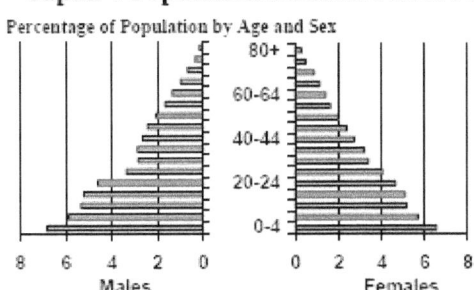

Watson Wyatt's 1950 population profile supports this analysis, since there is a dent in the male population trend between the ages of 25 and 35, five years after the war ended. The male population drops precipitously for those born between 1916 and 1925, corresponding to the last cohort of the U.S.'s Greatest generation. In the U.S., the Greatests were a peak generation, but due to the war, this would not be the case for Japan.

In the U.S., there were far fewer births during the Depression and war than after the war. This was not the case in Japan, where with the exception of only three years, the Silents' population grew continuously. In the U.S., the war boom lasted nearly 20 years producing dramatically more births. Except for five years, births declined in Japan during the same period and were significantly less than those of the Japanese Silents.

In the U.S., the Greatests outnumbered the Silents, which was the opposite case in Japan where the Silents outnumbered the Greatests. Therefore, we do have a series of waves forming. The Japanese Greatests, depleted by the war, represent a trough followed by a Silent wave. Their Boomers, as pictured above, become a trough. Then, the Xers form a brief wave followed by a Millennial trough.

The Japanese experience is the reverse of the United States - like a negative photographic image. The generational names do not apply to the Japanese, but what is important are the wave-like patterns regardless of the names. Below is a table summarizing Japan's generations using the corresponding U.S. names.

Japanese Equivalent Generations

Generation	Average Births (000)	% of Silents	Type	Years	Dura-tion	U.S. Years
Greatest	1,800	80#	Trough	1901 -25	25	1901 -25
Silent	2,160	100	Wave	1926 -51	26	1926 -45
Boomer	1,693	78	Trough	195 2-66	15	1946 -64
Xer	1,862	86	Wave	1967 -81	15	1965 -79
Millennial	1,253	58	Trough	1982 -06	25	1980 - 04

adjusted for military war deaths

Notice how remarkably close the Japanese generations line up with the American generations. The only difference, and it is a major one, is that their peak generations are our trough generations, and their trough generations are our peaks.

Japanese Generations Names
Circa 2010
The Japanese have their own names for these generations. Those now in their sixties and seventies are known as "the generation that got away" before the problems occurred. Those in their forties and fifties are "the generation desperate to get away." And those in their twenties and thirties: "The generation that can't get away."

The graphic below represents a prototype of a simple version of the Japanese Financial Time Machine. If you compare this version to the U.S. time machine, you see that it is practically the inverse image with our peaks corresponding to their valleys and vice versa.

Japanese Financial Time Machine Prototype

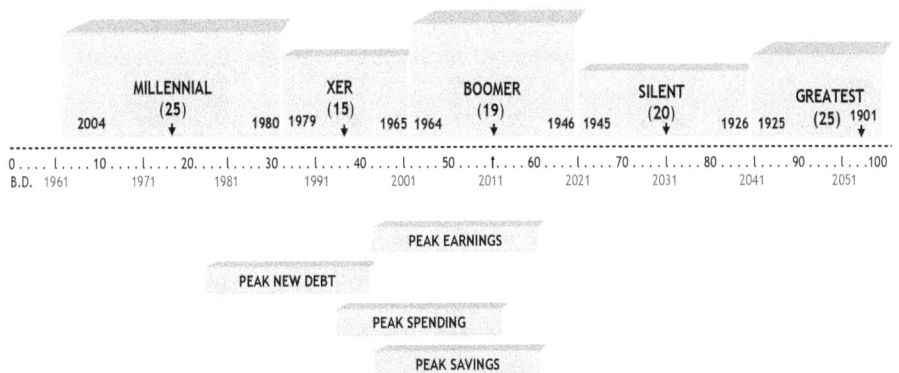

U.S. Financial Time Machine

According to the rough Japanese Financial Time Machine, we expect an extended period of economic growth from the long Silent generation when they are in their peak financial factors. Indeed, Japan's GDP growth averaged above 8% from 1956 until 1973, resembling the kind of robust growth we see in China over the two decades from 1992 to 2013. They did experience one brief recession in 1974, caused by the oil crisis. Afterwards, Japan continued to grow until the early 1990s.* Astoundingly, there was only one recession in **36** years. So, Japan's peak Silent generation led to an expansion similar to the Boomer's expansion, only longer, but they span an additional seven years.

Since the Japanese retire approximately five years later than U.S. workers do, the first Silents would exit their peak earnings and savings phases around 1987. The Financial Time Machine is not Japanese based, but according to the FTM, the trough Japanese Boomer generation would have started their peak earnings and savings phase. In just eight years, there was a precipitous 42% drop in the number of births from the peak of the Silents to the bottom of the Boomers. These reduced Boomers are the ones entering their peaks in 1992, which explain the severity of the economic reversal, with dramatically reduced generational stimulus to the economy.

According to the FTM, we expect an economic boom up until around 1992 and as expected, this is when Japan's asset bubble burst. Japan's annual GDP growth peaked in 1987 at 6.5% and then fell steadily until 1992. Up until this time, the Silent wave generation would have been accumulating wealth.

Since the Japanese save at a much higher rate than the U.S. and it was the second largest economy in the world up until 2012, their personal, corporate, and governmental retirement savings were massive. In addition, Japanese corporations provide more for employee retirement than those in the U.S. Like the U.S., there would have been an excess of savings looking for quality investments, since by the 1990s the peak wave would have been seeking safe investments and starting retirement. Climbing real estate investments would seem attractive, but starting in 1987 there would be continuously fewer buyers as the Silents commenced downsizing and there were dramatically fewer Boomers seeking residences.

From 1987 onward, the generational stimulus continuously declines, as does the demand for assets like stocks, and real estate. Therefore, these asset classes experience continuous devaluation.

Japan feared inflation at one time, but with an average retirement age of 68.5 (69.7 for males in 2009), the Silent wave generation who is currently 61 and older seek fixed assets, which enables their government to finance an oversized national debt, just as the later Boomer generations in the U.S. and Europe are doing.

As is the case in the U.S. with the Millennial generation, Japan's larger Xer generation is riding to the economy's rescue, with consistently more generational stimulus to help the economy. This stimulus is not yet enough to offset the loss of Boomer stimulus, but as we saw in the Super Financial Time Machine, it is enough to maintain minimal growth. This generation is larger than the Japanese Boomers, but not nearly as large as the Silents. Therefore, generational stimulus declined slowly starting around 2007.

Looking at the graph of births from earlier in the chapter, we see a spike resembling an Arizona mesa formation from 1947 until 1952 when the number of births suddenly rises by over a third. The last of the Japanese Silents (the tsunami-like crest of the wave) will reach the average retirement age in 2016. Lacking a better term, let's call these distinctive members of the generation the "Crestors." By then, the Xers enter their peak years, but they are 25% smaller than the Crestors are and the Millennials, early in their careers, are half their size. Therefore, even though a peak Xer generation is on the horizon, ready to ride to the economic rescue, this stunning population spike presents an unusual problem. The Financial Time Machine predicts that the period from 2016 through at least 2021 will be an exceptionally challenging one for Japanese leadership.

In the U.S., the Super Financial Time Machine accounts for all of the generations simultaneously. Even though the Boomer stimulus declines rapidly, when combined with the stimulus from the other generations, there is still a small positive stimulus. Without building a similar complex model for Japan, it is easy to see that their generational stimulus will decay at a very rapid rate, once the Crestors retire en masse, because there is no comparable wave to offset their declining stimulus.

Japan managed its debt well over the last 20 years, but the Japanese leadership faces a challenging period going forward. Absent courageous leadership, like in the U.S., the FTM predicts the Japanese debt crisis to unfold after 2016. Digesting the tough to swallow retiring Crestor pill will take approximately five years.

Japan is an island nation with a limited amount of space and resources, so stagnant growth, whether conscious or not, may be difficult to avoid. At 127 million, their population is three times what it was in 1900, yet it has only grown 0.5% over the last 10 years. From the Financial Time Machine's perspective, Japan's rapid population growth during their "Silent" generation provided an immense force of productive human resources to power their emergence as the second largest world economy of the 20th Century – an amazing accomplishment.

Adding credibility to the FTM's analysis, the previous central bank governor Maasaki Shirakawa credits Japan's declining population as the source of their problems. With fewer consumers, the demand for everything is declining. He says that the problem cannot be solved by flooding the market, with money because there are not enough people or companies looking to borrow it.*

Japan's story is not all bad. Over the last 20 years, their unemployment rate ranged between 2% and 5.6%, an enviable position for either the U.S. or Europe, but the number of workers is declining.

Their Debt to GDP ratio has exceeded 90% since 1996 and true to the Reinhart/Rogoff analysis, their average GDP now averages about 2%. Japan struggles with moderate deflation, but there is no immediate danger of inflation. Even with a mind boggling Debt/GDP of 212%, their bond rates remain minimal. This is because their people own their debt. According to the Bank of France, in 2011, the Japanese private residents owned 85% of Japanese sovereign debt; the central bank owned 9%, whereas foreigners owned only 6%.

Thus far, Japan has avoided a PIIGS-like debt crisis with a near 0.0% interest rate and mild deflation. Servicing their large debt has been inexpensive, but as aging continues, government social security and medical coverage costs will rise. With a declining ratio of workers, the highest number of old people, a mountain of debt and a slow rate of growth, Japan's prospects do not look bright.

Their long-term trade surplus allowed them to accumulate a large quantity of foreign financial assets, which provide needed income. At some time, they may be forced to sell some of these assets to support their retirees. Like the U.S., their retirees will cash in bonds, reducing the demand for these, which will likely lead to the debt crisis. The first Crestor hits the retirement age of 68.5 in 2016, which is the expected onset of the debt crisis. As the Japanese Silents pass away they will transfer the remainder of their wealth to the subsequent generations easing their financial burden.

Solutions

Considering the severity of the population drop, the Japanese government, companies, and people have done a remarkable job navigating through their fiscal problems. Many, who hedged against Japanese debt over the last decade expecting a crisis, lost those bets. Japan may be able to delay the crisis by selling assets like the $1+ trillion of U.S. treasuries and other foreign assets, since in effect, what they have done is save for retirement. The PIIGS did not have this option.

Another option utilized by many of the PIIGS nations is for Japan to increase the average retirement age. As recently as 1993 that age was a startling 71.4 for men, nearly 10 years later than the U.S.'s.

A possible long-term solution for Japan is to increase the number of births to the point where their population stabilizes over time (an easy thing to say, but not easy to implement.) Up until now, the Greatest generation, whose numbers were diminished by the war, has been passing on. From now on, the more voluminous Silent generation will pass. If Japan adopted incentives for parents to have more children, this might increase population growth, and help replace expiring Silents.

Japan's Child Care and Family Care Leave Law went into effect in 2010. "The law provides fathers with an opportunity to take up to eight weeks of leave after the birth of a child and allows employees with pre-school age children the following allowances:

- up to five days of leave in the event of a child's injury or sickness,
- limits on the amount of overtime in excess of 24 hours per month based on an employee's request,
- limits on working late at night based on an employee's request, and
- opportunity for shorter working hours and flex time for employees."

Such policies make it easier for Japanese parents to have children.* Unfortunately, it will take 20 years before newborns start working and during that time, they are dependents like the Silents. Japan faces tough times ahead and such a policy would help them maintain instead of lose population and workers, as they will be doing at an accelerating rate.

Another unlikely solution is to increase immigration, something which has helped the UK increase its population by 7% over the last decade, thereby helping to avoid its own aging and debt crisis. As an island locked country, Japan has never encouraged immigration, but the UK is also an island nation and they encouraged immigration. With huge neighbors like the Philippines, Indonesia, China, and Korea there are plenty of potential immigrants nearby, from whom to choose, although cultural norms may make it understandably difficult to do so.

Japan could limit immigration to the type of workers they need most (physicians, nurses, technicians, engineers, laborers.) In the U.S., new immigrants reproduce at a substantially faster rate. The immigrants could be in their twenties and thirties, who would help plug the gap left by the passing Silents, without waiting for a new generation. Immigrants could be temporary workers with no guarantee of permanent residence. Immigration is not a panacea. The U.S., France, Germany, UK, Dubai, and Norway have struggled with resultant immigration problems, but perhaps Japan can learn from their travails and create an enlightened policy.

A well thought out immigration strategy could greatly help Japan to lessen the pending debt crisis, increase its GDP, provide needed workers, taxes, and reduce its Debt/GDP. With limited space and having to import many resources, Japan probably does not want to grow much more than its current population, which the strategy can accomplish. Such a scenario is not ideal, but in a crisis, ideal solutions seldom appear.

Robots

Japan, the leader in robotics, is investing in robots to care for the elderly. Japan uses robots in manufacturing, which in essence makes their declining workforce more productive. There are already robots that:

- Lift patients
- Vacuum floors – Roomba
- Wash floors – Scooba
- Clean gutters
- Cut lawns
- Navigated by an adult child, move through a parent's apartment to see the parent, and like Skype can be seen and talk to the parent
- Interact with elderly, like pets or babies

The Elderly Robot Assistant (ERA)

With today's technology, it is relatively easy to create a robot to care for and perform chores for a non-ambulatory elderly person. It is really just a matter of combining current technologies towards a new application.

An elderly person could direct such a robot with a remote control and camera on the robot, so it could navigate from room to room. They would see what the robot sees and guide its motions on a tablet. There are already robots that perform a similar function attending school for ailing students. Let's call the robot the Elderly Assistant Robot or ERA. ERA would have typical robot extendable arms and hands that could open cabinets and grab any object and sensors to detect objects in the way. ERA would have the capability to fetch required items, make meals, and perform daily chores, according to its operator's tablet touches on the touch-screen.

A remote relative, friend, or healthcare professional could also control the ERA remotely and simultaneously interact with the elderly. The controller could be an iPad or Droid app, which could also record its activities. Soon ERA could learn established patterns and react to verbal commands like Siri, such as, "ERA take my robe and put it on the hook," "ERA take my glass and get me some water," "ERA call my daughter," "ERA turn down the heat two degrees and turn off the lights," or "ERA call an Ambulance." All the technology exists today to create such a device by integrating hand-held devices and apps with robotics through wireless communications.

ERA could also remember and dispense medications, based on bar coded medicine bottles. It could take, record, monitor, and transmit vital data such as temperature, blood pressure and pulse on a prescribed basis. With face recognition, it could monitor patient's mood and communicate these through the app to relatives or healthcare professionals. It could also detect skin abnormalities like bedsores and call for help in an emergency.

A more advanced robot could be trained to assist patients to get out of bed, which the Japanese have developed. It might also assist with cleaning and hygienic chores typically performed by, soon to be rare, aids. One remote operator, such as an aide could care for several patients who live in their homes from a central location, thereby avoiding non-productive travel.

Japan has produced robotic pets and is experimenting with robots that provide companionship to the elderly. Recognizing how much people interact with their hand-held devices, it may not be too much of a stretch to imagine robots with a semblance of personality like Siri's and pleasing design to combat loneliness.

All the technologies currently exist to build the initial version of

ERA. Considering the potential demand, the price could eventually be in the thousands of dollars. According to the Genworth 2012 Cost of Care Survey, the average nursing home cost of a single room is $6,750 per month.* ERAs costing perhaps two to three month of care ($15,000 - $20,000) could keep people in their homes for years, thereby saving Medicare, Medicaid, and the economy billions of dollars in the U.S. and Japan. Considering the future dearth of health care workers versus the looming demand, such solutions will soon become necessary.

Thanks to the Internet, seniors can order practically anything on-line and have it delivered usually without shipping charges. Fresh food delivery is even available in some U.S. cities.

With one out of four Japanese over 65 by 2015, Japan will become the leader in elderly robotics, pioneering the way for Europe and the U.S. This in itself will become a growing and highly profitable industry for Japan.

There is already a shortage of nursing home aids in the U.S, a problem that will only become more severe over the next 20 years. The aids literally perform the heavy lifting of the elderly and dirty jobs. In December of 2012, the demand for such aids was up 120% from a year earlier. With low pay, turnover rates averaging over 50%, and a high rate of injuries, finding enough aids to staff nursing homes is problematic. According to the Census Bureau, the number of people over 65 is projected to nearly double from 40 million in 2010 to 73 million in 2030. The nursing home aids are the type of jobs the ERA will perform, emphasizing the critical need for this device.

Parallels

The parallels between Japan and the U.S. are striking. The major macro difference is that their generational waves are the U.S.'s troughs and their troughs roughly line up with the U.S.'s waves. As a result, we are about 15 years out of synch with Japan. What they experienced in 1992 is the equivalent of what we experienced in 2008. The generational economic similarities are striking, as are the causes, results, and chosen solutions.   2013 in the U.S., is 1997 in Japan.   Japan has had five recessions over the last 20 years and the Financial Time Machine predicts three or four for the U.S.

Similarities:

- Waves – negative image of each other
- Long boom period during the peak generation's peak
- Wave generation generates high investment demand
- Crash when wave generation starts to retire as the trough generation enters their peaks

- Real estate bubble and crash when wave generation downsizes
- Severe stock crash
- Recession, which can be severe according to size of wave
- Declining birth rates
- Inclining mortality rates
- Declining worker/retiree ratio
- Negative or near zero generational stimulus
- Prolonged period of economic hardship
- Deflating real estate value
- Quantitative easing
- Keynesian stimulus does not end contraction period
- Nothing seems to bring back sustained growth
- Large deficits
- Low GDP growth rates
- High Debt/GDP ratio
- Near zero interest rates for years
- Successive recessions or near recessions

There is much to learn from Japan and how they manage their crisis.

Thankfully, the U.S. has the Millennial generation now in the workforce, which should lessen the financial hardships and recessions for the U.S. A large portion of the reason the U.S.'s population is growing is because of immigration, but the U.S. also has more land and resources. Japan has its Xer wave generation entering the workforce, which is 86% the size of the Silent wave. This generation should provide some offsetting stimulus for the Japanese economy. In the U.S. the Millennials should end the contraction period, but the Japanese Millennials are much smaller than the preceding generations, which represent an extremely difficult long-term generational economic problem to solve.

Given the rough hand they were dealt, Japanese leadership, companies, and their people have done an amazing job of providing high employment for their people, profits for the companies and care for those in need, all while avoiding an expected debt crisis. The U.S. leadership even though they have a better hand has not yet demonstrated they are equal to the task. Both nations face a debt crisis in 2016 - 2018. There is time, but not much. There are viable alternatives, but a decreasing set.

The Japanese debt crisis intersects U.S.'s debt, because Japan, its companies, and its people own over a trillion dollars of U.S. public debt plus numerous U.S. companies. As of May 2013, the Treasury reports that Japan owns $1,111 billion of U.S. treasuries versus $1,315 billion for China. China has been divesting its stake, so Japan could soon become the largest foreign creditor again. Starting around 2016 more Japanese retirees will cash in fixed assets to live on. Companies will cash in bonds to pay pensions and the government will cash in assets to pay for Social

Security payments.   This will decrease the demand for U.S. treasuries likely leading to increased rates.

So it now looks like the U.S. faces a triple threat to its debt from:

- Boomer investors and corporate pension funds cashing in U.S. debt.
- A European debt solution leading to less competitive U.S. debt,
- Japan and China's divestiture of U.S. debt,

When Japan starts cashing in its U.S. securities, where will the U.S. go to finance its mountainous debt?   The likely answer is China, the now second and soon to be largest world economy, but how about the rest of the BRICs nations (Brazil, Russia, India, and China.) We will examine these nations in the next chapter to see if the FTM applies to them, which we think will likely not be the case, but there are still may be some surprising revelations ahead.

21

Global Implications – The BRICs

The BRICs consist of Brazil, Russia, India, and China, the large developing nations, whose economies exhibited rapid expansion in the 2000s. With growth sometimes in double digits, their story has been a positive one versus the tragedy of the PIIGS and Japan of late. Jim O'Neil, former chairman of Goldman Sachs Asset Management coined the term BRIC in the early 2000s, spotting the tremendous potential of these nations that investors largely ignored,.*

BRIC Growth from 2001 - 2012

Brazil	*337%*
Russia	*537%*
India	*299%*
China	*523%*

For a number of reasons, the BRICs do not match the demographic and economic patterns of the previously explored economies. Applying the principles of the Financial Time Machine (FTM) as a long-term indicator will, however, provide insight into the long-term prospects of these economies. In previous chapters, it was important to not only look at the FTM, but also account for other more immediate indicators. As a long-term indicator, the FTM is a heavy force, but not the only one. For the BRICs, other indicators and behaviors will carry proportionally more weight.

Many of the now developed nations in Europe and North America emerged in the 18th, 19th, and 20th centuries. These four developing nations have many similarities to the U.S. in the early 20th century and to Japan in the last half of the 20th century. As such, they experience rapid growth followed in some cases by frequent wrenching recessions, but overall the trend line still climbs. So it has been with emerging nations in the past - rapid growth followed by recessions, rapid inflation, deflation, and even depressions.

They intricately link to the global economy. Much of their success stems from outsourcing, in the case of China or India; and from oil wealth in case of Brazil and Russia. China depends largely upon Europe and the U.S. to buy its manufactured goods. India depends largely upon the U.S. to buy its services. When the developed nations' economies sputter, the developing nations experience slower growth rates.

Since there are fewer great investments in the developed nations, record levels of Boomer driven funds flow to the BRICs, who offer potentially higher returns. Part of the problem for the BRICs has been managing all of the investment funding flowing their way, which periodically cause rampant inflation, particularly in the real estate sector and in Brazil. We know where that leads. All of the BRICs also struggle with graft and corruption to various degrees, but so does the U.S.

It seems a little odd to call the BRICs developing economies, since China and India are two of the oldest cultures in the world. Russia through the Czar and later the Soviet Union dominated much of the world. Brazil has been emerging for 40 years now.

While China, Russia, and India are not new economies, they are newly capitalistic. China and Russia were communist nations who later embraced capitalism in the 1980s and 1990s. India toyed with Soviet-style economic management resisting foreign interaction until the 1990s. All three of these potentially massive economies did not fully engage in global trade until recently. Here are the key economic indicators for the BRICs.

BRIC Economic Indicators

Statistic	Brazil	Russia	India	China	BRIC Ave
GDP (trillions)	2.4	2.0	1.8	**8.2**	3.6
GDP Growth %	1.9	1.6	4.8	**7.5**	4.0
Unemployment %	6.0	5.4	**3.8**	4.1	4.8
Inflation %	6.3	6.5	4.9	**2.7**	5.1
Interest rate %	8.5	8.3	7.3	**6.0**	7.5
Debt/GDP %	65	**8**	68	23	41.1
Confidence	110	-6	**118**	97	73.6
Recessions/yrs.	5/20	3/16	0/8	**0/23**	2/16

From Trading Economics, August 2013, Leader in **bold**

At 14.4 trillion dollars, the combined BRIC economies rapidly approach the size of the U.S. economy and could exceed it by 2015. It already exceeds the EU's by 20%. As expected, these economies are all fairing well with generally healthy growth rates and low unemployment. Like most developing economies, they also have higher interest and inflation rates. With frequent recessions and a lower current rate of growth, Brazil is the most volatile.

Generational Economic view of the BRICs

Generational economics is a large-scale leading economic indicator, which applied remarkably well to the developed economies in the U.S.,

EU, and Japan.   Since developing economies are more vulnerable to external forces, will it apply as well to the BRICs? The FTM will provide long-term insight into the future of these economies, but analysis of other factors must be considered concurrently, especially in these changing economies.

With huge populations, added population may be more a detriment than a benefit as more people compete for fewer available resources and are not able to save, but rather live at a subsistence level. China, the largest nation, undertook a campaign to reduce its population through its one-child program. The reason China and India were so competitive was because their wages were so low, starting out at near subsistence levels. Now, wages in Chinese cities are rapidly rising, as are the wages in regions of India like the tech center of Bangalore. These economies are becoming less competitive and in the future will depend more upon internal consumption from their burgeoning middle and upper classes.

In a sense, free trade worked. By buying trillions of dollars of goods and services, the developed economies of the world helped the BRICs grow their economies to the point where they can soon sustain themselves. Developing economies are typically more protective. China and India are continually, and rightfully, criticized for being protect-tionist. But Japan was protectionist in the last half of the 20th century, as was the U.S. in the early part of the century, and stepping back a little further, Great Britain in the 19th Century.

The chart below summarizes the BRIC's generational economic data.

BRIC Generational Economic Data

	Brazil	Russia	India	China
Median age	30	38	26	35
Peak median age	49	45	None	50
In year	2080	2035	None	2065
Life expectancy	74	64	66	74
Average Retirement age	53	58	59	51
Fertility rate	1.9	1.44	2.73	1.64
Worker/retiree in 2012	8:1	5:1	9:1	7:1
In 2030	4.5:1	3:1	7:1	3.8:1
Population (million)	196	142	1,242	1,344

Primarily from United Nations, Department of Economic and Social Affairs, Population Division (2011): World Population Prospects: The 2010 Revision. New York

Below is a graph displaying births for Brazil and Russia along with the U.S. for comparison purposes.

Brazilian and Russian Births

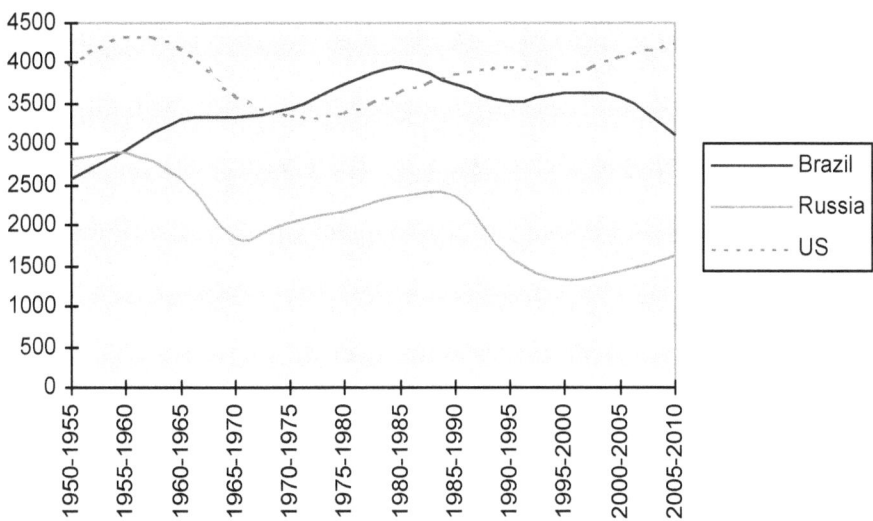

Based on data supplied by UN Population Division in 5-year increments

Brazil presents a building wave in population, reaching its peak in 1985, after which it declines. Overall, it resembles one giant swell.

Russia exhibits a wave pattern comparable to that of the U.S., or Europe who also fought in World War II although its general population trend is declining.

India and China Births

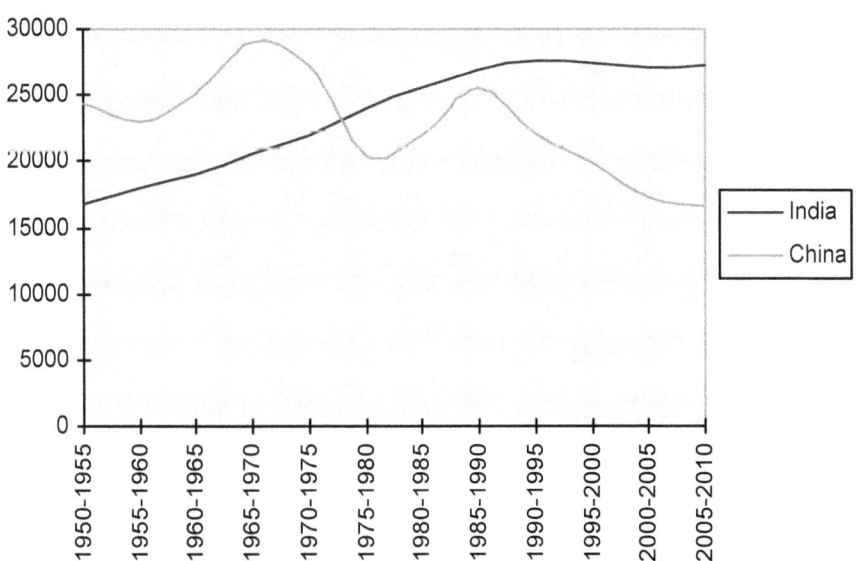

The graphs for India and China are displayed separately, since as the largest nations, the scale vastly differs.

India has one continuously increasing wave until 1995 when its births finally start to flatten at a remarkable 27 million a year.

China's births have a distinct wave pattern with peaks and troughs appearing about every 10 years, a remarkably short period of time. After 1990, as its one-child policy unfolds, its population steadily declines. Up until the late 1970s, their births were higher than India's, but now are 39% lower. This explains why China's worker to retiree ratio will be an unsustainable 1.75 in 2060.

BRIC Economic Cycles

The characteristics of BRIC economies differ from those of the developed nations. For instance, the retirement age for Brazil is 53 and China's is 51. The U.S. based FTM assumes the peak wealth accumulation years for its workers are in the fifties, a time when these nation's workers are already retired and out of the productive economy. So, the FTM principles require some adjustment.

As developing nations, their economies are more subject to volatility versus the more predictable and regulated developed nations. Just look at the risk factors associated with emerging funds. One year these funds may grow 40%, and lose 30% the next.

Based on generational economic principles, the FTM showed us that booms in the U.S. and developed European nations occur when a wave generation occupies its peak financial factors. Busts happen when these generations retire as their financial factors decline and the next smaller generation occupies their peaks.

To determine how economic cycles form in the BRIC nations, we examined the first members of each generation. Shortly after a peak generation's first members enter their peaks, we have a boom. When the first members of a lull generation hit their peaks, we have a bust. Looking at the 20th Century, U.S. generations for guidance, we find the following:

Age of Dominant Generation at Transition Point

Economic Period	Dominant Generation	Age of First Members
Great Depression & WWII	20th Century Millennials	44
50s/60s Boom	Greatest	45
70s Malaise	Silents	44
80s/90s Boom	Boomers	37
Great Recession	Xers	43
Post Recession	Millennials	43

Interestingly, we notice that in every case except the Boomers, the next financial period commences when the dominant generation was 43 - 45. The average age for these six generations is 43. This is not when the generation crosses into the quadruple peak zone, but when a substantial number of its members are there, since it will take a critical mass for the generation to flip the cycle.

Adding 43 years to the start of the peak and trough generations for Brazil, Russia and China, results in the chart below portraying the expected economic cycles for these nations. As illustrated in their population chart, India does not exhibit any generational wave characteristics since their population continuously increases, so there is no corresponding generational economically induced cycle.

Predicted BRIC Cycle Start Dates

	First Cycle		Second Cycle	
	Boom	Bust	Boom	Bust
Brazil	1993 →	2028 →	2038 →	2045 →
Russia	→	2003 →	2013 →	2031 →
China	2003 →	2013 →	2023 →	2033 →

Start date of each period, which ends on start date of the next period
Based on 5 year periods: deviation +/- 2 yrs

Many factors influence the economies of these developing nations beyond FTM-based generational economics. As discussed earlier, generational economics is a major leading indicator, but there are certainly others, particularly for developing economies. They are more subject to the economic winds such as political change, international conflict, monetary fluctuations, urbanization, and commodity prices.

What do the cycles above portend for the selected BRIC nations in light of their individual economic characteristics? A discussion of each follows.

Brazil

	Boom	Bust	Boom	Bust
Brazil	1993 →	2028 →	2038 →	2045 →

As in the developed economies, the number of Brazilian births declined and now is 20% below its peak, but according to generational economics, it takes time for these shifts to influence the economy. The time machine predicts a sustained boom for Brazil until the late 2020s when this population decrease will play out. So it projects a sustained boom period of 33 years. We saw extremely long boom periods play out in Japan and currently China.

As it has over the last decades, Brazil will likely face periodic recessions and inflation, a problem it repeatedly struggles to overcome, but is grappling with. Due to its exceptional energy program, Brazil is able to supply much of its energy demands by turning sugar cane into biofuel. There are also rich offshore oil deposits that Brazil is tapping, which will greatly enrichen its economy, since the state owns the largest oil producers.

Brazil had a relatively short increase in births around the turn of the century, so there should be a brief boom period commencing in the mid 2030s. Shortly afterwards expect another decline.

The average retirement age of 53 will likely become a problem as Brazil's life expectancy grows. Currently the average retiree can expect to live over 21 years after retirement, which with a high worker to retiree ratio, is feasible, but eventually this will become a concern. A relatively easy fix is to increase the retirement age, which the current president, Dilma Rousseff, supports.

Russia

	Boom	Bust	Boom	Bust
Russia		2003 →	2013 →	2031 →

Russia is physically the largest nation in the world, so unlike Japan, space, or resources do not limit the size of its population. As Russia's births graph shows, up until the 1990s, the shape of Russian peaks and troughs were very similar to that of the U.S. because they too experienced a large post war baby boom and Millennial echo. Prior to World War II, Russia had the highest population in Europe. The war was horrific for Russia, in which she lost a tragic 14 million people or 13% of her population, two-thirds of whom were civilians. Then In the early 1930s, there was a famine that killed approximately three million Russians. The number of births never recovered and by 1999, births were only a quarter of what they were in 1929.

Because of the hollowing out of the Russian Greatest generation, the Russian Boomers represent an even more powerful economic stimulus for the Russian economy. During the period when the U.S. Boomers were in their peak earnings, spending and wealth creation in the 1990s, the Soviet Union was breaking apart. Perhaps the force of Russia's large Boomer wave aided the revolution. The transition from state ownership to capitalism in the 1990s was yet another wrenching experience for the Russian populace when the number of births plummeted again. Economic stress continued until 1999. Oddly, those who benefited most from the collapse of communism in Russia are the "Russian Oligarchs" who now own the previously state run industries and are some of the richest billionaires in the world. In 2012, Moscow had more billionaires than any city in the world. This represents an odd turn of events, since oligarchy is the antithesis of communism.*

The FTM indicators show Russia's economy building from 1993 until 2003 and then declining until 2013. This is a good example of how geopolitical events trump generational economics predictions. Obviously, the seismic political and economic shifts of the 1990s did more to shape the economic outcome than generational economics.

Due to Russia's Xer population drop, the Financial Time Machine predicted a downturn starting around 2003. Russia did have a recession in 2009, but as a radically evolving political system and economy, this cannot be attributed to declining generational stimulus. Due to its emerging oil wealth, Russia's economy fared well during the 2000s.

As in the U.S., the first cohort of the Russian Millennials was forming a population wave, but around the time of the break up of the Soviet Union in December of 1991, the births declined to half of what they were previously. Under Communism, before 1990 only 1.5% of the people lived under poverty, whereas approximately 50% were in poverty by the end of the decade. By 2007, the births started inclining again.

The Russians do not have the same retirement problem as their European neighbors. With an average retirement age of 58 and an average life expectancy of 64, the average Russian can expect to retire for only 6 years. This explains why even though approximately six years of Russian Boomers are now retired, Russia's debt to GDP ratio is remarkably less than 10%, so retirement payments are not a burden.

China

	Boom	Bust	Boom	Bust
China	2003 →	2013 →	2023 →	2033 →

When the communists took over China in 1949, China was an agrarian economy reminiscent of those in the mid-nineteenth century. At the time, the life expectancy was 35 and the average woman had six children, favoring sons who would work the farm and later take care of their parents in their old age. Due to the social revolution, the Korean War, and a severe famine, the number of births plunged to nearly half of what they were earlier by 1961. Thanks to modern health care delivery, by 2000, just 50 years later, the life expectancy doubled to 71 and infant mortality vastly improved. China passed its one child policy in 1979.

Similar to Russia in the 1990s, it is difficult to compare China to developed countries until the end of the 20th century. The 1950s, 60s, and early 70s with Social Revolution, Anti-Rightist purge, and Cultural Revolution were tumultuous. During this time, political turmoil dominates generational economics. China had a nascent economy then that did not participate in the global economy.

Mao Zedong died in 1976, leading to the modernization of China. The Four Modernizations summed up the goals of the subsequent reforms:

The modernization of agriculture,
industry,
science and technology,

and the military.

Nixon visited China in 1972 and finally Carter recognized China in the late 1970s. In 1979, China went to war with Vietnam over their relationship with Russia; therefore, China no longer thought of the U.S. as worse than Russia, allowing China to open up to the Americans.*

After 2013, the U.S. based time machine predicts a financial decline. In 2012, the size of the Chinese working age population fell for the first time by 3.5 million signaling the reversal. When the world economy slows and exports to the U.S. and Europe decline, China's growth prospects dim. China has wrestled with an overheated real estate market and building boom partially supported by a shadow banking system estimated to be up to $5 trillion. This sounds similar to what occurred in the U.S. and Europe with an overheated housing market supported by subprime loans. The slowdown may result in recession or substantially lower growth rates.*

Depending upon the unknown structure of China's shadow banking system, the recession could be severe, resembling the European and U.S.'s bursting housing bubbles. Reaping low returns from traditional banking systems, unsophisticated newly rich Chinese investors have plowed funds into structural and real estate development projects with higher returns. Since these banking systems are unregulated, the likelihood of fraud is high. Once the bubble bursts, and fraud is revealed, investors could loose hundreds of billions of dollars worth of yuan.

An obvious way to stimulate continued economic growth in China is to increase consumer spending. Similar to Russia, and curious for a communist nation, the top 1% of China's households control 70% of the nation's private financial wealth. In 2011, there were 271 billionaires in China.* With new leadership, China is considering ways to distribute more income to a broader population, thereby creating more consumer consumption and providing more social benefits.

Having a Debt to GDP ratio of just 25% and owning trillions of dollars of U.S. and European debt, China has plenty of capital available to stimulate their economy when needed. The time between China's waves and troughs is a very short 10 years, so they should be able to weather the projected downturn with their immense reserves.

The expected mid-2030s decline in generational stimulus may be more challenging for China's leadership. By then, the nascent Chinese modern economy will be the largest in the world and no longer developing. As such, it will be improbable to maintain continuous GDP growth rates of 7-10-% and recessions will become more likely. The effects of the one child policy will start to unfold with fewer workers to support the retiring larger generation.

China's situation resembles their Asian neighbor Japan who entered the global stage 30 years earlier, thrived, and then due to rapidly declining births stagnated for over 20 years. Like Japan, they are saving furiously and beginning to buy worldwide industries. Limiting population in Japan makes sense considering its limited space and recourses. With over a billion people, limiting population in China made some sense too; however, the manner in which they did so with millions of forced abortions raises serious concerns. There are economic consequences to these decisions, but for a nation with a 5,000-year history, a 20-year adjustment period may seem negligible.

China currently has an unusually low average retirement age of 51, because they want to make room for younger workers to enter the workforce. With a rapidly increasing life expectancy, the time a retiree lives is currently a remarkable 23 years and climbing. By 2030, the number of workers per retiree will be nearly half of what it is now, but still relatively high, so increasing the retirement age may solve much of China's potential debt problems.

China is also considering revamping its one child policy to perhaps a two-child policy. There are currently exceptions to the policy for rural populations. Even if implemented immediately, China will still face a period of decline in the 2030s, because it will take time for these children to enter the economy.

The following concluding section summarizes the generational economic lessons learned from studying the U.S. and 13 other nations. It also looks towards the future.

22

Conclusion

The previous three chapters applied the type of generational economics found in the Financial Time Machine (FTM) to Europe, Japan, and the BRICs. The relative earning, spending, debt, and saving propensities for each no doubt vary resulting in varied peak periods. We did not perform detailed calculations or build voluminous models for each of the discussed nations; instead, we employed generalizations regarding population waves and generational stimulus. In essence, we retrofitted the U.S. FTM in order to study the thirteen nations.

Due to World War II, most of the developed European nations and Japan exhibit population wave patterns similar to the U.S.'s, at least for the first couple of generations after the war. The adapted FTM performed remarkably well predicting the boom periods and periods of decline. There were distinct differences between the developed nations in terms of the length of their generations, their retirement ages, and life expectancies, which the FTM methodology accommodated. Having accounted for these adjustments, the FTM predicted past economic cycle transitions nearly to the year, enhancing the credibility of future projections.

Generational Economics as portrayed through the Financial Time Machine is a powerful force. Its predictions can be delayed, as done by ramped up consumer spending by the U.S., but not abrogated. It accurately predicted four economic cycles for America over 140s years, consisting of four expansions and four contractions. In addition, it correctly predicts dozens of similar cycles for thirteen other nations. It is perhaps the most powerful long-term leading economic indicator.

The EU nations and Japan are very similar to the U.S., since they all are developed, democratic nations with varying degrees of socialization. The characteristics of the BRICs differ from those of the developed economies. Still an analysis of their cycles and corresponding generational stimulus variations provide insights into important factors regarding their economic growth prospects.

Some of the differences include:

- Changing the economic system from communism to capitalism or pseudo-capitalism – a painful transition.
- Natural disasters like famines in Russia and China that killed millions of people and the tsunami in Japan.
- Extremely large populations in India and China with masses of people not participating in the modern economy.

- Rapid assent from an agricultural economy to a manufacturing or service oriented economy.
- Political forces, such as massive purges, and cultural reforms.
- Decisions to open up to the global economy.

These forces may trump generational economics. Other factors may certainly play a role, such as the drastic political and economic philosophical changes in China, Russia, and to a lesser extent India. As these economies become fully developed, they will start to more closely fit the patterns exhibited by the developed economies. Brazil, Russia, and China are already displaying the declining population characteristic of developed economies. Examination of these nations also shows that major political decisions can alter the prescribed fate dictated by generational economics. Similarly, a lack of courageous political leadership can lead to more dire consequences.

Comparable to Japan in the late 20th century, China has gone 23 years without a recession. They are building large reserves, which can sustain them during lean times. Like Japan, these savings consist of U.S. and European treasuries, but they are starting to diversify by buying interests in U.S. industries such as energy and banking. Japan utilized reserves it built up to sustain itself over the next 20 years of declining births. Thus far, China has invested $60 billion in the energy industries of Africa, the Middle East, Brazil, Canada, and the U.S.

With treasury returns so low, and risks eventually rising, this trend will likely accelerate as China becomes more experienced at acquisitions and buys more American companies. Plus, China is constantly looking for new technologies to assume, facilitated by an acquisition from another nation. Some say that the U.S.'s focus upon Iraq and Afghanistan opened the door for Chinese economic colonization in Africa, South America, and Asia.

We have seen how population waves in developed nations lead to prosperity followed by economic decline. The Financial Time Machine goes into great depth to explore this phenomenon, but it is only logical. When a developed society has a large number of people in their most productive years, they will prosper. As the society ages, it will become less prosperous. From a long-term historical perspective, this is a new phenomenon, because in the past, the average person did not live much beyond their productive years and if they did, their relatively large families provided for them.

In the past, when life expectancies were in the 40s and 50s most of the work was in farming and manufacturing, which become more difficult and less productive with age. With the vast majority of people in the developed nations working in the services, working into the 60s or beyond is less burdensome, especially if there are plentiful part-time positions. With worker to retiree ratios declining, it will become increasingly more essential for nations to facilitate older workers and not waist this potentially valuable productive resource.

Prosperity Age

The average life expectancy for developed nations ranges from 78 for the U.S. to nearly 83 for Japan. When a nation has more older citizens than younger citizens, the economy will likely stagnate. A median age that is over half of the life expectancy (about 40) indicates a nation in danger of entering a period of stagnation. So as a nation's age approaches roughly 40, challenges loom ahead. Let's call this the prosperity age limit.

Below is a list of the nations with the highest median age by decade with their rank listed in the cells. Japan ranks first throughout the analysis. Later, some of these nation's median ages grow to over 45 and even 50.

Ranking of Nations with Oldest Median ages

Nation	Over 40		Over 45		Exceeded Prosperity Age
	2000	2010	2020	2030	
Japan	1	1	1	1[1]	1994
Germany	3	2	2	4	1997
Italy	2	3	3	2	2000
Portugal		14	6	3	2005
Greece		11	10	9	2005
Spain		19	11	5	2020

1. Over 50

Source: United Nations, Department of Economic and Social Affairs, Population Division (2011): World Population Prospects: The 2010 Revision. New York

Notice how Japan, Italy and Germany consistently rank in the top three nations with a median age over 40 and then over 45. These were the first three nations to exceed their prosperity age limit, all by 2000. Interestingly, these countries were allies during World War II, who experienced large losses and dealt with defeat. Perhaps the defeat led to declining birth rates, but it is beyond the scope of this book to speculate upon this. Notice also that the other PIGS including Portugal, Greece, and Spain consistently rank high on the list. The situation does not improve for Japan, Italy, Germany, or Portugal, whose median age is above 45 in 2030.

Japan, the first nation to exceed its prosperity age limit in 1994 was the first to stagnate at that time. Portugal, Italy, Greece, and Spain, the PIGS, are four of the oldest nations, who now face an elongated stagnation similar to Japan's, in some cases dealing with a triple dip recession.

France and the UK will reach their prosperity age limit around 2015, but the U.S. will not until 2030. Surprisingly, due to the one child policy,

China will reach its prosperity age limit by 2025, potentially shortening a boom cycle.

Future

Over the last 150 years, our global civilization evolved from an agricultural based economy, to an industrial based one, and now to a service based economy. Technological innovation led to vast productivity improvements shared by many of the world's inhabitants. Humanity profited from the vast agricultural and manufacturing improvements over that time, such that in the developed economies, only one out of six of us provide all the food and manufactured goods. In 1929, three and a half out of six of us provided these. In addition, the quality, quantity, variety, and power of these goods are immense.

As a result, the number of hours humans need to work to provide such largess declined by at least a third from 60 to 40 hours a week. Thanks to the innovations, women who toiled 80-hour weeks caring for their homes and large families were freed to work and contribute to this progress, accelerating the pace of innovation. Globalization transferred the benefits of the productivity improvements to the much of the rest of the world. In addition, the new civilization was able to supply benefits to people in need such as medical care, food, and shelter for the poor or disabled, a bridge during periods of unemployment, and retirement for the elderly.

At the root of the developed world's current problem is a declining population. According to the Population Reference Bureau's 2012 report, until 2050, only 3% of the world's population growth will come from Europe and North America. The European, Japanese, and Chinese populations will decline. This not only portends declining worker to retiree ratios, but potentially a reduction in productivity improvements. According to economists Esther Boserups and Julian Simon, growing populations lead to increased innovation.*

The developed nations face tough challenges over the next 20 years. Since we exist in a global economy, these challenges are universal in scope. Developing nations such as the BRICs should fair better, but since much of their growth depends upon the global exports to the developed nations, they too face headwinds.

It is possible that the developing nations will take the place of the developed nations, since this has happened throughout the world's history. What is more likely over the next 50 years is that the influence and power Europe and America enjoyed over the last century will diminish, while that of some developing nations will rise. Much depends upon each areas leadership and political system. Many developing nations have been developing for decades, but the greed of their leaders repeatedly prevents them from becoming all they might be.

During stressful times, nations frequently turn to wars to add scarce resources and "living space." Hopefully, this will not occur. The elderly nations cannot afford such endeavors and even China is aging rapidly. Plus, with an older population, it would be difficult to field an army while caring for the elderly who did not exist in such large numbers during the last world war.

The global quest for dwindling worldwide resources to feed increasing demands, hopefully, will subside as a cause of war. Most of the wars over the last 30 years originated in the Middle East and surrounding environs. The Arab Spring represents the most recent conflagrations. The median age for these countries is under 25 with Syria having the lowest age of 22, a likely contributor to the Syrian Civil War. Younger nations seem more likely to engage in conflicts.

Due to worldwide demand, OPEC and the western oil companies successfully raised the price of oil above $100/barrel, which made technologies that are more expensive profitable and alternative energy sources practical. Now, U.S. oil and gas reserves soar at the fastest rate in history, alleviating the pressure in the volatile Middle East. Soon similar discoveries around the world will further decrease pressure upon the Middle East as the world's prime energy supplier. Nations like Brazil, Mexico, Canada, Russia, and Iraq are already supplying more energy.

If, unfortunately, a major war does ensue, the Financial Time Machine's clock resets, generating a new wave pattern. Without a major war, the constant pace of productivity improvements should produce more goods, allowing even more people to provide services to their fellow man. The major area of improvement will continue to be services, so that the vast majority of those who work in the sector will provide continuously more value to their fellow man.

A couple of global problems will provide opportunities for major global technological developments, the first of which is caring for the aged. Japan and Germany with their older populations and technical skills will lead the way, followed closely by the other developed nations in Asia, America, and Europe. The leading nations will not only find considerable financial incentives for themselves, but a lucrative global export market. Eldercare will represent a trillion dollar, worldwide market when the world's first Boomers enter mid-retirement in five years. Later, China and the U.S. will face an aging problem too, but by then the automated eldercare industry will begin to supply their needs.

Technological development follows a predictable cycle as portrayed in *2020 Web Vision, How the Internet will Revolutionalize Future Homes, Business, and Society*, by this author. Usually, technologies such as e-mail (1971), the Internet (1969), or television (1925) are invented one or two decades before the consumers broadly adopt them. Interestingly, the economics of the aging of the world's developed populations will lead to a boom in the application of home robotics, similar to the home PC.

The other continuing technology will be resource exploration and development. Worldwide, developed nations demand for resources will slow, but the huge developing nations like China and India will demand constantly more resources for burgeoning internal consumption. Today, China is scouring the earth for such resources. Like in the Middle East, and as emerging conflicts in the South China Sea exemplify, resource shortages could lead to conflict escalation, as these have throughout the last 10,000 years. The digital technology the world depends ever more upon devours rare earth metals, which China controls. One potential source of such increasingly valuable metals may be the moon, mars, asteroids, or another planet, which may finally expedite space travel.

Productivity improvements will continue to provide more food, goods, and services for less labor. The rate of productivity improvement may slow due to the extended contraction. Until the mid 2020s, there will be an adjustment, as over promised social benefits adjust to economic realities. After that time, baring major wars, as the Millennials come into their most productive years there will be an economic resurgence with more rapid growth. They will invent and implement more than we can imagine and we will be able to afford more with less effort. The devices invented to care for the aging Boomers will usher in yet another generation of digital/robotic improvements that will eliminate much of the drudgery of daily living and commuting. This technological generation will extend to most of humanity through the global economy.

Afterword

There is a generational economic storm blowing and numerous ships of state must face its fury, or be washed up upon the rocks of economic hardship. How various nations weather the storm depends upon their captain of state's navigational abilities and their crew.

We have seen in the United States during the late 1990s that bipartisan leadership recognized the gravity of the approaching storm and took precautions to batten down the hatches and close the hurricane shutters while the sun still shone. They reformed welfare, shored up Social Security, and balanced the budget. They even started saving during the longest boom period in U.S. history - a wise strategy led by Republicans.

The Bush administration took the reins and surprisingly lowered taxes while spending $7 trillion on defense for the two of the longest wars in U.S. history, and increased retirement spending on Medicare by another $7 trillion through part D. They relied upon consumer spending, an escalating housing bubble, and a spiraling, out-of-control financial industry, now the largest in the nation whose army of lobbyists swarmed D.C., to keep the economy afloat. Instead of encouraging saving, they encouraged spending and debt accumulation on both a personal and a national level to keep the economy afloat.

They did little to prepare for the category 5 economic hurricanes that would hit during their watch. They did not need the Financial Time Machine to see this; after all, their predecessors in Washington saw it a decade earlier. The first of 70 million Boomers would start to retire during the last year of their administration, collecting under-funded Social Security payments. During the longest expansion in U.S. history, they might have thought the cycle would eventually reverse course and plan for the decline; instead, they doubled down on the national debt with the Obama administration continuing along the same course stimulating the economy to keep afloat during the worst recessionary period in 80 years.

Taking the hurricane analogy a little further -- the weather station shows the second fiercest hurricane in history is only a few days away and it is bearing down upon your outer banks retreat. Because it is a beautiful late summer day, instead of packing up their valuables, your neighbor opens up the hurricane shutters to let the sun in. Instead of leaving while there is still plenty of time, they call you and other neighbors to invite you all over for a hurricane party, after which they put out the patio furniture, tiki bar, and torches. Then instead of going to the store for emergency supplies, they go to the party center for decorations and the market for wine, beer, steak, and snacks.

As the storm approached, D.C. held a hurricane party of spending and deficits rather than preparing for the storm, facing into the economic wind, and battening down the debt hatches. In 2008 when the full force of the Recession's waves hit, we nearly capsized, but now that we are in the eye of the storm, the current bipartisan leadership has done little to prepare for the next onslaught other than jostle with each other.

Unfortunately, the global economy is intricately interrelated. Because of World War II and the consequent post war baby booms, nearly the entire developed world faces the same calamity at approximately the same time. Only a few followed Joseph's example and prepared for the storm. China saved trillions and our neighbor, Canada, also prepared. In Canada, only 50% of homes have mortgages, which require a 25% down payment. The Canadian's saving rate is twice the U.S.'s.

Other nations unwisely buoyed by incremental productivity improvements and the record economic stimulus of the Boomers, provided overly generous social spending policies, most evident in their early retirement programs. During the record boom period, their debts seemed reasonable, but then largely due to these retirement policies, the record number of highly-paid, skilled workers started retiring, downsizing their abodes, and withdrawing their accumulated wealth from the economy. As a result, many economies devolved into a long-term recession that they should have expected. Then, the Social Security payments rose, unemployment climbed, tax revenues declined, stimulus spending increased, and national and bank debts went to unsustainable levels.

The neither good nor bad news is that nearly the entire developed world will experience the same stagnation at the same time, allowing the G-20, interconnected, global banking system to moderate interest rate payments on burgeoning national debts. Like the Great Depression, we will all be relatively poor. The result will be to provide the developing world an opportunity to ratchet up their status in the global economy, likely supplanting developed nations; comparable to the rich industrial Midwestern cities decline in the latter half of the 20th century and the ascendance of southern and western cities.

Controlling global interest rates through coordinated national banking system's efforts will have one unfortunate consequence - reduced interest payments to retirees and stressed corporate and public pension funds. Ironically, however, it will provide a means to fund promised social security payments without escalating interest and inflation rates, leading to national defaults.

Since most large economies face a similar scenario, coordinated global banking efforts will be successful in keeping interest rates tamped down thereby lowering individual nation's debt payments. But, since the G20 nations are also competitors, there will be rewards for those who manage the looming crisis better. To the extent they can keep their Debt/GDP ratio down, they will be rewarded with lower debt rates and have more to invest in it items such as infrastructure, research, and education, which will build future competitiveness.

In a sense, the next ten years will be a contest. Imagine the G20 nations lined up at the start line of an Olympic marathon in order of their economies size with the U.S. wearing number one, China two, Japan three, etc. How they finish the grueling race, depends on how well they prepared, how they manage the race, and their resources. To the winners goes prestige, a higher share of the global economy, lower unemployment, growing GDP, the ability to attract and retain needed skilled human resources, and prosperity.

When things are tough, we tend to live one day at a time and hope for a better day tomorrow. We should realize that unlike the past, we will not recover to booming growth immediately, but we can still expect moderate growth over the next ten years. The predictions of the Financial Time Machine are not dire, but these are not rosy either. We can expect a decade of sluggish economic growth with frequent recessions or near recessions and a bursting bond bubble. Excessive stimulus spending or tax cuts are only temporary fixes and will only make things worse in the long-term, leading to drastic austerity measures like those in the PIIGS.

What we need is a balanced approach similar to Gramm-Rudman and prudent decisions. The political leadership implemented tough decisions in the late 1990s. If the national leadership maintained that course, we would be in much better shape now. If they had adopted such measure in 2010 when they voted down Simpson-Bowles, we would still be experiencing rough times, but headed for better times. The longer they wait to act, the worse our prospects will become and the longer it will take to emerge from the extended downturn.

GDP to Debt ratios above 90% compare to weather patterns off the northwestern coast of Africa that will eventually lead to multiple hurricanes bearing down upon the Gulf and Atlantic coasts of the U.S. The tropical storms lined up one after another throughout the southern Atlantic repeatedly morph into hurricanes. This is already occurring in the PIIGS, some of whom are facing their third recession in five years and Japan facing its sixth in 20 years. It may be sunny now, but the tropical depressions are out there gathering energy from high debt. They will hit furiously one after another unless we do something to dissipate their energy – unless we ratchet down the GDP/Debt ratio. We may have up to 2018 to do so, but no longer and we may have less time if Europe somehow gains financial ground or nearly a quadrillion dollars of derivatives again lead to serious calamity.

Like something out of a global warming, sci-fi movie, nearly every major European nation faces the same economic storm of the century. Much depends upon the quality of their leadership to steer the ship of state through the storm and the navigational policies they choose. But since these are democracies, it also depends upon the character of each nation's people and their ability to pull together versus tear apart.

With relentless dust storms ravaging the south and unemployment at a debilitating 25%, Roosevelt inspired the American people with his fireside chats during the Great Recession. Britain and the American leadership admirably inspired their people to pull together through the darkest nights of World War II. Such leadership is again essential. The difficult message starts by saying that the times will be difficult for a few years and we need to pull together so that our life and those of our children will improve in the future.

Eventually the economic storms will clear and by the mid-2020s, we will enter a period of economic stability. Productivity improvements and digital technology will continue to provide more goods and services for less. By then, we should experience remarkably stable economic conditions comparable to San Diego's warm days with clear blue skies.

Population Growth

The Financial Time predicts that population waves are the primary indicator of long-term economic expansions and contractions. One logical supposition is that countries should strive to increase their population continuously. Some nations who have long population increases such as Japan or China experienced unusually long expansions of 30 or more years. There are limits to how much a nation can grow its population especially for an island-based nations like Japan or the UK, or for extremely large populations such as China or India. Part of the reason these nations experienced such long expansions was that they were morphing into a developed economy, and in China's case, they restricted population growth.

There are certainly limits to population growth where available resources will no longer support the population. The population of Europe in the 19th Century had grown too large, but many of the people in these overcrowded nations immigrated to the United States, thereby relieving the pressure.

It is beyond the scope of this book to enter the world overpopulation debate. Many are concerned that the population will soon grow too large for the earth's resources to support, while others argue that continuing productivity gains will provide continuously more. There is, however, a natural tendency for birth rates to decline as a nation's population grows, and the economy matures. Birthrates in most of Europe, the U.S., China, and Japan are barely above replacement levels and in some cases below. Many of the developing nations in South and Central America experience this phenomenon too. Such was the case with France in the 19th century and even the Roman Empire in the 3rd - 7th centuries.* As the next crop of nations such as the Philippians, South Africa, Mexico, and Turkey develop, and more nations enter the global economy, the world population may again stabilize.

Appendix A.
Financial Time Machine

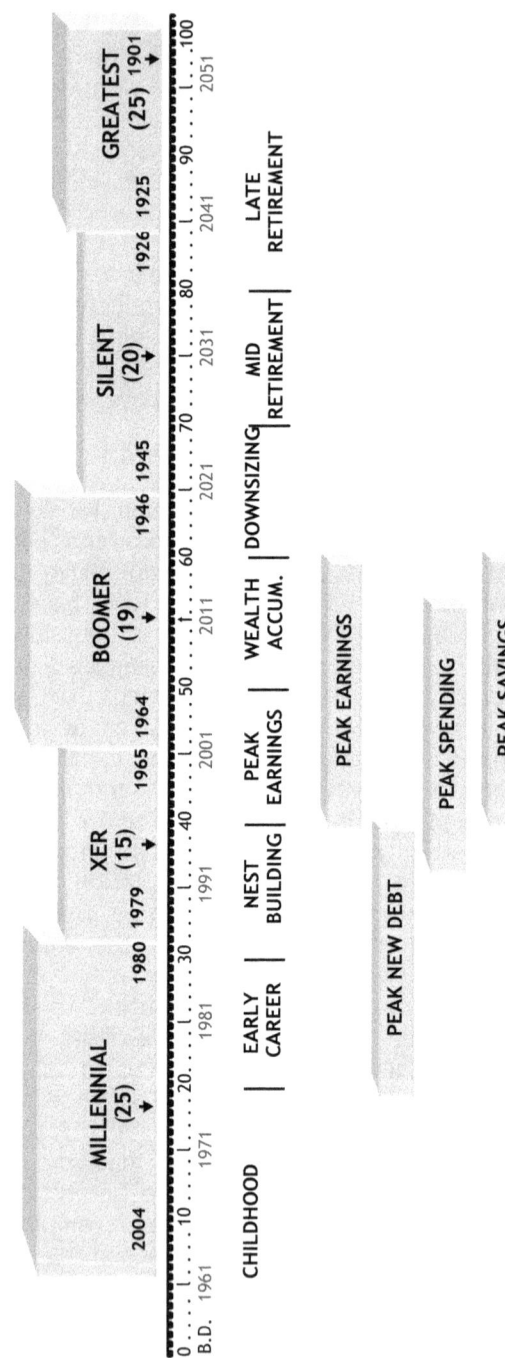

Appendix B:
What can Government do to encourage 20-hr positions?

1. The first thing they can do is eliminate irrelevant taxes for retirees and their employers. Disability insurance, workers compensation, and unemployment do not make sense for a retiree. If you are not working, you receive retirement payments. Similarly, if you are over 65 you receive Medicare and full Social Security over 66, so you and your employer should not contribute to these after those ages for part-time positions. This will create an incentive for retirees to continue working and for employers to employee them.

2. Change the definition of employee and unnecessary legislative requirements. Most of the Wage and Hour rules apply to the 20th Century concept of a 40-hour workweek. In the 19th Century, it was a 60-hour week. To avoid regulations and benefit requirements, companies hire contractors, which are not employees. Many benefit and employment laws apply to employers with over 20 or 50 employees, which discourage small business hiring above those levels. 401(k) and Section 125 flexible benefit discrimination tests apply based on number of employees. Change the definitions to allow for part-time employees without penalizing the employer. Someone that has given 30 years to the company should not have to be a contractor; they should still be an employee with the corresponding rights, privileges, and respect.

3. The government discourages retirees from working. If you are retired and you work, your earnings offset your social security benefits. Therefore, you earn less, which is an incentive not to work. At a time when we need more people in the workforce this is ridiculous. These laws have improved, but they can be better. Although typical, it is shortsighted for the government to offer incentives for people not to work. With more workers, the governments receive more federal, state, and local taxes and society has more workers providing goods and services to all of us. The Federal government would not receive more Social Security payments, but if they incent people not to work, they won't receive much any way and should not plan on it. Anyone who works up to 20 hours a week regardless of their hourly rate should have their payments reduced.

Take my father, Gene, as an example. The two-sport world-class athlete, who in addition to a national football championship, won the

U.S.'s first Olympic medal in the Javelin. After 25-years of coaching jobs and a stint as the university's Athletic Director, he found a position he loved as a Political Science and History professor. When he turned 65, the university had a forced retirement policy and initiated the retirement process even though the students elected him the professor of the year. The students loved his classes, because he told stories to make history come alive. Upon hearing of his pending retirement, they mounted a petition campaign that garnered over 50% of the student body's signatures and presented this to the President. The President relented and allowed Gene to teach until he was 70 as a part-time professor.

At the time, professors were paid perhaps half of what they are today, adjusted for inflation. You did not become a professor to become wealthy. When he was 64, he taught four classes. Afterward, as a part-time professor, he taught three large classes with more students than professors with the standard four. The University paid him about 30% of his full-time salary. Of this, half offset his Social Security payments. So he effectively made 20% of what he earned before. He did not really care though, because he loved teaching, the students, the university, and his colleagues. He would have taught for nothing. Still paying him 1/5th of the standard Professor's salary for teaching more students was unfair.

In ancient Greece, you could not be a leader until you were at least 60, because they felt wisdom was an acquired skill. In many rural Asian cultures, there is no retirement. You work as long and to the degree, you are able.

The government should not discriminate against retirees for working part-time. They should be encouraged to do so. The time to change the policies is now, not after most of the Boomers retire and it is too late for them to go back to work. The retirement paradigm that took hold in the 1950s represents a major societal shift. It is time for another concerted effort to shift into a new retirement paradigm. This is not an option; it is considering our circumstances, a necessity.

4. Start the part-time concept at all levels of government. Government employment makes up one-sixth of the total jobs, so this would be a great place to start. Many government positions are amenable to such positions. Here are just a few:

Retirement Jobs

Mail delivery	Lawyer
Teacher	Physician
Social Security administration	Researcher
Any of the millions of	Economist
administrative positions	Accountant
Garbage collection	Health workers
- using automatic pickers	Park ranger
Programming	Park staff
Analysis	Environmentalist
Economic analysis	Judge

If we apply the same savings to public positions as we do to private positions, the various levels of government receive a **30-40%** cost reduction for the part-time positions. These savings would go a long way towards balancing the budget. Plus, the various levels of governments get employment taxes from a segment they would not otherwise tax.

Many of these positions are amenable to telecommuting thereby saving transportation costs, reducing energy demands, and adverse environmental impacts. The savings should appeal to the Republicans with the green and social aspects appealing to the Democrats. The Government spends hundreds of billions on outside contracts ($500+ billion on defense alone) that they could instead utilize cost effective retirees to fill.

5. Lead the way: The government should set the example for the positions and then tout their budget savings to employers. Through industry associations, it will not take long for businesses to appreciate the cost savings and implement the positions. Associations like SHRM (the Society of Human Resource Management) with 100,000 members would rapidly adopt an idea like this. Good ideas spread like wild fire in business. We cannot afford to waste this valuable Human Resource in the future.

Notes

Chapter 1: The Financial Lifecycle
Years 1-20, Childhood
1. CNN Money, Cost of Rasing a Child, 9/21/2011, http://money.cnn.com/2011/09/21/pf/cost_raising_child/index.htm.
2. U.S. Department of Agriculture, "A Child Born in 2012 will cost $226,960 to raise," June 9, 2011.
Years 20 - 30, Early Career
3. Charles Murray, "The New American Divide," *Wall Street Journal*, January 21, p C1 -C2.
4. Len Serafino, "High Unemployment: Are IQ Scores to Blame?," *The Observer*, quoting Time Magazine, Tuesday, January 31, 2012, http://serafino1.blogspot.com/2012/01/high-unemployment-are-iq-scores-to.html.
5. David Wessel, "The Long-Term Economic To-Do List," *Wallstreet Journal*, 11/8/2012.
Years 30-40, Nest Building
6. Phil Izzo, "Pay Fell 7% in Last Decade and Economists Say It Won't Catch Up Before 2021; Even College Graduates See Salaries Slide," *Wallstreet Journal*, 10/14/2011, http://online.wsj.com/article/SB1000142405297020477460457662898120 8827422.html.
Years 40-50, Peak Earnings
7. U.S. Census Bureau, "American Community Survey," 2009.
Years 60-70, Downsizing
8. Adam Shell, "Will stocks' 'Lost Decade' usher in another bull market?," USA TODAY, 1/4/2010, http://usatoday30.usatoday.com/money/markets/2010-01-03-2010-outlook-stocks_N.htm.
9. Bureau of Labor Statistics, Unemployment Statistics, 2010, http://www.youtube.com/watch?v=FIJNqPTs_p0.
Years 80 and beyond, Late Retirement
10. David Demko, "How Many Seniors Really End Up In Nursing Homes?," AgeVenture News Service, www.demko.com.

Chapter 2 Generations
The Greatest Generation
1. History Channel, "Men Who Built America," November, 11, 2012.
2. Wikipedia, "World War II Casualties," http://en.wikipedia.org/wiki/World_War_II_casualties.
3. Wikipedia, "Strauss/Howe Generational Theory," http://en.wikipedia.org/wiki/Strauss-Howe_generational_theory.
The Silent Generation
4. Wikipedia, "Silent Generation," http://en.wikipedia.org/wiki/Silent_Generation.
5. Divorce Info Center, "US Divorce Rate Over Time," http://www.divorceinfo.com/statistics.htm.
Boomers

6. Wikipedia, "Vietnam War Casualties,"
    en.wikipedia.org/wiki/Vietnam_War_casualties.
7. Mary Louise Kelly, McNamara, "Vietnam-Era Defense Secretary, Dies,"
    National Public Radio, July 06, 2009 4:00 PM.
    Generation X
8. Wikepedia, "First reference to Gen X by Coupland in Tales for an Accelerated
    Culture, 1991,"
    http://en.wikipedia.org/wiki/Generation_X:_Tales_for_an_Accelerated_Cult
    ure.
9. Wikipedia, "Deming and Shewhart,"
    http://en.wikipedia.org/wiki/W._Edwards_Deming.
    The Millennial Generation
10. Scott Keeter and Paul Taylor, "The Millennials," *Pew Researh*, December 10,
    2009, http://pewresearch.org/pubs/1437/millennials-profile.

Chapter 3: Generational Megatrends
World War II
1. USGovernmentSpending.com, "Defense Spending,"
    http://www.usgovernmentspending.com/spending_chart_2001_2017USr_13s
    1li111mcn_30t.
    Life Expectancy
2. CDC, "National Vital Statistics Report, United States Life Tables," January
    11, 2012, Table A,
    http://www.cdc.gov/nchs/data/nvsr/nvsr60/nvsr60_04.pdf.
    Declining Birthrates
3. Sharon Jayson, "Is this the next Baby Boom?," USA Today, 7/17/2008,
    http://www.usatoday.com/news/nation/2008-07-16-baby-boomlet_N.htm.
4. US Census Bureau, "US Population From 1900,"
    http://www.demographia.com/db-uspop1900.htm.
    Delayed Marriage
5. Kay Hymowitz, W. Bradford Wilcox, and Kelleen Kaye, "The New Unmarried
    Moms," *Wall Street Journal*, 3/16/13, p C3.
6. Unmarried.org, "Statistics," http://www.unmarried.org/statistics.html..
7. Government Accountability Office, "RETIREMENT INCOME Intergenerational
    Comparisons of Wealth and Future Income, " April 2003, GAO-03-429
8. Conor Dougherty, "For Many Adults Marriage Can Wait, Census Shows," *Wall
    Street Journal*, September 29, 2010,
    http://online.wsj.com/article/SB100014240527487038824045755198714
    44705214.html.
9. Charles Murray, "The New American Divide," *Wall Street Journal*, January
    21, p C1 -C2.
    Changing spending and savings habits
10. The People's History, "Money And Inflation 1930s,"
    http://www.thepeoplehistory.com/1930s.html.
11. Retirement Income, "Average Retirement Savings," http://www.retirement-
    income.net/blog/retirement-savings-statistics/average-retirement-savings-
    all-measurements-lead-to-the-same-conclusion/.
12. Chris Isidore, "America's Lost Trillions," *CNNMoney*, June 9, 2011.
13. Bureau of Labor Statistics, "Current Population Survey, Unemployment By
    Age," July 2010.
    Expanding Productivity

14. Growing Nation, The Story of American Agriculture, "Historical Timeline - Farmers and the Land,"
http://www.agclassroom.org/gan/timeline/farmers_land.htm.
15. Robert D. Oberst, "2020 Web Vision, How the Internet Will Revolutionize Future Homes, Business & Society," July 2001, p 110.
16. Growing Nation, The Story of American Agriculture, "Historical Timeline - Farmers and the Land,"
http://www.agclassroom.org/gan/timeline/farmers_land.htm.
17. Jeremy Sherk, "Technology Explains the Drop in Manufacturing Jobs," *The Heritage Foundation*, October 12, 2010,
http://www.heritage.org/research/reports/2010/10/technology-explains-drop-in-manufacturing-jobs.
18. By Michael Schuman, "Can China compete with American manufacturing?," *Time Business & Money*, March 10, 2011,
http://business.time.com/2011/03/10/can-china-compete-with-american-manufacturing/.
19. Mark J. Perry, Phenomenal Gains in Manufacturing Productivity," June 15, 2011, http://seekingalpha.com/article/274917-phenomenal-gains-in-manufacturing-productivity.
20. Wikipedia, "Economy of The United States – Manufacturing,"
http://en.wikipedia.org/wiki/Economy_of_the_United_States#Manufacturing.
21. Christopher Davies, "China vs US Manufacturing comparison," 16 March 16, 2011, *Manufacturing Digital*,
http://www.manufacturingdigital.com/news_archive/tags/us/china-vs-us-manufacturing-comparison.
22. Barry Ritholtz, "The Shift from Manufacturing to Service Economy," *The Big Picture*, January 26th, 2012,   http://www.ritholtz.com/blog/2012/01/the-shift-from-manufacturing-to-service-economy/.
23. Robert D. Oberst, "2020 Web Vision, How the Internet Will Revolutionize Future Homes, Business & Society," July 2001, pp 89-93.
Utopia?
24. Divya Pakkiasamy, "Saudi Arabia's Plan for Changing Its Workforce," *Migration Policy Institute*, November 2004,
http://www.migrationinformation.org/Feature/display.cfm?ID=264.
25. SUSPS, "U.S. Birth Rates and Population Growth,"
http://www.susps.org/overview/birthrates.html.
26. Wikipedia, "Quality of Life Index," http://en.wikipedia.org/wiki/Quality-of-life_Index.
27. World Press, "2011 Quality of Life Index," 6/3/2011,
http://nationranking.wordpress.com/2011/03/06/2011-qli/.

Chapter 4: Building the Financial Time Machine
Financial Life Cycle Propensities

1. Over 80 references were researched in the building of the *Financial Time Machine* model resulting in the Financial Life Cycle propensities.
2. Neil Shah, "Freshly Flush, the Consumer Is Back," *Wall Street Journal*, 2/8/2013, p A3.
3. Min Zeng, "The BRIC Builder," *Wall Street Journal* Money, March 2013.

Chapter 5: Taking the Time Machine back in time for the Boomers
1981
1. Carolyn C. Rodgers, "Age and Family Structure by Race/Ethnicity and Place," *USDA Economic Research Service*, http://www.ers.usda.gov/publications/aer731/aer731d.pdf.
1991
2. Wikipedia, "Savings and Loan Crisis," http://en.wikipedia.org/wiki/Savings_and_loan_crisis.

Chapter 6: How The Financial Time Machine Predicted the Great Recession
What happened?
1. US Government Spending, "State Government Spending," ttp://www.usgovernmentspending.com/spending_chart_1980_2016USp_13s1l i011mcn_F0s_US_State_Government_Spending.
2. Ralph Smith , "Average Federal Salary: $83,679 and Lowest Average Pay Increase in 10 Years," March 25, 2012, http://www.fedsmith.com/2012/03/25/average-federal-salary-lowest-average-pay/.
3. Michael Hirsh, "Capital Offense: How Washington's Wise Men Turned America's Future Over to Wall Street," 2010, p 128.
4. Michel Lewis, "The Big Short," 2010.
Why not Earlier?
8. ES Browning, "New Wave of Workers Tries Novel Approach: Save More," *Wall Street Journal*, 9/25/12, p1.

Chapter 7: The Greatest Generation and Parallelism
1959
1. US Government Spending, "GDP History," USgovernmentSpending.com.
1970
2. Wikipedia, "List of Recessions in the United States," http://en.wikipedia.org/wiki/List_of_recessions_in_the_United_States.
Greatest generation's Greg Ostrum
2. Wikipedia, "TRW," en.wikipedia.org/wiki/TRW.
Stagflation
3. E.S. Browining, "Despite Gains, Many Flee Stock Market," *Wall Street Journal*, 10/8/2012, p 1.
4. ES Browning, "New Wave of Workers Tries Novel Approach: Save More," *Wall Street Journal*, 9/25/12, p1.

Chapter 8: Generational Waves and the Civil War Generation
The Great Depression
1. Wikipedia, "Economic History of the United States," http://en.wikipedia.org/wiki/Economic_history_of_the_United_States.
2. Michael Phillips, "Baby Boom Two: Projections for the 1990's," 1984.
3. US Census Bureau, "Population Distribution by Age, Race, and Nativity, 1860–2010," *Infoplease*, http://www.infoplease.com/ipa/A0110384.html#ixzz2OqblsiyS.
4. Wikipedia, "Economic History of the United States," http://en.wikipedia.org/wiki/Economic_history_of_the_United_States.

5. Bureau of Labor Statistics, Wikipedia, "US Unemployment measures (U-6)," http://en.wikipedia.org/wiki/File:US_Unemployment_measures.svg
6. Wikipedia, "List of US Recessions in the United States," http://en.wikipedia.org/wiki/List_of_recessions_in_the_United_States.
Expansion
7. US Government Spending, "US Real GDP," USGovernmentSpending.com.
8. Wikipedia, "Savings and Loan Crisis," http://en.wikipedia.org/wiki/Savings_and_loan_crisis.

Chapter 11: Generation X
1990

1. Wikipedia, "Savings and Loan Crisis," http://en.wikipedia.org/wiki/Savings_and_loan_crisis.
Looking forward for the Xers
2. Social Security and Medicare Trustees, "A SUMMARY OF THE 2012 ANNUAL REPORTS," http://www.ssa.gov/oact/trsum/index.html

Chapter 12: Onward to the Future

1. Bureau of Economic Analysis St. Louis Federal Reserve, "Real GDP Growth," http://research.stlouisfed.org/fred2/categories/18.
2. Rana Foroohar and Bill Saparito, "The 97-lb Recovery," Time April 2 2012, p 28.
3. Bureau of Labor Statistics, "Labor Force Statistics from the Current Population Survey," March 23, 2013, http://data.bls.gov/timeseries/LNS14000000.

Chapter 13: The Millennials to the Rescue?
Time Machine and Millennials

1. David Wessel, "Big U.S. Firms Shift Hiring Abroad" *Wall Street Journal*, April 19, 2011, http://online.wsj.com/article/SB1000142405274870482170457627078361182 3972.html.

Chapter 15: Future Implications
Corroboration for the FTM predictions

1. "United States, GDP Growth" Trading Economics, January, 2013, http://www.tradingeconomics.com/united-states/gdp-growth.
2. Sundeep Reddy, "Economic Growth Stays Soft," *Wall Street Journal*, April 27, 2013, 1.
Stimulus and GDP
3. Ben Casselman, "Fewer Workers Limit Growth," *Wall Street Journal*, Oct 28, 2012, page A2.
4. Damian Palleta and Jon Hillesnrath, "Economic Uncertainty Looms After Campaign," *Wall Street Journal*, 11/7/2012, pA14.
Corollary to Change
5. Haya El Nasser and Paul Overberg, "Census estimates show slow US population growth," USA Today, Dec 21, 2012, p3A.
Immigration
6. Unemployment from Bureau of Labor Statistics, "Labor Force Statistics from

the Current Population Survey," February, 2013,
http://data.bls.gov/timeseries/LNS14000000.

7. U.S. Bureau of the Census, Table 7. Age and Sex of the Foreign-Born Population: 1870 to 1990, March 9, 1999,
http://www.census.gov/population/www/documentation/twps0029/tab07.ht ml.

8. U.S. Bureau of the Census, Population by Sex, Age, Nativity and U.S. Citizenship Status: 2010,   September 2011,
http://www.census.gov/population/foreign/files/cps2010/T1.2010.pdf.

Retirement Implications

9. Save and Conquer, *History of Retirement in the US*, p 48,
http://www.saveandconquer.com/.

Wall Street

10. Social Security and Medicare Boards of Trustees, "A SUMMARY OF THE 2012 ANNUAL REPORT", Social Security Administration,
http://www.ssa.gov/oact/trsum/index.html.

China

11. "Wall Street Execs not Prosecuted," *Frontline*, Jan 22, 2013,
http://www.pbs.org/wgbh/pages/frontline/business-economy-financial-crisis/untouchables/blowing-the-whistle-on-the-mortgage-bubble/.

12. Lingling Wei and Bob Davis, "An 'Invisible' Hand Steers Beijing's Cash," *Wall Street Journal*, July 17, 2013, P 1.

Chapter 16: Leadership Implications

1. Bureau of Ecconomic Analysis, Gross Domestic Product, 11/8/12,
http://www.bea.gov/national/.

2. Joe Light and Ben Levisohn, "What a Trip." Wall Street Journal, 10/6/12, P A7.

The Deficit

3. Trading Economics, "China's Balance of Trade," March 25, 2013,
http://www.tradingeconomics.com/china/balance-of-trade.

4. Ibid.

States

5. "State Spending", October 2012, http://www.usgovernmentspending.com/.

6. Kris Maher, Bobby White and Valerie Bauerlein, "Hard Times Spread for Cities as Health," Pension Costs Rise, 8/11/12, pA1.

7. Michael Corkery, "Pension Crisis Looms Despite Cuts," *Wall Street Journal*, 9/22/2012, p A1.

How bad is the current downturn?

8. Spencer Jakab, "Fed's Long-Running Show goes On and On," *Wall Street Journal*, 1/30/13, pC1.

Stimulus

9. Liz Ann Sonders, "Schwab Investing Insight," 6/8/2012.

10. USA today, "Treasury sells AIG stake for $22.7B profit," December 11, 2012,
http://www.usatoday.com/story/money/business/2012/12/11/treasury-sells-aig-stake/1760625/.

Financing the debt - when will the bond bubble burst

11. Joe Light and Ben Levisohn, "What a Trip," *Wall Street Journal*, 10/6/12, pA7.

12. Liz Ann Sonders, "Schwab Investing Insight," 6/8/2012.

13. Bryan Olson , "Staright Talk: Looking through DC Fog to a brighter 2013," *Schwab*, 2/4/2013.
    Banks
14. Lawrence Lessig, *Republic Lost*, page 83.
15. Victoria McGrane and Jean Eaglesham, "Election Shifts Dodd-Fank Battle Plan," *Wall Street Journal*,
11/9/12 p C1, 2.
    The Corruption of Congress
16. Lawrence Lessig, *Republic Lost*, page 83.
17. TW Farnum, "Revolving door between Congress, Lobbying, Study Shows," *Washington post*, Sept, 12, 2011,
    http://www.washingtonpost.com/politics/study-shows-revolving-door-of-employment-between-congress-lobbying-firms/2011/09/12/gIQAxPYROK_story.html.
18. Lawrence Lessig, *Republic Lost*, p 123.
19. Ibid, 184, 202.
    How to Skirt Anti-lobbying Laws
20. www.ALEC.org.
21. Bill Moyers, "Moyers & Company," Update on ALEC, *PBS*, 6/23/13.
    Staglonation
22. Tom Lee U.S., "Oil Sector Notches Historic Annual Gusher," *Wall Street Journal*, 1/19/13, p B1.
23. Liz Ann Sonders, "Straight Talk Election Results — Impact on Markets and Policy," *Schwab*, 11/8/12.

Chapter 18: Recommendations

Regulation
1. Lawrence Lessig, *Republic Lost*, quoting David Moss, page 69.
2. Ibid., quoting Professor Frank Partnoy discussion, page 76.
3. Victoria McGrane and Jean Eaglesham, "Battle Plan Shifts on Dodd-Frank," 11/11/2012.
4. Lauren Weber, "Americans Rip Up Retirement Plans," *Wall Street Journal*, 1/1/2013, p B1.
    Financial Time Machine Based Recommendations
5. Dennis Cauchon, Federal workers' numbers decline," USA Today, June 1, 1012.
6. Fox news report, 6/12/12.
7. US Government Spending, "Federal spending,"
    http://www.usgovernmentspending.com/spending_chart_1997_2017USb_F 0f.
8. Garbiele Parussini and William Horodin, "France Take Aim at Jobless Payouts," *Wall Street Journal*, 1/31/2013, p 10.
    Working retirees
9. Michael Kinsman, "Hidden pay quite often overlooked," Quoting Robert D. Oberst, *San Diego Tribune*, November 9, 1998, p C 2.

Chapter 19: Global Implications - Europe

1. Ainsley Thomson, "U.K. Birthrate Keeps Rising," *Wall Street Journal*, August 9 2013, August 9, 2013, p A10.

2. United Nations, Department of Economic and Social Affairs, Population Division (2011): "World Population Prospects: The 2010 Revision. New York." http://esa.un.org/wpp/JS-Charts/aging-median-age_0.htm.

Worker to retiree ratio

3. Ibid. http://esa.un.org/wpp/unpp/p2k0data.asp.

Europe's Prospects

4. Matthew Ballton, Martina Stevis and Brian Blackstone, "Europe Cuts Growth forecasts," *Wall Street Journal*, p A26.

5. Ainley Thomson and Casell Bryan-Low, "UK Economy Turns Back Down," 1/28/13, A11.

6. Paul Hamon and Ainsley Thompson, "Population Increases," *Wall Street Journal*, July 17, 2012, p A11.

7. European Commission, "2009 European Aging report," http://ec.europa.eu/economy_finance/publications/publication14992_en.p df.

Women Freed from Housework

8. Dennis Cauchon, "More Americans leaving the workforce," *USA TODAY*, 4/15/11, http://www.usatoday.com/money/economy/employment/2011-04-13-more-americans-leave-labor-force.htm.

European Boomers to the Rescue?

9. European Commission, Eurostat, "File:Number of live births, EU-27, 1961-2010," http://epp.eurostat.ec.europa.eu/statistics_explained/index.php?title=File :Number_of_live_births,_EU-27,_1961-2010_(1)_(million).png&filetimestamp=20111130165640.

Social Expenditures

10. European Commission, Eurostat, "Total social protection expenditures," http://circa.europa.eu/irc/dsis/esspros/info/data/esspros_public_data/publi cation/Pub/P_b1 _1.html.

11. OECD, "Social Expenditures - Agrigated data, US," 2007, http://stats.oecd.org/Index.aspx?QueryId=4549.

12. US Government Spending, "Government Spending Details," 2010, http://www.usgovernmentspending.com/year_spending_2009USpn 13ps1n _50402010#usgs302.

13. European Commission, Eurostat, "File:Number of live births, EU-27, 1961-2010," 11/30/11 http://epp.eurostat.ec.europa.eu/statistics_explained/index.php?title=File :Number_of_live_births,_EU-27,_1961-2010_(1)_(million).png&filetimestamp=20111130165640.

14. Blogspot, Demographic Resources, "Births in Europe In the Twentieth Century," June 16, 2007. http://demoblography.blogspot.com/2007/06/births-in-europe-in-twentieth-century.html.

15. European Commission, "2009 European Aging report," http://ec.europa.eu/economy_finance/publications/publication14992_en.pdf.

16. European Commissions, "Autumn Economic Forecast 2012," January, 2013 revised estimate.

Chapter 20: Global Implications - Japan

1. Social Security and Medicare Boards of Trustees, "Status of the Social Security and Medicare Programs, A SUMMARY OF THE 2012 ANNUAL REPORTS," 2012, http://www.ssa.gov/oact/trsum/index.html.
2. Jonathan V. Last, "America's Baby Bust," *Wall Street Journal*, 2/2/13, p C1.
3. Prhed Dvorak and Elenor Warnock, "Stagnant Japan Rolls Dice on New Era of Easy Money." *Wall Street Journal*, 3/2013, P1.
4. Wikipedia, "Economic History of Japan," http://en.wikipedia.org/wiki/Economic_history_of_Japan#Timeline.
5. Prhed Dvorak and Elenor Warnock, "Stagnant Japan Rolls Dice on New Era of Easy Money," *Wall Street Journal*, 3/2013, P1.
6. Ibid.
7. James R. Hagerty, "As America Ages, Shortage Of Help Hits Nursing Homes, *Wall Street Journal*, April 16, 2013, p A1.
   Generational Economic Parallel?
8. Wikipedia, Cabinet office, Government of Japan, "Real GDP Growth Rate in Japan," http://www.google.com/imgres?imgurl=http://upload.wikimedia.org/wikipedia/commons/4/46/Real_GDP_growth_rate_in_Japan_(1956-2008).png&imgrefurl=http://en.wikipedia.org/wiki/File:Real_GDP_growth_rate_in_Japan_(1956-2008).png&h=532&w=755&sz=83&tbnid=BMvprJvgJJ5TGM:&tbnh=90&tbnw=128&prev=/search%3Fq%3Djapan%2Bgdp%2Bhistory%26tbm%3Disch%26tbo%3Du&zoom=1&q=japan+gdp+history&usg=___5WOGnjlxWbvKyw7cJ3ymfokU7K4=&docid=a4vRswKupVIcxM&sa=X&ei=rS4EUID4EeqA2AXmmYWmCw&ved=0CF0Q9QEwAQ&dur=1625.
9. Prhed Dvorak and Elenor Warnock, "Stagnant Japan Rolls Dice on New Era of Easy Money. *Wall Street Journal*, 3/2013, P1.
   Solutions
10. Wikipedia, "Aging of Japan," http://en.wikipedia.org/wiki/Aging_of_Japan.
    The Elderly Robot Assistant (ERA)
11. Skilled Nursing Facilities.org, "Nursing home costs," http://www.skillednursingfacilities.org/articles/nursing-home-costs.php.

Chapter 21: Global Implications - The BRICs

1. Min Zeng, "The BRIC Builder," *Wall Street Journal Money*, March 2013.
Russia
2. Wikipedia, "Demographics of Russia," http://en.wikipedia.org/wiki/Demographics_of_Russia.
China
3. Wikipedia, "History of the People's Republic of China, 1946 -1976, 1976 on," http://en.wikipedia.org/wiki/History_of_the_People's_Republic_of_China_(1976%E2%80%931989)#Reform_and_opening_up.
4. Tom Orlik and Bob Davis, "Relief on China Growth Comes With Caveats," *Wall Street Journal*, 1/19/2013, p A10.
Future
5. Jonathan V. Last, "America's Baby Bust," Wall Street Journal, 2/2/13, p C1.

www.ingramcontent.com/pod-product-compliance
Lightning Source LLC
Chambersburg PA
CBHW051443170526
45166CB00001B/99